AF844052

HANDBOOK OF RESEARCH ON STOCK MARKET GLOBALIZATION

Handbook of Research on Stock Market Globalization

Edited by

Geoffrey Poitras

Simon Fraser University, Vancouver, Canada

Edward Elgar
Cheltenham, UK • Northampton, MA, USA

© Geoffrey Poitras 2012

All rights reserved. No part of this publication may be reproduced, stored in a retrieval system or transmitted in any form or by any means, electronic, mechanical or photocopying, recording, or otherwise without the prior permission of the publisher.

Published by
Edward Elgar Publishing Limited
The Lypiatts
15 Lansdown Road
Cheltenham
Glos GL50 2JA
UK

Edward Elgar Publishing, Inc.
William Pratt House
9 Dewey Court
Northampton
Massachusetts 01060
USA

A catalogue record for this book
is available from the British Library

Library of Congress Control Number: 2011925768

FSC
www.fsc.org
MIX
Paper from
responsible sources
FSC® C018575

ISBN 978 1 84720 756 2

Typeset by Servis Filmsetting Ltd, Stockport, Cheshire
Printed and bound by MPG Books Group, UK

Contents

PART III EVALUATING STOCK MARKET GLOBALIZATION

Figures

Tables

Contributors

Youssef Cassis, Professor of Economic History, European University Institute, Florence, Italy; Youssef.Cassis@eui.eu.

Augusto de la Torre, Regional Chief Economist, Latin America and the Caribbean Region, World Bank, Washington, DC, USA; adelatorre@worldbank.org.

Manuela Geranio, Department of Finance, Università Bocconi, Milan, Italy; manuela.geranio@unibocconi.it.

Daniel J. Harty, Corporate Expert, Federal Deposit Insurance Corporation, Washington, DC.

Iftekhar Hasan, Cary L. Wellington Professor of Finance, Lally School of Management and Technology, Rensselaer Polytechnic Institute, Troy, NY, USA; hasan@rpi.edu.

Elaine Hutson, Associate Professor, Department of Accounting and Finance, Faculty of Business and Economics, Monash University, Melbourne, Australia; elaine.hutson@gmail.com.

Jerry W. Markham, Professor of Law, College of Law, Florida International University, Miami, FL, USA; markhamj@fiu.edu.

Ranald Michie, Professor of History, Department of History, University of Durham, UK; R.C.Michie@durham.ac.uk.

Geoffrey Poitras, Professor of Finance, Faculty of Business Administration, Simon Fraser University, Vancouver, Canada; poitras@sfu.ca.

Alexandru Preda, Professor, Department of Sociology, School of Social and Political Science, University of Edinburgh, UK; A.Preda@ed.ac.uk.

Janette Rutterford, Professor of Financial Management, Open University Business School, Milton Keynes, UK; j.rutterford@open.ac.uk.

Heiko Schmiedel, European Central Bank – Securities Settlement Systems Policy Division, Directorate General Payment Systems, Frankfurt am Main, Germany; heiko.schmiedel@ecb.int.

Sergio L. Schmukler, Lead Economist, Development Research Group, Washington, DC, USA; sschmukler@worldbank.org.

Liang Song, Michigan Technological University, Houghton, MI, USA; songl@rpi.edu.

Giovanna Zanotti, Associate Professor, Dipartimento di Economia aziendale, University of Bergamo, Italy; giovanna.zanotti@unibocconi.it.

Prologue: events from February to July 2011

Geoffrey Poitras

The first half of 2011 produced an apparent acceleration in the already rapid pace of stock market globalization. Since the 'Introduction' to this volume was completed in early 2011, there has been a flurry of activity covering four continents. This brief prologue is provided to benchmark the contents of this collection of academic contributions against significant recent events. Included in these events are the final resolution of a bid by the Singapore Exchange Limited (SGX), initiated in October 2010, to take over the Australian Securities Exchange (ASX). Significantly, this bid was voided in April 2011 by Australian regulators under foreign investment review legislation requiring such transactions to be in the national interest. Facing a decision under similar investment review legislation, the Canadian government ultimately did not have to determine whether a 'merger' proposed in February 2011 between the London Stock Exchange (LSE) and the Toronto Stock Exchange (TMX) to form the 'LTMX' exchange would be in the national interest. Based on early returns from a TMX shareholder vote on the LTMX deal, the merger proposal was withdrawn in June 2011. The proposed LTMX transaction was complicated by the presence of a hostile and vigorous competing bid made in May 2011 from the 'Maple' group led by prominent Canadian chartered banks and investment dealers. Friendly talks between Maple and TMX commenced following failure of the LTMX merger proposal. If successful the Maple bid would be subject to overview by the Canadian government under competition legislation.

On the global playing field, the LSE, TMX, SGX and ASX deals are small relative to the friendly Deutsche Bourse bid to merge with NYSE Euronext announced in February 2011.[1] In April 2011, this bid was challenged by an unfriendly takeover bid made by a combination of NASDAQ OMX and ICE. Based on discussions with the US Department of Justice associated with antitrust and other competitive considerations and a unanimous rejection of the bid by the NYSE Euronext board of directors, NASDAQ OMX and ICE withdrew the unfriendly bid in May 2011 allowing the Deutsche Bourse and NYSE merger to proceed to the last stage of shareholder approval in July 2011, with only final approval by US and European Union (EU) regulators as the last hurdle. This continues the trend to consolidation of the major continental European exchanges initiated by a number of EU Directives. In contrast, progress toward consolidation of important exchanges in East Asia has been much slower. The Tokyo and Osaka stock exchanges entered merger talks in July 2011 while the Hong Kong Exchange is exploring expanded consolidation with the two important exchanges in Mainland China.

The flurry of proposed mergers and takeovers occurring in the first half of 2011 serves to reinforce the relevance of the contributed chapters in this book. For example, a key theme associated with Part I of this volume is that stock market globalization is an ongoing historical process with roots stretching back to the beginnings of exchange trading. Recent events are now part of the history of that process. Advances in trading and communication technology have induced fundamental changes in regulatory structures that govern exchange ownership and stock market organization. Stock exchange demutualization has facilitated the ability of exchanges to consolidate and merge both national and internationally. Traditional stock market regulation, organized along national lines, is increasingly being challenged by the globalization of trading and ownership. These changes did not just appear in 2011. While contributions in Part I of this volume demonstrate that close parallels arising from the impact of advances in trading and communication technology can be found in the stock market globalization process of the nineteenth century, Parts II and III of this volume explore other key aspects of the globalization process.

The public debates surrounding the merger and takeover proposals from the first half of 2011 illustrate the need for solid academic research on the issues associated with stock market globalization. Shareholders of demutualized exchanges seek guidance on whether to tender to bids from other exchanges against a backdrop of national regulators reflecting a bewildering assortment of views. In rejecting the SGX bid under federal investment review legislation, Australian Treasurer Wayne Swan referred to the decision as a 'no-brainer'. Given the deal involved the ASX becoming a junior partner to a smaller regional exchange, the SGX, 'the deal would risk us losing many of our financial sector jobs . . . it's a takeover that would see Australia's financial sector become a subsidiary to a competitor in Asia' (*Sydney Morning Herald*, 21 April 2011). In contrast, since the inception of the EU, regulators have actively promoted international exchange consolidation. All the while, the progress of communications and trading technology have produced a dramatic erosion in the traditional profit drivers for exchanges. The significant benefits of reduced execution costs and enhanced liquidity produced by technological change have in turn created serious gaps in the regulatory framework that threaten the stability of the price discovery process. This volume provides reasoned and insightful treatments by leading academic researchers on important issues associated with the progress of stock market globalization.

NOTE

1. As discussed in more detail in the 'Introduction' to this volume, NYSE Euronext is the result of combining a number of exchanges including the US-based New York Stock Exchange (NYSE), Archipelago Holdings and the American Stock Exchange, together with five European-based exchanges in Paris, Brussels, Lisbon, Amsterdam and the London International Financial Futures exchange (LIFFE). NASDAQ OMX was formed as a combination of the US-based electronic National Association of Securities Dealers Automated Quotation exchange and a combination of smaller Northern European exchanges. ICE is the Intercontinental Exchange, a relatively new exchange initiated in 2000 that focuses on commodities and related derivative security trading.

Introduction: stock market globalization, past and present

Geoffrey Poitras

THE CURRENT STATE OF STOCK MARKET GLOBALIZATION

The first decade of the twenty-first century has witnessed historic changes in the stock market. From the nineteenth century until near the end of the twentieth century, stock exchanges were organized nationally and featured mutual ownership by exchange members.[1] In conjunction with a technological revolution in trading systems and communications, stock exchanges have also demutualized, that is, converted from mutual to corporate organization with publicly traded common stock. Following demutualization, various exchanges have engaged in an ongoing series of international mergers and acquisitions involving other exchanges, electronic communications networks (ECNs) and multilateral trading platforms (MTFs), derivatives exchanges, alternative trading systems and clearing organizations. In addition, the stock trading business has become increasingly competitive and a range of new products, such as exchange traded funds, have been introduced. New electronic trading platforms have emerged that are making the exchange trading floor obsolete for all but a small number of large block trades.

The changes that have taken place in the organizational structure of stock exchanges are illustrated in the 2009 10-K audited financial statements for the largest global exchange group, NYSE Euronext:

> NYSE Euronext is a leading global operator of financial markets and provider of innovative trading strategies. We offer a broad and growing array of products and services in cash equities, futures, options, swaps, exchange-traded products, bonds, market data and commercial technology solutions, all designed to meet the evolving needs of issuers, investors, financial institutions and market participants. We are also the world's leading, most liquid equities exchange group. With more listed issues than any other exchange group, trading on NYSE Euronext's equity markets represents approximately one-third of the world's cash equities volume. As of December 31, 2009, 64 of the 2009 Fortune Global 100 companies were listed on NYSE Euronext.

At the end of 2010, NYSE Euronext (NYX) was a holding company composed of a US component: the original New York Stock Exchange (NYSE); NYSE Arca, formed by a merger between the NYSE and Archipelago Holdings, Inc. in March 2006 that coincided with the demutualization of the NYSE; and NYSE Amex, formed by the acquisition of the American stock exchange in June 2008. The European component of NYSE Euronext comprises five European-based exchanges: the Paris, Amsterdam, Brussels and Lisbon stock exchanges, and NYSE LIFFE which has derivatives markets in London, Paris, Amsterdam, Brussels and Lisbon. There is also a relatively small US futures market component, NYSE LIFFE US. NYSE Euronext was formed in a merger on 4 April 2007 of NYSE Group and Euronext. NYSE Euronext common stock is dually listed on the NYSE and Euronext Paris under the symbol 'NYX'.

Similarly from the 2009 10-K for the next largest global exchange, NASDAQ OMX (NDAQ), which identifies:

> a leading global exchange group that delivers trading, exchange technology, securities listing, and public company services across six continents. Our global offerings are diverse and include trading across multiple asset classes, market data products, financial indexes, capital formation solutions, financial services and market technology products and services. Our technology powers markets across the globe, supporting cash equity trading, derivatives trading, clearing and settlement and many other functions.

The development of NDAQ is similar to that of NYX, with the proviso that the original NASDAQ (National Association of Security Dealers Automated Quotations) stock market started with a different organizational structure. From its original formation in 1971 until 2000, NASDAQ operated as a subsidiary of FINRA (formerly the National Association of Security Dealers). A restructuring of FINRA's NASDAQ ownership in 2000 started a process that resulted in the demutualization of NASDAQ from FINRA in 2006 and the conversion of NASDAQ to national securities exchange status in 2007. In February2008, NASDAQ OMX was created by the merger of NASDAQ and OMX AB, a Swedish–Finnish exchange group that, like Euronext, was the result of the stock market globalization process in Europe. In comparison to Euronext, OMX AB is a more modest exchange operation.

The beginnings of the stock market globalization process in Europe can be traced to the formation of the European Union in 1993 and subsequent initiatives to harmonize financial markets within the Union. This process facilitated the creation of Euronext in September 2000 that involved the merger of the stock exchanges in Amsterdam and Brussels with the Paris Bourse. Of these, the Amsterdam stock exchange can claim an historical pedigree as the first stock exchange trading venue starting in the early seventeenth century. The Paris bourse has origins in the early eighteenth century. In December 2001, Euronext acquired ownership of the London International Financial Futures Exchange (LIFFE), though the exchange governance remained with Liffe. In 2002, Euronext merged with the Lisbon Stock Exchange. The natural progression toward a pan-European stock exchange generated discussions between Euronext and the largest German stock exchange, Deutsche Bourse, starting in 2005. A bidding competition emerged with the entry of the NYSE, resulting in an agreement in 2006 producing the merger of the NYSE and Euronext in April 2007. Further merger negotiations between NYSE Euronext and Deutsche Bourse ended unsuccessfully in late 2008.

In contrast to the size and historical roots of Euronext, OMX AB is more modest. OM AB was founded during the 1980s as an exchange to trade option contracts in Sweden. In 1998, OM rose to significance with acquisition of the Stockholm Stock Exchange. Following this came an unsuccessful attempt in 2001 to buy the London Stock Exchange and another unsuccessful attempt to establish a fully electronic European stock exchange (Jiway) with some American investment banks that ended in October 2002. In September 2003 a significant step was taken when the Helsinki Stock Exchange merged with OM. With this merger, OMX also acquired interests in the Baltic stock exchanges in Latvia, Estonia and Lithuania. The combined exchanges assumed the name OMX in August 2004. In Jan 2005, OMX acquired the Copenhagen Stock Exchange and in September 2006, the Iceland Stock Exchange agreed to be acquired. Other OMX initiatives include: purchase of a 10 per cent stake in the Oslo Stock Exchange, October 2006; and, acquisition of the Armenian Stock Exchange in November 2007. With this foundation, the electronic Nordic Stock Exchange was launched in October 2006, trading securities from the three Nordic exchanges. This merger and acquisition activity by OMX set the stage for the merger with NASDAQ in February 2008.

A failed bid by NASDAQ to acquire the London Stock Exchange (LSE) provides a backdrop to the NASDAQ merger with OMX. Starting with a Deutsche Bourse bid in 2001, a number of unsuccessful efforts were made to acquire the LSE. The NASDAQ bid to acquire the LSE was advanced in early 2006 and rejected by the LSE shareholders in April 2006. NASDAQ responded by withdrawing the bid and proceeding to purchase shares in the LSE. After accumulating about 30 per cent of LSE shares, NASDAQ made another bid to acquire the LSE in December 2006 that, again, failed to gain shareholder approval. This bid was withdrawn in February 2007. Faced with serious competitive challenges posed by the NYSE Euronext merger in April 2007, NASDAQ agreed to buy OMX in May 2007. This precipitated a higher bid in August 2007 for OMX from Borse Dubai that, ultimately, led to Borse Dubai acquiring a 20 per cent stake and 5 per cent of voting shares in NASDAQ as well as all the NASDAQ stake in the LSE. The complicated deal was completed in February 2008.

Since the creation of NASDAQ OMX the expansion process has continued. In July 2008, there was the acquisition of the Philadelphia Stock Exchange which has a significant presence in the derivatives market, primarily in options. This move complemented the NASDAQ Options market that was launched in March 2008. The move into derivatives trading has continued with a number of further acquisitions. A stake in Nord Pool ASA was acquired in October 2008, adding clearing and international derivatives activities. Nord Pool was fully acquired in May 2010. The initial Nord Pool move was followed quickly by the acquisition of a controlling interest in the International Derivatives Clearing Group in December 2008, and in January 2009 a stake in the European Multilateral Clearing Facility was acquired. In December 2009, a controlling stake in a commodities trading ECN, Agora-X, was added. With this build-up, by 2010 NASDAQ OMX Commodities featured the world's largest power derivatives exchange and a European carbon exchange. Expansion in stock trading continued with the acquisition of the Boston Stock Exchange in August 2008 that was relaunched as NASDAQ OMX BX in January 2009.

Despite the considerable progress toward stock market globalization, much stock trading is still organized along national lines. As discussed, the two largest and most global stock exchange groups, NYX and NDAQ, have activities concentrated primarily in Europe and the US. Integration with stock markets in East Asia, South Asia, Latin America, South Africa and other geographical regions is limited. Capital market liberalization initiatives have all exchanges actively competing with each other for listings, cross-listings and trading volume at a time when market share in trading for listed securities by traditional exchange platforms is falling considerably. In particular, the market share of NASDAQ trading in NASDAQ listed stocks fell from 46.1 per cent in 2007 to 33 per cent in 2009, and the share of NASDAQ in all trading of US listed stocks fell from 29.1 per cent in 2007 to 23 per cent in 2009. There is even erosion of market share

Table I.1 Rankings of stock exchanges by total capitalization

Exchange	US$ millions
NYSE Euronext (US)	12 423 557
Tokyo Stock Exchange	3 534 685
NASDAQ OMX	3 500 875
NYSE Euronext (Europe)	2 793 199
London Stock Exchange	2 773 395
Shanghai Stock Exchange	2 630 841
Hong Kong Exchanges	2 325 349
TSX Group	1 817 263
Bombay Stock Exchange	1 373 016
National Stock Exchange India	1 338 495

Source: World Federation of Exchanges (31 March 2010).

in Europe where the share of the Nordic and Baltic exchanges fell from 100 per cent in 2007 to 88 per cent in 2009. NYX is experiencing similar results with the trading share of NYSE listed securities falling from 45.6 per cent in 2008 to 38.4 per cent in 2009. Though precise numbers are not reported, the market fragmentation generated by the Markets in Financial Instuments Directive (MiFID) in Europe has produced similar shrinking of trading share of Euronext in Euronext listed securities.

NYX and NDAQ have pursued mergers and acquisitions to deal with the competitive pressures of the stock market globalization process. In contrast, numerous important Stock Exchanges around the globe, such as the Tokyo Stock Exchange (TSE), Toronto Stock Exchange (TSX),[2] London Stock Exchange (LSE), and Hong Kong Stock Exchange (HKX), are not currently part of a global exchange group but have still had to deal with globalization forces (see Table I.1). Such major exchanges have reacted to the global growth of NYX and NDAQ by engaging in alternative approaches to deal with globalization, such as joint ventures with other exchanges. Regulatory change generated by technological advances in trading and communications technology, such as Regulation NMS (National Market System) in the US and MiFID in the EU, has been accompanied by similar legislation in other major countries. While all major stock exchanges have demutualized, there are other forces impeding the march to globalization. In addition, the related process of dominant national exchanges absorbing smaller regional exchanges has progressed at different rates in different countries.

The response of the Hong Kong Exchange (HKX) to the ongoing globalization process reflects the substantive segmentation that still characterizes the global stock market. HKX is acutely aware of the competitive issues raised by technological advances, as reflected in the 'CEO Review' from the HKX Annual Report (2009, p. 13):

> As we look ahead to the future, we see 2 major forces of opportunity and competition at play – opportunities resulting from the further opening of the Mainland market and more intense competition from exchanges and trading venues around the world and in the region . . . On the competition front, we believe that the advancement of financial technology is rapidly changing the competitive landscape. We must ensure that the capabilities and functionalities of our own trading platforms well equip us to compete with other global players. Further, we need to

> provide a full suite of products that meets the growing expectations of our current and future customer base, as well as continue to enhance the cost and operational efficiency for parties trading with us.

Despite such statements, HKX is relatively insulated from global competitive forces due to inherent advantages in the Chinese stock market. As a consequence, HKX has pursued a strategy of expanding in the market for Chinese stocks and defending the competitive position that it has in that market. Expanding connections with the Shanghai and Shenzhen stock exchanges in 2009, offering of new products such as a range of ETFs and actively pursuing Mainland initial public offerings (IPOs) are understandable and predictable developments. Initiatives to globalize outside of China do not make much strategic sense at this point for HKX.

In contrast to HKX, the second-largest stock exchange in the world, the Tokyo Stock Exchange (TSE), does not have significant inherent advantages supporting expansion in mainland China. Cross-listings of major TSE listed stocks on alternate exchanges also pose a significant competitive challenge. The Tokyo Stock Exchange demutualized in November 2001 and the exchange has moved recently to expand ETF trading. However, Japan has also been relatively slow in implementing Regulation NMS and MiFID-type reforms and the TSE has not moved significantly into derivative security trading. Arguably still the financial centre for East Asia, the Tokyo Stock Exchange still retains a 95.8 per cent share of the trading value of listed stocks in Japan. While faced with limited internal competition within Japan, developments by NYX and the NDAQ present growing external pressure due to the progress of stock market globalization. In response, the TSE entered an agreement with the LSE in October 2007 to extend the Alternative Investment Market (AIM), a market for growing companies founded by the LSE in 1995, into Japan and East Asia. Progress on this initiative has been relatively slow. AIM received an exchange licence in May 2009 and in November 2010 announced a framework for bond trading.

With a stated vision to be the 'World's Capital Market', the LSE is near the epicentre of the globalization process. Various exchanges, including NASDAQ and Deutsche Bourse, have attempted to acquire the LSE only to be rebuffed by the shareholders, ostensibly because the bids were insufficient. Competitive pressures compelled the LSE to merge with Borsa Italiana (BI) in 2007. This merger included the BI ownership of MTS, an electronic bond trading platform. Further developments followed in 2009 with the LSE entering into strategic partnerships with the Toronto Stock Exchange (TSX) and the Oslo Bourse. This move was also a strategic first step for TSX that has been primarily focused on the exchange consolidation process within Canada that took form in 1999 with the creation of the Canadian Venture Exchange (CDNX) from the merger with the Vancouver and Alberta stock exchanges and movement of CDNX trading to Toronto. The Winnipeg stock exchange and the equities portion of the Montreal exchange joined CDNX soon after. Despite being ahead of the curve in the move to fully electronic trading in 1997 and demutualization in 2000 (completed in 2002), TSX has been somewhat insulated from competitive pressure by the strength and specialized character of the Canadian equity market. In 2006, TSX expanded bond market trading with the acquisition of Shorcan Brokers. In 2008, the completion of the merger with the derivatives-based Montreal exchange to form the TMX finalized the exchange consolidation process in Canada. In September 2009, TSX announced that co-location services for high-frequency traders were available.

CONTENTS AND CONTRIBUTORS: THE *HANDBOOK OF RESEARCH ON STOCK MARKET GLOBALIZATION*

The stock market globalization process has produced historic changes in the structure of stock markets. Though this process has proceeded at different rates geographically, the effects are evident in stock markets throughout the globe. The process has been most pronounced in the US and Europe where competitive pressures have been greatest. Despite these historic changes, there are relatively few sources examining the historical connections between the globalization process currently under way and previous periods of stock market globalization. Part I of the *Handbook* details these connections with five historical contributions covering previous globalization periods. In particular, by the end of the nineteenth century a global network of national stock exchanges, centred in London, had evolved. In addition to trading on national exchanges, stocks and shares from around the world were traded in international 'capitals of capital'. Though this last period of globalization came to an end with the Great Depression, the 'capitals of capital' have survived to form key parts of the current globalization process.

The five chapters in Part I are contributed by the editor and four eminent scholars who have made outstanding contributions to the history of financial markets, stock markets and the corporate economy. To those familiar with this area of study, Youssef Cassis, Professor of Economic History at the European University Institute, Florence, Italy, needs no introduction. Chapter 1 summarizes the historical insights about 'capitals of capital' contained in the influential Cassis (2006) and related contributions including Cassis (1997, 1994) and Cassis et al. (1995). More precisely, the first chapter examines:

> these 'capitals of capital', the world's leading international financial centres, from the late eighteenth century to the present. Given the transformation of the world economy, their number has remained remarkably stable, yet without being rigid. In Europe, barely half a dozen centres have really made a difference in the financial field: London and Paris; Berlin, followed by Frankfurt after the Second World War . . . At world level, New York should of course be added from the end of the nineteenth century and, much more recently, Tokyo, Hong Kong and Singapore.

This chapter uses a historical approach to identify factors that contribute to the rise and decline of particular financial centres within the global stock market.

Chapter 2 is contributed by another eminent scholar in the history of financial markets: Professor Ranald Michie, University of Durham, UK. In addition to producing the definitive history of the London Stock Exchange (Michie 1999), Professor Michie has authored numerous insightful works on the history of financial markets in general, and the stock market in particular, for example Michie (2009, 2007, 2006, 1986, 1981). Chapter 2 takes an 'alternative perspective' to the history of stock market globalization which recognizes that 'the stock market serves a number of different masters'. Instead of focusing on the ability of the stock market to obtain corporate financing through the issue of transferable stocks, 'the needs of the investor must also be taken into account'. The accumulation of savings needs an outlet, producing variation in the investment from small amounts for short periods to large amounts over long periods. The needs of investors also varied according to whether regular income was desired over long-term capital gains. The more complex and sophisticated the economy the greater the need there was for a financial system that 'continually responded to the ebb and flow of credit and capital both over time and space and between individuals, institutions and businesses'. Confidence of investors in the stock market as a forum to trade stocks is essential. Erosion of this confidence underpins market disruptions such as the global financial crisis of 2007–09.

Though not as global in reach, precursors of the nineteenth-century stock market globalization process emerged as early as the sixteenth century. The third chapter, contributed by the editor, discusses the history of stock trading from the sixteenth century until the emergence of globalized exchanges in the late twentieth century. The initial development of essential institutional elements of the early trade in stocks is traced to the Renaissance Antwerp exchange. Subsequent speculative trading on the Amsterdam and London stock markets in the seventeenth and eighteenth centuries is closely reviewed. The emergence of a global trade in stocks and shares in the nineteenth century is reflected in the evolution of the New York Stock Exchange, together with the centralization of global stock trading in London. Following a disruption of the globalization process during the Great Depression and the Second World War, the last half of the twentieth century has seen an unprecedented acceleration of equity security market globalization. The chapter concludes with an overview of factors contributing to this acceleration, including exchange demutualization and the revolution in communications and information technology.

The fourth chapter in Part I is not directly concerned with the history of the stock market. Rather, this chapter, contributed by financial historian Janette Rutterford, is concerned with the historical evolution in the methods used to value common stocks and how investors have changed the way in which they value shares over time. This chapter is based on a number of insightful works on this subject, for example Rutterford (2006, 2004), Rutterford and Gregory (1999) and Laurence et al. (2009). Professor Rutterford identifies four key methods used to value common stocks: book value; dividend and earnings yields; price–earnings ratios; and discounted cash flow. The chapter identifies 'an early dependence on book value, the assets to back the nominal value of the shares, and on dividend yields, with shares, being valued as bonds, with a higher yield to reflect their more uncertain income. As firms became more profitable, dividends no longer represented the underlying earnings of firms. This was particularly true in the US'. The chapter demonstrates that the appearance of earnings yields and price–earnings ratios came into common use in the US during the Wall Street boom of the 1920s, while the transition was much slower in the UK where these valuation methods did not take hold until the 1960s.

One important aspect of the current stock market globalization process is the proliferation and increased importance of new 'diversification' products, such as exchange traded funds. Building on Hutson (2005), the fifth and final chapter in Part I, by Elaine Hutson of Monash University, Melbourne, Australia examines a similar historical occurrence that appeared during the second half of the nineteenth century: the investment trusts that traded in the British stock market. These funds were precursors to the professionally managed stock funds that rose to prominence in the US market following the First World War. This chapter traces the pedigree of the nineteenth century funds to the 1770s when a number of such schemes appeared in Paris, Amsterdam and Geneva. One such fund, the Eendragt Maakt Magt, originating in Holland in 1774, bore striking similarity to the British investment trusts that first appeared 1868. This chapter examines the history of these trusts from 1868 until the Barings crisis in the 1890s. Factors contributing to the growth in investment trusts are identified. While most funds were well managed, this chapter also details a number of investment trust scams that emerged during the speculative boom of the 1880s.

In contrast to the historical chapters of Part I, Chapters 6 to 9 in Part II of the *Handbook* are concerned with the current state of stock market globalization. Overwhelmingly, available studies on the current state of such globalization use an economic or financial perspective. While three of the four chapters in Part II also employ this approach, Chapter 6 by Alexandru Preda of the Department of Sociology, University of Edinburgh, UK continues the sociological approach to evaluating the stock market. This approach to analysing the stock exchange has an intellectual pedigree stretching back to Max Weber (1894 [2000]). Professor Preda has made numerous significant contributions to the recent revival of interest in financial markets by sociologists, for example Preda (2009, 2006, 2007) and Cetina and Preda (2004). The chapter focuses on 'social closure', or 'the processes through which institutional control mechanisms are set in place. These mechanisms contribute to providing stock exchanges with a distinct institutional identity, while integrating them within the social fabric.' While the technological revolution, shifts in the ownership structure and the emergence of alternative trading platforms would seem to have weakened the stock exchange as a social institution and, hence, to have made social closure superfluous, this chapter argues that the situation is much more complex.

One essential characteristic of the modern stock market globalization process is the change in the corporate governance and exchange ownership associated with demutualization. From the Antwerp bourse in the sixteenth century until 1773 when a group of brokers in London acquired a building in Sweetings Alley off Threadneedle Street that was called the 'Stock Exchange', venues for trading stock were owned separately from those involved in the actual trading of stock. From this point until the end of the twentieth century, most stock exchanges came to be owned by the members, that is, to have a mutual form of organization. Direct access to trading on the exchange was increasingly restricted to members only. The value of exchange membership was reflected in the price of 'seats' on the exchange (for example Davis et al. 2007). The demutualization of stock exchanges that began at the end of the twentieth century has, not surprisingly, generated a large number of studies on various aspects of this process that are usefully summarized and analysed in Chapter 7 by Giovanna Zanotti of the University of Bergamo, Italy. This chapter concludes from the various studies of the demutualization process that the emergence of the for-profit model for stock exchange governance was a consequence of the competitive pressures arising from the rapid change in trading and communications technology that characterized the last two decades.

In contrast to Chapter 7 which summarizes a large number of studies, Chapter 8, by Iftekhar Hasan, Heiko Schmiedel and Liang Song, empirically investigates the effects of stock exchange mergers and acquisitions (M&As) on the value of competitor shares. The sample consists of 63 M&As of stock exchanges paired with the respective competitors in the same region during the 2000–2007 period. As reflected in Francis et al. (2010), Hasan et al. (2003) and Schmiedel et al. (2006), the authors of this chapter are well suited to the task of investigating the short-run performance (share-price responses) of these public stock exchanges. The results indicate that, in general, when a stock exchange is merged with another exchange, its competitor significantly loses shareholder value. In particular, when a stock exchange is involved in a horizontal (cross-region) transaction instead of a vertical (within-region) one, the competitor loses even more shareholder value than the average loss. Further, if the stock exchange is merged with another stock exchange in a country with a more developed stock market or with higher governance, the competitor's shareholder value will also fall more.

The final chapter in Part II concerns a central factor in the competitive forces driving stock market globalization, both past and present: the trading of stocks outside the resident country of the corporation. In the nineteenth century, this was facilitated by the widespread use of bearer securities. In modern markets, this trading requires cross-listing. Though demutualization significantly reduced the incentives to cross-list, as reflected in the stagnant to decreasing share of foreign shares being traded on the major markets, there still remains an active literature on the subject. In Chapter 9, Manuela Geranio of Università Bocconi in Milan, Italy provides an insightful summary of this literature and, in the process, identifies important new avenues of trading that are replacing traditional cross-listing which took place primarily on US markets. These avenues include: the growth of cross-listing on East Asian, as opposed to US stock markets; demutualization of exchanges leading to non-resident, primarily US, broker-dealers becoming members of European exchanges increasing opportunities for trade internalization, that is, crossing of trades within the book of the broker-dealer; and advances in trading technology permitting the development of proprietary trading systems designed specifically for trading cross-listed stocks.

Part III of the *Handbook* is concerned with the regulatory challenges that are posed by stock market globalization. There are constant pressures on regulators from rent-seeking stock market participants to change rules or interpret rules favourably. In the US, from the introduction of Regulation ATS (alternative trading system) in 1998 to the Regulation SHO (short selling) amendments of July 2007, there was a radical restructuring of the US stock market that, ultimately, created large gains for certain stock market participants. The dismissal in July 2008 by the New York State Court of Appeals of all claims in the $140 million compensation law suit against Richard Grasso, former chairman and chief executive officer (CEO) of the NYSE from 1995 to 2003, is evidence of such legitimate gains. Like the economic rents created by demutualization, there is constant pressure for large stock market participants to obtain as large a share as possible of the gains from technological progress in communications and trading. As demonstrated in the 'flash crash' of 6 May 2010, this tendency can have disturbing implications. Increased competition from globalized stock exchanges able to benefit most from enhanced technology may also work to the detriment of stock markets in emerging economies.

Chapter 10 of Part III, by Augusto de la Torre and Sergio Schmukler, deals with the implications of stock market globalization for Latin America. Being senior economists in the Development Research Group and for the Latin America and the Caribbean

Region at the World Bank, the authors have essential practical experience enabling them to analyse specific problems in Latin American stock markets. Chapter 10 combines this experience with results from a long list of impressive and influential academic contributions in this general area, for example de la Torre et al. (2010, 2007) and de la Torre and Schmukler (2006). The conclusions reached in Chapter 10 are too familiar: 'One important feature of the current globalization process is that it is characterized by segmentation across countries and firms. This is relevant because if countries and companies benefit from access to foreign capital, only a small group of countries and firms reap most of the benefits.' Chapter 10 illustrates that the gains from reform have been illusive for countries and firms in Latin American stock markets.

Chapter 11 is the second of two chapters in the *Handbook* contributed by the editor. Though events surrounding the 'flash crash' of 6 May 2010 are the central concern, this chapter also details the significant, primarily US, regulatory and stock market evolution that occurred from the crash of 1987 until the flash crash. As such, the chapter continues the narrative from Chapter 3 to include the most recent events in the stock market. In response to requests from Congress, two reports produced jointly by the staffs of the Securities and Exchange Commission (SEC) and the Commodity Futures Trading Commission (CFTC) provide insight into the workings of the stock market that only becomes available in the aftermath of severe market disruptions. While the flash crash was a contained downside event that lasted about 15 minutes in the highly liquid markets for E-mini futures and the Standard & Poors S&P 500 ETF, the extension into the broader market lasted about a half hour with, ultimately, over 20 000 cancelled trades concentrated mostly in less liquid ETFs. The chapter concludes that, while helpful, the single stock circuit breakers introduced in response to the flash crash ignore the problems associated with short sale exemptions given to intermarket arbitrageurs. More importantly, advances in trading and communications technology could be employed to tighten restrictions on short sales needed to avoid liquidity problems associated with downside disruptions in the price discovery process witnessed in the crash of 1987 and the flash crash of 2010.

The final chapter in the *Handbook*, by Jerry Markham and Daniel Harty, examines the development and regulatory concerns associated with the replacement of exchange trading floors by electronic communications networks (ECNs). This fascinating chapter deals with two key elements in the current stock market globalization process: the impact of technological change on stock trading, and the legal and regulatory responses to this change. The lead author, Jerry Markham, Professor of Law at Florida International University, USA brings to this chapter an exceptional background in both legal studies and the history of financial markets, as reflected in the monumental, three-volume *Financial History of the United States* (Markham 2002), Markham (2006) and Markham and Harty (2008) This concluding chapter provides a fitting snapshot of the current state of stock market globalization in the world's most important stock market. As this chapter demonstrates, the technological revolution in trading and communications extends beyond the stock market to include other important interconnected security trading venues, especially derivatives exchanges. The ongoing acquisition of derivatives exchanges by global stock market groups, such as NYSE Euronext and NASDAQ OMX, provides further evidence of the impact of technological change on the stock market globalization process.

NOTES

1. The most important of recent initiatives in the US is Regulation NMS passed in 2005 and, in Europe, the Markets in Financial Instruments Directive (MiFID), initially introduced in 2004. Regulation NMS is discussed in Chapters 11 and 12 of this volume. Consistent with the overall goals of the European Union (EU), the MiFID was introduced to harmonize capital markets across the EU. Despite the intentions of both initiatives, the proximate result has been an ongoing fragmentation of market liquidity.
2. In June 2008, following a merger with the Montreal exchange, the TSX Group was renamed the TMX Group.

REFERENCES

Cassis, Y. (1994), *City Bankers, 1890–1914*, transl. M. Rocques, Cambridge: Cambridge University Press.
Cassis, Y. (1997), *Big Business: The European Experience in the Twentieth Century*, Oxford: Oxford University Press.
Cassis, Y. (2006), *Capitals of Capital: A History of International Financial Centres, 1780–2005*, Cambridge: Cambridge University Press.
Cassis, Y., F. Crouzet and T. Gourvish (eds) (1995), *Management and Business in Britain and France: The Age of the Corporate Economy, 1850–1990*, Oxford: Oxford University Press.
Cetina, K. and A. Preda (eds)(2004), *The Sociology of Financial Markets*, Oxford: Oxford University Press.
Davis, L., L. Neal and E. White (2007), 'The Highest Price Ever: The Great NYSE Seat Sale of 1928–1929 and Capacity Constraints', *Journal of Economic History*, **67**, 705–39.
de la Torre, A., J. Gozzi and S. Schmukler (2007), 'Stock market development under globalization: whither the gains from reforms?' *Journal of Banking and Finance*, **31**, 1731–54.
de la Torre, A., M. Martínez Pería and S. Schmukler (2010), 'Bank involvement with SMEs: beyond relationship lending', *Journal of Banking and Finance*, **34**, 2280–93.
de la Torre, A. and S. Schmukler (2006), *Emerging Capital Markets and Globalization: The Latin American Experience*, Stanford, CA: Stanford University Press and the World Bank.
Francis, B., I. Hasan, J.R. Lothian and X. Sun (2010), 'The signaling hypothesis revisited: evidence from foreign IPOs', *Journal of Financial and Quantitative Analysis*, **45**, 81–106.
Hasan, I., M. Malkamäki and H. Schmiedel (2003), 'Technology, automation, and productivity of stock exchanges: international evidence', *Journal of Banking and Finance*, **27**, 1743–73.
Hutson, E. (2005), 'The early managed fund industry: investment trusts in 19th century Britain', *International Review of Financial Analysis*, **14**, 439–54.
Laurence, E., J. Maltby and J. Rutterford (eds) (2009), *Women and Their Money 1700–1950. Essays on Women and Finance*, New York: Routledge.
Markham, J. (2002), *A Financial History of the United States*, 3 vols, Armonk, NY: M.E. Sharpe.
Markham, J. (2006), *A Financial History of Modern US Corporate Scandals: From Enron to Reform*, Armonk, NY: M.E. Sharpe.
Markham, J. and D. Harty (2008), 'For whom the bell tolls: the demise of exchange trading floors and the growth of ECNs', *Journal of Corporation Law*, **33**, 865–939.
Michie, R. (1981), *Money, Mania and Markets: Investment, Company Formation and the Stock Exchange in Nineteenth-Century Scotland*, Edinburgh: J. Donald.
Michie, R. (1986), 'The London and New York stock exchanges, 1850–1914', *Journal of Economic History*, **46**, 171–87.
Michie, R. (1999), *The London Stock Exchange: A History*, Oxford: Oxford University Press.
Michie, R. (2006), *The Global Securities Market: A History*, Oxford: Oxford University Press.
Michie, R. (2007), 'The City of London as a global financial centre, 1880–1939: finance, foreign exchange and the First World War', in P. Cottrell, E. Lange and U. Olsson (eds), *Centres and Peripheries in Banking: The Historical Development of Financial Markets*, Aldershot: Ashgate Publishing, pp. 44–79.
Michie, R. (2009), *Guilty Money: The City of London in Victorian and Edwardian Culture, 1815–1914*, London: Pickering & Chatto.
Preda, A. (2006), 'Socio-technical agency in financial markets: the case of the stock ticker', *Social Studies of Science*, **36**, 753–82.
Preda, A. (2007), 'The sociological approach to financial markets', *Journal of Economic Issues*, **21**, 506–33.
Preda, A. (2009), *Framing Finance: The Boundaries of Markets and Modern Capitalism*, Chicago, IL: University of Chicago Press.

Rutterford, J. (2004), 'From dividend yield to cash flow: a history of US and UK equity valuation techniques', *Accounting, Business and Financial History*, **14**, 115–49.
Rutterford, J. (2006), 'The world was their oyster: international diversification pre-World War I', in J. Rutterford, M. Upton and D. Kodwani (eds), *Financial Strategy: Adding Stakeholder Value*, 2nd edn, Chichester: John Wiley & Sons, pp. 5–24.
Rutterford, J. and A. Gregory (1999), 'The cost of capital in the UK: a comparison of the perceptions of industry and the city', London: Chartered Institute of Management Accountants.
Schmiedel, H., M. Malkamäki and J. Tarkka (2006), 'Economies of scale and technological development in securities depository and settlement systems', *Journal of Banking and Finance*, **30**, 1783–1806.
Weber, M. (1894), 'Stock and commodity exchanges', transl. S. Lestition (2000), *Theory and Society*, **29**, 305–38.

PART I

HISTORICAL PERSPECTIVES ON STOCK MARKET GLOBALIZATION

1 Capitals of capital[1]

Youssef Cassis

International financial transactions have always been organized within a given geographical space, usually an urban area, in other words in the leading international financial centres. Their role is candidly described by David Scholey, a former chairman of SG Warburg & Co., a renowned City of London merchant bank now incorporated into UBS, who acknowledged in 1987 that: 'Although we would like to pretend otherwise, the financial markets are, basically, pretty simple things. All they require is a surplus of capital, a roughly offsetting deficit of capital and an intermediator or intermediation process.'[2] The definition is clear, though it could be somewhat extended by considering a financial centre as the grouping together, in a given urban space, of a certain number of financial services; or, in a more functional way, it can be defined as the place where intermediaries coordinate financial transactions and arrange for payments to be settled. In both cases, this concentration can chiefly be explained by external economies, in particular in terms of liquidity and efficiency of markets, diversity and complementarity of financial activities, workforce skills, and high-quality information. Stock markets have been at the very heart of international financial centres and part of their global development: they cannot be understood independently from one another.

This chapter is thus concerned with these 'capitals of capital', the world's leading international financial centres, from the late eighteenth century to the present. Given the transformation of the world economy, their number has remained remarkably stable, yet without being rigid. In Europe, barely half a dozen centres have really made a difference in the financial field: London and Paris; Berlin, followed by Frankfurt after the Second World War; then, to a lesser extent, Zurich (which can be coupled with Geneva), Amsterdam (before 1800 and in the 1920s), Brussels (especially before 1914), and perhaps Luxemburg (as an offshore centre). At world level, New York should of course be added from the end of the nineteenth century and, much more recently, Tokyo, Hong Kong and Singapore.

On which basis these centres should be considered as the leading ones is not entirely clear, though there is a consensus around them. In the first place, the concentration of financial services in one centre can be found at national, regional and world levels, depending on the extent of the geographical area served by one financial centre or another. All financial centres do not, therefore, have the same functions or the same importance. The more or less explicit hierarchical order of the international financial centres has become one of the main themes of the literature devoted to the subject. Economists have proposed various quantitative measures in order to rank them. They usually include the number of foreign banks attracted to a centre, the number of multinational banks based in a centre, and the relative amount of non-residents' banking deposits existing in a centre.[3] Such approaches have their limits. They allow a large number of centres to be compared, but the indicators used give only limited information on the true nature of the centres.

A different approach has been adopted in this chapter. It does not attempt to draw up a ranking or taxonomy based on quantitative measures, but rather it undertakes a comparative and historical analysis of the leading international financial centres over the last 200 years or so, with particular emphasis on the dynamics of their rise and decline. It is not only a matter of ranking them according to predefined criteria, since the reasons for a centre gaining or losing influence are complex, and can only be understood within the economic, political, social and cultural context of a particular age.

The chapter is divided into two main sections. The first briefly surveys the leading centres, with their main characteristics, at seven moments in history:[4] 1780, at the onset of the industrial revolution; 1860, in the early stages of the concentration of capital; 1900, at the height of the first globalization; 1930, on the eve of the Great Depression; 1960, in the 'Golden Age' of economic growth; 2000, at the height of the second globalization; and 2010, to take account of the effects of the most severe financial crisis in history. The second section tries to explain the reasons for their rise and decline, and to assess what the financial literature can actually teach us on this matter.

I

In 1780, Amsterdam, London and Paris were the three great financial centres upon which, in the words of a Scottish merchant: 'Europe's trade depended'.[5] Amsterdam came top with a leading position in the two main activities of an international financial centre until well into the twentieth century: financing world trade and providing capital worldwide.[6] London had already overtaken Amsterdam as a trading centre in the second half of the eighteenth century, though British traders continued to be dependent on Amsterdam for finance. Moreover, its position was enhanced by the modern financial system which had been established in Britain in the course of the eighteenth century, based on the centralization of tax collection and the institutionalization and partial securitization of public debt with a redemption plan controlled by Parliament.[7] Paris relied on the state's financial needs and the possibilities of subscribing to its numerous loans, but it was also a very cosmopolitan centre and the importance of its financial institutions should not be overlooked.[8] Behind these three centres, a number of lesser ones followed in a ranking that is difficult to determine, and which included Antwerp, then Belgium's leading financial market; Frankfurt and Hamburg in Germany; and Geneva in Switzerland.

By 1860, London had been the world's leading financial centre for about 50 years, having overtaken Amsterdam during the French Wars. London's role had its roots in Britain's dominant position in the world's economy, its share of world trade, and its exports of capital.[9] Amsterdam's decline had been very brutal, and from the turn of the nineteenth century it was reduced to the status of a lesser centre, acting as a secondary rather than a primary market.[10] The main characteristic of the mid-nineteenth century, the Second Empire in France, was the rivalry between London and Paris – not in trade finance, which remained the preserve of the City, but in capital exports. France actually exported more capital than Britain in the early 1850s and during the 1860s, although London remained the main issuing centre.[11] Interestingly, one of the most striking signs of Paris's new ambitions was the proposal made by France in December 1866 to introduce a universal currency, based on the franc, a year after establishing the Latin

Monetary Union with Italy, Belgium and Switzerland. But it came to nothing, as Britain and Prussia refused the plan. However, France's defeat by Prussia in 1871 put an end to Parisian ambitions.[12] There was no other centre of real significance in the mid-nineteenth century. The three main German centres, Frankfurt, Hamburg and Berlin, were not integrated and none of them came close to London and Paris. Frankfurt specialized in state loans, Hamburg in trade finance, and Berlin in the nascent domestic industry. Brussels took over from Antwerp in the 1830s and Belgian capital exports resumed from 1850 onwards. Geneva retained some significance through its close links with France.

The years between 1870 and 1914 were the classical period of London as the world's financial centre – not only in quantitative terms, but also in qualitative terms.[13] The City was the first modern financial centre where an unrivalled range of services were provided. In the first place, the bill on London, accepted and thus guaranteed by the merchant banks, was the main instrument for financing international trade.[14] These bills of exchange lay in turn at the heart of the huge London discount market, in which the banks of the entire world participated directly or indirectly.[15] London was the main centre for the issue of foreign loans, with Britain accounting for some 40 per cent of the stock of foreign investment in 1913.[16] The London Stock Exchange was larger than the Paris Bourse and the New York Stock Exchange combined, and one-third of all the world's negotiable instruments were quoted there.[17] The City hosted major commodity markets, such as the London Metal Exchange and the Baltic Exchange; it was the world's leading insurance market, in particular with Lloyd's of London; and it provided specialized professional services, especially legal and accounting.[18] And sitting at the apex of the system, the Bank of England was the 'conductor' of the international monetary system, the gold standard.[19]

Paris's position in the belle époque has been accurately described by Alain Plessis as that of a 'brilliant second'.[20] As in the mid-nineteenth century, its strength lay above all within its long-term capital market. The big banks were the main actors and were involved in all types of international financial activities, in particular the placing of foreign issues. And the Banque de France played a key role in the international monetary system, maintaining regulation and stability by allowing its gold to flow to London when the need arose.[21]

By the turn of the twentieth century, two new centres had established themselves in the top tier of the international hierarchy. One was Berlin.[22] The capital of the Reich not only replaced Frankfurt as Germany's main financial centre, but also became far more important at both national and international levels in the wake of the rise of Germany as a major industrial power. The big universal banks were the main players, in both international and industrial finance. However, Berlin was not in a position to rival seriously London or even Paris, if only because Germany invested far less abroad than Britain and France did. The other newcomer was New York. Interestingly, its arrival among the leading financial centres was more as an entry point for foreign funds than as the point of departure for capital exports, even if the United States had by then started to export capital.[23] New York was still dependent upon the City of London, but the institutional foundations of its future predominance were laid during these pre-war years. Amsterdam, Brussels, Zurich and Geneva could not compete on all fronts with the leading centres and specialized in certain niches where they had a competitive advantage. Finance companies, also called holding companies, were the most important in that respect, especially in Brussels and in the Swiss centres. They were set up with foreign, especially German, capital in order to finance the development of the power industry.[24]

London still ranked first in the hierarchy of international financial centres at the end of the 1920s. Of course, London's position was weakened by the First World War. Britain lost some 20 per cent of its foreign assets and, more importantly, found it increasingly difficult to regain its role of exporter of long-term capital because of the constraints weighing down its balance of payments, especially due to the lack of competitiveness of its traditional industries. It is in this particular field that London had to cede first place to New York. During the second half of the 1920s, foreign issues placed in New York generally exceeded those offered in London by 50 per cent.[25] In other activities, in particular trade finance, London regained its predominance, despite the success of acceptances drawn on New York, thanks to the establishment of the Federal Reserve in 1913, which allowed national banks to accept bills of exchange.[26] Moreover, the pound remained the main trading currency and London was far ahead of New York in international banking. In the end, as has often been argued, if capital was henceforth in New York, London had the experience and expertise, and this could still be of some use.

New York ranked number two overall and number one for foreign issues. However, it should not be forgotten that in spite of its new world role, New York remained as much an American as an international financial centre. Foreign issues played a secondary role to domestic issues and accounted for only about 15 per cent of the total amount of new issues in the.1920s. In addition, foreign capital continued to be invested in the US economy; not only long-term investment, but also short-term funds as foreign investors were attracted by American stocks, especially with the bullish trend that marked the decade. This interaction between national and international business was one of the main characteristics of New York when compared to London.[27]

Paris was weakened by the war and dropped from second to third place. France lost 80 per cent of its foreign assets following sales and, in particular, the default by the Russian and Ottoman borrowers, and the franc was swept along in the monetary upheaval in the early1920s. However, the stabilization of the franc by Raymond Poincaré in December 1926 marked a turning point: Paris recovered part of its pre-war vitality, rekindling ambitions to compete with London and New York. Paris's main asset was in fact the amount of gold and foreign claims, mainly in pounds, held by the Banque de France as a result of the surplus in the French balance of payments. The pound's fragility and the franc's strength altered temporarily the balance of power between London and Paris and put the Bank of England on the defensive. But it was above all a matter of international financial diplomacy. Paris was far behind London and New York in terms of range of financial services and networks of relationships, despite talk of a 'fight for financial supremacy' between the three centres in the early1930s.[28]

Berlin paid the price of defeat and hyperinflation. Germany became a capital-importing country, and it is mainly in this capacity that the German capital remained a significant international financial centre.[29] Amsterdam, on the other hand, was commonly described as Germany's effective financial centre during the years of inflation and hyperinflation. All the major German banks set up there after the end of the war. They were active not only in the foreign exchange market, but also in Amsterdam's own financial activities, especially the acceptance market, which enjoyed spectacular growth during the 1920s and established itself as the foremost in continental Europe.[30] Zurich and the other Swiss centres (Geneva and Basel) played a lesser, though not insignificant role in attracting foreign capital and redirecting it abroad.[31]

New York emerged as the world's financial centre after the Second World War and its position remained undisputed until the 1960s.[32] The dollar had become the main reserve currency and the linchpin of the Bretton Woods system. Even more than in the 1920s, New York was the main centre for international issues. It also reached maturity during the 1950s, with a broad range of financial institutions: the Federal Reserve Bank of New York; the commercial banks, which became the largest in the world; the New York Stock Exchange; and an extensive range of specialized firms typical of a large international financial centre. However, New York's pre-eminence corresponded to a period in which the level of international capital flows was far lower than before 1913 or after 1960, and especially 1980, mainly because of the inconvertibility of most European currencies.[33]

This was the case of the pound, though it did not apply to the sterling area. During the 1950s, it was the sterling area that gave the City the chance to remain a major international financial centre, because of its part in international trade and the pound's role as the system's anchor currency, with half of all international trade still denominated in pounds.[34]

The years that followed the Second World War opened up an unprecedented period for the Swiss centres – especially Zurich, one of the rare financial markets, along with New York, to strengthen their international position. Taken together, the Swiss centres probably ranked third, behind New York and London, in the 1960s. Switzerland's competitive advantage derived from its currency, the Swiss franc being the only convertible currency with the dollar; and the Swiss markets quickly developed their role for accommodating and investing foreign capital, through bond issues and wealth management.[35]

Paris's international position after 1945 was a mere shadow of what it had been only some 30 years earlier. More than in Britain, the state's grip, not least with the nationalization of the big commercial banks, ended up stifling the Parisian capital market. In the end, only international banking networks maintained a certain status to Paris as an international financial centre.[36] In Germany, Frankfurt, which took over from Berlin, remained a centre of national rather than international significance until the late 1970s.[37]

By the turn of the twenty-first century, New York was still in first place, even if London had the edge in direct international activities.[38] The weight of the American economy still dominated the way that its financial institutions operated, as well as the activity and turnover of its markets, which thus effortlessly outperformed the City. In any case, it was New York which set the tone in international banking and financial business, if only because of the might of the American banks, mostly based in New York, and moreover on which a great deal of London's international influence depended.

London followed in second place, thanks to Britain's policy of opening up to the world, starting with the emergence of the Euromarkets in the 1960s, which quickly made London their natural home. This policy had borne fruit at the cost, however, of a certain eclipse of British financial institutions and the City's dependence on foreign banks.

As a result of Japan's rise to the rank of economic superpower, Tokyo established itself as a major international centre during the 1970s, going in 20 years from being a regional financial centre to a centre of world dimensions. The slump of the Japanese economy in the 1990s had severe repercussions for Tokyo's international position. However, as the financial capital of the world's second economic power, Tokyo continued to play a far from insignificant role in international finance, though like New York and Frankfurt it was a centre dependent on the domestic economy.

Frankfurt only overtook Zurich and Paris to become continental Europe's leading financial centre in the late 1980s and was given a further boost by being chosen as the location for the headquarters of the new European central bank, though a decade later it appeared unlikely to overtake London. Paris had been regaining some ground since the 1980s, though it still had not really found its role. Zurich and Geneva had somewhat dropped in the ranking and had been increasingly specializing in wealth management.

Finally, one of the most striking differences with earlier periods was the rise of centres in non-Western countries. Tokyo's arrival in the 1970s reflected Japan's new economic superpower status at that time; Singapore and Hong Kong's arrival in the 1980s and 1990s was connected with the emergence of newly industrialized countries in South-East Asia.[39]

The financial debacle of 2007–08 did not fundamentally change the hierarchy of international financial centres. By 2010, the top eight centres were the same as a decade earlier and London and New York remained the two leading global centres, with Hong Kong and Singapore, ranked respectively third and fourth according to some estimates, somewhat closing the gap.[40] The transformation that the financial world was facing – regarding, in particular, its economic significance, its regulation and supervision, and its profit expectations – did not seem to affect each of the leading centres very differently. Beyond the competition still existing between them, they were all facing the same challenges.

II

How can the rise and decline of the international financial centres be explained? Contemporary economic and financial literature has identified conditions that are necessary, if not sufficient, for their development. The most important and most frequently debated of these include: stability of political institutions; strength of the currency; sufficient savings that can readily be invested abroad; powerful financial institutions; firm, but not intrusive, state supervision; light tax burden; highly skilled workforce; efficient means of communication; and plentiful, reliable and widely accessible information.[41] This list may not be exhaustive, yet it is hard to refute it. These various elements, or most of them, can be found in the centres that, at one time or another, have held a dominant position in the international hierarchy. Conversely, those centres that have seen their international influence fade lack one or several of these elements.

Yet, another analytical grid, or at the very least a different departure point, seems more apt for understanding the changes in fortune of the capitals of capital over more than two centuries. In the final analysis, the elements of explanation most commonly put forward appear to be short- and medium-term rather than the underlying causes of the relative success or failure of the main international financial centres.

I would like to propose four elements of explanation, based on long-term historical analysis. First, the rise of a major centre is closely linked to the economic power of the country that hosts it. This may seem an obvious thing, yet it is often overlooked. Each of the three cities (Amsterdam, London and New York) successively ranked top in world finance since the end of the eighteenth century has at the same time been the financial centre of the dominant national economy of the day. The same goes for Berlin's emergence in the last third of the nineteenth century, as well as for Tokyo's and Frankfurt's 100 years later, as Germany and Japan in turn acquired an economic standing that gave their respective financial centres an international dimension. Even Hong Kong owes, indirectly at least, its recent rise to the growing weight of a China that is opening up to the world economy. Nor is it by chance that in 1913 London, Paris, New York and Berlin were the four leading international financial centres, and that in 2000 the five leading centres were New York, London, Tokyo, Frankfurt and Paris. They happened to be the financial capitals of the four largest economic powers in 1913 and the five largest in 2000.[42] The ranking of the centres and that of the economies do not match exactly, since the emergence of a major international financial centre follows, with some degree of time-lag, a nation's rise to being a great economic power. Britain had already overtaken Holland when London replaced Amsterdam as the world's financial centre at the turn of the nineteenth century, while the United States was largely ahead of Great Britain when New York began to supplant London in the 1920s. Similarly, it took Tokyo about 20 years to transfer the feats performed by Japanese industry in the post-war period on to the level of international finance. This time-lag can be explained in terms of stages of economic development; of industry's gradual transition to services and finance; or of simply the force of inertia of entrenched positions.

As usual, there are exceptions that prove the rule. There is Switzerland from the 1950s to the 1990s, during which time the financial sector held a position in the hierarchy of international financial centres – probably third – that was out of all proportion to the size of the country. This position was due to exceptional circumstances arising from its neutrality during the war, capital inflows and the role of refuge currency played by the Swiss franc, as well as to the relatively weak activity of other financial centres in continental Europe, especially Paris and Frankfurt, prior to the early 1980s. Since then, whilst remaining a centre of considerable importance, Switzerland has somewhat retreated.[43] There is Singapore, able to take advantage of the emerging Asian dollar market from the late 1960s and the absence of a major financial centre in South-East Asia, but which might be threatened by the development of new centres in the region.[44] And, of course, there is London. The City's rebirth in the 1960s and its persisting rank of leading financial centre for international activities are out of all proportion to Britain's economic weight in the world. Nor can this be considered, at least not in 2010, as resulting from its role as Europe's financial centre, even if its location in the European time zone has something to do with it. This success can be explained by its still recent world pre-eminence and by its unrivalled international openness. Yet one should not forget that, although London holds top ranking for international financial activities, it drops back to third place, behind New York and Tokyo, if national financial activities are included.

A second explanation is that the fall of an international financial centre is usually triggered by a military cataclysm – irrespective of the outcome, victory or defeat. Amsterdam's demise at the turn of the eighteenth century is probably the classic example of such a path, but there are others. After the 1870 defeat, Paris marked time before beginning its long decline after the First World War, aggravated by the 1940 defeat and German occupation. The City came out of the First World War weakened and its decline seemed irreversible after the Second World War. A variation on this theme, owing to its mainly national dimension, was Frankfurt's eclipse following Austria's defeat by Prussia in 1866.[45] As for Berlin's fall, this was a direct consequence of the German defeat in 1945.

A third explanation is path-dependency. International financial centres have experienced remarkable longevity, in spite of the phases of boom and bust in the course of their existence. Once established, they kept up with the frontrunners, or caught them up again after being left behind – even though the internal ranking within the group changed and there were significant differences among the leading centres. The exception here is Berlin. This can be explained by the unique circumstances surrounding the collapse of the Third Reich and was offset by the path followed by Frankfurt, which returned to the limelight after some 80 years of obscurity. Brussels certainly lost a fair amount of ground, but Amsterdam regained an appropriate position during the course of the twentieth century. Staying power through changes in the world economy as well as the traditions of the cities of finance have played a role here.

A crucial contributory factor in the financial centres' development, and this is the fourth element of explanation, is the arrival of new talent to replenish their energy and their capacity to innovate. It is not a one-sided relationship. A centre needs to be dynamic enough to attract foreign bankers and financiers; but in return it benefits enormously from this intake. Such immigration decisively shaped the Parisian *haute banque* in the first half of the nineteenth century and swelled the ranks of international finance in London throughout the nineteenth century.[46] In New York, an entire area of investment banking was built up during the second half of the nineteenth century by German Jewish immigrants.[47] These migrations carried on during the twentieth century. The most dynamic centres continued to exert their appeal, as the anti-Semitism of the Nazi regime made numerous Jewish bankers from Germany and Central Europe leave, mainly bound for New York and London. The small centres had their intakes too, particularly Brussels in the nineteenth century and Geneva after 1945; to say nothing, of course, of the Huguenot refuges in the sixteenth and seventeenth centuries.[48] These migratory shifts have changed in nature since the 1960s, but without disappearing, and typically involve foreign bank managers settling in the main centres. Their presence is more short-lived and more impersonal, whatever their impact on business life.

These are the more long-term foundations underpinning the financial centres' development. What, then, is to be made of the conditions usually considered as decisive for their success? Inasmuch as they provide explanations that are valid mainly in the short or medium term, taking them into account serves to compensate for the apparently deterministic nature of the long-term approach and undoubtedly leads to a better understanding of the phases of boom and bust that have marked the main centres' existence. At the same time, the longer historical perspective allows us to assess the role of these factors in a given spatial and temporal context and to test their degree of universality. Two of them in particular demand a closer look: the strength of the currency and the extent of state regulation.

National currency status is an interesting case. The generic label of a strong currency, which is usually considered as conducive to the success of an international financial centre, can be described in various ways. It can be a stable currency. It can be a convertible currency. It can be a reserve currency, which works as an instrument of exchange and a unit of reserve on international level. Finally, it can be the leading currency at world level, namely the pound sterling until 1914 or even until 1931, and the dollar since 1945.

Each of these statuses has its advantages and occasionally its disadvantages, depending on the period, or more precisely the monetary regime, and on the financial centre.

During the classic age of the gold standard between 1880 and 1914, the criterion of the stability of the currency was hardly applicable insofar as exchange rates were fixed and it seemed inconceivable that one of the main currencies might one day devalue. A reserve currency undoubtedly boosted an international financial centre's activities, as shown by the franc's and the mark's contributions to the rise of Paris and Berlin. As for the distinction of being a leading currency, this meant a critical advantage for the City of London.[49]

A stable currency represents a trump card in a period of monetary instability, a period that can exist even under a fixed exchange rate system as in the 1920s. Centres like Zurich, Geneva or Amsterdam took advantage of this, in contrast to Paris (until 1926) or Berlin. The City continued after 1914 to benefit from the pound sterling's status as a world currency, but at the same time it was put at a disadvantage by the difficulties that the British economy had in preserving this status.[50]

For London, this situation went on but with difficulties mounting in the 1950s and 1960s, during which time the pound's status was reduced to that of a reserve currency. At that time, New York fully enjoyed the advantages accorded to it by the dollar's status as the leading currency. The Swiss franc's strength was undoubtedly an asset for the Swiss financial centre, strengthening its appeal and its role of refuge. The strength of the mark and the yen, on the other hand, did not play such a crucial role for Frankfurt and Tokyo. Their international development remained slow, considering the weight of the German and Japanese economies – a gap that can be explained partly by these countries' leaders opting to give priority to the expansion of the national economy.

From the 1960s onwards, an international financial centre's activity became less linked to the status of the currency of the country hosting it. The City's rebirth and then its formidable rise, based on transactions in dollars and in other foreign currencies far more than in pounds, was of course the most obvious example of this new order of things; but it can be found elsewhere, primarily in the offshore centres. The fact that there was no longer any connection between the leading currency and the leading financial centre offered development opportunities to the main international financial centres, whilst relieving them of the burden that a reserve currency might represent.

More than any other factor, state intervention and the regulatory framework have been put forward to explain the performance of financial centres. The assertion that the state should limit its interference to guaranteeing conditions that allow the market to function properly has been commonly acknowledged in the financial literature. There are countless examples showing that state interference harms financial markets' competitiveness – even without taking into account wars, when economic activities everywhere were subject to far tighter control, and other interventionist measures such as credit control or nationalizations. One only need think of the various measures intended to channel or limit international movements of capital: the need for a green light from the political authorities to list a foreign security on the Paris and Berlin stock exchanges before 1914; the embargo on foreign issues in London in the early 1920s; exchange controls in post-war Europe; the introduction of the Interest Equalization Tax in the United States in 1963; measures aimed at curbing the development of euromarkets in continental Europe in the 1960s; and so on.[51]

As we know, all these measures were more or less detrimental to the financial centres of the nations that introduced them, and they benefited rival centres. Two questions should thus be considered. First, were there any other options? And second, what damage did these measures actually inflict on the financial centres? The answer to the first question is that, in almost every case, another option was practically and, above all, politically hard to achieve. The answer to the second question is that it is doubtful whether another non-interventionist path would have made any difference at all to the medium- and long-term development of the financial centres concerned. The political authorities' meddling in the international capital market in Paris and Berlin before 1914 did not have any real repercussions on their role as international financial centres. Paris remained the 'brilliant second' and could not aspire to any other role; nor could Berlin, whose leanings were in any case national rather than international. Great store has been set by the American regulations that led to international finance's centre of gravity shifting from New York to London in the 1960s. These were political decisions whose justification or even economic effectiveness in limiting capital outflows is open to debate. It is nevertheless a fact that these measures barely penalized American banks' international activities and did not really jeopardize New York's position as a financial centre, where domestic activities had traditionally prevailed and which had always had the ability to recover at least part of its lost international business. Would Paris or Frankfurt have been able to accommodate the euromarkets and experience development comparable to London's from the 1960s onwards if the monetary authorities had shown more flexibility? That seems highly improbable.

All this does not mean that state intervention in financial matters has no effect; but it rarely determines the destinies of international financial centres in a lasting or fundamental way. It is more likely to accentuate conditions that already exist, and it is on this level that political decisions become all-important. The British authorities' firm stand on eurodollars greatly contributed towards the City's recovery, but London was much better equipped than any other centre to take charge of these operations. In Switzerland banking secrecy, introduced in 1934, strengthened the competitive advantage, if only through its neutrality, that the country already had when it came to accommodating foreign capital. The Singapore government's effort to turn the city into an international centre was far more directive, but Singapore was not lacking in financial traditions and, at that time, conditions were particularly favourable in South-East Asia. It is the same for the regulatory frameworks set up over the last 25 years as state intervention has become less direct. It was widely acknowledged until the financial crisis of 2008 that with the Financial Services Authority, founded in 2000, London had a regulatory environment that was superior to that of its main competitors, especially New York, Frankfurt and Paris. This appeared as an appreciable advantage, but it was undoubtedly as much the consequence as the cause of the City's international pre-eminence – and the big banks are unlikely to leave London with the end of 'light-touch' regulation.

What about the future? International financial centres experienced an unprecedented rise during the 25 years or so preceding the financial crisis of 2007–08, with the globalization of the world economy and the advent in Western countries of a post-industrial society, which made their services even more valuable. Nevertheless, even in their heydays, international financial centres were confronted with the criticism – muddled and not always well founded, but felt by many people – that they were responsible for the most harmful effects of globalization, especially the excessive pay of some individuals, job losses attributed to relocations, and the exploitation of the Third World. Criticism became more damning with the financial crisis: bankers in the world's financial capitals were accused of wealth destruction on a massive scale for which they earned huge and totally undeserved remuneration, before being bailed out by taxpayers' money. The world of finance will have to rebuild its reputation. In the medium and long term, however, the success of international financial centres will mainly depend on the recovery of the world economy and the maintaining of its openness, which could be threatened by a prolonged downturn, let alone a depression. International finance can only strive in a globalized economy.

On the other hand, the financial crisis should not disrupt their hierarchical order. In the medium term, New York and London are unlikely to be toppled by Hong Kong, Shanghai, Singapore or Dubai. New York took 30 years to replace London as the world's financial centre, at a time when the American economy was already far larger than the British one; and the same applies to the change of leadership between Amsterdam and London. Emerging markets will have to meet several conditions, not least in terms of wealth and openness, before claiming the mantle. On the other hand, the growing weight of a number of emerging economies, above all the BRICs (Brazil, Russia, India and China) will enable them to host a financial centre of world significance, as did Germany and the United States in the nineteenth century and Japan in the twentieth. So Shanghai, Mumbai, Moscow and São Paolo should in due course, though not necessarily at the same time, rank alongside New York, London, Tokyo, Frankfurt and Paris.

One may also speculate whether the real risk faced by international financial centres is that of becoming obsolete. This spectre has often been raised, and there is awareness of both the reasons potentially hastening their disappearance – amazing progress in long-distance communications enabling firms to access information and execute transactions from anywhere in the world – and those so far ensuring their survival: external economies, the effect of emulation and the importance of personal connections and networks of contacts. The arguments in favour of their survival are more plausible. Whilst there is a noticeable historical trend towards change in the hierarchy of the main centres, it is more difficult to discern any trend leading to their disappearance. The telecommunications revolution may certainly seem like a phenomenon without precedent, but the cities of finance have continually had to grapple with transformations in ways of exchange. These cities' layout, their functions and their organization have ended up vastly altered. Tomorrow's financial centres will reveal a different face, which will require new efforts of adaptation; but as the nerve centres of international financial activity, they remain hard to replace.

NOTES

1. This chapter is primarily based on my recent book *Capitals of Capital: The Rise and Fall of International Financial Centres, 1780–2009*, 2nd edn, Cambridge, 2010.
2. D. Scholey, 'Essential features of international financial centres', in Swiss Bankers' Association (ed.), *International Financial Centres: Structure, Achievements and Prospects*, Proceedings of the 40th International Summer School, Interlaken/Basel, 1987, p. 12.
3. See in particular H.C. Reed, *The Preeminence of International Financial Centres*, New York, 1981. For 1980, he divided the 80 centres under consideration into five ascending categories: 40 were classified

as host international financial centres; 29 as international financial centres; 8 (including Hong Kong, Frankfurt, Paris and New York) as supranational centres of the second order; 2 (New York and Tokyo) as supranational centres of the first order, and 1, London, as the supranational centre par excellence.
4. Further developments can be found in Cassis, *Capitals of Capital* as well as in the references given in this chapter.
5. S.R. Cope, *Walter Boyd: A Merchant Banker in the Age of Napoleon*, London, 1983.
6. See J. de Vries and A. Van der Woude, *The First Modern Economy: Success, Failure and Perseverance of the Dutch Economy, 1500–1815*, Cambridge, 1997; J. Jonker and K. Sluyterman, *At Home on the World Markets: Dutch International Trading Companies from the 16th Century until the Present*, The Hague, 2000; J.C. Riley, *International Government Finance and the Amsterdam Capital Market, 1740–1815*, Cambridge, 1980.
7. See in particular P.G.M. Dickson, *The Financial Revolution in England: A Study in the Development of Public Credit, 1688–1756*, London, 1967; L. Neal, *The Rise of Financial Capitalism: International Capital Markets in the Age of Reason*, Cambridge, 1990.
8. See H. Lüthy, *La banque protestante en France de la Révocation de l'Edit de Nantes à la Révolution française*, 2 vols, Paris, 1959–61.
9. See P. Matthias, *The First Industrial Nation: An Economic History of Britain, 1700–1914*, London, 1969; F. Crouzet, *L'économie de la Grande-Bretagne victorienne*, Paris, 1978; R. Floud and P. Johnson (eds), *The Cambridge Economic History of Modern Britain. Volume I: Industrialisation, 1700–1860*, Cambridge, 2004.
10. See J. Jonker, *Merchants, Bankers, Middlemen: The Amsterdam Money Market during the First Half of the Nineteenth Century*, Amsterdam, 1996.
11. A. Imlah, 'British balance of payments and the export of capital, 1816–1913', *Economic History Review*, 2nd ser., **5** (2), 208–39, 1952; M. Levy-Leboyer, 'La balance des paiements et l'exportation des capitaux français', in M. Levy-Leboyer (ed.), *La position internationale de la France. Aspects économiques et sociaux XIXe–XXe siècles*, Paris, 1977.
12. See L. Einaudi, *Money and Politics: European Monetary Unification and the International Gold Standard (1865–1873)*, Cambridge, 2001.
13. See H. Withers, *The Meaning of Money*, London, 1910; Y. Cassis, *La City de Londres, 1870–1914*, Paris, 1987; R. Michie, *The City of London. Continuity and Change, 1850–1990*, Basingstoke and London, 1992; D. Kynaston, *The City of London, Vol. II: Golden Age, 1890–1914*, London, 1995.
14. See S.D. Chapman, *The Rise of Merchant Banking*, London, 1984.
15. See W.M. Scammell, *The London Discount Market*, London, 1968.
16. See United Nations, *International Capital Movements during the Interwar Period*, New York, 1949; A.R. Hall (ed.), *The Export of Capital from Britain*, London, 1968; I. Stone, *The Global Export of Capital from Britain, 1865–1914: A Statistical Survey*, London, 1999.
17. R. Michie, *The London and New York Stock Exchanges, 1870–1914*, London, 1987; R. Michie, *The London Stock Exchange: A History*, Oxford, 1999; R. Michie, *The Global Securities Market. A History*, Oxford, 2006.
18. See Kynaston, *City of London, Vol. II*; H. Barty-King, *The Baltic Story: Baltic Coffee House to Baltic Exchange, 1744–1994*, London, 1994; B. Supple, 'Corporate growth and structural change in a service industry: insurance 1870–1914', in B. Supple (ed.), *Essays in British Business History*, Oxford, 1977; D.E.W. Gibb, *Lloyd's of London: A Study in Individualism*, London, 1957; E. Jones, *Accountancy and the British Economy, 1840–1980: The Evolution of Ernest and Whinney*, London, 1983.
19. See R.S. Sayers, *The Bank of England, 1890–1944*, 3 vols, Cambridge, 1976; B. Eichengreen, *Globalizing Capita. A History of the International Monetary System*, Princeton, 1996.
20. A. Plessis, 'When Paris dreamt of competing with the City . . .', in Y. Cassis and E. Bussière (eds), *London and Paris as International Financial Centres in the Twentieth Century*, Oxford, 2005.
21. See M. Flandreau, 'Central bank cooperation in historical perspective: a sceptical view', *Economic History Review*, **50** (4), 735–63, 1997.
22. See H. Pohl (ed.), *Geschichte des Finanzplatzes Berlin*, Frankfurt, 2002.
23. See M. Myers, *The New York Money Market*, Vol. I, *Origins and Developments*, New York, 1931; V. Carosso, *Investment Banking in America*, Cambridge, MA, 1970; S. Fraser, *Wall Street: A Cultural History*, London, 2005.
24. See S. Paquier, 'Swiss holding companies from the mid-nineteenth century to the early 1930s: forerunners and subsequent waves of creation', *Financial History Review*, **8** (2), 163–82, 2001.
25. K. Burk, 'Money and power: the shift from Great Britain to the United States', in Y. Cassis (ed.), *Finance and Financiers in European History, 1880–1980*, Cambridge, 1992.
26. B.H. Beckhart, *The New York Money Market*, Vol. III, New York, 1932; T. Balogh, *Studies in Financial Organization*, Cambridge, 1947.
27. M. Wilkins, 'Cosmopolitan finance in the 1920s: New York's emergence as an international finan-

cial centre', in R. Sylla, R. Tilly and G. Tortella (eds), *The State, the Financial System and Economic Modernization*, Cambridge, 1999.

28. See Plessis, 'When Paris dreamt of competing with the City . . .'; M. Myers, *Paris as a Financial Centre*, London, 1936; E. Moreau, *The Golden Franc: Memoirs of a Governor of the Bank of France: The Stabilization of the Franc (1926–1928)*, Boulder, CO, 1991.
29. See H. James, 'Strukturwandel im Kriegs- und Kriszeiten 1914–1945', in H. Pohl (ed.), *Geschichte des Finanzplatzes Berlin*, Frankfurt, 2002.
30. J. Houwink ten Cate, 'Amsterdam als Finanzplatz Deutschlands (1919–1923)', in G.D. Feldman, C.-L. Holtfrerich, G.A. Ritter and P.-C. Witt (eds), *Konsequenzen der Inflation*, Berlin, 1989; P. Einzig, *The Fight for Financial Supremacy*, London, 1931.
31. M. Perrenoud, R. Lopez, F. Adank, J. Baumann, A. Cortat and S. Peters, *La place financière et les banques suisses à l'époque du national-socialisme*, Zurich, 2002.
32. See M. Nadler, S. Heller and S. Shipman, 'New York as an international financial center', *The Money Market and Its Institutions*, New York, 1955.
33. M. Obstfeld and A. Taylor, *Global Capital Market: Integration, Crisis and Growth*, Cambridge, 2004.
34. See C. Schenk, *The Decline of Sterling: Managing the Retreat of an International Currency 1945–1992*, Cambridge, 2010.
35. See M. Iklé, *Die Schweiz als internationaler Bank- und Finanzplatz*, Zurich, 1970.
36. See O. Feiertag, 'The international opening-up of the Paris Bourse: overdraft-economy curbs and market dynamics', in Y. Cassis and E. Bussière (eds), *London and Paris as International Financial Centres in the Twentieth Century*, Oxford, 2005.
37. See C.-L. Holtfrerich, *Frankfurt as a Financial Centre: From Medieval Trade Fair to European Banking Centre*, Munich, 1999.
38. See R. Roberts, *Inside International Finance*, London, 1998; R. Roberts, *Wall Street*, London, 2002; R. Roberts, *The City*, London, 2004.
39. See Y.S. Park, 'A comparison of Hong Kong and Singapore as Asian financial centres', in P.D. Grub, C.H. Tan, K.C. Kwan and G. Rott (eds), *East Asia: Dimensions of International Business*, Sydney, 1982.
40. *The Global Financial Centres Index*, 5, March 2009; 6, September 2009; 7, March 2010. The ranking of the GFCI is based on measures of competitiveness.
41. See R. Roberts (ed.), *International Financial Centres: Concepts, Developments and Dynamics*, Aldershot, 1994.
42. A. Maddison, *The World Economy*, OECD, 2006.
43. See B.V. Christensen, 'Switzerland's role as an international financial center', Washington, DC, IMF Occasional Paper 45, 1986.
44. See R.C. Bryant, 'The evolution of Singapore as a financial centre', in K.S. Sandhu and P. Wheatley (eds), *Management of Success: The Moulding of Modern Singapore*, Singapore, 1989.
45. Holtfrerich, *Frankfurt as a Financial Centre*.
46. See M. Levy-Leboyer, *Les banques européennes et l'industrialisation internationale dans la première moitié du XIXe siècle*, Paris, 1964; L. Bergeron, *Les Rothschild et les autres . . . La gloire des banquiers*, Paris, 1991; Chapman, *Rise of Merchant Banking*.
47. B. Supple, 'A business elite: German-Jewish financiers in nineteenth century New York', *Business History Review*, **31** (2), 143–78, 1957.
48. S. Tilman, *Les grands banquiers belges (1830–1935). Portrait collectif d'une élite*, Brussels, 2006; Lüthy, *La banque protestant en France*.
49. See P.H. Lindert, *Key Currencies and Gold 1900–1913*, Princeton, 1969; M. de Cecco, *Money and Empire: The International Gold Standard, 1890–1914*, Oxford, 1974.
50. See S. Pollard (ed.), *The Gold Standard and Employment Policies between the Wars*, London, 1970; B. Eichengreen, *Golden Fetters. The Gold Standard and the Great Depression 1919–1939*, Oxford, 1992.
51. See S. Battilossi and Y. Cassis (eds), *European Banks and the American Challenge: Competition and Cooperation in International Banking under Bretton Woods*, Oxford, 2002.

2 The stock market and the corporate economy: a historical overview

Ranald Michie

INTRODUCTION

An 1874 study of stock exchange speculation voiced the opinion that: 'Very few persons, if any, will be found to dispute the statement that speculation on the Stock Exchange is gambling.'[1] Such a view has existed from the very beginning of the modern stock market, according to Raines: 'In popular imagery, stock markets represent the most exciting aspect of capitalism . . . where soaring bull markets bring sudden wealth only to subsequently wipe it out during spectacular crashes with the bursting of speculative bubbles.'[2] The eminent American economist Robert Shiller has employed the term 'irrational exuberance' to categorize stock markets as perennially exposed to speculative outbursts, of which the Mississippi Bubble in Paris, the Railway Mania in London, the Wall Street Crash in New York and the global financial crisis of 2007–08 are the most prominent examples. In these speculative bubbles temporarily high prices for stocks were sustained more by investor enthusiasm rather than fundamentals. These bubbles then burst when prices reached unsupportable levels and selling began to outweigh buying. In turn that had enormous consequences for the regular supply of credit and capital as banks collapsed because borrowers defaulted on loans taken out to buy stocks and savers withdrew their deposits, leaving the entire financial system in a highly weakened state for years to come.[3] In a recent study British economist and *Financial Times* columnist John Kay concluded that: 'Securities markets are better described as arenas for sophisticated professional gambling than as institutions which minimize the costs of risk bearing and allocate capital efficiently among different lines of business.'[4]

Though it has been argued that a dynamic stock market is the hallmark of a successful capitalist economy, many warn that its uncontrolled operation has the potential to inflict serious damage. To others the stock market appears to be almost irrelevant. Such a verdict is supported by evidence that shows that very little of the finance required by business is obtained through the issue of stocks. The principal sources of business finance have long been personal savings, reinvested earnings and bank borrowing, while governments have the ability to fund investment out of taxation.[5] Furthermore, the stock market is not where these stocks are issued on behalf of business, but the place where subsequent buying and selling takes place. As such, it has no direct connection to the whole process of providing the economy with the finance it requires.

However, these views derive from a standpoint that sees the relationship between the stock market and the corporate economy solely in relation to the needs of business in its quest for capital. That aspect of the stock market is important. The issue of stocks provides business with a source of long-term capital which, in turn, can leverage additional funds from banks and encourage others to extend credit. However, as the ownership of these stocks can be easily transferred, this form of financing can force management to focus on short-term profits rather than long-term growth. Hence the criticisms made of the stock market by those who view it solely from the perspective of business. There is an alternative perspective, which recognizes that the stock market serves a number of different masters. If that is followed, then the contribution of the stock market to the operation of advanced economies can be more fully understood. Important as is the ability to obtain finance through the issue of transferable stocks, that is only one of the functions that the stock market performs. The needs of the investor must also be taken into account. At all times those accumulating savings need an outlet that suits their needs, ranging from the ability to invest small amounts for short periods, to the ability to invest large amounts over long periods. It also varies according to whether they seek regular income or look for long-term capital gains. The more complex and sophisticated the economy, the greater the need there is for a financial system that continually responds to the ebb and flow of credit and capital over both time and space and between individuals, institutions and businesses.

By providing a flexible interface between borrowers and lenders the stock market ensures that the needs of all can be met in a way that maximizes the returns to savers and investors and maximizes the supply of funds available, while minimizing the costs of obtaining credit and capital and minimizing the risks involved. This means that the continuous buying and selling found on stock markets, and the accompanying volatility of prices, is normally not the product of speculation or manipulation but the process through which investors can constantly respond to their own changing needs and perceptions about the future, driven by either adverse or positive flows of information. The stock market allows investors to anticipate the future and so make provision against its consequences, rather than being caught unawares and so being forced to make rapid adjustments. Inevitably in any market economy, mismatches occur within the financial system, leading to speculative peaks and troughs. This has to be accepted as a cost incurred by any financial system where the stock market plays a central role. In return, however, the stock market provides an economy with a mechanism that continuously transmits signals to both the business and the financial community. These signals facilitate a process of adjustment both within and between business and finance. The rising stock prices of successful businesses make it easier for them to issue new stock and borrow from banks, so allowing them to expand rapidly. The converse is also true for failing businesses. Included within that is a means through which the control of a business can be transferred, so bringing in new management or creating new groupings. It is the flexibility provided by the stock market that has led to growing appreciation of the contribution it has made to a dynamic economy, because that requires change if high rates of economic growth are to be sustained over time.[6]

Finally, it must be recognized that stock markets are man-made creations that involve costs and require participants to submit to enforceable codes of behaviour. To function successfully stock markets must provide a mechanism through which buying and selling can be conducted, and that involves a cost, whether it is for a room in which to meet or for an interactive trading network. In addition, any transaction involves an element of counterparty risk that can prevent trading taking place if it is too great. In order to counteract that risk, those involved in the process of buying and selling create rules and regulations that determine which practices are acceptable and which are not. Organized stock markets offer a certainty of payment and delivery that encourages buying and selling to take place. They also provide a guarantee that the prices produced are both accurate and reliable, which means the signals being transmitted to the business and financial community reflect current supply and demand conditions. The enforcement of these rules and regulations creates a cost which also has to be met. The consequence of this is that those who meet these costs are in a position to influence the organization and development of the stock market. It also means that those who meet the costs have to receive some reward for doing so, for otherwise they would refuse to pay. The outcome of this is that stock markets have to be understood in terms of both the facilities they provide and the interests of those who pay for those facilities.

CORPORATE ECONOMY

The stock market plays its central role through its relationship to corporate enterprise. A prominent feature of an advanced economy is the important role played by corporate enterprise. Though many areas of economic activity remain the preserve of individuals and closely knit groups, or are provided on a mutual basis or by governments, it is companies that increasingly dominate the production and/or distribution of commodities, the manufacture and sale of products, and the provision of all types of services. Across the world the company has replaced the individual to become the key player in economic activities as diverse as mining, manufacturing, distribution and banking, and companies have taken over from many governments the provision of such essential services as the supply of gas, water and electricity, and the provision of telecommunication networks. With the advance of companies into retailing, education, health and business services, the role of both individuals and governments is being continually squeezed. By 2009 the market capitalization of the 45 328 companies listed on the world's stock exchanges had reached $79 trillion dollars or 109 per cent of global gross domestic product (GDP) ($72.5 trillion).[7] This can be compared to the 1913 position using the estimates of Lyndon Moore. He calculated that the value of corporate stocks quoted on the world's stock exchanges was $41.1 billion for 1913. Adjusted for 2009 prices this is equivalent to $918 billion, indicating that there had been an 86-fold increase in the absolute value of quoted corporate stocks in the course of approximately 100 years. In relative terms corporate stocks were only equivalent to 17 per cent of global GDP in 1913 when compared with Angus Maddison's global GDP figure for that date. This implied a sixfold increase in the importance of corporate stocks, which was achieved against the background of an enormous destruction of stock market value during two world wars and successive bouts of government confiscation of privately held assets and the state ownership of many areas of business activity.[8]

This growth in the absolute and relative importance of corporate enterprise was achieved through its extension into ever more diverse areas of economic activity. The changing contribution of corporate enterprise to advanced economies can be traced through the business undertaken by the world's largest 100 companies over the twentieth century, with relative importance measured by their share of the combined market capitalization. At the beginning of the twentieth century the composition of corporate enterprise was heavily orientated towards railways, because they needed to raise enormous

Table 2.1 *The 100 largest companies in the world, by market capitalization, 1912 and 2010: by activity*

Activity	Total 1912	Total 2010	% 1912	% 2010
Total	\$280 billion	\$11 843.5 billion	100	100
Mining and oil	\$28.0 billion	\$2963.3 billion	10.0	25.0
Banking/finance	\$20.0 billion	\$2795.4 billion	7.0	23.6
Manufacturing/retailing/media	\$53.0 billion	\$2176.9 billion	19.0	18.3
Telecommunications/utilities	\$179.0 billion	\$1175.5 billion	64.0	9.9
Pharmaceuticals	–	£1122.1 billion	–	9.5
Technology hardware and equipment	–	\$859.4 billion	–	7.3
Structure and Computing	–	\$750.9 billion	–	6.3

Sources: The 1912 data come from P. Wardley, 'The world's 100 largest capitalist enterprises of 1912' (forthcoming). I am grateful to Dr Wardley for permission to use his data. The 2010 data are from the *Financial Times*, 29 May 2010.

amounts of capital very quickly in order to build and operate an entire network if they were to be in a position to generate profits. A similar position prevailed with telecommunication networks, the supply of gas, water and electricity, and mass transit systems in urban areas. In all these cases an incomplete system could not provide the service required or attain the economies of scale necessary for financial viability. As a result, 64 per cent of the market value of the top 100 companies was located in the field of railways, telecommunications and urban utilities in 1912. Another 19 per cent was in manufacturing, especially such basic industries as brewing, steel production and chemicals, and 10 per cent in financial activities, particularly the large European retail banks. With only 10 per cent in mining and oil this suggests that the stock market largely appealed to the conservative investor who focused on income and security rather than capital gains.

Over the next 100 years corporate enterprise then invaded areas of business that did not require large inputs of capital delivered over a short period of time. By 2010 the proportion of the market value of the world's 100 largest companies taken by railways, telecommunications and utilities had shrunk to 10 per cent, with railways being totally eliminated. In contrast, the mining and oil sector had risen to 25 per cent, while financial services had grown to 23.6 per cent. Manufacturing had remained roughly constant in relative terms, even if extended to include retailing and media, though companies were prominent in a number of sectors that combined high levels of research and marketing with manufacturing, such as pharmaceuticals, electronics and information technology. From this it appears that roughly half the market capitalization of the top 100 companies in the world was found in high-risk sectors involving the exploration for and production of oil and minerals, or the development of new products and services at the cutting edge of technology. Companies that relied on the issue of stocks to fund growth and then rewarded risk-taking investors through high capital gains, or punished them through large losses, had become much more prominent over the course of the twentieth century (see Table 2.1).

The geographic area of operation for corporate enterprise had also widened considerably from its base in Western Europe and North America. In 1912 only 1 per cent of

Table 2.2 The 100 largest companies in the world, by market capitalization, 1912 and 2010: by location

Country	Total 1912	Total 2010	% 1912	% 2010
USA	$143 billion	$4986.6 billion	51	42.1
China	–	$1527.9 billion	–	12.9
UK	$81 billion	$1221.5 billion	29	10.3
France	$28 billion	$641.5 billion	10	5.4
Switzerland	–	$532.1 billion	–	4.5
Japan	–	$472.1 billion	–	4.0
Brazil	–	$437.6 billion	–	3.7
Australia	–	$386.4 billion	–	3.3
Russia	–	$287.3 billion	–	2.4
Germany	$8.0 billion	$284.4 billion	3.0	2.4
Spain	$3.0 billion	$217.9 billion	1.0	1.8
Canada	$11.0 billion	$147.7 billioOn	4.0	1.2
Netherlands	$3.0 billion	$118.5 billion	1.0	1.0
South Korea	–	$117.3 billion	–	1.0
Italy	–	$94.1 billion	–	0.8
Belgium	–	$81.0 billion	–	0.7
Saudi Arabia	–	$79.6 billion	–	0.7
India	–	$76.7 billion	–	0.6
Norway	–	$73.9 billion	–	0.6
Israel	–	$59.4 billion	–	0.5
South Africa	$3.0 billion	–	1.0	–
World	$280 billion	$11 843.5 billion	100	100

Sources: The 1912 data come from P. Wardley, 'The world's 100 largest capitalist enterprises of 1912' (forthcoming). This was in UK pounds. It was converted to US dollars at the prevailing exchange rate of £1 = $4.86. It was then adjusted to 2009 prices using the Measuring Worth inflation converter. The 2010 data are from the *Financial Times*, 29 May 2010 (the capital of the two UK/Australia and one UK/Netherlands companies is split equally).

the market value of the world's 100 largest companies was found outside these regions. Though large companies were found in the likes of Argentina, Australia, Brazil, India, Russia and South Africa, they were largely owned and run from head offices in Western Europe, especially London, Paris and Brussels. In contrast the position by 2010 had been transformed. By then large companies were owned and managed from head offices scattered around the world, with those in China having risen to a position of major importance. The Far East provided 17.9 per cent of the total market capitalization of the top 100 companies in 2010 compared to nothing in 1912; whereas those from Western Europe had shrunk from 44 per cent to 27.5 per cent over the same period. The one area of consistency was the USA which was the location for roughly half the market capitalization of the top 100 companies in the world in both 1912 and 2010, despite the fact that the composition had been totally transformed (see Table 2.2).

Indicative of the increasing importance of corporate enterprise for the world economy was the diminishing share of market capitalization taken by these top 100 companies. In 1912 the market value of the 100 largest publicly quoted companies was $280 billion, adjusted to 2009 prices, which was approximately 30 per cent of total stock market capitalization at that time. By 2010 the market value of the top 100 companies reached $11.8 trillion but this was only 15 per cent of total stock market capitalization, or half the level of 100 years before. What this indicates is that corporate enterprise had spread across the globe, had expanded into ever more diverse areas of business, and had penetrated much deeper into economic activities.[9] By 2009 large multinational corporations were responsible for approximately one-third of international trade as products flowed between subsidiaries located in different countries, but all integrated into global production and sales networks.[10]

For corporate enterprise to have achieved this position against, at times, such adverse conditions as war, state control and government confiscation, provides a strong basis to suggest that companies whose stocks were traded on the stock market must have possessed intrinsic merits as they were the preferred means through which a growing volume and variety of products and services were provided. These merits are associated with the organization of business into joint stock companies. In a joint stock company there was a separation between the investors, who provided the capital required by the business, and the managers, who conducted its operations. Though day-to-day control was in the hands of those who managed the company, ultimate control rested with those who owned the stocks. Hence, of fundamental importance to the growth and success of corporate enterprise in advanced economies was the role played by financial instruments known as stocks.

STOCKS

Companies sold stocks, otherwise known as shares or equities, to investors. The use of stocks and their subsequent trading made a number of specific contributions to the operation of a market economy. In essence a stock was a promise of future reward for current expenditure. The two advantages that stocks possessed, over a direct investment that would achieve the same end for both participants, were divisibility and transferability. Divisibility expanded the number of potential participants whereas transferability permitted change to take place in their composition. Both these attributes had far-reaching consequences for the financial system, though it took centuries before their full potential was realized. Divisibility expanded the absolute amount of finance that could be raised at any one time, through the ability to access the pool of passive investors. This made it possible for business to fund large infrastructure projects such as canals and railways, as their financial requirements were beyond that available to an individual or even those who might directly benefit from the project. Divisibility also mobilized funds for high-risk ventures through the ability to spread the investment among numerous individuals. This contributed to the finance of such activities as mining, where profitable discoveries were something of a lottery, or the development of new products, processes or services whose success was uncertain.

Transferability changed the time horizon associated with an investment as no repayment was promised, as with a bank loan, mortgage or the issue of a fixed interest bond redeemable at a future date. What transferability permitted was a better matching between the needs of the business and those of investors. Those who purchased corporate stocks were not locked into a long-term relationship even though the money they invested was used for long-term purposes. After the initial issue of stocks by a company, the subsequent buying and selling neither increased nor diminished the capital available to it. It involved a change of ownership, not a withdrawal or increase in the funds available to a business. That was the situation in a partnership where the retirement of a partner led to the withdrawal of capital. It was also the case in a business when a bank loan had to be repaid or a bond reached its maturity date. Instead, the buying and selling of corporate stocks was dictated by expectations, preferences and changing circumstances of different investors. Those with funds to invest and/or impressed by the business prospects of the company bought stock, whereas those in need of funds and/or worried by future performance sold. Transferability of stocks thus lowered the cost of capital as it allowed a company to attract the interest of those investors with available funds and a belief in its potential, and then their replacement by others when those investors wanted to employ their funds elsewhere or changed their opinions.

Transferability also meant that control of a business was divorced from the way it was financed. This permitted the employment of professional management and their replacement over time. No longer was the duration of a business dependent upon the individual who had founded it, and the chance that the same family would continually produce future generations of successful entrepreneurs and managers. Instead, a corporate enterprise could enjoy a permanent existence as it had the capacity to renew itself through the training of future leaders or the recruitment of such personnel from an external talent pool. This permanence gave companies the ability to reshape themselves over time through the direction of funds internally. Profits generated in one sector could be used to develop another that was seen to offer future potential. Externally, the ability to expand into new areas or create larger units through mergers and takeovers was facilitated by the ability to offer stock in the enlarged enterprise to all involved. Conversely, particular sectors could be converted into separate companies with the stock issued to the existing holders, so spawning new enterprises that then enjoyed a life of their own. A particular division of a company could also be sold, if it was valued more highly by another business, and the funds obtained either returned to the stockholders or used to finance the expansion of the remaining business. Overall, the separation of ownership and control that was a major feature of corporate enterprise meant that business could be conducted in ways that were beyond the scope of any individual or even extended family, no matter how dynamic and cosmopolitan it was. Though the Rothschilds remain a power in banking they have been eclipsed, even in the niche area of investment banking, by those who have embraced the corporate form, such as Goldman Sachs, J.P. Morgan Chase, Bank of America Merrill Lynch, Barclays, Deutsche Bank, UBS, Nomura and the like.

The combination of divisibility and transferability meant that the trading of stocks generated constantly changing prices as investors bought and sold. This price information transmitted signals which informed decision-making in business, whether regarding investment or control. Pricing signals were also of value in the wider financial community, permitting banks and others to anticipate problems among their business customers and adjust accordingly, though never eliminating the risks that were always attached to any lender–borrower relationship. This contributed to overall economic stability. In the 2007–08 global financial crisis it was not corporate stocks that created the problems, but the securitization of debt, interbank lending and the finance of long-term investment using short-term funds without an adequate capital reserve. In contrast, the issue of stocks provided companies with capital that did not have to be repaid, no matter the economic conditions. The divisibility and transferability possessed by stocks made them highly flexible financial instruments. Through the issue of stocks business was provided with a permanent source of finance, while the ownership of these stocks could be easily changed without affecting the management and operation of the business. From this analysis corporate stocks emerge as central components of financial systems within advanced economies, and have been increasingly recognized as such in the recent literature.[11]

However, none of the characteristics possessed by stocks had only positive consequences. The very divisibility of securities created an anonymity to investment which could be exploited by business. Managements could pursue irresponsible and even fraudulent strategies resulting in eventual financial collapse, as they had little to lose and much to gain. Despite such safeguards as external audits, the lack of personal oversight from investors meant that it was possible for managements to conceal their actions. Similarly, the very transferability of stocks lent itself to market manipulation, with the result that the wrong price signals were transmitted. Even if that was not the case, the constant fluctuation in the market price of corporate stocks induced short-term horizons among management as they strove to produce immediate returns, and so avoid a predatory takeover, rather than devising a long-term business strategy. This trading of stocks could also degenerate into a speculative frenzy where values became divorced from the underlying reality regarding the prospects for future growth. The outcome was windfall gains for the lucky few but the loss of savings for the many, accompanied by the destabilization of the financial system and the distortion of financial flows, none of which was conducive to the finance of long-term economic growth.[12] Thus, the very advantages that could be claimed for stocks could also be seen as their disadvantages, lending credence to the attractions possessed by alternative means of providing finance and organizing business, such as through individual enterprise, bank intermediation or state control. Such a division on the merits of stocks lies at the heart of the debate on the relative merits of different financial systems.

Comparisons have been drawn, for example, between the Anglo-American financial system, in which stocks were central, and that of continental Europe and Japan, where banks were dominant. As Germany and Japan experienced more rapid rates of economic growth in the 35 years after the Second World War than either Britain or the United States, a causal connection was drawn between the financial systems they employed and the economic success they enjoyed. Banks then emerged as the clear winners. However, a reversal in relative economic performance since 1980, and the results of research casting doubts on marked differences in bank behaviour across countries, has undermined the previous conclusion, though without reversing it. Nevertheless, a recent view is that the faltering of the growth rate of continental European economies is the result of their financial systems coming more to resemble that of Britain.[13] Furthermore, as the world enjoyed historically high rates of stable economic growth between 1950 and 1973, and these were not years marked by a heavy reliance on the use of stocks, banks and governments were credited with the success. Conversely, the years since have been ones of crisis, instability and slower economic growth when corporate stocks grew rapidly in importance, both absolutely and relatively.[14]

However, it is hazardous to draw firm conclusions about the merits of stocks from either cross-national or cross-period comparisons, considering how much else differed between countries and across time. Financial systems were only one of the variables at work, and possibly not the most important one, considering the impact made, for example, by two world wars in the twentieth century, and effects of government control and management of economies since 1945. Though it is increasingly accepted that differences between financial systems do contribute to a faster or slower rate of economic growth, identifying the precise relationship and its direction is very difficult and defies simple generalizations based on either national performances or comparisons over time. What is required is a balanced assessment of the contribution made by corporate enterprise to the operation and growth of advanced economies, recognizing both advantages and disadvantages. No financial system is perfect and none are free from both abuse and instability.

MARKETS/EXCHANGES

For corporate stocks to be of value they had to possess a market in which they could be readily bought and sold. Unlike physical assets such as land, property or commodities, stocks had no value in themselves. Their value was found in the rights the owner of the stocks possessed and the ease with which they could be acquired or disposed of. For stocks to displace direct sources of finance and bank borrowings, in the operations of business, and real property and other types of financial assets, among the portfolios of investors, there had to exist a market that maximized their advantages. There needed to exist a high level of confidence among actual or potential holders that any transfers of ownership would be fully honoured in terms of the amount, price, time, type and location. Such transfers were often part of a rapid sequence of buying and selling that was integrated into other financial transactions, such as employing borrowed funds, investing temporarily idle money or transferring ownership of assets. That meant that the existence of a market in which stocks could be easily, quickly and cheaply bought and sold was critical to their use. This made stocks and the market in which they were traded highly interdependent, with the growth in the use of the former being dependent upon the development of the latter. Though the appearance of stocks clearly predated the development of specialist markets in which they were traded, these specialist markets made an essential contribution to the increasing use made of stocks in advanced economies. Though trust was an ever-present element in all transactions it was at its extreme in the purchase and sale of stocks, given the intangible nature of the asset and the requirement for speedy transaction. The greater the delay, cost and complexity involved in arranging the transfer of stocks, the less value it possessed compared to a direct participation in a business.

However, there was always a tension between a business and the stock market. The greater the size of the business unit the more it was able to internalize market activities. Big companies were able to mobilize finance from retained earnings and then internalize the flow of funds from one sector to another, with the added advantage of minimizing the taxation that they had to pay. Multinational companies were able to do this internationally, for example. Similarly, as banks increased in size through mergers and acquisitions, they were in a position to provide more diverse financial services on an increased scale, so meeting the needs of ever bigger companies. Similarly, as institutions replaced individuals as investors they possessed a scale that allowed them to finance a business directly rather than confining themselves only to holding stocks. Businesses could raise substantial funds from banks and investment institutions or grow organically within a larger organization and so bypass the stock market. Nevertheless, the role of the stock market remained crucial for both investors in and issuers of stocks. Through an initial public offering (IPO) those who had backed a new enterprise were able to realize the profits they had made and so release funds for use elsewhere. The existence of the market provided by the stock market was essential because it provided the confidence that a profitable exit was possible, if the business prospered. At the exit stage the market provided was also essential as it allowed the participation of new investors. Many investors were not willing to finance a new enterprise, because of the risks involved, but were keen to buy stock in a business with a proven track record. Essentially, what the stock market provided was a means of matching investors with stocks across the entire risk profile. As the constant buying and selling that took place on the stock market produced authoritative prices, this matching could take place on a continuous basis.

To achieve this result required the stock market to exist on a permanent basis, and to be organized in a way those buying and selling had confidence that delivery and payment would take place, and that the price paid or received reflected current market conditions. It was this that stock exchanges delivered. By restricting entry to the market a stock exchange could impose rules of behaviour on those who bought and sold. If the rules were broken the offender could be expelled and so lose the opportunity to buy and sell in the market. Conversely, by charging for entry a stock exchange could generate the revenue required to provide and maintain not only a trading facility but also the staff required to police the regulations imposed. Those who paid to join an exchange accepted the rules governing the conduct of business there and, in return, gained direct entry to the trading community and immediate access to the constantly changing prices being generated. Both these were denied to those who did not pay for access. What this meant was that the authoritative prices generated by the trading taking place through an exchange were not a free good, but one that cost money to create in the form of the infrastructure and staffing of a stock exchange and those who policed its activities and so prevented manipulation. These costs were accepted by those using the exchange because it gave them privileged access to the trading forum and knowledge of current prices, both of which were denied to others. These costs could also be passed onto the ultimate buyers and sellers of securities because stock exchanges usually provided the best market for the most heavily traded stocks.

Buying and selling of stocks took place on stock exchanges not simply because its members might offer the cheapest transaction cost. Membership of a stock exchange gave brokers access to the market with the greatest liquidity, allowing them to transact business for their customers quickly and with the least effect on current prices. The ability to buy and sell quickly at current prices, no matter the amount, was a service valued by the largest investors, especially institutions like banks and insurance companies. This did not mean that stock exchanges were immune to competition. It was important for stock exchanges and their members to disseminate prices as that informed investors and banks of the market value of particular stocks and bonds, and so generated ongoing interest and repeat orders. These prices could be used by non-members to undercut the charges made by exchange members as they did not pay the charges levied and need not obey the rules and regulations. As communications technology improved with the telegraph and the telephone, this dissemination of prices became a growing issue for stock exchanges and their members. The solution adopted was to delay the dissemination of prices. By doing so exchanges balanced the need to disseminate prices, and the interests of members. The former was essential if stocks were to remain widely used financial instruments. The latter was essential if the charges made on members, which were responsible for the continuing existence of the exchange and the market it provided, were to continue.

Stock exchanges also brought order to battles for corporate control. There was little incentive for others to pay a premium to buy control unless there were advantages to be gained, and these were limited when the commonest form of corporate stock was that issued by railways and utilities. That began to change when all types of business adopted the corporate form, as this created opportunities for one business to expand by taking over another and so integrating its operations with its own. Management of rival companies could compete for ownership of shares and thus control, in the expectation that they would be able to generate increased profits from the combined operation. In turn, this generated increased activity on stock exchanges both through rumours about expected mergers or acquisitions and when actual bids emerged. This created a relatively new dimension to the role played by stock exchanges and they had to devise rules of engagement covering such activities as the use of inside information, stake-building and the timing of announcements. Thus, added to the traditional role of stock exchanges in creating and supervising a market for transferable assets was one of providing a means through which the control and organization of business could be continuously challenged and changed in an orderly way.

BEGINNINGS OF THE STOCK MARKET

The origins of the stock market are to be found in late medieval Italy. Emerging out of the growing trade between East and West that was taking place at that time, there was a flowering of modern finance in the city states of Venice, Genoa and Florence. Advances included such developments as deposit banking, marine insurance, bills of exchange, and joint stock companies. These companies issued either bonds (called *sopracorpo*) paying a fixed rate of interest or stocks (*corpo*) claiming a share of the profits in the shape of an annual dividend. However, these developments did not lead directly to the development of markets through which stocks could be bought and sold. The companies that existed in medieval times were small-scale enterprises owned by a few people often closely related through blood and marriage. As such they were little more than extended partnerships with no active trading in the stocks that they issued. Most activities were undertaken by individuals, families or a few partners who combined the financing and the management of the enterprise in one. It was only in a few areas of business that a need existed to form a company, such as mining and long-distance trade from the thirteenth century onwards, as these were both high-risk enterprises and required an amount of capital that few individuals possessed and were willing to lose totally. Even in these areas the companies formed were of a closed nature, with the result that transfers of stocks were private affairs with only known and trusted individuals permitted to participate. By the sixteenth century the number of stockholders remained small and little trading took place.

Out of this situation emerged in 1602 the Verenigde Oostindische Compagnie (VOC) or the Dutch East India Company. This was a well-capitalized joint-stock company that intended to send a fleet of ships to the Far East for trading purposes, returning with goods for resale in Europe. It was thus a high-risk venture that employed the joint-stock form both to obtain the level of capital required and to minimize the possible losses incurred by any single individual. From the outset VOC stock attracted the attention of Dutch investors, with at least 1000 subscribing. Each share was for 500 guilders and had an equal claim to the profits of the company. This appealed to both speculators and investors. The results of each voyage were uncertain, dependent as they were upon the survival of the ships on both the outward and homeward journey and the sale of goods both in Asia and Europe. Until each trip was completed the level of profit or loss was a complete unknown, and thus the value of the shares was like a lottery ticket, but one that had a residual value as it could be resold at any time at a price reflecting current expectations. The shares also appealed to the investor as they possessed an active market, and so could be easily bought and sold.

Turnover rose from around 100000 a year between 1603 and 1607 to 400000 per annum over the 1608–12 period. If the stock was bought for immediate delivery and simultaneously sold for future delivery (spot and forward) or an option was purchased, money could be profitably employed in holding these shares with little risk. Though the government attempted to ban such practices as early as 1610, regarding them as encouraging speculation, it proved unable to do so because of the role they played in assisting the short-term investor to cover their exposure to any sudden drop in value. Such devices as these also made the shares excellent collateral for loans, for they could be quickly sold if repayment was required or they could be held on borrowed funds in the expectation that the profits would cover the interest paid. As a result even the stock of an intrinsically risky trading venture like the VOC could serve the interests of those who had temporarily idle funds at their disposal, such as merchants and bankers. Consequently, an active stock market developed in Amsterdam as much in response to the needs of investors for a liquid asset as to provide the capital for long-distance trade and shipping. With the success of the Dutch East India Company other heavily capitalized joint-stock companies were formed in Amsterdam. Among the most notable were the Dutch West India Company formed in 1621, whose shares were also actively traded.

By the end of the seventeenth century a small but relatively sophisticated stock market existed in Amsterdam, and certainly one of sufficient importance as to be worthy of a description by a contemporary, Joseph de la Vega, in 1688. What emerges from that description is that the main stock traded remained the shares of the Dutch East India Company but the techniques in use included spot and future contracts; call, put and straddle options; margin trading, hedging and short-selling; and the ability to defer both payment and delivery. Such was the level of trust that existed in this market that buying and selling was done for a monthly settlement when the outstanding differences in the money owed were cleared through the debiting and crediting of accounts at the Bank of Amsterdam. There also existed specialist intermediaries (rescounters) who could meet any deficiency in the supply of shares either from their own holdings or by anticipating the fact that they could buy them in the market before the settlement date, indicating the importance of active trading. Most, though not all, of this trading took place through a small group of largely Jewish brokers who both acted for investors and dealt on their own account, so helping to ensure that the market was a highly liquid one. Where this market remained undeveloped was that it lacked any specific location, with trading taking place not only in the Exchange itself but also outdoors in various parts of Amsterdam. That in turn created a major weakness in the market as anyone could participate and there was no way of excluding those who did not make good their promises, as de la Vega himself notes with some concern.

The next major advance in the development of a stock market took place in London with the formation of the Bank of England in 1694. It was not the formation of the bank that was novel, for similar institutions had been formed in other parts of Europe in the past. Instead, it was the intention of the Bank of England, once formed, to lend its entire capital of £1.2 million to the British government in perpetuity in return for a guaranteed interest of 8 per cent per annum. Investors were presented with the opportunity of participating in an enterprise that would not only enable them to enter the potentially profitable world of banking, with guaranteed business from the government, but also to gain a return of 8 per cent on their money, with some reduction for the expenses of running the company. The result was a great success with the Bank of England attracting all the capital it required from numerous investors largely located in London. Whereas the Bank of England had 1509 shareholders in the early 1690s other London based joint-stock companies had many fewer: the British East India Company had only 449 and the Royal African Company only 213. What the Bank of England had done was quickly copied by others. As a result of these developments the London stock market was transformed. Between 1694 and 1709 the number of investors doubled from around 5000 to 10000 and this drove up the number of transactions. Practices in use in Amsterdam were also quickly introduced such as options and dealing for time. Dealers or jobbers also appeared who bought and sold securities on their own account, and not for clients. Nevertheless, the size of the London stock market remained small, as in Amsterdam, and had no permanent place in which trading took place. There were possibly fewer than 50 active traders in 1712, only three stocks commanded a regular market, and international interest was confined to the Dutch.

THE FIRST STOCK MARKET BUBBLE

Though the formation of joint-stock companies played a prominent role in the first stock market bubble, with the fevered buying and selling of shares, at its heart were the actions of governments in France and then Britain. The Scotsman John Law proposed to the French government a simple and quick solution to its financial difficulties through the formation of a note-issuing General Bank in 1716. Stock in this bank was offered to investors in exchange for government debt, which was accepted at face value even though it could be bought at a discount of 60 per cent. This made the stock very attractive to investors and demand was further stimulated by the payment of generous dividends to shareholders, at the same time as the ability to buy shares was increased by a great expansion in the money supply through the issuing of a large volume of new bank notes. Such conditions as these whetted the appetite of investors for stocks.

This was met by transforming a number of existing French joint-stock companies into attractive investment vehicles. This was done through the exchange of government debt for shares and then the use of those shares in the master company to take over other companies. None of these companies had attracted investor interest in the past or enjoyed much in the way of trading success, unlike their counterparts in Amsterdam or London.

The first to be given the 'Law' treatment was the Mississippi Company. This had begun as a company with a charter giving it a trading monopoly in French Louisiana, which was the entire area of North America accessible via the Mississippi–Missouri river systems. Law then proceeded to merge the Mississippi Company, renamed the Compagnie des Indes, with a series of other French companies through a series of leveraged buyouts. The result was the creation of a huge joint-stock company that had monopoly rights not only over much of French trade with Asia, Africa and North America, but also to sell tobacco and mint coins within France. This convinced investors that it was capable of generating huge profits and this belief was fuelled by a proposed dividend of 12 per cent for 1720. By November 1719 the company had a market value of 5 billion livres. However, it was not simply expectation about the company's prospects that generated investor enthusiasm. This enthusiasm was also cleverly manipulated by the actions of John Law. In 1719 the General Bank was converted into the Royal Bank which extended almost unlimited credit to those wishing to buy shares in the Mississippi Company. These shares were available in a partly paid form so they could be bought by investors of limited means in the expectation that they would be paid up over time or, hopefully, sold at a great profit before further instalments were required. This was not all. It was stipulated that only holders of existing shares could subscribe to new issues, which were expected to offer even better returns. This caused a scramble for the existing shares which drove up their price, as those holding them were reluctant to sell as they hoped for even greater gains in the future.

The shares in the Mississippi Company rose from around 500 livres each in middle of May 1719 to around 5000 livres by the end of August, with hopes that they would rise even higher as the company was to refinance the entire French national debt. By then a speculative mania was in full swing, sustained not by any realistic prospects of future profits but by the money to be made through buying and selling the shares as the price rose, which sucked in more and more investors from throughout France and even Europe. In December 1719 the price of the shares reached about 10 000 livres. Attempts by Law to restrain speculation through limiting bank lending proved unsuccessful, and the boom continued into 1720. By then the Mississippi Company itself was supporting the market by buying in shares and guaranteeing a minimum price of 9000 livres, so simultaneously reducing supply and limiting the risk of loss. A price of 12 500 livres was reached in March 1720, with many confidently expecting it to go much higher still. This confidence was based on the supposed prospects of a giant joint-stock company formed through the merger between the Mississippi Company and the Royal Bank. However, the bubble was on the point of bursting. Fearing that the situation was out of hand the French government attempted to reduce the paper money in circulation, as that was leading to rampant inflation, and to dampen speculation by removing the guaranteed price to Mississippi shares. Investors were now faced with tighter credit and a falling share price, and so sought to sell rather than buy. In the course of two weeks in May the share price halved, reaching 4200 livres by the end of the month. The speculative boom was truly over and a panic had ensued as investors recognized that there was now no reason to hold for a gain, and instead attempted to sell so that they could pocket their profits or simply repay their borrowings. Fearing the vengeance of impoverished investors, John Law fled France in December 1720.

Contributing to the collapse were developments in London where attempts by the British government to convert more of its debt into corporate stock also led to a speculative bubble. In particular, the South Sea Company converted itself into a vehicle through which money raised from investors was used to purchase government debt bearing a fixed rate of interest. To encourage people to buy its stock the South Sea Company lent out the money it received from investors buying its shares, to those shareholders who then bought more shares in the expectation that the price would rise and they could sell out at a large profit. Their very actions then drove up prices, encouraging shareholders not to sell but to make additional purchases, while new investors were attracted because of the prospect of gain. These investors came not only from within Britain, with British investors selling Mississippi stock in Paris to purchase South Sea stock in London, but also from across Europe, such as the Netherlands and Switzerland. French investors were also switching from Paris to London, so weakening the demand for Mississippi stock. The speculative boom also spilled over into other investments with a wave of new joint-stock company promotions in London. During 1719–20 around 190 new joint-stock companies were proposed and they expected to raise £220 million. Apart from London Assurance and Royal Exchange Assurance most came to nothing. Nevertheless, before they disappeared there was great activity in the securities market as shares changed hands at greatly inflated prices. Though Paris and then London were the centres of speculation in Europe in 1720 they were joined by Amsterdam, Geneva, Hamburg, Lisbon and Vienna. However, these speculative booms elsewhere in Europe were both short-lived and limited in scope, with collapse following shortly upon the ending of the boom in London. By October these speculative booms had petered out across Europe. In France, the epicentre of the bubble, the government liquidated the Mississippi Company, dissolved the Royal Bank, cancelled the paper currency and issued government debt to cover part of the losses incurred by investors.

POST-BUBBLE

In the wake of the collapse of Mississippi and South Sea bubbles, investor interest in corporate stocks waned. Most forms of business could be financed from personal savings and informal networks while investor demand was satisfied by the issue of growing amounts of public debt. In 1750 the Amsterdam stock market traded the shares of only three Dutch companies. In the late eighteenth century there was some renewed interest in stocks in both Britain and France. In England in the 1780s this focused on the promotion of canal companies, as these required a large initial investment but promised safe and steady dividends from the tolls paid by the users. Speculators were also attracted to canal shares because of the unknown prospects of profit once in operation due to the potential traffic they could carry. However, this interest in corporate stocks quickly died away once government borrowing resumed its upward trajectory in the 1790s, with the need to finance the wars that ravaged Europe until the defeat of Napoleon at the Battle of Waterloo in 1815. It was not until after investors had absorbed the debt created by governments to finance these wars, including French reparations, that the formation of joint-stock companies resumed. This was the case across Western Europe and in the USA. This even led to a speculative bubble in London with an estimated 624 joint-stock companies promoted in 1824–25 with a nominal capital of £372.2 million, or four times the number and eight times the capital of those already in existence at the end of 1823. These joint-stock companies covered a wide range of activities, ranging from domestic canal and railway projects to financial concerns aiming to channel British savings abroad. Among those that attracted the greatest interest from speculators were foreign and domestic metal mining companies. This speculative boom collapsed towards the end of 1825, in the wake of a tightening of credit due to a poor harvest, leaving investors with large losses. Of the joint-stock companies, 80 per cent had disappeared by the end of 1826.

In the 1830s there was another flurry of joint-stock company formation, though on a much smaller scale, which resulted in a further addition to the number in operation. However, neither the number of companies nor the field of enterprise within which they operated had been much extended. Though numerous joint-stock companies were formed, most were little more than extended partnerships, being owned by relatively few investors. Of the larger ones few survived long, as in the case of the French companies formed in both the 1820s and 1830s. Of those that did banks, insurance and gas lighting companies were prominent examples. Along with Western Europe, joint-stock company formation grew rapidly in the USA at this time. The continuing decline in the level of the US national debt, which had become almost negligible by the mid-1830s, meant that there was considerable investor interest in corporate stocks. Joint stock companies also offered a means of mobilizing collective savings to finance all types of enterprise in a rapidly growing economy that was short of finance. However, even among the joint-stock companies that did appear only a few were of such a size as to attract numerous investors. Most numbered their shareholders in the hundreds, with only an institution like the Second Bank of the United States having widespread investor appeal. It had 4145 domestic shareholders in 1831, while there were also many others from abroad. Nevertheless, in both Western Europe and North America the growing number of joint-stock companies by the 1830s did lead to the establishment of organized markets where stockbrokers could regularly meet so as to buy and sell.

In addition to the long-established exchanges in London and Paris, where corporate stocks were traded along with bonds and government debt, stock markets appeared in a growing number of cities, providing a forum through which locally held stocks could be regularly traded. Major American cities all had stock exchanges by the 1830s, such as New York, Philadelphia, Baltimore and Boston. The number of stocks listed on the New York Stock Exchange rose from 28 in 1820 to 112 in 1840, for example. In turn, the existence of such markets encouraged the formation and growth of more companies, which in turn stimulated the creation of additional markets, improvements in the facilities they provided, and refinements in the rules and regulations under which trading was conducted. No longer was the buying and selling of corporate stocks dependent upon an informal market where much was left to chance, prices were exposed to manipulation and counterparty risk was high.

RAILWAYS AND THE GROWTH OF CORPORATE CAPITALISM

It was the financial need of railways that was to take the stock market to an entirely new level by the eve of the First World War. Only by issuing stocks could railways obtain the long-term finance they needed, as the amount required was too great for any individual or even extended partnership. Even banks were not in a position to provide the finance, given the length of time before any loan could be repaid. In the years from 1843 to 1845 there was a railway mania in Britain as investors became ever more enthusiastic about the prospects of each line proposed. As in the past, this speculative boom had its origins in a temporary mismatch between the growth of savings and the existence of remunerative openings. Under these circumstances investors turned eagerly to the stocks issued by railway companies. These appeared to offer investors an almost guaranteed return as, once built, a railway line had a near monopoly of transport between the towns that it served. As in past speculative bubbles this growing enthusiasm among investors for stocks developed a momentum of its own that eventually became a mania. The stocks issued by railway companies, usually in a part-paid form, became speculative counters being held for future gain rather than because of intrinsic worth. This situation was fuelled by generous bank lending using inflated share values as collateral.

Eventually the boom came to an end towards the end of 1845. Triggering the collapse was a poor harvest, as this led to a tightening of credit. This brought the boom to an abrupt end as a wave of selling overwhelmed the market, bankrupting those who had overextended themselves by borrowing extensively and bringing down the most exposed banks. Nevertheless, the result was to leave a permanent expansion of corporate stocks in Britain. The very vitality of local investment by local investors in local stocks, combined with the excitement of speculation in the 1840s, drove the formation of additional stock markets outside London. By the end of 1845 there were some 18 provincial stock exchanges in existence in Britain compared to three at the beginning of the decade, and most major towns possessed at least one.

Though the railway mania of the 1840s was very much a British affair it was mirrored in a number of other countries, though never reaching the same extent or intensity. By 1847–48 railway shares had become as popular as government debt in France, attracting around 200 000 investors. The result was to transform the French stock market not only in terms of the level of activity but also geographically, as exchanges were formed outside Paris in such places as Bordeaux, Lille, Lyons, Marseilles and Toulouse. The same process took place in a number of other countries around the world in the 1840s and 1850s, as in the USA, where railway stocks helped expand an already thriving stock market. It was in the years after 1850 that the world's railway system expanded enormously, with a large proportion being provided by joint-stock companies, though governments also played an important role. By 1900 the length of track opened had reached 765 222 kilometres compared to 38 152 in 1850. In addition to railways, joint-stock companies also provided tramways, subway systems, telephone networks and electricity generation and distribution. Also, in many rapidly developing economies the joint-stock form was used as a way of mobilizing scarce finance for mining and manufacturing as well as urban facilities. The use of the joint-stock company form and the issue of shares offered a way of both sharing risk and raising capital, and so it was adopted in many countries around the world when new capital-intensive methods of production were introduced. In Russia the development of both the cotton textile industry and the iron and steel industry was done through joint-stock companies and the issue of stocks and shares. Similarly in Japan the country's early industrialization was aided by the ability of the cotton spinning companies to issue shares. In India the development of industries as diverse as tea planting, textile production and coal mining was heavily dependent upon the formation of joint-stock companies and the issue of shares.

The most prominent area of economic activity where this took place was in mining. Throughout the Americas, Australia, Asia and Africa, and even in Europe, and ranging from gold and silver to copper and oil, joint-stock companies were formed to explore and develop mineral resources. Mining was an industry that delivered large gains to a fortunate few accompanied by total loss for the great majority, especially in the early development phase. Mining companies both appealed to the gambling instincts of investors and also required their financial support if output was to move beyond the stage of individual effort. One measure of the increasing volume of corporate stocks in existence, as well as their diversification, comes from the USA. Between 1860 and 1912 corporate stock outstanding in the USA grew from $0.7 billion to $32 billion. Whereas railway stocks comprised 15 per cent of the total in 1860 they had grown to 39 per cent by 1900, but then fell back to 26 per cent by 1912. In contrast, the stocks of mining and manufacturing companies grew from 34 per cent in 1900 to 52 per cent in 1912, with the emergence of such giant industrial companies as US Steel.[15]

Overall, it can be seen that from the 1840s corporate stocks grew steadily in importance as a proportion of national assets. This was despite competition from governments with their need to finance wars and their investment in railway infrastructure, either through new build or by purchasing the assets of existing companies. Where railway systems were taken into state ownership the advance of stocks as a proportion of national assets could be reversed, as investors were given bonds in exchange. Banks were also growing rapidly in this period as they spread into new areas and deepened their penetration of existing markets. The growing scale of banks also gave them the ability to finance larger projects for longer periods, with Germany being the main location for universal banks. These met the need that business had for both short-term and longer-term capital. Though always a small percentage of national assets, stocks had grown in significance in countries as diverse as Japan, Russia and Switzerland, and played an important role in the USA, the UK and South Africa (see Table 2.3).

With this huge increase in the amount and distribution of corporate stocks worldwide there was a corresponding need for formal markets within which they could be traded. As each of these markets was a product of local conditions, the outcome was a great diversity among the exchanges in which stocks were traded. Despite this diversity each stock exchange was increasingly drawn into a worldwide network that integrated them all into a single global securities market. Most of the stock exchanges that were established around the world before 1914 provided a local market for a restricted range of locally held corporate stocks and the interests of local investors ranging from banking and insurance companies through local utilities providing gas, water, electricity, railways and urban transport to the growing number of industrial, commercial and mining concerns. In 1900 the Shanghai Stock Exchange listed 68 companies and the Tokyo Stock Exchange 130.

What developed in the half-century before 1850 was the spread of stock exchanges

Table 2.3 Corporate stocks as a percentage of national assets, 1850–60 to 1937–40

Country	1850/60 (%)	1875/85 (%)	1895/1900 (%)	1912/14 (%)	1927/30 (%)	1937/40 (%)
Belgium	6.5	6.5	5.1	8.34	7.9	3.5
Denmark		9.2	8.8	8.8	13.0	7.3
France	1.0	2.7		5.1	2.7	
Germany	0.5	1.7	2.7	3.2	3.0	2.5
India	0.2	0.2	0.3	0.5	0.6	0.8
Italy	1.8	0.9	1.2	0.8	3.8	3.0
Japan		0.5	3.8	4.7	6.8	11.8
Norway		1.7	3.1	4.5	4.7	3.5
Mexico					6.4	11.9
Russia				2.1		
South Africa				16.4	12.0	17.5
Switzerland		4.7	6.2	7.5	10.6	9.5
UK	3.0	4.0	16.1	14.0	15.7	17.6
USA	5.5	9.2	9.2	12.5	19.4	11.5

Source: R.W. Goldsmith, *Comparative National Balance Sheets*, Chicago, IL: Chicago University Press, 1985 – national tables.

throughout the globe. Whereas the major stock exchanges of Western Europe combined trading in both government debt and corporate securities, those that were established elsewhere in the world were really only markets for the stocks and bonds of joint-stock companies. Some only traded shares, such as the numerous mining markets and the many stock exchanges located in the smaller cities of the world. This was even the case for the New York Stock Exchange. An estimate made in 1911 suggested that whereas the annual turnover in stocks on the New York Stock Exchange was $15.5 billion, that for bonds was considerably less at $0.8 billion, or 5 per cent of the total. This led to a fundamental division between those exchanges that traded both fixed interest securities – especially those issued by governments – and corporate stocks, and those that confined themselves to stocks. Underpinning this difference before 1914 was the fact that investors in Western Europe owned a large proportion of the securities in existence in the world, especially government debt and corporate bonds. This left exchanges outside Western Europe to focus on stocks.

This was not the only substantial difference between exchanges at this time. There also existed two major types of stock exchange. In continental Europe and a number of Latin American republics stock exchanges were, on the whole, subjected to a great deal of government intervention, even leading to control. This was often driven by a desire by government to eradicate market abuses and limit speculative outbursts. However, the result was to limit the business that passed through the exchanges, forcing it to take place outside or through banks. In contrast, in most of the rest of the world, and especially in Britain, its Empire and the United States, the growth and operation of stock exchanges was largely free of government intervention, being driven by the needs of the market participants to provide a means whereby trading could take place easily, cheaply and securely. There were, of course, exceptions to this, with the Dutch and then Belgian stock exchanges operating largely free of central government control, while in Japan the reorganization of the stock exchanges after the crisis of 1893 resulted in the government acquiring an element of control. Nevertheless, the consequence of all this was to establish a fundamental divide between the stock markets of continental Europe and those of the Anglo-Saxon world. In turn, this intervention had wider implications for national financial systems, which was manifested by the somewhat different roles played by banks and securities markets.

By 1914 stock markets played a key role in the financial systems of most advanced economies and had also established a niche position within less developed countries. Though far from becoming the universal means through which business raised funds or people employed their savings, stocks had achieved a high level of penetration among the most sophisticated borrowers and investors. Internationally, stock markets were no less important, being instrumental in the worldwide movement of funds that provided the finance for major infrastructure projects and the development of the earth's minerals and oil.

THE FIRST WORLD WAR AND ITS AFTERMATH

Within seven days of the outbreak of the First World War the stock exchanges of the world had ceased to function. Though far removed from the scene of conflict the Johannesburg Stock Exchange, for example, closed on the 1 August 1914, faced with an avalanche of selling of South African mining stocks from abroad, which threatened to ruin their members as prices fell precipitously. These closures were not to be brief, considering the worldwide nature of the conflict and its growing intensity. The nature of modern warfare required the mobilization of all resources available to each nation state and that had implications for the domestic and international operations of stock markets. Consequently, there was a general reluctance among governments to condone a quick reopening even though buying and selling took place elsewhere, such as on the street, in offices or via the telephone. Even when stock exchanges did reopen the level of business remained low. In Canada there was little interest in mining and oil stocks, for example, as investors placed their savings in government debt, and this was typical of the situation around the world. Contributing to this low level of activity were the restrictions imposed by governments and the actions of the stock exchange authorities themselves, which had the aim of reducing market volatility as that might undermine the national war effort.

A more long-term consequence of the war was the sale by Western Europe investors of the stocks of companies operating elsewhere in the world. In particular, US and Canadian corporate stocks, which were extensively held in Europe, were sold back to investors in these countries and the proceeds used to finance the war. In other countries, such as Russia, regime change led to the confiscation of corporate enterprise and the repudiation of the holdings of investors, whether domestic or foreign. The result was the eclipse of stock markets around the world as investor interest focused on the more immediate wartime needs, especially the issue of debt by governments (see Table 2.3). Though inflation and defaults made the return on bonds negative over the 1910 to 1919 period it was little better for corporate stocks, and they lacked the patriotic appeal of government debt for investors at a time of war (see Table 2.4).

Table 2.4 Real return on assets: world average by decade (geometric mean, % per annum)

Period	Bonds	Stocks
1900–1909	0.3	5.4
1910–1919	−7.9	−3.7
1920–1929	5.5	13.0
1930–1939	5.3	1.7
1940–1949	−4.8	1.0
1950–1959	−0.4	17.1
1960–1969	0.6	5.5
1970–1979	1.6	0.9
1980–1989	6.6	13.5
1990–2000	5.8	5.4
1900–2000	1.2	5.8

Source: E. Dimson, P. Marsh and M. Stanton, *Triumph of the Optimists: 101 Years of Global Investment Returns*, Princeton, MA: Princeton University Press, 2002, p. 313.

However, this was to change in the 1920s as investors who had bought government debt during the First World War switched to the growing number of stock issues by industrial and financial companies. These offered the prospect of avoiding the consequences of inflation, as in Germany or France, or participating in potential capital gains where deflation prevailed, as in the USA and the UK. This trend was most apparent in the USA where the number of shareholders in major US corporations grew rapidly between 1910 and 1930. The number of shareholders in American Telephone & Telegraph rose from 35 823 to 469 801, US Steel from 22 033 to 167 951 and Pennsylvania Railroad from 65 283 to 196 119. Comparing 1925 with 1913, Moore calculated that the global market value of corporate stocks rose from $41.1 billion to $61.8 billion or by 50 per cent, though in real terms there was a decrease to $33.8 billion at 1913 prices. In both Germany and France there was even a decline in nominal terms because of the considerable disruption that their economies experienced during and immediately after the First World War, along with the large loss in the holdings of foreign corporate stocks. It was the USA that experienced real growth, with the $9.1 billion of 1913 becoming $12.2 in 1925, even after adjusting for inflation.[16]

THE WALL STREET CRASH AND ITS AFTERMATH

In the light of the gains made by investors holding US corporate stocks, and the prevailing low interest rates, American investors became active purchasers. This both pushed up the price of existing stocks and encouraged ever more businesses to convert into joint-stock companies and to issue stock. New stock issues in the USA grew from 1822 in 1921 to 6417 in 1929. As stock prices rose and the volume of available stock expanded, investors borrowed ever more money from banks and brokers in order to participate in the capital gains to be made. The risk in this situation was that a sudden collapse in prices would leave banks holding stocks as collateral whose value no longer covered the amount of the loan. As a result, a highly dangerous situation was building up in the United States in the 1920s and the longer the boom went on the more likely it was that the collapse would be sudden and steep, as it was based more and more on expectations that were becoming daily less and less realistic. The call loan market in New York grew rapidly in the 1920s with the money coming from the largest banks in the city. These New York banks employed not only their own money in this way but also the large balances maintained with them by correspondent banks from across the United States. By September 1929 a total of $6.5 billion was lent out to New York brokers and dealers. In 1920 the estimated turnover in outstanding stocks was put at $39 billion and this had risen to $157 billion in 1929.

Inevitably, the speculative boom came to an end as the cost of borrowing rose and the level of selling grew as the more cautious among the investors sought to realize their gains. That came in the course of 1929 in response to a gradual tightening in the money market. Faced with rampant speculation the Federal Reserve Bank began raising the interest rate charged on loans, and this was a signal to the market as a whole. As it was, stock prices peaked on 3 September 1929, when the Dow Jones Industrial Average reached 381, and then began to fall. This prompted a build-up of sales as investors tried to realize their holdings. The Crash began on 24 October 1929 (Black Thursday) when sales reached almost 13 million shares on the day, with a sharp fall in prices. On 29 October (Black Tuesday) sales reached almost 16 million shares with another sharp fall in prices. Eventually the bottom of the market was reached in July 1932 when it was down 89 per cent from the 1929 peak.

The result was to leave many investors much poorer as the stocks they held had collapsed in value. Much more pervasive was the fact that banks were left holding both overvalued stocks and loans with inadequate collateral and little prospect of repayment, especially as the stock market collapse was so prolonged and deep. The result was a sequence of crises and banking collapses as depositors rushed to make withdrawals when the precarious situation of individual banks became known or even rumoured. By the end of 1931 a total of 2290 banks had failed in the United States, while a further 1450 failed in 1932. Under these circumstances savers were reluctant to trust banks and banks focused on ensuring a high level of liquidity so that they could meet sudden panic withdrawals. They thus restricted all types of investing and lending at home and abroad. This severe credit contraction created temporary but serious difficulties within the USA. It also had major international implications as both banks and governments around the world had come to rely upon borrowing from US investors to cover deficits. As a result there was a slow unravelling of the complex web of financial links that had supported the international economy during the 1920s as each crisis came and went.

Faced with the actual or imminent closure of their national banks in the wake of the Wall Street Crash, governments around the world intervened to prevent a complete financial collapse. In the USA the Securities Exchange Act was passed in 1933 and that was followed by the establishment of the Securities and Exchange Commission in 1934. The result was a radical transformation in the relationship between stock exchanges and the government in the United States. Generally, the stock market was perceived to be the immediate cause of the financial crisis, rather the ongoing instability caused by the First World War, and so governments felt justified in placing controls on its operation in most countries or even closing them down completely. As stock exchanges already existed to regulate the market they were the obvious mechanism through which this control could be exercised. The result was to discourage the use of the stock market by business in comparison to the funds provided by banks. Even where new stock issues continued to take place, as in the USA, they were often confined to the over-the-counter (OTC) market rather than on a formal stock exchange. Whereas in 1920 the OTC market commanded only 6 per cent of all trading in corporate stocks, and 14 per cent in 1929, this had reached 23 per cent in 1939. Overall, estimated turnover in outstanding stocks fell from $157 billion in 1929 to $14.8 billion in 1939.

Around the world in the 1930s governments imposed controls on the financial system, blaming it for the global financial crisis and subsequent economic depression. Internationally these controls limited the free movement of funds around the world, and domestically circumscribed both banks and the stock market. Thus, even in those countries where the stock market was allowed to operate relatively freely it was subjected to external scrutiny and regulation. As a result the stock market increasingly lost a number of its traditional functions. Banks were less willing to lend to those providing stocks as collateral, having witnessed the consequences of such policies in the wake of stock market collapses. Stock market authorities also became more conservative, being less willing to offer a trading opportunity for speculative enterprises, as in those companies involved in mining and the development of new technology. The effect of this was to push such business towards banks, governments and existing companies, or into unregulated areas of the stock market.

THE SECOND WORLD WAR AND ITS AFTERMATH

On top of all this came the Second World War, in which government borrowing was again prioritized. Though the stock market in such countries as the USA and the UK continued to function throughout the war, elsewhere many stock exchanges were closed and even destroyed. Whatever the position, the result of the war was to relegate the stock market to a very minor role in the financial system, as governments absorbed all available savings and banks became the main instruments through which financial flows took place in market economies. Even in neutral countries governments imposed controls in the interests of preserving stability and limiting the effects of events taking place in the war zones. This then created a precedent which was followed once the war came to an end. In the new world that existed after 1945, governments dictated not only whether stock markets were allowed to exist in their country but also the scope of their activities, when they did exist. Whereas the stock market had been an important source of corporate finance in Japan before the Second World War, it ceased to be for many years afterwards, having been replaced by retained earnings, bank loans and business networks. The cause of that can be traced directly to the monopoly given to the organized stock exchanges and the costly and rigid regulations imposed by the government. Similarly two-thirds of the finance used to finance investment by corporate enterprises in Germany came from internal sources between 1950 and 1969, with most of the rest being provided by banks. In France business relied on reinvested profits and bank loans for most funding in the 1950s and 1960s.

From the perspective of many investors, though, the increased supervision of stock exchanges by government increased the appeal of the stocks that they quoted. Corporate stocks had traditionally been regarded as involving greater risk than bonds because their return was not guaranteed. The return generated from ownership of corporate stocks depended upon the ability of the business to generate profits greater than the amount required to pay interest on borrowings, whether from banks or via the issue of bonds. Railways and public utilities were able to do so with a high degree of regularity because demand for the service they provided was almost constant and costs varied little. Conversely, there were corporate stocks that involved a high degree of risk, with those dependent upon exploration for oil and minerals, developing a new product or technology or supplying a new service being at the most extreme. Such companies attracted investors because of the potentially high gains to be made if the results were successful. If unsuccessful, a total loss could result. However, in the more highly regulated era that followed the Second World War such stocks became more respectable in the eyes of investors. Careful vetting removed those that were fraudulent, dubious or highly risky to the advantage of those that offered investors an attractive combination of income and capital appreciation. Such a combination proved to be increasingly popular among investors as inflation became a feature of most economies beginning in the 1950s.

Inflation created a real predicament for investors as it led to returns falling in real terms. In contrast, corporate stocks could offer the prospect of a return that would keep pace with inflation as earnings grew through the ability to pass on rising prices to customers. In turn, that was reflected in the value of the business and the dividends paid, which would result in rising share prices. In the 1950s global equity returns averaged 17.1 per cent per annum compared to a loss of 0.4 per cent per annum for bonds. Though these equity returns fell in the 1960s, and those for bonds rose, they continued to be more attractive investments. The effect of this recovery on the stock market can be seen in the case of the New York Stock Exchange where the turnover of shares rose from 0.8 billion shares in 1960 to 2.9 billion in 1970. Similar growth was observed in other leading stock exchanges like London and Tokyo. Trading on the Tokyo Stock Exchange grew from 1.3 million shares per day in 1949 to 130.4 million in 1963.

However, not all stock exchanges benefited. Trading in stocks gravitated away from the smaller stock exchanges. By 1970, the Tokyo Stock Exchange handled 72 per cent of the total volume of securities trading in Japan compared to 63 per cent in 1960, and this was typical of the process taking place around the world. In the past, investors in stocks had favoured both local and national exchanges. Investors used familiarity as a guide at a time when the science of investment was still rudimentary. In addition, there remained advantages to local management, local production and local services until full economic integration was achieved. However, that situation was transformed after the Second World War. In addition to greater economic integration encouraging the growth of ever larger companies, the process was also responsive to the great increase in government intervention after 1945. The increased level and complexity of legal requirements and the taxation system imposed a growing burden of compliance on business. That burden fostered a growing scale of enterprise as only the largest companies possessed the managerial structure and staffing that could cope. Through mergers and acquisitions, businesses grew bigger as a result, and so the market for their stocks gravitated to the largest exchanges. In countries as diverse as Australia, South Africa, India and Peru, trading increasingly converged on a single stock exchange encouraged by national governments as an easy solution to the problem of ensuring that the national securities market was an orderly one, relatively free of excesses and scandals.

Law and taxation also changed investment behaviour as it encouraged collective rather than individual activity. The rise of the institutional investor was a marked feature of the post-war years. Institutional investors had long existed in the form of the insurance company and the investment trust, but they really flourished after 1950, when there was an expansion in pension provision by both business and quasi-official bodies. In this, they were emulating the state-financed schemes that relied on taxation, as well as responding to the emerging complexity of investment. In the past, an individual or institutional investor purchased government debt, mortgages or corporate bonds and then lived on the regular income they produced. In contrast, corporate stocks required both more active and more expert management because the return was unknown and the risks greater. To minimize these risks a diverse portfolio was required, and this was best done collectively for all but the exceptionally wealthy. The effect was to move control over the sale and purchase of corporate stocks from the individual using their knowledge and connections, often on a local basis, to trained fund managers. Reflecting the growing popularity of corporate stocks among investors was the fact that their market value in the USA grew from $110 billion in 1946 to $859 billion in 1970. At the same time the proportion owned by institutional investors tripled from 7 per cent to 21 per cent. In Japan institutions held 39 per cent of listed stocks in 1950 but 57 per cent in 1970.

The rise of the institutional investor had consequences for the stock market, as finance professionals had a preference for those stocks that justified analytical research and could be bought and sold easily and quickly. These were the stocks of the larger companies. The market for such stocks was usually found in the largest stock exchange located within any country. In contrast, the market provided by the local stock exchanges was often too shallow and too narrow to cope with the buying and selling needs of institutional investors. As trading activity in stocks was increasingly generated by institutional investors this favoured the expansion of the largest stock exchanges at the expense of the smaller. By 1975, 75 per cent of trading on the New York Stock Exchange was on behalf of institutions. This phenomenon was observable across the world from 1950 onwards to a lesser or greater degree. The number of individual stock exchanges began to shrink as they either closed down or merged. In the USA there was a steady decline in the number of exchanges, while in both France in 1966 and Britain in 1973 a single organization emerged.

These mergers were also defensive measures as stock exchanges strove to improve the quality of the market they could provide to institutional investors. The risk always existed that investors would bypass the stock exchange. The matching of sales and purchases was made easier when investors were few and large. Such conditions had existed before exchanges came into existence, when the ownership of stocks was in the hands of a few wealthy individuals. It reappeared in the age of the institutional investors, as they could trade with each other directly or use the services of interdealer brokers. What made this difficult to do in corporate stocks was the problem of pricing. Stock exchanges were the source of the most reliable current prices for a wide range of stocks and their members were reluctant to make these immediately available. If institutional investors had access to current prices and a mechanism for trading between each other they could bypass the stock exchange and save on the charges made. However, as the composition of investors increasingly diverged between the large institution and the single individual, it created tensions with the stock market community. With the objective of creating an orderly market for stocks, exchanges had long imposed rules that dictated who was eligible for membership, the minimum and maximum size of the unit, the scale of charges for business done, and the degree of competition permitted. Many exchanges also had a cap on membership, excluded deposit banks, and imposed a fixed scale of charges. In the face of an increasingly diverse investing community and, especially, the emergence of institutions controlling very large portfolios of stocks, these rules were no longer appropriate in all cases. However, there was a reluctance to change as many members of stock exchanges benefited from the existing situation. Where stock exchanges enjoyed a national monopoly and the support of the government there was also no need to change, as demands for reform from the large institutional investor could be ignored.

That was not the case in the USA where a number of separate stock exchanges remained in existence and investors were numerous, wealthy and spread throughout the country. Though supervised by the Securities and Exchange Commission (SEC), stock exchanges did not have a monopoly of trading in stocks. Under these circumstances the New York Stock Exchange faced growing competition from OTC markets, which harnessed new developments in communications and computing technologies to create alternative trading systems. In 1971, the National Association of Securities Dealers had created their Automated Quotations system (NASDAQ). NASDAQ delivered instantaneous quotes, provided by authorized market-makers, on over-the-counter stocks allowing all participants to trade by telephone on the same basis, wherever located. This concerned the SEC because it was no longer certain that individual investors, in particular, had full access to a properly regulated market in which their interests would be safeguarded.

MAY DAY IN NEW YORK AND ITS AFTERMATH

Driven by demand from investors rather than the financial needs of business, by the 1970s corporate stocks had become a favoured investment among fund managers. Their inclusion in pension funds allowed assets to grow in line with liabilities and so meet the needs of the retired population that they catered for. Insurance companies, investment trusts and mutual funds also had a growing demand for corporate stocks as they could be included in a balanced portfolio comprising government debt and corporate bonds as well as property and mortgages. Wherever pensions and insurance was the responsibility of the individual or the employer there was a necessity to ensure that the assets were available to meet future liabilities. Increasingly, this could only be done by investing in corporate stocks. Fixed-interest securities provided no guarantee against inflation, and property lacked flexibility. Matching this demand from investors was the growth of big business. In the past the likes of railways and urban infrastructure had provided attractive investments for those needing a combination of income and capital growth, but much of these had either been taken into state ownership after the Second World War or were no longer the secure investments that they had been in the past. Railways, for example, were no longer immune from competition given the advances made in road and air transport in the 1950s and 1960s. With inflation becoming rampant in the 1970s many of those managing collective investments had little alternative but to turn more and more to corporate stocks, despite the risks involved. These risks were being lessened with the growth of ever larger companies whose activities were spread over different sectors or different countries, or even both. As corporate enterprise grew in size each business was less vulnerable to sudden changes in fortune, though that could still occur. The development of branded products, with loyalty maintained through advertising, also helped to stabilize sales.

The result of this was to place the stock market centre stage in national financial systems and highlight the need for reform. During the 1950s and 1960s not only had the volume of business grown on many stock exchanges but its nature had changed considerably. Stock exchanges now had to meet the needs of financial institutions employing trained professionals who wanted a facility through which they could buy and sell stocks in large volume at close prices and at speed. These institutions preferred either to buy and sell directly, and so eliminate costs, or to operate through a small number of intermediaries who were in a position to provide them with the service they required. All this was very far removed from the world that stock exchanges had evolved to provide. That was a world where large numbers of individual investors paid brokers to buy and sell on their behalf, doing so on the floor of the stock exchange where they either transacted business with other brokers or used a dealer. What was required was change, and stock exchanges were ill equipped to undertake it because of the role they had acquired since the Second World War, which was the official or unofficial regulators of the stock market with or without an additional tier of statutory authority. Where stock exchanges possessed a monopoly position within the stock market, and were backed by government, they were under no pressure to respond to the need to change. It was this inertia which had to be overcome if the stock market was to respond fully to the opportunities available to it in the 1970s. Stocks were becoming the asset of choice, which business was supplying by adopting the corporate form. What was now required was for the institutional form of the stock market to respond.

That response eventually took place in the USA in 1975. Under pressure from the SEC the New York Stock Exchange (NYSE) agreed to end fixed commission charges on 1 May 1975. Though still denying institutional investors direct access to the market, this move did introduce a much more flexible charging structure or even the possibility of the largest investors avoiding commission payments entirely. Instead, they could trade directly with a dealer. This had major implications for the US stock market. It encouraged certain brokers to grow in scale so as to remain profitable at the lower or non-existent fees being demanded by the large institutional investors. As a result there emerged a small group of large and powerful Wall Street investment banks that combined the issuing of stocks on behalf of US corporations with the retailing of these to investors and their subsequent trading, whether for individuals or institutions. These Wall Street investment banks were also free from the competition of the large US commercial banks, including those with New York head offices. The Glass–Steagall Act, dating from the 1930s, stopped commercial banks from undertaking investment banking; while the New York Stock Exchange excluded them from membership, which denied them direct access to the trading floor. Commercial banks were also hampered by nineteenth-century legislation which prevented interstate banking, so that they could not create nationwide branch networks. Though the Wall Street investment banks had long played an important role in the US financial system, it was the ending of the minimum commission rules that allowed them to flourish as never before. Such firms had the ability to service both the increasingly dominant institutional investor and the expanding number of individual investors of modest means. This was a radically changed environment compared to the past, when the broker catered largely for a relatively small group of wealthy individuals, who were willing to pay the fixed commission charged.

Though driven by internal considerations this act of the SEC unleashed on the world the competitive power of the world's largest stock exchange and the world's most aggressive investment bankers. However, that competition could only be effective if strongly entrenched national and international barriers were overcome. In most cases that did not begin to happen until the 1980s. National stock exchanges continued to dominate national stock markets, operating as they did behind exchange controls and with the support of national governments. Nevertheless, one place where this competition was keenly felt was in London, where many US bankers and brokers were located, because of its role as an international financial centre. These competitive pressures became acute with the abolition of British exchange controls in October 1979. Without exchange controls it became easier for US investment banks to compete for business in the UK stocks, and encouraged UK institutional investors to press for the abolition of minimum commission charges in London. The eventual result in 1986 was a total revolution in the way the stock market operated in London. Not only was the regulation of the market placed under the control of a British equivalent of the SEC, the SIB, but membership was opened up to all financial institutions, fixed commission rates were abandoned, and trading moved from the floor of the London Stock Exchange to the screens and telephones located in the offices of large international banks and brokers. This was a far more revolutionary change than May Day in New York and had major implications for the global stock market, given the international role played by London as a financial centre.

Generally, in the 1980s there was a huge increase in the trading volumes experienced by stock markets around the world, with equity turnover in New York rising almost fourfold, Tokyo ninefold, and London seventeenth-fold. This was driven by the growing preference among institutional investors for corporate stocks. In contrast to fixed interest bonds stocks did appear to offer the solution to the funding needs of private pension funds, as they were required to match their long-term liabilities to an ageing population with assets that would not only generate an income but also grow in real terms over time. As governments began to cut back on the generous provision of pensions funded out of future tax revenues, stocks appeared to offer the ideal solution. By 1980 stocks already comprised 23 per cent of the global stock of financial assets, which totalled $12 trillion, and then rose to 27 per cent by 1993, when the total had risen to $53 trillion. In turn, this investment activity flowed ever more strongly in the 1980s to those markets that were the largest and most liquid, driven as it was by institutional investors. This was happening nationally with the stock exchanges in such cities as Frankfurt, London, Milan, New York, Paris, Sydney and Tokyo all becoming dominant within their own domestic market. In turn, this led institutional investors to put pressure on these exchanges to reduce their charges in the same way as happened in New York, and was then promised and later delivered in New York.

With the ending of most exchange controls around the world in the 1990s stock exchanges around the world either had to copy what had taken place in London or face the gradual loss of business. The forces of competition were inexorable, especially in the European Union where the gravitation of business to London could not be prevented by national governments. Consequently, there was a steady transformation of stock markets around the world, as stock exchanges lost their monopoly and governments and central banks stepped back from direct control, establishing regulatory authorities instead. The rewards that awaited those stock exchanges that abandoned restrictions, lowered charges and opened up membership was the ability to repatriate trading lost to London. This happened in the case of Frankfurt in the early 1990s and later Tokyo, when it rather belatedly followed suit in 1998–99. By 1990 the Tokyo Stock Exchange provided a market for 1627 companies with a market value of 379.2 trillion yen compared to 1280 companies with a market value of 16.2 billion in 1970.

What this represented was not just the return of the stock market to the centre stage of financial systems around the world. Unlike the era before the First World War, inflation was an inbuilt characteristic of most market economies even though the excesses of the 1970s had been brought under control in the 1980s. What inflation did was constantly to erode the value of both bank deposits and fixed interest securities such as government debt and corporate bonds. This was true even if the rate of inflation was relatively mild. Though the direct ownership of property offered protection against inflation it was not suitable for many investors, who required the flexibility that came with either bank deposits or transferable securities. Index linking of bonds also offered a means of protecting against the erosion of value due to inflation, but these involved risk of default and concerns about the measures used as well as no prospect of capital gains in real terms. In contrast, the stocks issued by large companies appeared to provide the perfect solution to the investor's dilemma at a time of inflation, even of a mild kind.

THE STOCK MARKET POST-1990

Whereas the stock market was well on its way to surpass its pre-1914 position by 1990, it had yet to incorporate those countries where the state largely controlled the economy. By domestic market capitalization, for example, only 0.2 per cent of the total market was located in Eastern Europe in 1990. Even in non-centrally planned economies the stock market remained of little significance, as was the case throughout Latin America and in Africa apart from South Africa. In those countries the provision of many services by government, the existence of closely knit groups that internalized financial flows, and the activities of banks limited the opportunities for corporate enterprise. There was thus no need for a stock market. North America, Western Europe and Japan provided the world's dominant stock markets in 1990 whether measured by domestic market capitalization or by the value of trading that took place (see Tables 2.5 and 2.6).

That was all to change after 1990 with the mass disposal of state assets by governments around the world. There was no need for such a process in the USA as the state had never extended far into the provision of goods and services. Instead, the process began in the UK in the 1980s. Its success there led to its emulation around the world as governments saw the double benefit of receiving the proceeds from the sale of assets and then the tax revenue generated by the more profit-orientated businesses that emerged. Between 1990 and 1999 a total of $850 billion in state assets was transferred from public to private

Table 2.5 Leading stock markets by domestic market capitalization, 1990

Stock market	Domestic market capitalization
Tokyo	$2928.5 billion
New York	$2692.1 billion
London	$850.0 billion
Deutsche	$355.3 billion
NASDAQ	$310.8 billion

Source: WFE Statistics.

Table 2.6 Leading stock markets by value of share trading, 1990

Stock market	Value of share trading
New York	$1325.3 billion
Tokyo	$1287.7 billion
London	$543.4 billion
Deutsche	$508.7 billion
NASDAQ	$452.4 billion

Source: WFE Statistics.

hands in the world. This privatization, combined with the expansion of joint-stock enterprise generally, resulted in an enormous expansion in the value of corporate stocks during the 1990s. Increasingly the corporate form of enterprise was favoured throughout the world because of the appeal of its stocks to all categories of investor and the flexibility of operation it provided to management. Over that decade, the market value of the corporate stocks quoted on the world's stock exchanges grew almost fourfold, from $8.9 trillion to $31 trillion. Across the world, more and more investors discovered the advantages of corporate stocks, especially those that possessed a liquid market. Stocks became the asset class preferred by all varieties of investors, ranging from the individual willing to speculate on the future value of a company developing a new product, service, technology or resource, to the institution needing to rebalance a portfolio in the light of changing circumstances. This drove up the value of quoted securities as investors searched for income, capital growth or their preferred combination of both in different countries around the world. By 2005 stocks comprised 31 per cent of all financial assets, compared to 27 per cent in 1993, while the value of such assets reached $140 trillion, or almost three times the amount of 2003.

One consequence of this growing investor interest in corporate stocks was a speculative boom which centred on those companies expected to profit most from new developments in information technology. Advances in computing and communications were transforming the nature of business, with enormous profits predicted for those companies supplying the equipment and software or creating new services. Unproven as these profits were, they tantalized investors, who backed every new issue of stock and then drove its price up to new heights. The 'dot.com' boom eventually peaked in 2000 as those investors with more realistic assumptions about the future level of profits sold out and

Table 2.7 Leading stock markets by domestic market capitalization, 2000

Stock market	Domestic market capitalization
New York	$11 534.6 billion
NASDAQ	$3597.1 billion
Tokyo	$3157.2 billion
London	$2612.2 billion
Euronext	$2271.7 billion

Source: WFE Statistics.

Table 2.8 Leading stock markets by value of share trading, 2000

Stock market	Value of share trading
NASDAQ	$19 798.8 billion
New York	$11 060.0 billion
London	$4558.7 billion
Tokyo	$2315.5 billion
Deutsche	$2119.8 billion

Source: WFE Statistics.

fewer were drawn in to replace them. As the balance between buyers and sellers shifted towards the latter, the valuation placed on the stocks of these new companies began to fall, prompting selling by those investors who had invested merely for a quick gain on a rising market. A sharp stock market correction followed in which many of the new 'dot.com' companies either collapsed, because they could not raise additional funding, or struggled to establish themselves. Despite these losses, the legacy of this speculative boom was a new generation of companies using the new technology to supply products and services to customers. Among the largest companies in the world by 2010 were pioneers of this new technology such as Microsoft, Google and Amazon. As with previous speculative booms – whether involving a technology like railways, automobiles and radio, or resources such as gold, oil and rubber – the irrational exuberance of the few did produce lasting benefits for the many. What the stock market provided, once again, was a means through which investors willing to take risks were matched by entrepreneurs seeking finance for their ideas. This reflected the return of the market to the role in which the divisibility and transferability of stocks was used to provide the funds required to develop new businesses rather than the conversion of existing ones.

All this meant greatly increased activity on those exchanges that already dominated the global stock market. By 2000 the domestic market capitalization of the New York Stock Exchange reached $11.5 trillion compared to $2.7 trillion in 1990. Even more spectacular was the situation of NASDAQ, which had become the market of choice for the wave of high-technology companies being promoted in the 1990s. The market capitalization of the US stocks it quoted rose from $0.3 trillion in 1990 to $3.6 trillion in 2000, by which time it had become the largest stock exchange in the world measured by turnover in stocks (see Tables 2.7 and 2.8).

However, it was not just the leading markets that attracted listings of new companies and increased activity in their stocks during the 1990s. New stock markets also appeared around the world. Despite the removal of exchange controls, the growing internationalization of investment in stocks, and the development of global investment banks able to conduct buying and selling on a global basis, most corporate stocks were owned by investors resident in the country where the business was based and operated. Even when there was considerable foreign interest in particular stocks, trading was often concentrated in the stock exchange where the company's head office was, as that was where the single greatest concentration of investors was found. The very existence of global investment banks made it easy for the buying and selling of stocks to be directed to the best market, wherever that was. As a consequence that market became the deepest and broadest market in that particular corporate stock, so attracting further trading activity. As a result there was a rash of stock market formation from 1990 onwards. These appeared especially in those countries were none had formerly existed, either because they had been communist states or because the level of economic development had been too low to support one in the past. In Eastern Europe, for example, stock exchanges appeared in Budapest in 1990, Warsaw in 1991 and Prague in 1992, often though the efforts of local financial institutions and the participation of foreign banks. Elsewhere in the world, stock exchanges were established in Botswana in 1994, Palestine in 1997 and Saudi Arabia in 2001, while two appeared in Dubai in 2005.

Even within those countries where stock exchanges were long established, new ones appeared to cater for particular segments of the market. Exchanges always had to strike a balance between providing a market for the stocks of unproven enterprises and those issued by long-established companies. Especially for individual investors in corporate stocks this listing acted as a signal that the business had good prospects and the securities could be easily bought and sold. Consequently, long-established stock exchanges like New York, London, Frankfurt, Paris and Tokyo were concerned about the reputational damage that would be inflicted if they became too lax in terms of the companies whose stocks they provided a market for. In the case of New York this was a gap that was quickly filled by NASDAQ. Elsewhere in the world established stock exchanges created separate markets for the stocks issued by companies judged to involve a greater degree of risk, as with those developing a new product or service. It was on these that many of the new 'dot.com' stocks were traded, and so it was these markets that suffered most when the boom ended. In Germany, for example, a very small proportion of the population owned stocks until the flotation of Deutsche Telecom in 1996. Such was the success of that issue that an enthusiasm for stocks was born throughout the German population, with the proportion of the population owning stocks rising from 5 per cent to 20 per cent as a result, reaching 12 million by 2001. This then flowed out into high-technology stocks catered for by a separate market created by Deutsche Borse. In the wake of the bursting of that bubble, the market was closed.

Dramatic as was the ending of the dot.com boom, global stock markets quickly recovered, driven by the increasing preference for stocks among financial institutions and ongoing privatization programmes around the world. This recovery favoured, especially, the most established markets as it was on these that the stocks of the largest and most stable companies were traded. In the USA, for example, the New York Stock Exchange not only retained its lead over NASDAQ in terms of domestic market capitalization but

Table 2.9 Leading stock markets by domestic market capitalization, 2006

Stock market	Domestic market capitalization
New York	$15421.2 billion
Tokyo	$4614.1 billion
NASDAQ	$3865.0 billion
London	$3794.3 billion
Euronext	$3712.7 billion

Source: WFE Statistics.

Table 2.10 Leading stock markets by value of share trading, 2006

Stock market	Value of share trading
New York	$21 789.5 billion
NASDAQ	$11 807.5 billion
London	$7571.7 billion
Tokyo	$5872.8 billion
Euronext	$3853.3 billion

Source: WFE Statistics.

also recovered its position as the most active stock market in the world (see Tables 2.9 and 2.10).

As in the past, the consequence of these developments was the concentration of trading in a few large stock markets as they could offer the depth and breadth of a market that appealed to financial institutions. The result was the domination of incumbent stock exchanges as they possessed the most liquid markets for the securities that they listed. In 2008 the Tokyo Stock Exchange was responsible for 89 per cent of all trading in domestic stocks, and this was typical of the position in those countries where more than one stock exchange existed. This was the product of a situation in which financial institutions not only owned most of the stocks in the major corporations, but also conducted most of the buying and selling. By the end of 2006 institutional investors owned 66 per cent of all US stocks compared to 37 per cent as recently as 1980. Also, these institutional investors increasingly took a global view of investment and so spread their holdings around the world. Foreign institutional investors owned 5 per cent of all Japanese stocks in 1987 but 27 per cent in 2007. The holdings of these institutional investors were also heavily concentrated in the stocks issued by the largest companies, as these were the most liquid. US institutional investors owned 76 per cent of the stock issued by the 1000 largest US companies. This meant that financial institutions dominated trading on the world's leading stock exchanges, including those that had grown rapidly since 1990 and then recovered quickly from the ending of the dot.com boom. In 2008, 65 per cent of all trading in shares on the Spanish stock exchange (Bolsas y Mercados Españoles or BME) was undertaken on behalf of foreign institutional investors, while the figure for the Tokyo Stock Exchange was 70 per cent. Catering for the global buying and selling activities of these financial institutions was a small group of global financial businesses led by US investment banks such as J.P. Morgan Chase, Morgan Stanley, Goldman Sachs and Merrill Lynch, but including others such as Citibank, Nomura, Deutsche Bank, UBS and Credit Suisse. In 2008 they were responsible for around half of all the business done on the major European stock exchanges, for example.

The consequence for many smaller stock markets was that they lacked the facilities to provide the trading facilities required by the world's financial institutions and the global investment banks through which they operated. What was required was a market of sufficient depth that would allow it cope with large-scale buying and selling orders, and the ability to operate at speed and at low cost. For those stock exchanges that could not provide this, survival depended on merging with a larger stock exchange. This was especially the case for stock exchanges located in small countries as they lacked the depth and breadth of corporate enterprise required to maintain an active market at a time of global financial flows. Contributing to the pressures faced by these smaller stock exchanges was their increasing conversion from mutual organizations to corporate enterprises in their own right. This created the opportunities for stock exchanges to create alliances in which they provided markets both for specific geographical areas and for particular types of stocks. In March 2000, for example, Euronext was formed as an alliance between the Paris, Amsterdam and Brussels stock exchanges, which was later extended to Lisbon. As a consequence Euronext became the fifth-largest stock exchange in the world, measured by either the market capitalization of the corporate stocks for which it provided a market, or the total value of trading (see Tables 2.9 and 2.10). Euronext captured the market that the smaller stock exchanges had previously provided for the stocks of a small number of national companies. What it was doing was matching the internationalization of corporate enterprise and the internationalization of investment by internationalizing the operation of the market on which stocks were traded.

However, there were limits to this process of internationalization. Though Euronext was later acquired by the New York Stock Exchange it retained its role as the market for a particular group of European corporate stocks, indicating that a global stock market had not yet arrived. National stock markets continued to dominate trading in the stocks of national companies; unless they were too small to offer adequate depth, but the ownership of these markets was now increasingly international. Even where the ownership of stocks was geographically dispersed there was always a single location in which it was densest. Consequently, underpinning the primacy of such stock exchanges as those in New York, Tokyo, London, Paris and Frankfurt was the market they provided for the stock issued by the world's largest companies. The same situation was apparent with the emerging Chinese stock exchanges as their importance was propelled by the market they provided for Chinese-owned companies. National stock markets continued to provide a market for the stocks of national companies because they were owned, in the main, by national investors. Across Africa, for example, it was the national stock exchange of each country that provided the market for the stock issued by companies based there, making the creation of a pan-African stock market very difficult to achieve.

This situation gave an advantage to stock exchanges located in the world's largest financial centres, as that was where so many companies had their head offices and where global fund managers maintained offices. In particular, this favoured New York as so many of the world's largest companies continued to be from the USA, when measured

Table 2.11 Leading stock markets by domestic market capitalization, 2009

Stock market	Domestic market capitalization
New York	$11 837.8 billion
Tokyo	$3306.1 billion
NASDAQ	$3239.5 billion
Euronext	$2869.4 billion
London	$2796.4 billion

Source: WFE Statistics.

Table 2.12 Leading stock markets by value of share trading, 2009

Stock market	Value of share trading
NASDAQ	$28 951.3 billion
New York	$17 784.6 billion
Shanghai	$5061.6 billion
Tokyo	$3990.9 billion
London	$3391.1 billion

Source: WFE Statistics.

by market capitalization, and their stock continued to be heavily owned by US investors, especially the institutions managing pension funds. This was the case even after the catastrophic fall in values during the global financial crisis of 2007–08 which involved the temporary bankruptcy of a major US company, General Motors, while a growing number of other companies were located in emerging economies, especially China. In 2010 almost half of the world's largest companies, measured by market capitalization, were still located in the USA whether they were in long-established activities such as oil (with ExxonMobil) and manufacturing (with General Electric), or rapidly expanding new sectors which included Microsoft in computer software, Apple in computer hardware, and Amazon in Internet retailing. In contrast, other countries hosted only a small number of the world's largest companies and could offer investors nothing like the depth and diversity found in the US stock market (see Table 2.2). In 2009 the domestic market capitalization of the two New York stock exchanges ranked first and third in the world. In terms of stock market activity they ranked first and second. By then the Shanghai Stock Exchange had emerged as the third-largest in the world by turnover, at the expense of European stock exchanges, London and Deutsche Borse. Euronext had also displaced London as the largest European stock exchange in terms of domestic market capitalization, though not in terms of trading, because of London's much larger activity in the stocks of non-British companies (see Tables 2.11 and 2.12).

This did not mean that these large stock exchanges were able to monopolize the stock market even in their own countries. In the course of the 1990s, the advances made in integrating computing and communications made it possible to set up interactive electronic trading platforms which not only displayed prices but also allowed participants to buy and sell on screen. Though existing stock exchanges increasingly embraced the new technology, new entrants appeared that offered investors faster and cheaper access to the stock market. These were known as ECNs (electronic communication networks) in the USA, MTFs (multilateral trading facilities) in Europe and PTSs (proprietary trading systems) in Japan. In addition, so big had become the financial intermediaries that conducted the buying and selling of stocks that they were in a position to complete many of the transactions internally, so saving on costs. Out of this developed 'dark pools', which were internal markets maintained by the largest banks, to which they allowed the largest investors direct access. These developments had the effect of reversing the trend towards the concentration of trading in the stock market into a small number of exchanges, leading instead to fragmentation. From the standpoint of these large banks the market provided by stock exchanges was no longer essential as it could be bypassed through either internal trading or the use of an independent electronic platform.

Thus, when these banks devised new financial products to match the needs of savers and borrowers, little thought was given to having them listed on exchanges where their robustness to different trading conditions could be tested. Instead, these products were traded in and between the banks. As long as confidence existed in these assets this system of trading was successful and banks profited from matching buyers and sellers. However, when the global financial crisis broke in 2007–08 the market for many of these new financial assets ceased to operate. Though believing them to be akin to the corporate stocks traded on exchanges, and thus liquid, banks found these assets to be the same as direct loans, as they did not possess a secondary market. In contrast exchange-listed corporate stocks continued to possess a market, and so they were heavily sold by those banks and investors desperately searching for liquidity. The result was a massive drop in the value of listed stocks between 2007 and 2008 of almost $30 trillion. As testimony to the resilience of exchanges at a time of crisis, the value of trading remained remarkably constant over 2007–08. What falls there were took place mainly on the newer exchanges, which was only to be expected as that was where the more illiquid stocks were to be found. In contrast, the highly liquid US markets experienced a higher level of trading as banks and other investors sold stocks because they could. Once those disposals were over, the value of corporate stocks then recovered because of their ability to offer both capital gains and revenue at a time of low interest rates, concerns over the security of sovereign debt and fears of inflation.[17]

What the global financial crisis of 2007–08 reaffirmed was the contribution made by stock exchanges to the functioning of the stock market. Freed from the costs required to enforce market discipline and police the pricing of stocks, electronic trading platforms and the internal markets offered investors a cheap means of buying and selling stocks. However, the contribution made by the stock market to the value attached to corporate stocks was not confined to the provision of a mechanism through which they could be bought and sold, though this was the judgement increasingly made by governments from the 1990s onwards. When the regulation of the stock market became the responsibility of the state, as with the Securities and Exchange Commission in the USA, and its various forms across the world, the role played by stock exchanges gradually disappeared. Associated with this was the growth of ever larger financial institutions. These had the scale and capital to guarantee to any counterparty that stocks bought would be paid for and stocks sold would be delivered. They also appeared to promise to investors that the markets they provided for the securities they created would always exist. Again, the implication of this was that stock exchanges were no longer necessary for the operation of the stock market. Instead, the market could be equally well provided by electronic trading platforms or 'dark pools'.

All that prevented the ability of investors gaining access to these newer and cheaper components of the stock market was the refusal of stock exchanges to make immediately available the current prices at which stocks were being traded. Perceiving that to be a restraint on the operation of a competitive stock market, governments took action to force disclosure. In 2005, the SEC introduced a requirement that not only were current bid/offer prices to be publicly displayed, but that all orders went directly to the market that could execute them at the best price. This was Regulation National Market System (Regulation NMS). At a stroke, it removed one of the key advantages that regulated exchanges could offer those who paid to use their trading facilities to buy and sell, which was access to current prices in advance of those who did not. Such a situation was akin to removing copyright or patent protection, leaving the originator of the idea or the product with no reward for past effort. The consequence was market fragmentation. The European Union quickly followed suit, introducing the Markets in Financial Instruments Directive (MiFID) in 2007. This emulated US practice and had the same consequences.

The problem was that the value of corporate stocks was the product of many diverse and individual influences. The strategy followed by individual managements, and the profit or loss resulting, was often a key feature in determining the value of a particular corporate stock, and this required constant monitoring, with the knowledge gained affecting prices. With the ownership of stock also went control, creating opportunities for the replacement of managements and a reordering of business activity through mergers, acquisitions, disposals, buyouts and buy-ins. Anticipation of events of these kinds were major drivers behind the constant fluctuations in the price of individual corporate stocks. Under these circumstances it was critical to have in place regulations that ensured both equal and universal price disclosure, that prevented the spread of rumour and the use of privileged information, and that monitored unusual price movements that might be the product of market manipulation. It was circumstances such as these that had long dissuaded investors from purchasing stocks. By eliminating such abuses stock exchanges had created a climate of trust in corporate stocks that contributed greatly to their growing popularity over time. This was why investors continued to use stock exchanges to buy and sell stocks, because that was the only way to guarantee that transactions were completed at the universally accepted current price. When stock exchanges were forced to make available these current prices, financial intermediaries and investors were then able to able benefit from the lower costs available elsewhere. This created the illusion that stock exchanges were no longer central to the stock market because regulation now lay with statutory authorities and large financial institutions stood behind all transactions. This illusion was shattered in the 2007–08 global financial crisis when particular components of the global securities market froze and one of the largest financial intermediaries, Lehman Brothers, failed leaving counterparties facing large losses and years of frustration before deals could be fully unwound. In contrast stock exchanges continued to provide a mechanism through which corporate stocks were traded at prices that were accepted as an accurate reflection of current supply and demand conditions. These were the reference prices against which all else was measured.

CONCLUSION

Corporate enterprise has made a major contribution to the growth of the modern world economy. Though the origins of the modern company can be traced back to long before 1800 it was only in the nineteenth century that it began to play a major role in economic activity. Prior to that individual enterprise prevailed, extended through family and religious networks. In the absence of government provision this changed with the coming of railways. Such was the level of their capital requirements, and the need for a large expenditure in a short period of time, that corporate enterprise became the chosen means for providing railway systems across the world. The result was an important contribution to the growth and development of the global economy. Over time, corporate enterprise was then extended to other forms of business activity because of the flexibility it provided. This flexibility extended far beyond access to capital to the ability to alter continually the shape of the enterprise and the employment of professional management that was distinct from the owners. What corporate enterprise brought to business was extended longevity, for success and growth were no longer dependent on a single person or even family but on the collective input of numerous investors and managers, generation after generation. This did not mean that any single business now enjoyed permanence, only that it possessed the ability to metamorphose over time.

Without the existence of the stock market, corporate enterprise would not have developed. What the stock market provided was a mechanism through which ownership and control could be constantly adjusted to meet changing circumstances, whether in business or among investors. The stock market provided a continuous stream of information to both parties which generated a response leading to some companies growing and other declining. This made the stock market a highly visible part of the financial system. It also led to criticism because the functions it performed were neither immediate nor direct. Instead, the role it played was indirect but pervasive. All that the stock market did could be done in other ways. Economic activities could be financed by individuals acting alone and in small groups or undertaken by governments. Investors could engage in direct participation in business or lend to the government. However, the result would be less satisfactory for both economic activity and investors, which is why a modern economy prefers the intermediation of corporate enterprise and the stocks it generated.

Finally, the stock market is a product of those who use it, for the regulations devised ensure that it meets the needs of both companies and investors. At one level the stock market was very simple. It was where buyers and sellers of stocks transacted their business. To achieve that, though, required an elaborate mechanism which ensured that the interests of all were preserved. It was this that stock exchanges provided through an ever-evolving compromise between the needs of buyers, sellers and the intermediaries they employed to act on their behalf. Long before the involvement of government, these intermediaries devised both trading forums and rules and regulations that gradually led to the creation of a market in which all could have trust. That trust encompassed both the permanence of a market in which corporate stocks could always be bought and sold, and the prices at which these transactions took place. From this trust sprang a confidence that encouraged investors to hold stocks as assets and so encouraged business to issue them. Without trust that confidence evaporates, and that is the lesson of the global financial crisis of 2007–08.

NOTES

1. A. Crump, *The Theory of Stock Exchange Speculation*, London: Longmans, 1874, p. 10.
2. J.P. Raines, *Economists and the Stock Market: Speculative theories of stock market fluctuations*, Cheltenham, UK and Northampton, MA, USA: Edward Elgar, 2000, p. 1, cf. pp. 1–2, 23, 28, 45, 54–7, 69, 73, 92–3, 99, 106, 109, 111, 149.
3. R.J. Schiller, *Irrational Exuberance*, Princeton, NJ: Princeton University Press, 2001, pp. 9, 12, 35, 38, 60–61, 182, 188–9, 193, 195, 228, 233, 246.
4. John Kay, *The Truth About Markets*, London: Allen Lane, 2004, pp. 10, 223, 249, 268, 335, 337, 339, 353, 357–8, 362–3, 370, 373.
5. See N. Dimsdale and M. Prevezer (eds), *Capital Markets and Corporate Governance*, Oxford: Oxford University Press, 1994; and F. Allen and D. Gale, *Comparing Financial Systems*, Cambridge: Cambridge University Press, 2000.
6. See R. Levine and S. Zervos, 'Stock markets, banks, and economic growth', pp. 537–58, and T.G. Rajan and L. Zingales, 'Financial dependence and growth', pp. 559–86, in *American Economic Review* **88** (1998); and P.L. Rousseaux and R. Sylla, 'Financial systems, economic growth, and globalization', in M.D. Bordo, A.M. Taylor and J.G. Williamson (eds), *Globalization in History*, Chicago, IL: NBER, 2003, and Cambridge University Press, pp. 373–415.
7. The Stock Market data for 2009 are taken from the historical time series maintained by the World Federation of Exchanges (see WFE Statistics). The global GDP data are provided by the World Bank, based on purchasing power parities and in current international dollars (see World Bank Statistics).
8. This is based on Dr Moore's calculations of the market value of the equities quoted on each stock exchange. It was in UK pounds and I converted it into US dollars using the prevailing exchange rate of $4.86 = £1 to make it comparable with the data produced by the World Federation of Exchanges. I have then converted it into 1990 dollars using the MeasuringWorth price index calculator so as to compare it with Angus Maddison's 1913 GDP data. The 1913 figure was $454 billion when converted to 1990 dollars, which was then compared to Angus Maddison's global GDP figure for that date of $2.7 trillion in 1990$s. I am very grateful to Dr Moore for his data. The most recent Maddison data is in A. Maddison, *Contours of the World Economy 1–2030 AD : Essays in Macro-Economic History*, Oxford: Oxford University Press, 2007, Table A.4. For an account of the growing importance of corporate stock over the twentieth century see R.G. Rajan and L. Zingales, *The Great Reversals: The Politics of Financial Development in the 20th Century*, Paris: OECD, 2000.
9. The 1912 data come from P. Wardley, 'The world's 100 largest capitalist enterprises of 1912' (forthcoming). The 2006 data come from the *Financial Times*, 10 June 2006. The 1912 data have been converted to 2006 prices using the Measuring Worth calculator and then compared to Maddison's 1913 data.
10. *Financial Times*, 25 November 2009.
11. For the recent debate on financial systems and economic growth see R. Levine and S. Zervos, 'Stock markets, banks, and economic growth', pp. 537–58, and T.G. Rajan and L. Zingales, 'Financial dependence and growth', pp. 559–86, *American Economic Review*, **88** (1998); P.L. Rousseaux and R. Sylla, 'Financial systems, economic growth, and globalization', in M.D. Bordo, A.M. Taylor and J.G. Williamson (eds), *Globalization in History*, Chicago, IL: NBER, 2003, and Cambridge University Press, pp. 373–415.
12. R.J. Schiller, *Irrational Exuberance*, Princeton, NJ: Princeton University Press, 2001, pp. 9, 12, 35, 38, 60–61, 182, 188–9, 193, 195, 228, 233, 246; N. Dimsdale and M. Prevezer (eds), *Capital Markets and Corporate Governance*, Oxford: Oxford University Press, 1994, pp. 14, 71–2, 80, 179–83, 191, 295–9; P.J. Drake, *Money, Finance and Development*, Oxford: Robertson, 1980, pp. 34–6, 192–3, 215.
13. See F. Carnevali, *Europe's Advantage: Banks and Small Firms in Britain, France, Germany and Italy since 1918*, Oxford: Oxford University Press, 2005.
14. For the changing nature of national financial systems see R.W. Goldsmith, *Comparative National Balance Sheets*, Chicago, IL: Chicago University Press, 1985. For comparative and historic growth rates see Maddison, *World Economy*.
15. R.W. Goldsmith (ed.), *Institutional Investors and Corporate Stock*, New York: NBER, 1973, pp. 38, 45. (The percentages are based on the total corporate stocks outstanding while the total for both stocks and bonds only include those issued by non-financial corporations.)
16. Based on Dr Moore's calculations of the market value of the equities quoted on each stock exchange.
17. WFE Statistics.

BIBLIOGRAPHY

This chapter draws heavily on my published work dating back many years. In that work will be found references to many books and articles of others who have contributed to my understanding of the role played by the stock market and how it developed over time. Among the most recent are the following.

The London Stock Exchange: A History, Oxford: Oxford University Press, 1999, 2001.

'One world or many worlds? Markets, banks, and communications, 1850s–1990s', in T. de Graaf, J. Jonker and J.J. Mabron (eds), *European Banking Overseas, 19th – 20th Centuries,* Amsterdam: ABN AMRO Historical Archives, pp. 227–48, 2002.

'Banks and securities markets, 1870–1914', in D.J. Forsyth and D. Verdier (eds), *The Origins of National Financial Systems: Gershenkron revisited*, London: Routledge, pp. 43–63, 2003.

'The City of London and British banking, 1900–1939', in C. Wrigley (ed.), *A Companion to Early Twentieth-Century Britain*, Oxford: Blackwell Publishing, pp. 249–69, 2003.

'The City of London and the British government: the changing relationship', in R.C. Michie and P.A. Williamson (eds), *The British Government and the City of London in the Twentieth Century*, Cambridge: Cambrige University Press, pp. 31–55, 2004.

'A financial phoenix: the City of London in the twentieth century', in Y. Cassis and E. Bussierre (eds), *London and Paris as International Financial Centres*, Oxford: Oxford University Press, pp. 15–41, 2005.

'Der Aufsteig der City of London als Finanzplatz: Vom Inlandsgeschaft zum Offshore-Centrum?' in C.M. Merki (ed.), *Europas Finanzzentren: Geschichte und Bedeutung im 20. Jahrhundert*, Frankfurt: Campus Verlag, pp. 23–51, 2005.

'The City of London as a European financial centre in the twentieth century', in *Europaische Finanzplatze im Wettbewerb*, Bankhistorisches Archiv-Beiheft 45, Stuttgart: Franz Steiner Verlag, pp. 51–81, 2006.

The Global Securities Market: A History, Oxford: Oxford University Press, 2006.

'The City of London as a global financial centre, 1880–1939: finance, foreign exchange and the First World War', in P.L. Cottrell, E. Lange and U. Olsson (eds), *Centres and Peripheries in Banking : The Historical Development of Financial Markets*, Aldershot: Ashgate Publishing Company, pp. 41–79, 2007.

'The City of London and the British regions: from medieval to modern', in Bill Lancaster, Diana Newton and Natasha Vall (eds), *An Agenda for Regional History*, Newcastle upon Tyne: Northumbria University Press, pp 201–15, 2007.

'Reversal or change? The global securities market in the twentieth century', *New Global Studies*, **2** (1), 2008.

Guilty Money: The City of London in Victorian and Edwardian Culture, 1815–1914, London: Pickering and Chatto, 2009.

'The London Stock Exchange and the British government in the twentieth century', in S. Battilossi and J. Reis (eds), *State and Financial Systems in Europe and the USA: Historical perspectives on regulation and supervision in the nineteenth and twentieth centuries*, Aldershot: Ashgate, pp. 79–96, 2010.

'The emergence and survival of a financial cluster in Britain', in 'Learning from some of Britain's successful sectors: an historical analysis of the role of government', BIS Economics Paper No. 6, Department of Business Innovation and Skills, pp. 89–111, 2010.

'Securities, markets, exchanges and the finance of economic growth: a global and historical perspective', in J. Morilla, J. Hernandez Andreu, J.L. Garcia Ruiz and J.M. Ortiz-Villajos (eds), *Homenaje A Gabriel Tortella: Las Claves del Desarrollo Economico y Social*, Madrid: LID Editorial Empresarial, pp.567–88, 2010.

'Gamblers, fools, victims or wizards? The British investor in the public mind, 1850–1930'. in D.R. Green, A. Owens, J. Maltby and J. Rutterford (eds), *Men, Women and Money: Perspectives on Gender, Wealth and Investment, 1850–1970*, Oxford: Oxford University Press, pp. 156–83, 2011.

'The battle of the bourses? Competition between stock exchanges in the 20th century', in Y. Cassis and L. Quennouelle-Corre (eds), *Financial Centres and International Capital Flows in the Nineteenth and Twentieth Centuries*, Oxford: Oxford University Press, forthcoming.

3 From the Renaissance exchanges to cyberspace: a history of stock market globalization

Geoffrey Poitras

The revolution in computing and communications technology that began in the 1980s has produced a radical realignment of traditional financial institutions. *Ex post*, the patchwork framework of regulatory oversight has proved incapable of adapting to these changes, resulting in systemic instability in the globalized financial system. Lessons gained from centuries of historical development are being ignored (for example Neal and Davis 2005). The current public debate on financial market reform reflects confusion about essential properties of trading stock in 'cash' and derivative security markets (for example Pirrong 2008 and CFTC 2008).[1] One of the casualties has been the collapse of the self-regulating, mutual form of centralized stock exchange organization, which has been replaced by a dispersed, demutualized opaque network of electronic trading networks (ETNs) and automated trading system (ATS) platforms (for example Markham and Harty 2008, and Chapter 12 in this volume; Kumpan 2006; Treptow 2006). The crude rationale given by regulators for such fundamental changes, and the relatively limited associated public debate, is disturbing.[2] Counterproductive regulatory arbitrage, fragmentation of market liquidity and undermining of the price discovery and dissemination function of important financial markets have been some implications of the changes.

Despite being fundamental to the market economy, the history of the globalization in trading for stocks and shares has received relatively limited academic attention.[3] The connections between public property rights, government regulation, exchange ownership, composition of the trading population and pricing efficiency have been generally ignored. Basic questions about the evolution of exchange trading remain unanswered, such as: does a globalized trading system of competing ETNs, electronic communications networks and dark pools represent a sustainable, liquidity-enhancing and risk-reducing evolution of traditional, centralized open outcry exchange floor trading of equity securities on national exchanges? What form of stock trading system takes greatest sustainable advantage of the potential social gains associated with the revolution in trading technology? By tracing the historical evolution of trading in stocks and shares, this chapter focuses on three key elements: the market participants involved in the trading process; the approach to regulating markets, for example registration and other barriers to entry; and the contracting, clearing and settlement methods employed. Where applicable, the public perception regarding pricing efficiency is also considered.

The following chapter first examines complications that arise with basic definitions for 'stocks', 'shares', 'stock exchange' and 'exchange traded'. Following this historical developments that surround the emergence of speculative exchange trading in 'to arrive' contracts on the Antwerp exchange during the sixteenth century are examined. The next section details the application of speculative exchange trading techniques to forward and option contracts for shares in joint-stock companies traded in seventeenth-century

Amsterdam and eighteenth-century London. Specific attention is dedicated to considering the regulation of trading in stocks and shares prior to the nineteenth century. The emergence of the global stock market centered on the London stock exchange during the nineteenth century, the subsequent emergence of the New York Stock Exchange and the erosion of globalization generated by the First World War and the Great Depression are subsequently considered. The concluding section examines the substantive reemergence of stock market globalization since the Second World War. This time period includes: the creation of the Chicago Board Options Exchange in 1973 and subsequent emergence of equity derivative trading, primarily on futures exchanges, and the demutualization of stock exchanges that commenced late in the twentieth century that is sustaining the ongoing mergers of major national exchanges.

BASIC DEFINITIONS

Any history of 'stock' market globalization prior to the twentieth century has to deal with semantic complications, with 'the perplexing habit of business nomenclature which seems to go out of its way to be unscientific and confusing' (Withers 1910 [1917], p. 33). In particular, the securities being traded, market terminology and trading conventions are often determined by the dominant trading venue. During the twentieth century, New York emerged as the centre of globalized stock trading and 'stock' came increasingly to refer only to equity securities, primarily 'common stock'. Withers (1910 [1917], p. 55) describes market terminology at the beginning of the twentieth century: 'Bonds are nearly always bearer securities, but are occasionally registered, and a bond necessarily implies debt. Shares are always portions of a company's capital, while stock may represent either capital or debt'. Observing that the 'word stock has meant many things in the course of its versatile career', Withers (1910 [1917], pp. 33–4) traces usage of term from Francis Bacon to Ben Jonson to Adam Smith, where 'stock' refers to 'the capital of a firm or company . . . the monetary resources which have been invested in its business or kept in hand for its daily needs'. From this point, 'stock' evolved to mean: 'securities received by those who subscribed the capital of companies, and then divided itself again to mean marketable securities in general, and a certain kind of marketable security in particular'.

Ultimately, Withers (1910 [1917], p. 34) decides that the definition of 'stock' 'is applied to all the securities dealt in on the Stock Exchanges'. This is consistent with referencing a 'stockbroker' as an individual 'who will buy and sell for you stocks, shares and bonds'. From this point, American practice has come to supplant the historical English convention of distinguishing between 'shares', which represent indivisible equity securities typically issued in bearer form, and 'stock', which represents a divisible equity security issued in registered or inscribed form. Such distinctions between different historical terminologies are not merely arcane historical details. As Withers (1910 [1917], p. 43) illustrates, the process of stock market globalization at the beginning of the twentieth century was intimately connected to the characteristics of the securities being traded and the conventions governing the exchange process:

> The quickness and cheapness of telegraphic and telephonic communication have knit the chief stock markets of the world into one, and a security thus has a great advantage which can be

> bought and sold not only in London, but in Paris, Berlin, Amsterdam, and other centres where the cravings of Continental capitalists for investments are satisfied. Owing to the Continental habit, this advantage can only be enjoyed by bearer securities, and where it is desired to create an international market, it is now general practice to give the security bearer form, or at least to give its holders the choice of being registered, or holding bearer securities, as they may choose.

The profound impact of technological change on the stock market globalization process is also a fundamental in the stock market globalization process currently under way. Distinct biases in the globalization process arise from different security market conventions employed by the dominant trading venues of the time.

A stock market where bearer securities are prevalent had advantages and disadvantages. The gains to clearing and settlement greatly facilitate international trading. However, the problems of dividend distribution, fraud, counterfeiting, theft and market manipulation are significant negatives. The current globalization process is conditioned on US registration requirements initially introduced in the Securities Act (1933) and the Securities Exchange Act (1934), that require publicly traded securities to be registered and for regular financial reports to be filed. This modern move to trading of registered securities has been accompanied by an incongruent segmentation of modern trading venues for fixed income and equity securities, and cash and futures markets. As a consequence, in modern times the 'stock' market has come to represent a cash market for trading common stocks. From an historical perspective, such an interpretation of 'stock' is too narrow and fails to capture essential elements of previous 'stock' market globalizations. A more appropriate historical approach is to interpret 'stock' to include tradeable securities used to raise firm capital. This is the approach employed in this chapter.

Given this, the history of stock market globalization can be closely connected to the evolution of 'exchanges' where stock is traded. Despite being a widely used term, it is difficult to define 'exchange traded' precisely. Though the roots of security trading stretch back to antiquity, the emergence of centralized venues where securities are traded is more recent. The economic basis for such trading evolved from the fundamentals of exchange in goods markets. This exchange process involves two steps. First, a buyer and a seller agree on a market clearing price for the goods involved in the transaction. Second, the transaction is completed, typically with a cash payment being made in exchange for adequate physical delivery of the goods involved. In many transactions, time can separate the pricing agreement, the settlement date and the delivery of goods. For example, a forward credit sale involves immediate pricing, delivery as specified in the forward contract and final settlement at an even later date. Because the earliest 'stock' markets were also venues for goods trading, trading practices associated with goods transactions were naturally adapted to the trading of 'stock'.

Commercial goods transactions in early markets often involved a rudimentary sale agreement structured as a forward contract with option features. The contract could vary from loosely structured to formal and notarized. Unstated terms and conditions of such agreements were often governed by merchant convention (for example Malynes 1622 [1979]; Peri 1638 [1707]). For example, because trading on samples was common in sixteenth- and seventeenth-century goods markets, an agreement for a future sale would typically have a provision that would permit the purchaser to refuse delivery if the delivered goods were found to be of inadequate quality when compared to the original sample. As reflected in notarial protests stretching back to antiquity, disagreement over what constituted satisfactory delivery was a common occurrence.[4] Contracting practices in the goods market were also employed in the early trading of 'stocks'. The history of stock market globalization demonstrates the importance of recognizing the connection between cash market trading and the corresponding use of forward sale contracts to facilitate such trade.

Following van der Wee (1977) and Gelderblom and Jonker (2005), the first instance where a contingent claim was unbundled and traded as a separate security on an exchange was the transferable 'to arrive' commodity contracts traded on the Antwerp exchange during the sixteenth century. This development signifies the depth of liquidity and degree of trading sophistication associated with commodity transactions at a time when commercial sales typically employed either outright cash sales or, where trading on samples was involved, non-transferable forward contracts with multiple delivery dates. Similar to modern over-the-counter (OTC) derivative transactions, these contracts were executed as private deals between two signatories, usually employing *escripen*, notaries and 'scriveners' to formalize the contract. As Malynes (1622 [1979], p. 126) observes, if a broker was involved, a verbal contact could be used:[5]

> Verbal contracts are made between party and party, or by means of Brokers or Mediators, and that only by word without writing. Such are the daily buying and selling of commodities either for ready money, or payable at some dates of payment, wherein the mediation of a Broker is most necessary: For as it would be troublesome to use Scrivners in every bargain; so is it commodious to use the means of Brokers, the commodities are not only bought and sold with more credit and reputation, but all controversies which do arise by misadventure or otherwise are sooner determined, and a sworn Broker is taken as a double witness, if he do produce his book, with a *Memorandum* of the bargain, as the same was agreed between both parties, whereby many variances are reconciled, and differences (like to fall out) are prevented.

This brief discussion on the use of brokers in commodities transactions follows a longer discussion by Malynes (1622 [1979], pp. 124–6) regarding the use of 'notarial contracts' in the trading business of the regulated company of 'Merchant Adventurers' where the systemic use of forward sale contracts in their commercial transactions is apparent.[6] In modern vernacular, the sixteenth- and seventeenth-century sales contracts that Malynes describes for the sale of English cloth goods arranged on the English bourse in Antwerp, the Bruges bourse and other important commercial centres, were structured as non-transferable forward sale contracts with option features.

Clarifying the definition of 'stock' permits the different trading venues for the 'stock market' to be identified. Since the seventeenth century, stock trading has been increasingly associated with 'stock exchanges', which requires 'exchange' to be defined. As painfully apparent in the difficulties confronting the Securities & Exchange Commission (SEC) since Reg ATS was contemplated in 1997 (see Markham and Harty, Chapter 12 in this volume), this is not as easy as might be expected. A number of conventional and technical definitions for an 'exchange' are possible, for example Lee (1998, pp. 322–3). Almost all modern academic definitions identify an exchange with a physical location or building. This creates problems when, say, the 'exchange' is in cyberspace. The Securities and Exchange Act (SEC 1934, amended 2010) currently identifies an exchange as:

> The term 'exchange' means any organization, association, or group of persons, whether incorporated or unincorporated, which constitutes, maintains, or provides a market place or facilities for bringing together purchasers and sellers of securities or for otherwise performing with respect to securities the functions commonly performed by a stock exchange as that term is generally understood, and includes the market place and the market facilities maintained by such exchange.

This expands the location of an exchange to be a 'market place' with 'facilities' which:

> includes its premises, tangible or intangible property whether on the premises or not, any right to the use of such premises or property or any service thereof for the purpose of effecting or reporting a transaction on an exchange (including, among other things, any system of communication to or from the exchange, by ticker or otherwise . . .)

Significantly, while recognizing the technological evolution of segmented exchanges into a market system of trading platforms, this definition fails to specify adequately 'the functions commonly performed by a stock exchange as that term is generally understood'.

Stock market history illustrates the relevance of accurately identifying stock exchange functions. Consider a general definition that treats 'bourse' and 'exchange' as synonyms that is provided by Ehrenberg (1928, p. 54):

> A bourse or exchange is an assembly meeting at frequent intervals, usually daily, consisting of the merchants and other persons, who meet for the purpose of dealing without exhibiting, delivering or paying for their goods at the same time.

This definition identifies essential characteristics that apply to 'bourse' and 'exchange', but in doing so ignores features that divide bourse and exchange trading. In a modern context, this definition is consistent with the location of an exchange in 'cyberspace'. It is also sufficient to distinguish an exchange from, say, a marketplace selling produce and is preferable to definitions that identify an exchange only as a physical location where buyers and sellers meet to trade goods.[7] However, this commonly used general definition fails to identify characteristics of an 'exchange' that facilitates 'speculative exchange trading'. In this chapter, characteristics associated with the contracts, clearing and settlement procedures are identified that make a distinction between centralized exchange trading and decentralized bourse trading. Identification of these differences clarifies fundamental difficulties confronting modern regulators regarding periodic market instability generated by trading in OTC derivative securities, and the associated price discovery distortions arising from unconstrained manipulative short selling.

Given this, the impact of exchange trading techniques on the historical evolution of the stock market can be more readily identified. In particular, speculative exchange trading of a transferable security contract needs to be distinguished from a situation where a buyer and seller meet at, say, the Royal Exchange and agree to a forward sale of goods with a contract then drawn up by a 'scrivner'. In this situation, it is the goods that are being traded, not the forward contract. Speculative exchange trading requires transferability and an exchange clearing mechanism to settle positions. In turn, transferability requires standardized contract terms and a relatively homogeneous deliverable commodity. A transaction where merchants meet at the Royal Exchange and agree to a non-transferable forward contract with multiple delivery dates would correspond, in modern terms, to an OTC commodity swap transaction. There is no exchange clearing mechanism for the transaction. The merchants that are party and counterparty to the trade are responsible for completion. As such, a technical distinction is being made that corresponds to the modern difference between trading derivative securities on exchanges or OTC. In addition to the clearing mechanism, there can be significant variation in the character of exchange speculation due to settlement practices, that is, between cash settlement and 'settlement by account'.

The beginning of purely speculative exchange trading occurs when the parties involved in the completion of the trade are different from those initiating the trade. This requires a traded contract to be created for which there is no intention of completing the underlying goods transaction; in effect, the seller may not have possession of the goods and the buyer may not intend to take delivery. In this case, a contract is created for which there is no resulting delivery of goods. This requires a clearing method for determining and settling gains and losses on contracts. Various prerequisite conditions are required for such trading to occur. The evolution was gradual, not dramatic, and depended on a range of informal restrictions on those participating in the trade. Recognizing that initial trade was in the bulk commodities of herring, whale oil and wheat – commodities that require special warehousing, grading and handling facilities – initial trade was associated with brokers and dealers directly involved in the bulk commodity trade willing to execute 'to arrive' forward contracts for which there was no associated goods transactions, seeking to offset the position prior to delivery or, if necessary, cover the position in the spot market upon arrival of the fleet. Given the vagaries of market liquidity, in the event that the contract could not be transferred both parties to the contract needed to be able to complete delivery.

THE ANTWERP EXCHANGE

The evolution of exchange trading techniques for bulk commodities revolved around two important elements: enhanced securitization of the transactions and the emergence of speculative trading. Both these developments are closely connected with the increasing concentration of commercial activity, initially at the large medieval market fairs and, later, on the bourses and exchanges. Securitization of bulk commodity transactions was facilitated by extending trading methods that had been in use for centuries in the market for bills of exchange.[8] Prior to the emergence of joint-stock companies, bills of exchange and related contracts were the primary methods of raising capital for business ventures. By implication, the early markets in bills of exchange were the precursors to modern stock markets. By the sixteenth century, the central role of bills of exchange in financing domestic and international trade was associated with the prevalence of partnerships to structure firm governance. The seasonality of the commodity businesses that dominated commercial trading and the 'localized' character of international trade did not require permanency in firm capital structure that the joint-stock company introduced in the following century.

In addition to being focal points for goods trading activities, the medieval fairs were also financial events. The fairs, such as those at Champagne, featured well-organized money markets conducting manual foreign exchange transactions and substantial dealings in bills of exchange (de Roover 1954, p. 204).[9] Because the larger fairs involved transactions between merchants from a number of different regions, it was not practical to settle all transactions using manual exchange of coin. This was a primary impetus for dealings on credit, as de Roover (1949, p. 110) observes:[10]

> Today banks discount the trade acceptances or the promissory notes of merchants who are in need of credit. Such a procedure was ruled out as long as contracts involving the payment of interest were unenforceable at law. It is true that usury laws could be circumvented by various subterfuges. However, the easiest method for securing short-term credit was for merchants to 'take up' money by exchange and not at interest. The result of this practice was that commercial credit was tied to the exchange. This point, although obvious, is so fundamental that its importance should be stressed . . . the credit system rested on the exchanges.

As such, methods for clearing and settlement of bill of exchange transactions were fundamental to the smooth operation of the international commercial and financial system.

Though the precise origin of the practice is unknown, 'arbitration of exchange' first developed during the Middle Ages. Around the time of the First Crusade (1095–99), Genoa had emerged as a major sea power and important trading centre (Einzig 1964). The Genoa fairs had become sufficiently important economic and financial events that traders from around the Mediterranean were attracted. To deal with the problems of reconciling transactions using different coinages and units of account, a forum for arbitrating exchange rates was introduced. On the third day of each fair at Genoa, a representative body composed of recognized merchant bankers would assemble and determine the exchange rates that would prevail for that fair. The process involved each banker suggesting an exchange rate and, after some discussion, a voting process would determine the exchange rates that would apply at that fair. Similar practices were adopted at other important fairs later in the Middle Ages. At Lyons, for example, Florentine, Genoese and Lucca bankers would meet separately to determine rates, with the average of these group rates becoming the official rate. These rates would then apply to bill transactions and other business conducted at the fair. Rates typically stayed constant between fairs in a particular location providing the opportunity for arbitraging of exchange rates across fairs in different locations.

The actual clearing process differed from fair to fair (Parker 1974, p. 546). At the Lyons fairs, clearing involved the participation of all merchants attending the fair. At other fairs, such as the fairs of Besançon or Medina del Campo, clearing was controlled by a restricted group of merchant-bankers who were responsible for setting exchange rates and for handling the book-transfers between the accounts of merchants at the various clearing member banks. Ehrenberg (1928, p. 284) describes the clearing process used in Lyons:[11]

> Before the merchants attended the fair they entered in their 'market book' . . . all the payments due from or to them in the fair. At the beginning of the fair these payments books were compared with one another. In the case of every entry found correct the person from whom the payment was due made a mark which was taken as a binding recognition of the debt; later he had to sign his whole name. The bill – for, generally speaking, there was no question of anything but bills – was *accepted* in this way. If an item was not recognized, the owner of the book would write by it 'S.P.' (*sous protest*).
>
> After the acceptance of the old bills there followed the new business with foreign markets, which originated [whether] at the preceding fair or as the result of the acceptance, or otherwise.

> Here we meet for the first time a peculiar arrangement, the settlement of an official average price for each species of bill, the so-called Conto.
>
> (T)he Conto in Lyons was done as follows: The bill dealers met on a certain day and formed a circle (*Faire la Ronde*); the Consul of the Florentines then asked the dealers of the different nations in turn what they thought the price ought to be. The answers were noted and an average taken. This was the official rate for bills which was noted in the bulletins . . . and sent abroad. The dealers themselves were naturally not bound by this, their business was left free to bargaining. Yet the Conto at the beginning had some meaning for the market itself, as previously many transactions had been concluded at the average rate which had not yet been settled . . .
>
> The payment proper closed the fair. It was affected chiefly by *viremant de parties*, *giro* or *scontro*, as follows: Two persons were commissioned to collect and compare . . . all the fair books. They then canceled the payments against one another, and only paid the balances in cash . . . The fair payments at Lyons owe their form to the Florentines, a fact which is clearly shown by the development of the Lyons Bourse.

Various features of the clearing process at Lyons were not only adapted for use at other important fairs, but also had an impact on the methods later employed on the Lyons bourse. The method of offset used in the end-of-fair settling process was later reflected in the *rescontre* system adopted to settle exchange trading of shares in seventeenth-century Amsterdam and eighteenth-century England.[12]

The Lyons fairs first assumed importance circa 1463 due to the explicit mercantilist policies of Louis XI. As early as 1419, various French kings had granted privileges to merchants doing business in Lyons in an attempt to counteract the success of the fairs held in Geneva. These privileges included freedom to engage in various financial transactions, such as manual exchange of coin and dealing in bills of exchange, activities that were tightly regulated elsewhere in France. Even more than the economic benefits associated with the commodities trade, the French monarchs were motivated by the gains associated with the financial dealings of the fairs. By the fifteenth century, the capital that could be raised at important fairs such as those of Geneva was substantial. This capital was essential to securing financing for the military adventures in which the national monarchs were almost continually engaged. The extension of commercial liberties beyond the time period of the fairs contributed significantly to the emergence of bourse trading. As early as the end of the thirteenth century, the dukes of Brabant encouraged the growth of Antwerp by granting privileges to alien merchants visiting the city (van Houtte 1966), such as not requiring that local brokers be used to transact commodity business. Such merchants trading in Bruges, the northern centre of European commerce during the fourteenth century, were required to use local brokers.

While the medieval fairs served as an important step in the growth of trade and payments, by the late fifteenth century economic activity was outgrowing the restrictions of the fixed fair dates. A network of international merchants had established permanent offices and warehouses throughout the key commercial centres of Europe. To support the associated trading activities, sizeable communities of foreign merchants were established. These changes meant that liquidity was sufficient to support trading throughout the year. This growth sustained the creation of bourse trading in various cities, designed to facilitate dealings in both physical and financial commodities. The bourses were, effectively, meeting places for merchants of various countries to transact financial and commodities business. The use of the term 'bourse' (*beurs*) is indicative of the historical development, the term being taken from a square in Bruges, named for an inn on the square owned at one time by the van Beurs family, where the Florentines, Genoese and Venetians had their consular houses. This inn was a popular meeting place for foreign merchants. Though exchange trading of free standing derivative securities was yet to come, some essential characteristics of exchange trading are discernible at the beginnings of the bourses: a self-regulating collection of merchants – both brokers and dealers – meeting for the mutual gain of enhanced liquidity. For the early bourses, access to credit and foreign exchange facilities were integral factors.

Bourse trading was a major development on trading at medieval fairs and local markets for at least two reasons. First, trading at the fairs was restricted to specific time periods. While initially useful as a method of concentrating mercantile activity, the growth of trade soon surpassed the narrow time windows provided by the individual fairs. Bourse trading involved both financial transactions and trading in goods. For the medieval fairs, these two activities were complementary. Commercial trade in goods generated financial transactions, activities that were facilitated by the concentrated activity of the fair. Yet, as evidenced in the activities of merchant bankers in centres such as Bruges (for example de Roover 1948), there were other reasons for financial activity independent of goods trading, especially trading in bills of exchange for investment and market-making purposes. These financial activities formed the basis of an element of bourse trading that can be traced back to the Middle Ages in Southern Europe, starting in the trading centres of Italy. By the fourteenth century, financial bourse trading can be found in certain Northern European centres, most importantly Bruges (Ehrenberg 1928, p. 55):

> in the trading cities of Italy, [bourse trading] arose from the business which developed at the banks of the money-changers native to the city, when the notaries likewise had stalls in the open air . . . there arose . . . the characteristics of the exchange business as early as the fourteenth century . . . In the countries north of the Alps bill business . . . developed in closest connection with the factories of the Italians. The streets and market places where they lived, and more especially where they had their consular houses or Loggias, were the localities where the bourse business first developed.

Bruges was geographically well situated to have the first significant bourse trading in northern Europe. The opening of seaborne trade routes through the Straits of Gibraltar contributed to the decline of fairs along the land trade routes, such as the Champagne fairs. In addition, the Hansards developed important seaborne trade from Northern Europe. This growth in seaborne traffic contributed to the initial rise of Bruges as 'the greatest market of Christendom in the fourteenth century' (van Houtte 1966, p. 37).

In addition to being a main seaport, Bruges was also the locale for one of the five fairs of Flanders. The importance of Bruges peaked in the mid-1300s with the comparatively faster growth of commercial markets and bourses in other centres being due to two primary local factors: the silting of the waterway connecting Bruges to the ocean, and the various restrictions imposed by Bruges on foreign merchants trading there. The international growth of trade meant that Portuguese, Spanish, South German and Italian merchants had sufficient reason to establish permanent colonies in locales such as Bruges and Antwerp where, before, these merchants sojourned to the fairs. In addition to geographical factors, the freedoms granted to alien merchants played a key role in determining where bourse trading was concentrated.[13] From the beginnings of bourse trading there was competition between geographical venues for business. A second factor favouring bourse trading was that fairs required goods to be transported to the fair's geographical location for inspection in order to conclude specific transactions. The goods were then transported to another district to be sold. As trade expanded, factors such as acceptable levels of standardization and the growth of mutual merchant confidence allowed goods transactions to be made without actual inspection of goods at the time the sale was completed. In turn, bourses and exchanges were located geographically close to the centre of the underlying bulk goods trade. Such factors significantly reduced transactions, transport and other costs. By providing enhanced liquidity and cheaper execution, bourse trading was an essential impetus to the emergence of speculation in commodities which, ultimately, progressed into speculative exchange trading of derivative securities on stocks.

Though the transition from discrete trading intervals at the medieval fairs to the regularity of bourse trading was gradual, the sixteenth century does provide a transition period: at the beginning of the century, the fairs still played an important role in providing fixed dates and locations at which concentrations of liquid capital were assembled; by the end of the century, general economic activity was such that bourse and exchange trading predominated. During the century, the emergence of exchange trading in Antwerp and Lyons was especially important, though by the end of the century both these centres were in decline. Of these two centres, Antwerp was initially most important for trade in commodities, and Lyons for trade in bills of exchange. In 1531, Antwerp opened a new exchange building designed exclusively for trading of commodities and bills of exchange.[14] Tawney (1925 [1962], pp. 62–5) describes the international money market of the sixteenth century:

> In its economic organization the machinery of international trade had reached a state of efficiency not noticeably inferior to that of three centuries later. Before the most highly-organized economic systems of the age were ruined by the struggle between Spain and the Netherlands, and by the French wars of religion, there were perhaps ten to twelve commercial centres whose money markets were the financial power-houses of European trade, and whose opinion and policy were decisive in determining financial conditions. In the Flemish, French and Italian cities where it reached its zenith, and of which England was a pupil, the essence of financial organization of the sixteenth century was internationalism, freedom for every capitalist to undertake every transaction within his means, a unity which had as its symptom the movement of all the principal markets in sympathy with each other, and as its effect the [mobilization] of immense resources at the strategic points of international finance. Its centre and symbol was the exchange at Antwerp, with its significant dedication, '*Ad mercatorum cujusque gentis ac linguae*' where . . . every language under heaven could be heard, or the fairs at Lyon which formed, in the words of a Venetian, 'the foundations of the pecuniary transactions of the whole of Italy and of a good part of Spain and of the Netherlands'.

The public-good characteristic of such a centralized exchange location was recognized and adapted in other centres, with Sir Thomas Gresham personally advancing the funds for the building of a similar exchange in London, the Royal Exchange, opening in 1571. With initial construction starting in 1611 on the new building for the Amsterdam Exchange, by 1613 the transfer of trading to the exchange from different venues around the city was completed.[15]

Fully developed speculative trading in commodities emerged in Antwerp during the second half of the sixteenth century (Tawney 1925 [1962], pp. 62–5; Gelderblom and Jonker 2005). The development of the Antwerp commodity market provided sufficient liquidity to support the development of trading in 'to arrive' contracts associated with the rapid expansion of seaborne trade during the period. Various sources report that speculative transactions in 'to arrive' grain that was still at sea were particularly active, with trade in whale oil, herring and salt also being important (Gelderblom and Jonker 2005; Barbour 1950; Emery 1896). Unger (1980) provides detailed information on the herring industry during this period. The Dutch herring trade to the Baltic was intimately connected to the grain trade to Southern Europe. Due to a number of technological developments introduced over the fourteenth to sixteenth centuries, the Dutch herring fleets dominated this trade until the second half of the seventeenth century. The evolution of the herring fishery depended on increased capital requirements; as a consequence the role of brokers also evolved: 'By the mid-fifteenth century the brokers were becoming owners and operators of ships as well. They were merchants with an interest in more assured supplies of preserved fish . . . even individuals with no direct connection with fishing can and did invest in the boats and their supplies' (Unger 1980, p. 258).

That 'to arrive' contracts came to be actively traded by speculators also directly involved in trading the underlying physical commodity is not surprising. Because transport by sea was a risky business and information about cargoes to arrive at a later date could be sketchy, the quality and quantity of physical commodity available for delivery could not be known prior to arrival of the fleet; a forward sale of such cargoes would be inherently speculative. The concentration of speculative liquidity on the Antwerp exchange centred on the important merchants and large merchant houses that controlled either financial activities or the goods trade (van der Wee 1977). The milieu for such trading was closely tied to medieval traditions of gambling and insurance where wagering on the safe return of ships, a rudimentary form of early insurance (Lewin 2003), was often connected with the conclusion of commercial transactions. A key step in the evolution of exchange traded contracts came when trading in 'to arrive' contracts involved standardized transactions in fictitious goods for a future delivery that was settled by the payment of 'differences'.[16] Purchasers of such contracts would speculate on the rise in prices before the due date. If such a rise occurred, the contract could then be sold and the speculator pocketed or paid the difference in price. This 'difference dealing' was also conducted by goods vendors selling for future delivery, betting that prices would fall.

The development of difference dealing was accompanied by the emergence of 'premium contracts' where: 'The buyer made a contract for future delivery at a fixed price, but with the condition that he could reconsider after two or three months: he could then withdraw from the contract provided that he paid a premium to the vendor (*stellegelt*)' (van der Wee 1977). Little is known about the precise evolution of the contracts used for speculative trading, but the premium contract appears well suited to difference dealing by speculators. The 'premium' form of contract for forward sale became a staple of the European securities trade into the twentieth century, for example the contract for the German *prämiengeschäfte* (Hafner and Zimmermann 2009). Such contracts differ from the options traded in modern markets which have inherited characteristics associated with historical features of US option trading. Following Emery (1896, p. 53), the *prämiengeschäfte* 'may be considered as an ordinary contract for future delivery with special stipulation that, in consideration of a cash payment, one of the parties has the right to withdraw from the contract within a specified time'.[17] As such, this option is a feature of a forward contract with a fee to be paid at delivery if the option is exercised. For example, on the nineteenth-century Paris and Berlin exchanges the premium payment at maturity was fixed by convention and the 'price' would be determined by the setting the exercise price relative to the initial stock or commodity price, for example Courtadon (1982).

Characteristics of trading in commodities and bills of exchange in Antwerp formed the basis for later trading at other venues. Some elements of that trade are still of contemporary relevance. While access to the Antwerp exchange was unrestricted, those unconnected to the bulk commodity trade and seeking to speculate required a broker to establish a position. Brokers could also be dealers in the commodity. The exchange was a largely self-regulatory entity with broker-dealers clearing speculative difference trades with other broker-dealers. Rules of conduct for trading were largely governed by merchant convention. Penalties for violations involved loss of reputation and an ensuing inability to conduct business. The state provided official recognition to certain 'sworn brokers' and established a civil court system for settling disputes. Physical infrastructure and a sympathetic legal and taxation environment were provided to promote the development of trade. Difference dealing was facilitated by the use of premium contracts. Following traditions developed in the bill of exchange market, the clearing and settling of positions in commodity difference dealing was done by brokers coordinating with other brokers. The 'hand-to-hand' settlement practices in Antwerp involved primarily cash settlement of contracts, eliminating the possibility of contract offset associated with 'settlement by account'.

EXCHANGE TRADING IN SEVENTEENTH-CENTURY AMSTERDAM

The collapse of Antwerp in 1585 and the resulting diaspora of important merchants contributed substantially to the rise of the important exchanges in Amsterdam and other centres such as London, where the Royal Exchange was established in 1571. While Amsterdam had developed as an important commercial centre prior to 1585 (van Dillen 1927; Gelderblom and Jonker 2005), the establishment of a permanent building for the Amsterdam bourse in 1611 marks a symbolic beginning of Dutch commercial supremacy. During the seventeenth and eighteenth centuries, speculative trading of forward and option contracts on the Amsterdam exchange developed many essential features of such trading in modern derivative security markets. By the middle of the seventeenth century speculative exchange trading in Amsterdam for shares in the Dutch East Indies Company (VOC) and, to a lesser extent, the Dutch West Indies Company, had progressed to where contracts with regular expiration dates were traded (Wilson 1941 [1966]; Gelderblom and Jonker 2005) and a clearing method with contract offset and settlement by account was fully developed.[18] By the eighteenth century, the trade involved both Dutch joint-stock shares and 'British funds'. This trading on the Amsterdam exchange is the first historical instance of speculative exchange trading in financial derivative securities. 'With the appearance of marketable British securities, and the application to them of a speculative technique that was already well understood, the Amsterdam [exchange] became the scene of international finance at its most abstract and most exciting – gambling in foreign securities' (Wilson 1941 [1966], p. 79).

Despite isolated instances of previous joint stock trading in other centres, the first developed market arose with trade in VOC shares in Amsterdam starting from the founding of the company by the States General in 1602.[19] At this time, the Amsterdam bourse was held in the open air near the New Bridge and in the church square near the Oude Kerk. It was not until 1613 that trading completely moved to a building dedicated to the Amsterdam exchange. Trading in shares was only a small portion of the general activity on the Amsterdam exchange, which was predominately in bills and commodities. Creation of the company led to a call for initial subscriptions of capital. Prospects for the company were generally perceived to be favourable among the moneyed individuals willing to invest in such a venture and the closing of the VOC subscription lists found numerous individuals still desiring shares. These individuals turned to the Amsterdam bourse to purchase shares and, when this could not be done at par, a 14–16 per cent premium emerged within a number of days (Ehrenberg 1928, p. 358).[20] With such immediate returns, the potential for gain became apparent to bourse traders and the speculative trade in shares began in earnest with the selling of shares for deferred delivery not owned at the time of the sale. This initial trade was conducted in bourse fashion using OTC-style forward contracting.

By the beginning of the seventeenth century, it was apparent that bourse trading in Amsterdam was becoming the successor to the Antwerp exchange that had fallen on hard times due to a combination of political, geographic and economic factors. In conjunction with the shift in trading activity, many of the traders also eventually relocated from Antwerp to Amsterdam and brought with them the trading techniques that had been successfully developed on the Antwerp exchange. Included among these techniques was speculative trading for future delivery. This technique, almost immediately, was applied to bourse trading in company shares. Ehrenberg (1928, pp. 358–9) provides some fundamental insight into methods used for trading in VOC shares:

> From the beginning, the speculation in shares . . . as a means of gain depending on taking advantage of future price changes, made it appear extremely desirable to postpone the fulfilment of the bargains. In the case of bears, who had sold shares which they did not possess, this was an absolute necessity.
>
> Speculative future dealings made possible a twofold simplification of the technique of dealing. First, speculative dealings could be realized before the date of delivery. Secondly, settling days made it possible to use the same procedure that had done so much in the methods of payment, namely, set off. Both together resulted in an incalculable increase in turnover, since now only a little ready money and stock were required for very large dealings.

Significantly, 'it was speculation which made the first modern stock exchange'. Speculators provided the liquidity essential for continuous trading and 'accurate' pricing. In turn, traders seeking to acquire or dispose of stock positions provided the 'honest' liquidity needed to clear the market. De la Vega (1688, p. 164) suggests that the relative composition of the speculative trading population changed over time reflecting the evolution from bourse to exchange trading: whereas 'formerly twenty speculators ruled the exchange . . . Today there are as many speculators as merchants'.

Kellenbenz (1957, pp. 139–42) provides a useful summary of de la Vega's discussion of the various types of transactions in the Amsterdam market:

a. There were sales of real stock against immediate payment of cash.
b. There were comparable sales where the money to cover payments was borrowed from individuals, up to four-fifths of its value.
c. There were transactions in which future settlement dates were specified – that is, beyond the regular monthly settlement dates. These future contracts were seemingly used for both speculative and hedging purposes, both by speculators and by the lenders on securities. De la Vega implies that the latter parties always hedged by means of such contracts. Hypothecation, which was mentioned as early as 1610 (in the edict of that year), was permitted to the seller presumably during the period of the forward contract. Arrangements also were possible, and were fairly frequently resorted to whereby the date of the termination of a future contract could be postponed, apparently by mutual consent of the parties. This action was called 'prolongation'. A large proportion of the foregoing future sales were really sales 'in blanco' – or short sales, as we would label them – even though such transactions were prohibited by laws of the state and of the city.
d. There were options contracts. These were at least of the 'call' and 'put' varieties, which have persisted ever since . . . Option contracts were utilized sometimes for hedging purposes by *bona fide* investors, but more commonly for mere speculation . . .
e. In addition there were purchases and sales of 'ducaton' shares. (Such transactions were of recent origin in 1688, and actually had been abandoned in the slump that had occurred just as de la Vega was writing his book.) What this 'ducaton' trading amounted to is a bit uncertain on the strength of what de la Vega actually says. Scholars who have worked on this period assert that the ducaton shares were fictitious . . .

Trading for forward delivery was essential to the seventeenth-century trade in shares on the Amsterdam bourse (Barbour 1950).[21] Such trading was of practical necessity because the delivery and settlement process for traded shares was much different than the modern process. Though shares could be transferred, the process required the seller to be present at the company offices to record the transfer in the 'book of shareholders' and to pay a transfer fee. The practice of same-day cash settlement, delivery and transfer was not usually possible – even for trades arranged at the transfer office.[22] Agreements to sell shares typically included a future settlement and transfer date which could be months in the future, though delivery dates longer than one month in the future were discouraged by statutes dating from 1610.

Perceptions of speculative abuse associated with the delivery process appeared almost from the start of bourse trade in VOC shares (van Dillen et al. 2006; Gelderblom et al. 2010 [2009]). A bear ring headed by Isaac Le Maire was formed around 1609 to gain by manipulating prices to fall using long-dated forward short sales in order to purchase stock in the cash market at lower prices. 'It is not clear that the ring did more than help to hold down the already slumping prices, but the company lodged a protest with the States of Holland and West Friesland in the summer of 1609 to have a ban placed on the sale of shares "in blanco"' (De Marchi and Harrison 1994, p. 51). The result was the Dutch edict of 1610 banning short sales *in blanco*, where, at the time of the short sale, the seller does not actually possess the shares being sold. In addition, the edict required that share transfers be made within one month of the sale date. The ban on short sales was not permanent and the 'occasion of renewal brought out anew sentiment for and against VOC' (p. 51). Despite opposition, the ban on 'selling in the wind', or *windhandel* trade, was repeated in 1624, 1630, 1636 and 1677. It is important to recognize that the de facto impact of the ban on *in blanco* short selling was to make such contracts unenforceable in the courts. There was no direct criminal penalty for entering into such contracts which provided the basis for difference dealing among the close knit community of brokers and dealers that dominated the stock and commodity trade on the Amsterdam exchange.

Though the ban on *in blanco* short selling technically applied to both commodities and stocks, the character of speculative trading in commodities was less affected due to the practical need for bourse speculators to have a connection to the underlying goods trade. No such constraint was associated with stocks. Without the discipline of exchange trading, the potential for abuse of non-transferable forward contracts with option features in the loosely organized Amsterdam share market was considerable. In turn, the ban did not eliminate speculative trading. Rather, the characteristics of trading were altered. Though the Amsterdam exchange had unrestricted access, the exchange also facilitated concentration of commercial activity. Exchange trading was primarily conducted by sworn and free brokers in combination with a group of dominant merchants. This provided a foundation for the introduction of trading conventions that constitute an early form of exchange self-regulation. The emergence of the *rescontre* settlement was a development on these early methods of exchange self-regulation. Such self-regulated trading in VOC shares on the Amsterdam exchange was further facilitated by the bulk of trading activity being conducted by Jewish traders of Iberian descent.

Modern knowledge about stock trading activity on the Amsterdam exchange at the end of the seventeenth century derives primarily from *Confusion de Confusiones* (1688; Fridson 1996) (Cardoso 2006). Though central concerns of this remarkable book are much broader, de la Vega does make a number of detailed references to speculative exchange trading practices on the Amsterdam exchange. For example, there is a general description (Fridson 1996, p. 155) of the potential gains to options trading: 'Give "opsies" or premiums, and there will be only limited risk to you, while the gain may surpass all your imaginings and hopes'. This statement is followed by a somewhat exaggerated claim about the potential gains: 'Even if you do not gain through "opsies" the first time . . . continue to give the premiums for a later date, and it will rarely happen that you lose all your money before a propitious incident occurs that maintains the price for several years'. Presumably, de la Vega has call options trading in mind, the possibility of trading put options appears later (p. 156).

The reference to extending contracts is further elaborated in de la Vega's discussion of the *rescontre* system (p. 181), a major technical evolution of the 'settlement by account' method of clearing trades that emerged between 1650 and1688, when the Dutch first introduced quarterly settlements of share transactions on the Amsterdam bourse. Prior to this time, settlement procedures had been less formal. Wilson (1941 [1966], p. 83) provides the following description of the settlement process:

> The technique of speculation in the British Funds at Amsterdam . . . was a kind of gamble carried on every three months: no payments were made except on *rescontre* (settlement or carry-over), i.e., the period for which funds were bought or sold and for which options were given or taken. *Rescontredag* (contango day) occurred four times a year, and on these occasions representatives of the speculators gathered round a table to regulate or liquidate their transactions, and to make reciprocal payments for fluctuations or surpluses. Normally these fluctuations were settled without the actual value of the funds in question being paid – only real investors paid cash for their purchases. Speculative buyers paid to sellers the percentage by which the funds had fallen since the last contango day, or alternatively received from them the percentage by which funds had risen in the same interval. After surpluses had been paid, new continuations were undertaken for the following settlement. In such a *prolongatie* (continuation) the buyer

granted the seller a certain percentage (a contango rate) to prolong his purchase to the next *rescontre*: in this way he stood the chance of benefiting by a rise in quotations in the interval, without tying up his capital: he was only bound to pay any possible marginal fall.

A key feature of the *rescontre* was the concentration of liquidity that, for example, permitted prolongations to be done more readily (Dickson 1967, p. 491; van Dillen 1927). The term 'rescontre' was derived from the practice of Dutch merchants to 'indicate that a bill had been paid by charging it to a current account – "solvit per rescontre" as distinct from "per banco", "per wissel" and so on' (Poitras 2009b; Dickson 1967, p. 491; Mortimer 1761 [1996], p. 28n).

In addition to the references to extension of the option expiration dates, with regular marking-to-market, de la Vega takes up the uncertain legal interpretation of option contracts at a later point (p. 183) and explicitly recognizes that the Dutch restriction on *in blanco* short sales could impact upon put and call options differently:

> As to whether the regulation (banning short sales) is applicable to *option contracts*, the opinions of experts diverge widely. I have not found any decision that might serve as a precedent, though there are many cases at law from which one [should be able to] draw a correct picture. All legal experts hold that the regulation is applicable to both the seller and buyer [of the contract]. In practice, however, the judges have often decided differently, always freeing the buyer from the liability while holding the seller [to the contract] . . . If . . . the opinion is correct that it applies only to the seller, the regulation will be of no use to me [as a person wanting to seek shelter] when I receive call premiums, for in this case I am in fact a seller; but it will help me if I have received a put premium, as I am then the buyer of stocks. With regard to the put premium . . . law and legal opinion, the regulation and the reasons for the decisions are contradictory. The theory remains uncertain, and one cannot tell which way the adjudication tends.

The bulk of option market participants appear to have been speculators, attracted primarily by the urge to gamble, usually 'men of moderate wealth indulging in a little speculation' (Wilson 1941 [1966], p. 105). In contrast, drawing from de Pinto (1771a, 1771b), Wilson (p. 84) observes that for trading conducted on the Amsterdam exchange during the eighteenth century: 'Options were the province of the out-and-out gamblers'.[23]

EXCHANGE TRADING IN EIGHTEENTH-CENTURY LONDON

Following the Glorious Revolution of 1688, many of the speculative practices used in Amsterdam were adopted in England where a bourse market for stock trading had developed by the mid-1690s with about 140 joint-stock companies available for trading by 1695. However, speculative share trading took a substantively different form than in Amsterdam. Despite the presence of the Royal Exchange, the development of speculative exchange trading of shares was hampered in England by a combination of factors. Houghton's 1694 contributions to his circular *A Collection for the Improvement of Husbandry and Trade* (1692–1703 [1969]) can be fairly recognized as containing possibly the first coherent and balanced description of early stock trading in London, for example Neal (1990, p. 17), though the description provided by Houghton is so brief that Cope (1978, p. 4) credits Mortimer (1761 [1996]) with being the 'first detailed description of the market'. In addition to providing a description of cash stock trading, the bulk of the contribution by Houghton is on the specific subject of share trading using option contracts. For seven weeks in June and July 1694, Houghton dedicated the first page of his circular to discussing various aspects of stock trading. About two and a half of the seven weeks are dedicated to trading in 'puts and refusals'. On 22 June 1694, Houghton provides the following discussion of the process for cash trading of shares at that time:

> The manner of managing the Trade is this: The Monied Man goes among the *Brokers*, (which are chiefly upon the *Exchange*, and at *Jonathan's* Coffee House, sometimes at *Garaway's* and at some other Coffee Houses) and asks how *Stocks* go? And upon Information, bids the Broker buy or sell so many Shares of such and such Stocks if he can, at such and such Prizes. Then he tries what he can do among those that have stock, or power to sell them; and if he can, makes a Bargain.

As with early Amsterdam share trading, there was no specific physical exchange location where the bulk of trading could take place.

Prior to 1696–97, there were two venues for London stock trading: the Royal Exchange and Exchange Alley. In the Royal Exchange, dealers in stocks and shares 'had a "walk" near the centre of the building between the salters, the Italian merchants and the Canary merchants' (Morgan and Thomas 1962). However, due at least partly to abuses arising from the 1696 price collapse of various joint-stock promotions, stock traders left the Royal Exchange, conducting business after that date in the environs of Exchange Alley.

> There is a certain amount of mystery about [the stock dealers] withdrawal [from the Royal Exchange]. Scott refers to their being turned out, whereas Duguid insists that they were so harassed by their fellow traders, and so short of space that they went voluntarily and in spite of the efforts of the City to prevent them. (Morgan and Thomas 1962, p. 27)

Until 1773, when a group of brokers acquired a building in Threadneedle Street that was, for the first time, called the Stock Exchange, the history of speculative trading in London for stocks was intimately connected to Exchange Alley. Not being associated with a single physical location where access to entry could be restricted, the coffeehouse trading in Exchange Alley was initially incapable of providing the clearing and settlement conditions needed to avert abuses associated with speculative trading of shares.

The separate trading venues represented by the coffeehouses in Exchange Alley and the company transfer offices cannot be considered an exchange. Without the structure of exchange trading, clearing and settlement posed problems for brokers and other stock traders. While it is not possible to date precisely the beginning of the regular three-month *rescontre* (called 'rescounters' in London) for settlement of stock trades in London, Dickson (1967, p. 508) 'tentatively' puts the date in the early 1740s. Dickson attributes the emergence of the rescounters to the impact of Barnard's Act on the use of option contracts and other time bargains and to the subsequent emergence of 'dealing on margins, where the penalties on the broker were less severe, and harder to enforce'. In turn, dealing on margins 'made the case for regular settlement days (like the Dutch Rescounters) increasingly urgent. The institutional development required for regular clearing to emerge contributed significantly to the formal establishment of the London Stock Exchange (1773).' Though standardized contracts were in use from the early beginnings of share trading in London, conditions were not sufficient to sustain speculative trading of standardized derivative contracts for shares until a method of clearing was in place. As such, the London experience prior to the introduction of the rescounters reflects the difficulties of permitting OTC-style trading of derivative securities. Attempts to suppress directly the contracts used for such speculative trading only led to trading of leveraged cash securities, for example Shea (2007).

Until well into the eighteenth century, the London stock market was impacted upon significantly by Dutch investors and speculators conducting a considerable amount of their British securities trading outside the Amsterdam exchange at various locations in London. By construction, such trades took time to complete – if only for the time needed to draw bills of exchange between Amsterdam and London. Trading in both 'time bargains' and option contracts was widespread.[24] These activities were the main components of the 'stockjobbing' associated with the trading of stock for future delivery. Following Mortimer (1761 [1996], p. 32):[25]

> the mischief of it is, that under this sanction of selling and buying the funds for time for foreigners – Brokers and others, buy and sell for themselves, without having any interest in the funds they sell, or any cash to pay for what they buy, nay even without any design to transfer, or accept, the funds they sell or buy for time. The business thus transacted, has been declared illegal by several acts of parliament, and this is the principal branch of *stock-jobbing*.

While stockjobbing would be considered a basic activity in the context of speculative exchange trading of derivative securities, the result of the widespread OTC trading of such securities is reflected in the infamous history of stockjobbing in England which was met with considerable and generally disapproving interest in Parliament.[26]

A number of attempts were made to regulate stockjobbing, starting in 1697 with an Act 'To Restrain the number and ill Practice of Brokers and Stockjobbers'.[27] In addition to restricting the number of practices of commodity brokers, this Act was designed to deal with three main difficulties associated with the trade in shares: unscrupulous promotion activities, manipulation of prices for shares and misuse of option contracts. The pressures to further regulate stockjobbers intensified, leading to the Bubble Act of 1720 and, following the South Sea Bubble, to the passage of 'An Act to prevent the infamous Practice of Stock-jobbing' in 1733, also known as Barnard's Act. While this Act contained substantial penalties for speculative trading in options, the primary contractual vehicle for speculators, the Act was quite ineffective in eliminating this trade. However, Barnard's Act was successful in removing legal protection for these transactions, making the broker a principal in speculative transactions, responsible for completion of transaction in the event of default by a client. In turn, this led to the increased use of 'dealing on margins' as a method of speculation and the subsequent introduction of the London rescounters. The increased need for honesty and integrity in the settlement process was a significant factor leading a loose-knit group of brokers to form the London Stock Exchange where access by the general public could be restricted.

That speculating in shares using option contracts was present from the beginnings of London share trading in the 1690s is evident from the discussion in Houghton (1694) (in 1692–1703 [1969]):

> Another time he asks what they will have for Refuse of so many Shares: That is, How many Guinea's a Share he shall give for liberty to Accept or Refuse such Shares, at such a price, at any time within Six Months, or other time they shall agree for.

> For Instance; When *India* Shares are at Seventy Five, some will give Three Guinea's [*sic*] a Share, Action, or Hundred Pound, down for Refuse at Seventy Five, any time within Three Months, by which means the Accepter of the Guinea's, if they be not called for in that time, has his Share in his own Hand for his Security; and the Three Guinea's, which is after the rate of Twelve Guinea's profit in a year for Seventy Five Pound, which he could have sold at the Bargain making if he had pleased; and in consideration of this profit, he cannot without Hazard part with them the mean time, tho' they shall fall lower, unless he will run the hazard of buying again at any rate if they should be demanded; by which many have been caught, and paid dear for, as you shall see afterwards: So that if Three months they stand at stay, he gets the Three Guinea's, if they fall so much, he is as he was losing his Interest, and whatever they fall lower is loss to him.
>
> But if they happen to rise in that time Three Guinea's, and the charge of Brokerage, Contract and Expence, then he that paid the Three Guinea's demands the Share, pays the Seventy Five Pounds, and saves himself. If it rises but one or two Guinea's, he secures so much, but whatever it rises to beyond what it cost him is Gain. So that in short, for a small hazard, he can have his chance for a very great Gain, and he will certainly know the utmost his loss can be; and if by their rise he is encouraged to demand, he does not matter the farther advantage the Acceptor has, by having his Money sooner than Three Months to go to Market with again; so in plain *English*, one gives Three Guinea's for all the profits if they should rise, the other for Three Guinea's runs the hazard of all the losses if they should fall.

This insightful description is quite remarkable in that, unlike de la Vega or de Pinto, Houghton was not an active participant in the market; Houghton was 'not much concern'd in Stocks, and therefore [had] little occasion to Apologize for Trading therein'. As Houghton does not provide a discussion concerning speculation using 'time bargains', it is likely that many speculations were executed using options contracts.

An important, but overlooked, feature of Houghton's 1694 discussion appears in the contributions of 29 June and 6 July where samples of put and call option contracts are given in detail (for example Poitras 2000, pp. 350–51; Poitras 2009a). The use of standard contracts indicates that contracting practices common in Amsterdam were adopted in London. As de la Vega (1688 [1996], pp. 181–2) observes for Amsterdam trade:

> For . . . time bargains the brokers use printed *contract forms* with the customary stipulations and conditions of the business. On these forms spaces are left only for names, dates, and prices . . . For the *option business* there exists another sort of *contract form*, from which it is evident when and where the premium was paid and of what kind are the signatories' obligations.

With standardized forms and *rescontre* clearing, brokers were the vehicles for executing trades. As to the types of brokers, practices similar to those in Amsterdam appear to have been adopted in London. On practices in Amsterdam, de la Vega (1688 [1996], p. 185) reports:

> There are two kinds of brokers. Some are appointed by the municipal authorities and are called 'sworn' brokers, for they take another to do business on their own account. Their number is limited, and it changes only in the case of death, or through special privilege, which is seldom conferred. The other class of brokers is called 'free' brokers . . . clemency and indulgence toward these brokers prevail, instead of the sworn brokers attending actively to their own interest.

Unlike Amsterdam where free brokers 'appear so faithful and concerned about their customers that they compensate by zeal what they lack in reputation' and where exchange clearing and settlement were well developed, the speculative trading activities of free brokers operating in the London share market almost immediately involved some unscrupulous activities.

During the emergence of trade in free-standing option contracts, the conventional legal view in both Holland and England was that, while technically a gambling transaction, such contracts could be entered into by private parties willing to conduct such business without the guarantee that the courts could be used to enforce such contracts. However, in periods of speculative excess, the abuse of derivative security contracts in general, and option contracts in particular, produced a subsequent demand for further regulation. As Houghton (1694 in 1692–1703 [1969]) reports, the organized use of options contracts that had emerged in London during the 1690s was a venue for market manipulation:[28]

> But the great *Mystery* of all is, That some Rich Men will join together, and give money for *Refuse*, or by Friendship, or some other way, strive to secure all the Shares in a Stock, and also give Guinea's [*sic*] for Refuse of as many Shares more as Folk will sell, that have no Stock: and a great many such they are, that believe the Stock will not rise so high as the then Price, and Guinea's receiv'd or they shall buy before it does rise, which they are mistaken in; and then such takers of Guinea's for Refuse as have no Stock, must buy of the other that have so many Shares as they have taken Guinea's for the Refuse of, at such Rates as they or their Friends will sell for; tho' Ten or Twenty times the former Price.

In modern parlance, this is a classic example of a short squeeze being executed against uncovered call option writers. The Act of 1697 limited some of the potential abuses that were perpetrated with options, but did not eliminate such trading. This left forward trading as the favoured vehicle for manipulating security prices, an undesirable outcome of the 'villanous' practice of stockjobbing.[29]

There was considerable disagreement in the London broker community about whether options transactions were reputable. While potentially useful in some trading contexts, reputable brokers felt that options contributed to the speculative excesses common in the early financial markets. While trading in options and time bargains did contribute to the most important English financial collapse of the eighteenth century, the South Sea Bubble of 1720, this event was due more to the cash market manipulations of 'John Blunt and his friends' (Morgan and Thomas 1962, Ch. 2) facilitating instalment purchases of stock by lending the margin needed to raise the initial instalment. In any event, dealing in time bargains and, especially, options were singled out as practices that were central to 'the infamous practice of stock-jobbing'. In 1721, legislation aimed at preventing stock-jobbing passed the Commons but was not able to pass the Lords. It was not until 1733 that Sir John Barnard was able to introduce a bill successfully under the title: 'An Act to prevent the infamous Practice of Stock-jobbing'. This Act is generally referred to as Barnard's Act. Unlike the Dutch regulatory actions aimed at *in blanco* selling, the British approach was designed to regulate those features of stock dealings associated with excessive speculation, for example Morgan and Thomas (1962, p. 62).

The main provision of Barnard's Act (1733) states:

> All contracts or agreements whatsoever by or between any person or persons whatsoever, upon which any premium or consideration in the nature of a premium shall be given or paid for liberty to put upon or deliver, receive, accept or refuse any public or joint stock, or other public securities whatsoever, or any part, share or interest therein, and also all wagers and contracts in the nature of wagers, and all contracts in the nature of puts or refusals, relating to

> the then present or future price or value of any stock or securities, as aforesaid, shall be null and void.

A penalty of £500 was levied on any person, including brokers, who undertook any such bargain. All bargains were to be 'specifically performed and executed', stock being actually delivered and cash 'actually and really given and paid', and with a £100 penalty for anyone settling a contract by paying or receiving differences. Consistent with the seventeenth-century Dutch restrictions on *in blanco* selling, it was further provided: 'whereas it is a frequent and mischievous practice for persons to sell and dispose of stocks and securities of which they are not possessed', anyone doing so would incur a penalty of £500. There is disagreement among modern writers, such as Cope (1978) and Dickson (1967), concerning the extent to which Barnard's Act actually limited trading of options and other time bargains for stock. That it had some impact is evident as the Act did produce a stock market dependent upon cash settlement. Speculation was conducted using margin purchases and cash market short selling of borrowed securities replacing trading of options contracts and time bargains. Instead of settling by account at the rescounters, differences and loans would be settled in cash and loans for securities renewed until the next rescounter.

By the middle of the eighteenth century, the more substantial securities brokers in London 'were looking for ways of conducting their business in greater comfort and away from the disreputable hangers-on of the market' (Morgan and Thomas 1962, p. 68). An attempt in 1762 by a club of 150 brokers to obtain exclusive rent of Jonathan's failed when the courts upheld the access rights of those being denied access. Subsequently, in 1773 a group of brokers acquired a building in Sweetings Alley off Threadneedle Street that was called the 'Stock Exchange'. However, while some trade did gravitate to the new venue, there were no formal rules regarding membership, trading and the like. Access was open to the public on payment of a daily admission fee. In addition, trading continued to take place at various locales around London, especially in the Rotunda of the Bank of England building that had opened in 1765. In addition to free admission, the Rotunda building was where transfers for Bank of England stock and, more importantly, government debt issues were executed. Though the volume of trade was much greater than in Paris, this London stock exchange was 'neither exclusive or dominant' in the London securities market (Michie 1999, p. 32).

The evolution of the London stock market took a dramatic turn starting with the French Revolution in 1789 and the closure of the Paris bourse in 1793. The subsequent occupation of Amsterdam by French troops in 1795 meant that two of the most important financial centres in Europe – Paris and Amsterdam – were disrupted. These events triggered an exodus of important bankers, brokers and other merchants to London, providing further impetus to the emergence of London as the dominant financial centre for global trading of stocks and shares in the period from the early nineteenth century until the First World War. Against this late eighteenth-century backdrop, the British government greatly expanded the stock of national debt to fund military expenditures.[30] The eventual result was that: 'on 3 March 1801 a London Stock Exchange formally came into existence that not only provided a market for securities but also incorporated regulations on how business was to be conducted'. With this move, the exchange moved from an open to a closed market designed to ensure: 'that all those who participated both obeyed the rules and paid for the necessary administration' (Michie 1999, pp. 35–6). In effect, the first modern stock exchange was born.

Despite Barnard's Act making options trading illegal, such speculative trading continued to the point where, in 1820, a controversy over the trading of stock options nearly precipitated a split in the London Stock Exchange.[31] A few members of the Exchange circulated a petition discouraging options trading. The petition passed, and members formally agreed to discourage options trading. However, when an 1823 committee of the Exchange followed up on this with a proposal to implement a rule forbidding Exchange members from dealing in options (which was already illegal under Barnard's Act), a substantial number of members voted against it. A dissident group even began raising funds for a new Exchange building. In the end, the trading ban rule was rejected because the options trade was a significant source of profits for numerous Exchange members who did not want to see that business lost to outsiders. The upshot is that speculative exchange trading of options on the London Stock Exchange was subject to the discipline of trading by a restricted group of traders – the exchange members – operating subject to explicit agreed-upon rules. Though such contracts were settled by the party and counterparty, because exchange members were involved on both sides of the trade, either as dealer or broker, the fortnightly clearing process for shares was sufficient to prevent the significant speculative abuses that had plagued the previous OTC trading of option contracts and time bargains.

Until the middle of the nineteenth century, development of the London stock market was profoundly impacted by the fallout from the South Sea Bubble of 1720. The South Sea scheme involved the conversion of government debt into shares in the South Sea Company. The fantastic promotion of John Law was in the process of unwinding just as the South Sea scheme was beginning, though the full extent of the financial market collapse in France could then only be guessed at. The markets in England and France were awash with speculative capital. In England, this produced a competing array of small joint-stock promotions, involving companies either acting without a charter or using a charter that was not granted for the firm's current activities. Scott identifies 120 such issues appearing between September 1719 and August 1720, with a potential market capitalization of £220 million. To stem the flow of speculative capital out of the market for South Sea shares, the South Sea Company was able to get the so-called 'Bubble Act' invoked.

The Bubble Act was not a specific Act, per se. Rather, the Bubble Act was some clauses attached to a bill enabling the charter for two insurance companies, the Royal Exchange Assurance and London Assurance Companies; yet another instance of the government exchanging exclusive rights in exchange for the paid-in capital of the venture. These clauses prohibited promoters from 'presuming to act as if they were corporate bodies and pretending to make their shares or stocks transferable or assignable without any legal authority'. The prohibition was extended to companies operating 'under the authority of charters that were obsolete or had been given for some other purpose'. The effect of this Act was to restrict joint-stock issues severely, leaving the two insurance companies, together with the Bank, the East India Company and what remained of the South Sea Company as the main components of the English market for joint stocks for the rest of the century and half of the next. Little progress was made in joint-stock company formation until the enabling of 'letters patent' in 1834 and passage of the Joint Stock Company

Act (1844) (for example Todd 1932; Alborn 1998). As a consequence, the London stock market during this period was largely concerned with government loan stock and the debts of private companies. Despite London being the centre of the global stock market until well into the twentieth century, developments in the US stock market have had the greatest impact on the current stock market globalization process.

THE US STOCK MARKET DURING THE NINETEENTH CENTURY

With the emergence of the London Stock Exchange to international prominence at the end of the eighteenth century, there developed during the nineteenth century an international network of stock exchanges, with London being the dominant exchange for international issues of stocks and shares, and Paris having a greater role for Europe and the Mediterranean. This growth was facilitated by the sometimes massive increases in government debt and corporate share issues due to events such as the Napoleonic Wars, the railway construction boom through much of the nineteenth century, the US Civil War, and the transition of businesses to publicly traded joint-stock companies. Changes in communication technology, such as the telegraph and the telephone, contributed to the evolution of the local and regional exchanges from being sources of capital for smaller, locally located enterprises toward national specialization in specific stocks traded in a global market – for example South African exchanges for gold mining stocks; New York for American securities. The exchanges located in national financial centres increasingly 'provided the most liquid market in which money could be readily employed or securities quickly sold' and so attracted business from throughout the country (Michie 1999, p. 6).

Accompanying the development of stock exchanges was a gradual transition in the sophistication of the investing public and the businesses seeking to attract capital. Shares in joint-stock companies came increasingly to be perceived as 'investments' instead of 'gambling' vehicles. The increasing liquidity of stock markets substantially reduced the difficulty of purchase and sale, further encouraging trade. These social transitions took place somewhat more quickly in Paris and London than in New York, and only by the beginning of the twentieth century was New York on a comparable footing. The development of US stock trading is roughly consistent with the growth of New York as the world's financial capital. As late as the 1820s, Philadelphia had as strong a claim as New York to be the nation's financial capital. In the period before the Civil War, London was still, by far, the world's dominant securities market. Even with the sizable influx of funding issues associated with the Civil War, around 1866 London still had a market capitalization of around $10 billion compared to $3 billion for New York (Gordon 1999, p. 123). Armstrong (1848), an essential source on US stock market practices at the middle of the nineteenth century, indicates that stock trading in the US was a gambling transaction conducted in a trading environment characterized by corners, bubbles and 'fancy stock manoeuvres'. Later biographical and autobiographical accounts of those involved in the industry in the second half of the century, such as Henry Clew's *Fifty Years in Wall Street* (1908) or Edwin Lefèvre's *Reminiscences of a Stock Operator* (1923 [1994]), present a similar picture.

This somewhat later social development is consistent with the 'dramatic expansion' that took place in US stock markets from the mid-1880s to the late 1920s (O'Sullivan 2007). Yet, these comparable historical developments mask fundamental differences in the workings of the financial markets in Europe and America. As it turns out, these differences – such as 'trading for account' versus 'daily cash settlement' – have had a significant impact on the development of the stock market that continues to the present. Fortunately, helpful primary sources that detail stock trading practices, such as Armstrong (1848) and Emery (1896), are available. Among other insights, these sources support the conclusion that early stock market trading practices in the US were transplanted from European centres, especially London. This is hardly surprising given that America was a British colony until the War of Independence. However, the lack of US stock market liquidity and sophistication produced a greater reliance on cash settlement. Despite the lack of sophistication, certain trading practices employed during the nineteenth century are closer to the modern US stock market than the highly regulated markets that prevailed from the Securities Act (1933) until the creation of the Chicago Board Option Exchange (CBOE) at the Chicago Board of Trade (CBT) and the International Monetary Market (IMM) division of the Chicago Mercantile Exchange (CME) in the 1970s. During this latter period, there were sharp restrictions on trading equity derivative securities. In addition, cash market short selling and buying on margin were subject to restrictions. Gradual removal of these restrictions since the 1970s places the modern stock market on a similar playing field to the nineteenth-century stock market where stock trading could involve cash, 'time contracts' or 'hypothecation'.

Armstrong (1848, pp. 9–12) details New York stock market trading methods used around the middle of the nineteenth century. 'When Stocks are bought and sold in "*the regular way*", the delivery and payment must take place the day after the sale is effected'. Trading by legitimate investors 'making or withdrawing investments . . . would seldom be on any other terms than in the "regular" way'. In addition to this legitimate cash trade, there was also considerable trading activity in 'time operations' that involved non-transferable forward sale contracts with a variety of delivery options, for example 'seller three days' where 'the seller has the right to deliver and demand payment for the Stock upon any day of the three':

> In all time operations, Contracts are generally exchanged which specify the terms of sale; and it is understood that either party has a right to call for a deposit as collateral security for fulfillment of the contract . . . the deposit most commonly desired is five per cent. and occasionally ten. This deposit is then generally deposited by each party in the hands of any third person who may be agreed upon.

In no case was a contract made for more than a year to delivery, nor could an increase in collateral be requested 'unless it was agreed upon at the time of sale'. In addition, time operations were 'not recognized by the law . . . upon a par with all other gambling operations . . . there is no other security for the performance of contracts than the laws of honor'. Yet, similar to trade in London, a network of brokers and influential speculators sustained a viable market in time contracts.

Armstrong (1848, p. 12) recognizes that the overriding purpose of time contracts was speculation:

> all those transactions called time operations, which are based on anticipated fluctuations in prices, are . . . essentially the same as so many bets upon what the future will bring forth, for hardly any one share out of fifty which is sold on time is actually transferred, the contract being 'settled' by one party paying to the other the 'difference' between the price specified at the time of sale and the market price at the time the stock is to be delivered and paid for.

Significantly, Armstrong also finds that, as a consequence of time operations: 'inevitable fluctuations [in stock prices] are aggravated, and unnecessary or unnatural actions and reactions are produced by the various manoeuvres resorted to' by those involved in time operations. For Armstrong: 'One prominent result of these time operations has been the formation of two opposing parties among stock operators – the Bulls, who have based their transactions upon their expectations of an advance in prices, and the Bears, who have sold stock which they are not in possession of, trusting to a decline'. Upon closer inspection, many of the mythic events of nineteenth-century US stock market history were conducted using time operations.

Not all time operations involved the use of time contracts. Similar to the practices in the London stock market after the passage of Barnard's Act, speculative dealings could also be conducted using 'hypothecation':

> When such a time operation as is desired cannot be conveniently obtained, it is customary to buy the stock for cash, and then borrow as much money upon it as possible, and deposite the certificate of Stock with the lender as security for repayment of the amount borrowed. The market value less five or ten per cent can almost always be obtained.

Various sources provided such loans: banks, 'professed money lenders' and 'any person who has got money to spare'. If the stock declined in value after the purchase then the loss would have to be paid or the stock would be sold. Short sellers that did not use time contracts were typically lenders against stock collateral that had sold the stock placed on deposit to secure the loan. A system of borrowing stocks that would then be sold, as described in Emery (1896, p. 77), is not mentioned by Armstrong (1848). Similarly, Emery (1896) observes that: 'time dealings have given place to dealings which are practically for immediate delivery'. Much of this evolution in US stock market trading practices over the last half of the nineteenth century can be attributed to the emergence of the New York Stock Exchange (NYSE) as 'far and away the most important exchange of the United States'.

In examining the various stories and historical accounts of early US stock market trading activities, it is conventional to go back to 1792 when the 21 individual brokers and three firms signed the Buttonwood Agreement: 'not to buy or sell from this day for any person whatsoever any kind of Public Stock, at a rate less than one quarter per cent Commission on the specie value, and that we will give preference to each other in our negotiations' (Eames 1894 [1968], p. 14). This arrangement was eventually to evolve into the NYSE, a name that was introduced in 1863 as a name change for the Regular Board of the New York Stock and Exchange Board. The New York Stock Exchange emerged as the dominant exchange for trading stocks in New York with its merger with the Open Board of Brokers in 1869 (Gordon 1999, pp. 95,124–5). The New York Stock and Exchange Board, formed in 1817 (Eames 1894 [1968], p. 18), could trace its pedigree to the Buttonwood Agreement. The Open Board was a relative newcomer that flourished in the face of the flood of issues arising from the Civil War. Armstrong (1848, p. 8) discusses the 'Old Board' and 'New Board', the latter composed of brokers that for various reasons could not gain a seat on the New York Stock and Exchange Board where admission required approval of the members. Prior to the 'memorable crash' of 1836, the number of members and volume of transactions on the New Board was larger than on the Old Board.

Even after the emergence of a dominant exchange, stock trading in New York was still scattered across a range of venues. For example, in 1856 Gordon (1999, p. 87) reports that there were 360 railroad stocks, 985 bank stocks, 75 insurance stocks, in addition to hundreds of corporate, municipal, state and federal bonds and other types of stocks being traded in New York. Of these most were not traded on the New York Stock and Exchange Board (NYSEB), the lineal precursor of the NYSE, as the board did not trade new and untested issues. These issues were 'curb-stone' traded. The primary venue for curb trading changed over time. Armstrong (1848, p. 18) refers to the trading taking place:

> when the two boards of brokers are not in session, the members, small operators, money lenders, toadies, and other interested, assemble promiscuously for the transaction of business at the corner of Wall and Hanover-streets; and it not unfrequently happens that more business is done at this place than at the board.

In severe weather, the business would 'cluster about the interior of the Exchange'. In 1836 the NYSEB prohibited members from street trading, so Armstrong is suggesting that this ban was not fully effective. Honourable brokers were essential to curb trading where time operations were conducted. Armstrong (1848, p. 24) observes: 'be very particular in selecting a broker as people very often lose by their agent . . . there are a thousand different ways in which a dishonorable broker can cheat his employer'. Later in the nineteenth century, the curb market expanded to various lamp posts in the Wall Street area. Throughout the nineteenth century, even though the volume of curb trading was usually higher than trading on the board, the market capitalization of curb issues was lower.

The tales of American stock operators predate the Buttonwood Agreement. Notoriety was, and still is, the result of doing something on a grand scale, often in conjunction with a massive bull market speculation, or the creation of a colossal conglomerate or the execution of an immense market manipulation. An early example is William Duer who was at the centre of a 1791–92 speculative scheme to inflate the value of bank stocks, particularly of the Bank of New York (Gordon 1999, pp. 40–45). The scheme was based on leveraged speculation, that is, making cash purchases using borrowed funds, and trading on insider information. At the height of the speculative frenzy, a number of banks were incorporated that, ultimately, did not open. As such, these stocks represent an early US instance of bull market 'paper hanging'. The collapse of the scheme resulted in bankruptcy of many of the players, including Duer. The scheme prompted Alexander Hamilton to write: 'Tis time there should be a line of separation between honest Men and knaves, between respectable Stockholders and dealers in the funds, and mere unprincipled Gamblers'. This seeking of the line of separation between legitimate trade and counterproductive speculation is a task that has occupied regulators up to the present day.

The formation of the New York Stock and Exchange Board in 1817 also marks the beginning of the Wall Street career of Jacob Little, the first of a long line of big-time Wall Street speculative operators (Gordon 1999, pp. 59–62, 89–90). Unlike Duer who only used Wall Street as a trading venue, Little made a career on Wall Street. Jacob Little & Co. is the first broker detailed in the 'sketches of the brokers' given in Armstrong (1848, pp. 32–9). As a broker, Little gained membership to the NYSEB in 1825. Yet, it is as a speculator that Little made his reputation, further supporting the view that some members of the NYSEB were involved in time operations. Little's trading strategies were typically short-term, aimed at anticipating market movements. During his career, Little made and lost four fortunes in speculative trading activities.[32] In the end, he was unable to recover from his last insolvency brought on by the market panic of 1857. From that time, until his death a few years later, Little ended his Wall Street career as a trader of penny stocks and odd lots.

Little was primarily a short seller, commonly using the collateral deposited against hypothecations. He was involved in lending to buyers of stock on margin, using the collateral deposited for the short sale. Oddly enough, Little's first fortune was made in a 1834 short squeeze involving the Morris Canal & Banking Company. The objective of a short squeeze in a stock issue is to gain control of the quantity of that stock available for trading (the 'float' or 'floating supply') at a time when a sizable amount of stock has been sold short by traders who do not have a sufficient amount of stock to deliver. As was the case in the squeeze on Morris Canal & Banking, the capital requirements for gaining control of the stock for delivery usually involves a group or pool of speculators operating in concert. When the time comes for the short to make delivery of the stock on a time contract or return the collateral on a hypothecation, the short has to enter the market to buy – but there is no supply available because the short squeezers have already gained control. The result is a rapid rise in the stock price as short sellers bid up the price to tempt new supply onto the market (either from accounts of long-term investors or from the short squeezers). At Little's time, most short sellers were brokers using time contracts that had sold stock they did not own to investors, speculators or other brokers. The short position was sometimes the outcome of longer settlement periods than in modern times. In other cases, the objective of both parties was to engage in speculative forward trading, resulting in delivery dates on the short that could be many months in the future.

Prior to the wide reaching regulatory reforms of 1933–34, stock market self-regulation was an important theme of government policy. Yet, self-regulation suffered from the conflicting interests of the legitimate brokers who recognized the negative impact associated with widespread unscrupulous trading activities, and the big-time speculators who saw the market as a conduit for achieving big profits from a range of trading schemes. As late as the Great Depression, many practices that are illegal in modern markets were considered fair game, such as trading on insider information, or the formation of pools to engage in manipulative trading activities aimed at creating price movements favourable to speculation on stock price changes. Though important changes were implemented from time to time, the process of reform using self-regulation was slow and problematic. One example of an important change happened in November 1868, just prior to the merger of the Open Board and the New York Stock and Exchange Board, when registration of securities and 30 days' notice of new issues was required of companies listed on the two boards. As is often the case, this change was precipitated by severe and adverse market events.

The imposition of the listing requirement had an immediate impact on the activities of the big-time speculators Daniel Drew, Jay Gould and James Fisk, involving the Erie Railway. The 1864–69 manipulations associated with the securities of the Erie are almost epic, reflecting the state of stock markets of that time. On one side of the struggle was 'Commodore' Cornelius Vanderbilt, a giant in the transportation industry, who wanted to control the Erie in order to be able to control the pricing of railway freight rates into and out of New York City. On the other side was a group including Drew, Gould, Fisk and other big-time speculators who were seeking to control the Erie as a vehicle for making speculative gains through manipulation of the companies security issues. The machination of these two camps has been captured in some of the early classics of business finance, for example Adams and Adams, *Chapters of Erie* (1871) and Henry Clews, *Fifty Years in Wall Street* (1908 [1973]). The struggle between these two groups is an epitome of the problems that prevailed in stock markets of that era, for example Medbury (1870 [1968], Ch.9), Gordon (1999, Ch. 6).

Vanderbilt was concerned with stock markets only as a vehicle for creating and managing a business empire, primarily involving railways. As part of the ongoing process of expanding this empire, Vanderbilt moved to acquire a controlling position on the Erie board of directors during the late summer and early autumn of 1867. Vanderbilt had been involved with the Erie as recently as 1865, when he resigned from the board over concerns about the evident manipulations in the stock that took place during 1864–65. A major player in these manipulations was Daniel Drew, also a board member, who conveniently served as treasurer. In his position as treasurer, Drew was able to issue securities, and in 1866 had done so by loaning the company $3.5 million in exchange for 28 000 unissued shares and $3 million in convertible bonds that had the provision that the 30 000 shares obtained from conversion could be reconverted back into convertible bonds. This provided Drew with the ability to expand and then contract about 10 per cent of the outstanding stock – providing effective control of the floating supply.

When Vanderbilt was unsuccessful in using his influence to control the Erie board of directors, starting in January 1868 he moved to gain control of the company by making purchases of as much of the outstanding stock as could be obtained. The speculators saw this as an opportunity to issue more convertible bonds that became a conduit to print stock certificates that were then sold to Vanderbilt. From late February to mid-March, Drew and his group were able to sell 100 000 newly issued shares. The absence of registration and listing requirements prevented the New York Stock and Exchange Board from knowing what was happening. All this was set against a backdrop of corrupt judges issuing injunctions and arrest warrants, and legislators being bribed to pass laws favourable to one or the other of these groups. On 19 April, Vanderbilt was able to strike a deal with Drew, Gould and Fisk and recoup his potential losses from his stock dealing. Following this, Gould and Fisk continued to manipulate Erie stock issues, until the listing and registration requirements were introduced by the two boards. Gould attempted to resist the requirements, even trying to establish a new exchange for the purposes of trading Erie stock. In September 1869, Gould capitulated and agreed to the new regulations. At that time, it was revealed that the number of Erie shares outstanding was around 700 000, about double the 351 000 shares outstanding at the time of the Vanderbilt agreement of April 1868.

To modern observers, events surrounding the Erie have the appearance of a classical farce. A business titan attempting to gain control of a railway company in order to implement a pricing cartel enters battle with a group of big-time speculators seeking to use the company as a vehicle for generating profits from stock price manipulation. Drew, Gould and Fisk are usually lumped in with Andrew Carnegie, J.D. Rockefeller and Commodore Vanderbilt and recognized as the 'robber barons' who dominated American industry through their financial dealings in the 1870–90 period (for example Geisst 1997, Ch. 3). The activities of the robber barons took place against a backdrop of increasing concentration of economic power in the hands of the trusts such as American Telephone & Telegraph, General Electric, Standard Oil and the American Tobacco Company. The trusts were formed largely as a way of dealing with the legal restriction imposed on corporations until around 1900 that prevented them from holding the stock of other corporations. During the 1890s there were about 50 trusts operating throughout the US, involving most of the major industries. This number includes some agricultural trusts that were concentrated primarily in the south.

Trusts were formed as a legal device largely to circumvent state corporation laws that restricted the ability of a corporation to expand using mergers and takeovers. Prior to the changes in state corporation law that started with New Jersey during the 1890s, the ability of a corporation to act as a holding company was quite limited. Trusts provided a legal avenue around these restrictions. In a trust, the companies being merged or taken over would exchange the common shares in the original corporations for trust certificates that possessed a claim to earnings of the trust as well as voting rights to elect the trustees that ran the trust. Standard Oil, for example, had nine trustees. Trust certificates traded like common stocks on the stock exchanges. The trust was a useful legal mechanism for the takeover ambitions of the emerging industrialists. Instead of having to issue new shares to raise new capital for a takeover, trusts could pay for the takeover using trust certificates or internal sources of funds.

Due to changes in various state corporation laws, the trusts had a relatively short life span. The legal status of trusts did not prevent various states from initiating legal actions on other grounds, such as the common law restrictions on monopoly, aimed at preventing the increasing monopolization of specific industries. In addition, the public perception of economic and social problems posed by the trusts was addressed in 1890 with the passage of the Sherman Anti-Trust Act. Though this Act did not result in many successful prosecutions, it did provide a federal definition and jurisdiction for what constituted a monopoly. The trusts gradually reorganized as holding companies and trust certificates were replaced by common shares. Standard Oil, for example, completed the shift in 1899. Whether it was trading in trust certificates or in common shares, the changes in American industrial structure were good for Wall Street. The importance of trading in shares of these industrial companies gradually came to surpass that of trading in shares of the railroads. The volume and value of trade on the NYSE doubled between 1875 and 1885, with more growth on the horizon.

Yet, despite the growth, the US stock market of that era justly deserved the public perception as a speculator's haven. Henry Clews (1908 [1973], p. 19), a veteran broker and investment advisor with 50 years' experience on Wall Street from 1857 to 1907, provides an informed view of 'How to Make Money on Wall Street':

> To the question often put, especially by men outside of Wall Street, 'How can I make money in Wall Street?' there is probably no better answer than the one given by old Meyer Rothschild to a person who asked him a similar question. He said, 'I buys "sheep" and sells "dear"'.
>
> Those who follow this method always succeed. There has hardly been a year within my recollection, going back nearly thirty years, when there has [*sic*] not been two or three squalls in 'the Street', during the year, when it was possible to purchase stocks below their intrinsic value. The squall usually passes over in a few days, and then the lucky buyers of stocks at panic prices come in for their profits ranging from five to ten per cent on the entire venture.
>
> The question of making money, then becomes a mere matter of calculation, depending on the number of squalls that may occur during any particular year.
>
> If the venture is made at the right time – at the lucky moment so to speak – and each successive venture is fortunate, as happens often to those who use their judgment in the best way, it is possible to realize a net gain of fifty per cent per annum on the aggregate of the year's investments.

Coming from an individual so intimately connected to the dealings of 'the Street', it is difficult to deny that speculation played an essential role in the US stock market of the time. Given the numerous abuses associated with trading common stocks, the disposition of the small investor to favour bonds over stocks during this period is understandable.

Many of the systemic problems raised by the predominance of speculators in the US stock market persisted until the regulatory reforms following the Great Depression. The introduction of legislation such as the Securities Act (1933) involved a radical realignment of the federal government's role in securities markets in general, and the stock market in particular. The collapse of the US stock market from late 1929 to early 1933 was sufficient to end the period of self-regulation that had largely governed stock trading up to that time. Yet, the period of self-regulation was not without contributions. Many of the trading tools needed to lay the foundation for sustainable stock trading had evolved without government intervention. The growth of stock markets witnessed the emergence of professionals who made their living in the market and had a vested interest in making sure the game was played, if not always fairly, at least according to accepted rules.

US EVOLUTION OF DERIVATIVE SECURITY TRADING

By the beginning of the nineteenth century, a number of characteristics associated with stock exchange trading had emerged in Europe. In particular, self-regulatory requirements needed to ensure settlement of positions were imposed on exchange participants. Both informal and formal rules were introduced by exchanges to control access to the trading process, for example restrictions on participation in the trading process through private ownership of the exchange building, and restrictions on membership. When speculative exchange trading was concentrated around a small group of merchants and brokers directly involved in the commodity trade of sixteenth-century Antwerp, self-regulation was generally sufficient to prevent speculative excesses and manipulation. However, as trading expanded to include joint stocks, government oversight was required to prevent speculative abuses and unscrupulous practices associated with OTC-style contract design, where deals were directly done between counterparties. The practical connection of speculative exchange trading for bulk commodities to the underlying goods trade restricted speculative participation in comparison to such trading in stocks and shares. Competition among exchanges was muted by the need to locate trading geographically close to the associated goods trade, for example the transfer offices for shares or the wholesale goods market for commodities.

Though primary sources are scarce, it is likely that some form of speculative trading with time contracts was present from the eighteenth-century beginnings of US trade in 'stocks', perhaps earlier in the produce markets, for example Markham (1987, 2002). Significantly, over time this trade developed differently from that in Europe due to differing settlement practices. In the US, 'each day is a settling day and a clearing day for transactions of the day before . . . This is a marked difference from European practice', where 'trading for the account' involves monthly or fortnightly settlement periods with allowance for continuation of the position until the next settlement date (Emery 1896, p. 82). Daily or short-dated settlement had dramatic implications for speculative trading in the US stock market. Instead of trading using time contracts, which was discouraged by the stock exchange, it was more expedient to speculate by selling (shorting) borrowed stocks and buying stocks on margin. As a consequence, the venue for evolution of speculative exchange trading in the US was in the bulk commodity markets which, during the nineteenth century, experienced a revolution that can be attributed to the subtle impact that American culture had on specific business practices. Writing in 1896, Emery (1896, p. 7) captures the main theme: 'The American people are regarded by foreigners as the greatest of all speculators'. This drive to speculate facilitated American innovations in commodity derivative security trading. 'It was not until the [nineteenth] century . . . that the system [of dealings for time] became widely developed and not until the great expansion of foreign trade in the last fifty years that it became of great importance'.

An important theme in the historical progress of stock market trading is the public-good benefits provided by enhanced participation of speculators in the exchange process. Among other benefits, enhanced speculation increases market liquidity and can improve price discovery. Yet, speculative activity can have decided disadvantages, such as the increased incentive and ability to manipulate markets resulting in sometimes severe distortions in the pricing process. Periods of turbulence in specific commodity markets – where price discovery apparently failed – are often associated with the entrance of speculators not directly connected to physical trade in the underlying commodity using the leverage associated with derivative contracts to distort market pricing for private gain. Though there were time dealings being conducted in a number of centres throughout the nineteenth century, the beginning of speculative exchange trading in the US commences with commodity futures contracts traded on the Chicago Board of Trade (CBT) in mid-nineteenth-century Chicago. First incorporated as a village in 1833, Chicago had a population of only 4107 by 1837. In order to promote commerce, the Board of Trade of the City of Chicago was founded on 3 April 1848 with 82 members. This event, in itself, was not particularly noteworthy. The usefulness of boards of trade in promotion had been recognized for quite some time. For example, around 1700 John Law of the infamous Mississippi scheme promoted the creation of a board of trade for the city of Edinburgh (Murphy 1997).

From the beginning, there were inherent conflicts between the exchange as a promoter of trade and promoter of the interests of (owner) members. The exchange as a self-regulatory entity was not recognized (for example Lurie 1972, p. 221):

> A basic purpose of the Board was to facilitate profitable economic activity by members. Thus its directors had to sense with some accuracy how far they could go in the areas of rule enforcement. If rules were enforced too harshly, board members could either ignore them or decline to remain in the organization. Yet, another purpose of the exchange was to rationalize the commodities market through efficient and effective regulation. The efforts of the directors to reconcile this inherent tension between private economic activity and an ordered national market represent a recurring theme throughout Board history.

The CBT initially served as a marketplace for members of the grain trade. A system of wheat standards was developed together with a system of inspecting and weighing grain. In 1859, the Board of Trade was authorized by the state of Illinois to engage in the measuring, weighing and inspecting of grain, effectively corn and wheat. As Hieronymous (1977, p. 73) observes:

> The development of quality standards and an inspection process and the substitution of weighing for the measurement of grain greatly facilitated trade. The substitution of weight for volume measures made the development of grain handling machinery possible. Increase in physical efficiency was important in the development of Chicago as a great grain terminal.

These developments facilitated the handling of grain in bulk, through the use of grain silos. This permitted interchangeable warehouse receipts to be introduced, instead of having to deal in unstandardized, specific lots. Not unlike the bulk commodity trade in sixteenth-century Antwerp and seventeenth-century Amsterdam, conditions in the goods market were evolving to where standardized contracts on physical commodities could be traded.

The grain trade of that time typically involved merchants at various points along major waterways such as the Illinois–Michigan canal purchasing grain from farmers which was then held in storage, often from autumn or winter into spring. In this operation, the merchants' capital investment involved: paying the farmers for their crops at delivery; costs of building and maintaining storage facilities; and providing funds for shipment of grain when required. In order to avoid the risk of price fluctuation and to satisfy bankers, merchants started to go to Chicago and make forward sale contracts for future, spring delivery of grain, at prices which were determined that day. While there was ad hoc OTC-style forward sale of grains previously, the first 'time contract' in Chicago was made on 13 March 1851, calling for delivery of 3000 bushels of corn in June at 1 cent below the 13 March cash price. The transferable time contracts called for delivery of a standardized grade at a later delivery date. Similar contracts for wheat appeared in 1852. However, while there were similarities to exchange traded futures contracts, other conditions were significantly different, such as: the absence of an exchange clearing mechanism; contracts that were specific to the original parties to the transaction; and contracts being created by parties able to ensure delivery. As such, the initial trading in time contracts did not have all the aspects needed to support speculative exchange trading.

The development of futures markets in Chicago was significant because, in the years immediately following the introduction of time contracts, individuals not connected to the grain trade became interested in taking positions. The resulting contracts often changed hands numerous times before being purchased by a market participant actually interested in taking delivery of the grain. This marks the introduction of a fundamental feature of speculative exchange trading: the essential participation of speculators not concerned with completing the underlying commodity transaction. Characteristics of speculative exchange trading were not associated with trading in the often non-transferable 'to arrive' contracts and 'privileges' which had characterized American commodities trading previously (Williams 1982). This trade was concentrated primarily in flour. 'To arrive' forward sale contracts in wheat, corn, rye and pickled hams were also conducted, with activity centring on New York. The contracts typically featured short delivery dates, limited standardization of the deliverable commodity and the expectation that delivery would be completed. While there is some evidence of limited speculative dealings in these 'to arrive' contracts and 'privileges' associated with the flour default of May 1847, participants to these transactions usually involved merchants directly involved in the commodity business.

The increasing speculative interest in time contracts led the Board of Trade to introduce a number of resolutions to curb abuses. Many of the abuses were consistent with speculative participation and longer delivery dates. 'It seems that when time for settlement arrived some of the contracting parties were difficult to locate' (Hieronymous 1977, p. 76). Out of the early self-regulatory process came the beginnings of formal trading rules for futures contracts. In 1863, the board adopted a rule which suspended the membership of anyone failing to comply with a contract, either written or verbal. On 13 October 1865 the General Rules of the Board of Trade explicitly acknowledged futures trading and adopted rules which included many essential elements required for speculative exchange trading, that is: standardized contract terms; restriction of futures contract trading to exchange members; margin deposits to guarantee performance; and standardized delivery procedures.[33] Prior to this date, individual traders had been responsible for establishment and enforcement of the terms of the contract. This development followed a similar move in 1864 by the Liverpool Cotton Brokers' Association, introducing formal regulations for 'to arrive' contracts in cotton (Forrester 1931).

Speculative exchange trading of commodities progressed dramatically since the first corn futures trade on the CBT in 1865. Many other commodity futures exchanges emerged in the period between the Civil War and the First World War. The New York Cotton Exchange was formed in 1870 and the New Orleans Cotton Exchange in 1871, though time contracts did not play an important role on the latter exchange for almost a decade. In 1874, the Chicago Produce Exchange was formed by dealers trading in produce of various kinds. The Coffee, Sugar and Cocoa Exchange was initially founded in 1882 as the Coffee Exchange of New York City with the specific intent of trading in time contracts for coffee. Initially founded in 1872 to trade in butter, eggs and cheese, a decade later the exchange acquired its current name, the New York Mercantile Exchange (NYMEX).[34] In 1898, a subgroup of the produce exchange known as the Produce Exchange Butter and Egg Board withdrew from the Produce Exchange and formed the Chicago Butter and Egg Board. This group is of present interest because it had established an active trade in time contracts for eggs, even though such trade was only a small proportion of the Butter and Egg Board's activity. When margin rules for time contracts were finally written in 1911 there was considerable controversy among the members. Finally, in 1919, a complete set of commodity futures trading rules was written and the mandate of the Butter and Egg Board was changed to include commodity futures trading. The end product was the emergence of the Chicago Mercantile Exchange, which started trading contracts for butter and eggs on 1 December 1919.

The late nineteenth-century renaissance in speculative exchange trading for commodities was accompanied by a rash of speculative manipulations that ultimately led to vociferous attacks from agrarians and Populists, for example Cowing (1895 [1965]) and Hicks (1961). Though referred to as 'anti-option' bills, the focus of the attacks was commodity futures contracts. The anti-speculation reasoning behind the attacks was described around that time by Cowing (1895 [1965], p. 5):

> The seemingly orthodox futures contract, occasionally used before the Civil War and an outgrowth of earlier 'to arrive', and 'forward delivery' agreements, began to receive unprecedented attention from speculators. Persons not previously connected with the commodities business had been attracted, and were buying and selling futures contracts in the central markets, especially in Chicago and New York. The number of bushels and bales traded on the exchanges exceeded the annual production from 1872 on and in several years toward the end of the century amounted to sevenfold the annual crop. Prices had moved widely before the war because of weather, economic instability, and imperfect crop information, but it appeared that the new volatility was due to maneuvers by speculators with large purses. Thus 'speculator' became more than ever a term of opprobrium; the physiocratic bias against those who produced no primary products was more bitterly asserted as the agrarian population shifted consciously to the defensive. The mysterious and remote commodity speculator seemed more of a parasite to the farmers than the local physician who was holding land for appreciation. Farmers identified the commodity speculator as the villain responsible for erratic price changes in Chicago, Minneapolis, and New York, especially around harvest time. The stage was set; the national crusade against the exchange speculator was about to begin.

Various efforts were made by the exchanges, as well as state and federal legislatures, to control the perceived market manipulations. At the federal level, between 1880 and 1920, there were some 200 bills introduced in the US Congress aimed at regulating derivative security trading, though few bills made it out of committee (Markham 1987, pp. 6–9). State legislatures that did pass bills, for example an 1874 Illinois statute prohibiting 'corners', were unsuccessful in curbing such activities. Various states passed laws prohibiting futures trading for which there was no intent to take delivery. Such laws were voided by the courts on grounds that: 'pro forma assertions of interest with respect to delivery were sufficient to preclude application of the statutes' (Markham 1987, p. 6; Lurie 1972).

The decline in agrarian conditions following the post-1886 droughts generated sufficient political will to produce the Hatch–Washburn bill of 1892, the most concerted effort at anti-speculation legislation prior to passage of the Grain Futures Act in 1922. Instead of outlawing futures trading, this bill aimed to impose a prohibitive tax on speculative dealings in futures contracts. The congressional debate on the issue surrounding the Hatch–Washburn bill is an essential primary source on nineteenth-century views on derivative securities. The committee meetings leading up to votes on the bill included testimony from important agrarians such as J.H. Brigham, Master of the National Grange, and C.W. Macune of the Farmers' Alliance and Industrial Union. Not only farmers were in favour of the bill: the testimony also included statements from millers such as Charles Pillsbury, as well as grain and hog merchants. Pillsbury held that: 'neither grower nor miller had as much influence over prices as a few men around the wheat pit in Chicago. Short selling by these few made prices erratic and unstable; opinions based upon supply and demand were worthless in the face of this manipulation' (Cowing 1895 [1965], p. 7).

Pillsbury also maintained that the use of futures to hedge would not be necessary if price volatility due to speculation was eliminated.

In 1893, the Hatch–Washburn bill successfully passed the House, 167 to 40, and passed the Senate, 40 to 29, though there were some amendments which had to be returned to the House for approval.[35] However, this placed the bill too far down the calendar to be dealt with before the end of the session. A suspension of House rules was required for the bill to become law. However, suspension of rules requires a two-thirds majority and the vote, 172 to 124, fell short by 26 votes. The gradual return of prosperity dampened, but did not eliminate, the drive of the anti-speculator forces. However, it was not until after the First World War that sufficient legislation, such as the Grain Futures Act (1922), was in place to curb the alleged abuses of the middlemen and speculators using the exchanges. By this time, the extreme anti-speculator position of the agrarians had faded. Though the Act did contain provisions against manipulation, these were largely ineffective, but the Act was successful in bringing the futures exchanges under federal supervision and in providing for 'continuous fact-finding and supply of continuous trading information' (Hieronymous 1977, p. 314). However, the failure to reinforce and exploit the fundamental role of exchange self-regulation in identifying and penalizing market manipulation still survives to the present.

The history of regulating speculation was primarily focused on time contracts. Though there were instances of earlier trading, initial US trade in commodity options is usually associated with the beginnings of the CBT, where options were known as 'privileges'.[36] Bid and offer privileges roughly corresponded to modern-day puts and calls. The similarity of privileges to gambling, as well as the prominent use of options in a number of market manipulations, led to numerous unsuccessful attempts by the CBT, various state and federal legislatures and the courts to halt commodity options trading. As early as 1865, the CBT introduced a rule which denied the protection of the exchange to privilege traders. This rule was found to be both unpopular and ineffective and was withdrawn in 1869, illustrating the ineffectiveness of self-regulation when the governance of the exchange is controlled by the members being regulated. Various legal challenges were launched to privilege trading, including an Illinois Supreme Court ruling which found privileges to be illegal. In 1890, the US Congress attempted to ban commodity options but was unsuccessful in getting the legislation passed. The trade in commodity options continued under different guises, for example calling the contracts 'indemnity of sale or purchase' (Markham 1987, p. 9), until the trade was banned by the Commodity Exchange Act (1936).

The social resistance to commodity option trading during this period was propelled by farm-based 'populist' political movements which associated erratic price behaviour with excessive speculation. These views were not without foundation. The limited amount of regulation of commodity and stock markets in the pre-First World War period permitted numerous corners and other market manipulations. Charles Taylor (1917) relates the role of privileges in one of the more

> outstanding of these [corners that] had to do with oats, and was operated by Mr Chandler, a prominent merchant. He peddled 'puts' about the city, inducing speculation on the part of a large number of people not ordinarily in the market. Chandler and his friends did not count on a large inrush of oats attracted to Chicago by the high prices and the corner failed. Many people lost money and there was much public indignation. (Hieronymus 1977, p. 85)

There was a prevailing belief among populists that brokers were using the exchange process to extract money from farmers. This view was carried forward into the Grain Futures Act (1922) which contained a section maintaining that futures contract prices were 'extremely sensitive to speculation and manipulation' (Markham 1987, p. 14). The social importance of many of the underlying commodities meant that commodity options received substantially more scrutiny and opposition than stock options.

US OPTION TRADING FROM THE NINETEENTH CENTURY TO THE CBOE

For a variety of reasons, including a history of speculative abuses, option trading was generally held in low esteem by the bulk of stock and commodity market participants in the US.[37] Until the emergence of the CBOE, there was no exchange trading of such contracts in the US. As a consequence, the trade was generally conducted by a specialized group of OTC dealers catering to a relatively small clientele. Circa the end of the nineteenth century, trading in privileges was only conducted in the after market and on 'the curb' as such trading was prohibited on all US stock and commodity exchanges. Evidence for such trade in stock options is provided by Kairys and Valerio (1997, p. 1709) where an 1873–75 sample of over-the-counter US option contacts is examined. This sample was obtained from advertisements in the *Commercial and Financial Chronicle*. The prices were only ask quotes, exclusive of bids, and were aimed at generating business from buyers of options. The option prices were found to favour the option writer. Following the European practice, these contracts determined prices by keeping the premium constant and adjusting the exercise price:

> Whereas current option prices are quoted after fixing the strike price, the cost of a privilege was fixed at $1.00 per share for all contracts and the strike price was adjusted to reflect current market conditions. Furthermore, the strike price was expressed as a spread from the current spot price of the underlying stock with the understanding that the spread was then the 'price' that was quoted for the privilege contract.

Based on Emery (1896), this method of pricing options was also customary in the Chicago grain markets where contract maturities varied from one day to a week. This indicates the prevalence of European practices in the US option market at this time.

Kairys and Valerio (1997, p. 1719) pose the question: why did the option markets fail to develop further given the apparent level of refinement? Unfortunately, the explanations provided are lacking. In contrast, Emery (1896, p. 80) provides a more insightful explanation for the disappearance of stock options trading:

> In the last few years . . . privileges have been less common than they formerly were. The trade in privileges depends chiefly upon a few men of large means. The public buy, but seldom sell, privileges, and if the men who are accustomed to dealing in that way stop selling, the field for such practices becomes very circumscribed.

The disappearance of the 'men of large means' in 1875 is possibly due to the substantial deterioration in the public perception of options, or to lack of profit from such ventures. This privilege trade is not to be confused with the stock projector Jacob Little's use of options to manipulate the price of Erie stock (see note 36). According to Clews (1908 [1973], p. 10): 'Mr Little had been selling large blocks of Erie stock on seller's option, to run from six to twelve months.' In this case, the seller's option permitted delivery on a date determined by the seller. Delivery was required. There was no 'privilege' to sell or not sell. The resulting attempt to corner the stock and squeeze Little is one of the fascinating stories of the nineteenth-century robber barons. The upshot was, yet again, a public black eye for speculative stock trading in the US, and the imposition of a restriction on the maximum term of stock 'option to deliver' contracts to 60 days.

Following the introduction of taxes on privilege earnings in 1921, the Grain Futures Act (1922) represented a significant step in curbing market abuses associated with derivative security trading. Following Markham (1987, p. 15): 'Although [the Grain Futures Act] was subsequently replaced by the Commodity Exchange Act of 1936, it nonetheless forms the core of the current regulatory scheme'. This Act required commodity exchanges and their members to maintain and file privilege trading reports. The Act also required commodity exchanges to act to prevent price manipulation. Combined with the authority of the Secretary of Agriculture to investigate exchange operations, this led to a substantial curtailment in commodity options abuses. However, some commodity options trading still continued and, following the collapse of agricultural prices associated with the Great Depression, pressure from farm lobbies led to the outright ban on commodity options trading, in selected commodities, legislated in the Commodity Exchange Act (1936). Included in the restricted list were wheat, cotton, rice, corn, oats and barley. However, despite the restrictions, considerable OTC trade continued in unlisted commodities such as coffee, silver, copper and platinum, together with commodity options trading offshore, especially in London.

In the US, trading in stock options began as early as 1790. Much as with commodity options, stock (privilege) option trading also played a significant role in market manipulations. As early as the 1890s, option pools were in operation.[38] Two general types of pools were present in the 1920s: trading pools and option pools, with the latter being the most common. While trading pools acquired stock on the open market, option pools would acquire all or most of their securities by obtaining call option contracts to purchase stock at favourable prices. These options were acquired OTC from various sources, such as the corporation, where the options took the form of warrants, as well as from large stockholders, directors, officers, large speculators and banks. While there was considerable diversity in the maturity of the options granted and the types of schemes involved, the primary objective of the option pool was to benefit through manipulation of the common stock price. In addition to speculative abuses of overleveraged positions, the option pools were symptomatic of the types of abuses that contributed to the 1929 stock market collapse. The regulatory response implemented in the 1930s, culminating in the Securities Act (1933) and the Securities Exchange Act (1934), was to prohibit all activities aimed at manipulating market prices and trading on insider information.

Franklin and Colberg (1958, pp. 29–30) illustrate the importance of stock options trading in the 1929 market collapse:

> Testimony before the Senate Committee on Banking and Currency in 1932 and 1933 disclosed that many of the financial abuses of the 1920s were related to the use of options. A favorite device of large stockholders was to grant options without cost to a pool which would then

> attempt to make these profitable by 'churning' activities designed to bring the general public in as buyers of the stock. In addition, long-term and even unlimited-period option warrants were issued frequently in connection with new stock issues.

During the wave of securities market reform following the market collapse of 1929–33, considerable attention was given to terminating option trading all together. One of the most profitable pools was the Sinclair Consolidated Oil option pool of 1929. While Sinclair stock was selling in the \$28 to \$32 range, a contract was obtained from Sinclair granting the pool an option to buy 1 130 000 shares at \$30 per share. The pool then purchased 634 000 shares in the open market to bid up prices. The pool exercised its option, then liquidated all its holdings while the stock was selling in the \$40 range. The pool also sold 200 000 shares short as the price fell. The pool's total profit was approximately \$12.5 million from the following sources: \$10 million profit from optioned shares purchased at \$30 per share, \$500 000 profit from shares purchased in the market and \$2 million profit from the short sales.[39]

In the process of developing a regulatory response to the market abuses which contributed to the financial market turbulence of 1929–33, it was accepted that the abuses associated with option pools would become illegal. However, in addition to the use of options in pool operations, there were other, more legitimate reasons for stock option trading. In the end, the brokerage industry was able to avoid the outright ban associated with commodity options. The initial legislation aimed at regulating the securities markets, the Fletcher–Rayburn bill (1934), called for a total ban on stock options. The brokerage industry was able to prevent this result. Instead, the Securities Exchange Act (1934) empowered the newly created Securities and Exchange Commission (SEC) to regulate the market and introduced the Put and Call Brokers and Dealers Association (PCBDA) (1934) which was designed to act as a self-policing agency, working closely with the SEC and other agencies to avoid further direct government regulation. It was member firms of the PCBDA which formed the basis for the OTC market trading of options which took place in the period leading up to the creation of the Chicago Board Option Exchange (CBOE) and the International Monetary Market (IMM).

THE EMERGENCE OF THE CBOE AND IMM

'The strategic direction of derivative security regulation, both in the US and internationally, is almost incoherent' (Poitras 2002, p. 22). The incoherence in the regulation of trading in derivative securities on common stock is apparent in the so-called 'flash crash' of 6 May 2010 detailed in Chapter 11 in this volume. The roots of the regulatory confusion can be traced to the creation of the Chicago Board Option Exchange and the International Monetary Market divisions of the CBT and the CME in the early 1970s. Various substantive questions can be used to identify some key issues. Why did a self-regulating futures exchange specializing in bulk commodities, the CBT, undertake and be permitted to trade options on stocks? Why did the trade in stock options not originate with the stock exchanges that trade the underlying stocks? Why did the CME, another exchange associated with trading in bulk commodities, create a division dedicated to the trading of financial futures? Why were currency futures (but not option) contracts, a commodity for which there was a well developed OTC market between financial institutions, the initial contract to be traded on the IMM? Why are two US regulators – the CFTC and the SEC – responsible for key elements in the speculative trading of common stocks?

The regulatory conflict between mutually owned exchanges as promoters of trade and as self-regulatory organizations responsible for protecting the interests of exchange members was addressed by the exchange demutualization process. The associated fundamental change in exchange governance required a transition in the self-regulatory oversight function. Compounded by the historic changes in communications and trading technology, the formulation of adequate changes confounds present regulators (for example Pirrong 1995; Mahoney 1997; Markham and Harty 2008, and Chapter 12 in this volume). Fortunately, the fear generated by the apparently inexplicable events of 6 May 2010 has provided a regulatory paper trail that gives unprecedented information about the workings of the modern stock market. Regulatory analysis of detailed information about the interconnection between the cash and futures markets for stocks produced an incremental move back toward restrictions that had been previously been removed, such as the use of circuit breakers and trading pauses. These changes coincided with changes to incrementally increase short selling restrictions that had been introduced following the global stock market collapse of late 2008.

To appreciate the major historical advance that the CBOE represented, it is necessary to consider the state of equity option trading prior to the CBOE. Franklin and Colberg (1958, p. 22) describe the general state of equity option trading at the end of the 1950s:

> Practically all of the Put and Call business in the US is handled by about twenty-five option brokers and dealers in New York City. The brokers operate through [the PCBDA]. All the contracts in which they deal are guaranteed or indorsed by member firms of the New York Stock Exchange . . . The Put and Call business is largely self-regulated, but a great deal of the aura of secrecy which surrounds this activity seems to stem from the early 1930s when the threat of strict regulation or even legislative extermination haunted the entire options trade. Testimony before the Senate Committee on Banking and Currency in 1932 and 1933 disclosed that many of the financial abuses of the 1920s were related to the use of options.

At this time, the options market was relatively small. Self-regulation, both by the exchanges and by the PCBDA, coupled with the ability of the SEC to require reporting of options trading, were sufficient to prevent the abuses of previous years. However, the markets were relatively illiquid and it was difficult to resell positions. Upon closer inspection, though the options being traded through the PCBDA were transferable and, in a sense, protected by a clearing mechanism, some common drawbacks of OTC trading of derivative securities were present. In addition to illiquidity, trading in the market primarily involved large institutional investors writing overpriced options to small investors seeking to gamble in stocks with limited capital. In effect, OTC trading was aimed at capturing rents from control of the information and transactions technology of options trading.

Among other significant regulatory changes introduced by the Securities Act (1933) was the requirement that all options sellers post margins. Unscrupulous activities such as granting brokers options for touting a stock were banned, together with the use of options to trade on inside information. In addition to the increased government regulation, self-regulation by the PCBDA also played an important role. While the options traded in the OTC market were often illiquid, in 1972 this started to change with the creation of the Options Clearing Corporation, as a subsidiary of the CBOE. In following years, the American, Philadelphia, Pacific and Midwest stock exchanges also introduced options trading. Trading on the CBOE commenced in April 1973 with 16 stock options. While initial interest in options trading was limited, by 1977 volume had increased substantially to the point where put options were introduced. The ensuing implications of interexchange competition undermining the self-regulatory function of exchanges, a phenomenon which has overtaken derivative markets in recent years, was not adequately appreciated at the time. The advantages associated with combining options with cash trading, a tradition on European exchanges stretching back to early nineteenth-century France (Viaene 2006), is unrecognized.

The implications and advantages associated with exchange trading of options are much as with futures. Strike prices and expiration dates of contracts are standardized to facilitate liquidity. The security of doing trades with the clearing-house instead of a specific counterparty means positions are easier to unwind. Transactions and other costs are also lower. The subsequent profitability of stock option trading was reflected in the cost of exchange seats: before the recent wave of exchange demutualization and mergers, seats on the CBOE were the most expensive of any exchange in the world. The successful introduction of exchange trading for stock options was not, initially, matched by commodity options. The creation of the CFTC in 1974 in combination with a number of large commodity options frauds originating in London commodity options led, in 1978, to the CFTC banning all London options, dealer options and domestic exchange traded options, except under certain restrictive conditions.[40] These rules were altered substantially in 1981 when new regulations on trading in commodity options were introduced. In 1982, trading began with options on futures for gold, heating oil, sugar, US T-bonds and certain stock indices. Over time, stock index option trading has been extended to a variety of national stock markets.

Despite having decades to deal with the problem, there is still regulatory confusion over how to deal with speculative exchange trading in the stock market. The confusion is apparent in the regulation of options where the SEC has jurisdiction over trading in derivative securities on common stocks. In addition, the SEC is responsible for regulating stock exchanges, broker-dealers and other traders in the stock market. In contrast, the CFTC is generally responsible for regulating trading on the commodity futures exchanges where important derivative security contracts for stocks are traded. The CFTC is also responsible for regulating futures and options contracts for a range of financial 'commodities' such as currencies and government debt. The situation has become even more complicated with Congress granting regulatory authority to entities for regulating specific commodity markets, such as the Federal Energy Regulatory Commission (FERC). The competition between exchanges for business that characterized the emergence of the CBOE is reflected in the experience of the IMM division of the CME where financial futures first appeared in 1972 in the guise of foreign currency futures contracts, followed shortly thereafter by interest rate futures and, eventually, stock index futures. Demutualization transformed the competition between exchanges into competition between the exchanges and OTC trading platforms – a theme which continues to the present with the competition between exchanges and OTC ETN and

ATS trading platforms (for example, Domowitz and Lee 2001). Against this backdrop, various important market participants such as hedge funds are seeking and exploiting exemptions from regulatory oversight leading to situations such as the Amaranth Advisors LLC in 2006 where both the FERC and CFTC battled over jurisdiction to prosecute for market manipulation involving trading across both futures exchange and OTC ETN platforms (for example Cuillerier and Fleitas 2008).

The history of speculative exchange trading contains numerous lessons being largely ignored in the current calls for regulatory reform. There is limited recognition of the danger to market liquidity and oversight from the fragmenting of trading activity through the emergence of dark pools and other manoeuvres aimed at capturing the economic rents associated with control over information and transactions technology. Given the historical difficulties with legally proving manipulation in courts, the role of the self-regulatory exchange in maintaining 'fair and orderly' markets is being threatened by an ongoing process of trading platform fragmentation. Regulators have failed to provide rules for resolving the conflict between the private and public functions of the self-regulating exchange. With the economic rents from the demutualization process largely dissipated, profit-maximizing exchanges will understandably seek to reduce the costs of maintaining the public self-regulatory function. Where trading is still concentrated on exchanges, regulatory costs can be reduced by exempting important traders and not incurring assorted costs associated with determining the composition and strategies of market participants. Despite claims by large investment banks and other self-interested stock market participants, speculative OTC trading of derivative securities is not 'innovative' and 'flexible'. The history of speculative exchange trading suggests, instead, that encouraging such OTC trading will only lead to counterproductive regulatory arbitrage, fragmentation of market liquidity and undermining of the price discovery and dissemination function of important commodity and financial markets.

NOTES

1. The current debate on financial market reform is widespread and has filled many volumes of contributions. Relevant parts of the debate of immediate interest about clearing mechanisms are reviewed in Pirrong (2008) where the misconceptions of the US regulators are identified. Even Pirrong (2008) does not make a sufficient connection between the self-regulatory function of exchanges and the mechanisms for clearing and execution. CFTC (2008), prepared against the backdrop of escalating oil prices, is a further example of the confusion among regulators. The conclusion of the Interagency Taskforce employs Granger causality tests to support the view: 'based on available evidence to date . . . changes in futures market participation by speculators have not systematically preceded price changes'. Leaving aside the questionable relevance of using Granger causality tests in this instance, as many hedge funds and other alternative investment vehicles currently operate under exemptions from reporting requirements, it is difficult to see how key speculative players have been identified.
2. Treptow (2006, Ch. 3) and Pirrong (1999) review many available studies. Hart and Moore (1996) demonstrate theoretically that closed ownership structures for exchanges, such as the mutual form, can result in inefficiencies in governance leading to economic inefficiencies. Lack of technological innovation, higher transactions costs, reduced liquidity and monopoly rent extraction are a number of undesirable outcomes. However, Hart and Moore fail to consider the gains associated with using self-regulation to restrict manipulation. Both empirically, for example Pirrong (1995), and theoretically, for example De Marzo et al. (2005), it has been demonstrated that self-regulation can only be effective with accurate government oversight.

3. Weber (1894 [2000]) is an early exception. Modern exceptions include Gehrig and Fohlin (2006), Neal and Davis (2005), Rajan and Zingales (2003), Michie (1986), Lurie (1972) and the references cited in Markham and Harty (2008, pp. 867–82).
4. Some of the earliest examples of written language, the Sumerian cuneiform tablets, contain such notarial protests. See, for example, http://www.sfu.ca/~poitras/Brit_Mus.ZIP which provides a picture of a Sumerian tablet circa 1750 BC from the British Museum collection: 'A letter complaining about the delivery of the wrong grade of copper after a Gulf voyage.'
5. In the following quotes, the old English spelling used by Malynes in the original text has been modernized, for example 'booke' to 'book', 'necessarie' to 'necessary'. No alternations have been made to grammar.
6. 'In 16th century England, the bulk of the export trade was in the hands of the Merchant Adventurers, but the import trade was largely controlled by the merchant strangers, especially Italians, Spaniards and Flemings' (de Roover 1949, p. 110). The Merchant Adventurers were an important English regulated company, a guild association of merchants with a royal charter providing a grant of monopoly for the export of cloth from England. Regulated companies differ from joint-stock companies in that each merchant member provides capital and conducts business on an individual basis. Admission to the Merchant Adventurers could be obtained by patrimony or apprenticeship or by paying an admission fee. It was also possible to obtain admission by 'free gift'.
7. Max Weber (1924 [2000], p. 339) provides an example of such a definition: 'A stock or commodity exchange is a *market* in which the purchase and sale of large quantities of goods and money, of stocks and commercial bills of exchange, take place between professional businessmen'. Weber (1894 [2000]) aims to defend the exchange process from the view that: 'one is dealing with an wholly dispensable organization – one that must be judged by its very nature to be a sort of "conspirators club" aimed at lying and deception at the expense of honest laboring people'.
8. The term 'bill of exchange' is being used loosely. The subtle differences in the features of the bill of exchange contract, for example transferability, that evolved over time are being ignored. Munro (2000) and de Roover (1949) discuss these differences in some detail. Until the latter part of the sixteenth century, the bill of exchange was the dominant means of settlement in Southern Europe, while the bill obligatory (letter obligatory, writings obligatory) was prevalent in the north: 'The bill of exchange was definitely not unknown in the north; on the contrary. But before 1550 the bill of exchange was certainly not yet the characteristic, dominant instrument of foreign trade. Within the Hanseatic League the bill of exchange remained marginal. From the second third of the sixteenth century . . . use of the bill of exchange quickly became general in the north . . . The letter (or bill) obligatory, based on extension of payment, had from the late Middle Ages been the characteristic, dominant security in the foreign trade of the north. It continued to hold this position in the fifteenth and sixteenth centuries' (van der Wee 1977, pp. 324–5).
9. De Roover (1954, p. 205) traces the progression of the banking practices from the fairs to fixed metropolitan locations: 'By 1325 . . . the role of the fairs of Champagne was played out, both as trading and financial centres. In the fourteenth and fifteenth centuries, the banking places of Europe were: Bologna, Florence, Genoa, Lucca, Milan, Naples, Palermo, Pisa, Siena, Venice and the court of Rome in Italy; Avignon, Montpelier, and Paris in France; Barcelona, Valencia, and Palma de Mallorca in Spain; Bruges in Flanders; and London in England . . . Paris declined shortly after 1400 . . . and its place was taken by the fairs of Geneva and, after 1465, by those of Lyons. There were no banking places east of the Rhine, although the fairs of Frankfort-on-the-Main began to emerge as a clearing centre toward the end of the fifteenth century.'
10. Relevant English legislation on enforce-ability of interest payments is detailed in de Roover (1949, p. 110, n. 31). Henry VIII made the first substantive effort in 1545.
11. A similar description can be found in van der Wee (1977, pp. 318–19).
12. The contrast in settlement practices between different trading venues is a historical theme that continues to the present. Lyons was an important Renaissance financial centre for trading in bills of exchange while Antwerp was an important commercial centre. From the settlement practices employed at Lyons, the Continental and British practice of 'settlement by account' developed. In contrast, commercial trading in Antwerp was primarily based on cash settlement and short-dated forward contracts. It was this general 'cash' approach to settlement that emerged in the US stock market.
13. Buckley (1924, p. 590) makes the following observation about the treatment of the English merchants of the Staple in Bruges: 'It was, apparently, an important concession which the city Bruges made to the English merchants of the Staple in 1559, when it was agreed that the latter should be free of brokers when buying. It was asserted in 1562 that in most foreign countries no "stranger" bought or sold except through a sworn broker, and the English Statute Book contains a number of regulations of similar import. Such arrangements were general, being due to the universal prejudice against foreigners'.

Buckley (p. 591) also makes another observation which is indicative of the pervasiveness of brokers at Gresham's time: 'Dealings in Bills of exchange without the intervention of a broker were exceptional'.

14. This statement disguises a number of characteristics of bourse trading in Antwerp. Following the practice in Bruges, which preceded Antwerp as the centre of economic activity in Northern Europe, bourse trading consisted primarily of dealings in money and bills of exchange located in a building around a specific square ('Beurs' square named after the van Beurs family which owned a meeting house on the square where Italian financiers would conduct business). Trade in commodities was conducted 'either in the large "Halles" or in the houses and warehouses where the goods were stored' (Ehrenberg 1928, p. 237). In 1531, the Antwerp City Council opened a building dedicated exclusively to bourse trading. While intended to accommodate both trading in bills and commodities, the Antwerp bourse emerged as the venue for trading in bills while bourse trading in commodities was conducted on the 'English bourse'. Whereas in Bruges and other medieval trading venues traditional bourse trading was organized along national lines, in Antwerp trade was segmented by the type of transaction. An impediment to trading in Antwerp was the rudimentary settlement practices. In contrast to the clearing-house methods that sustained the importance of Lyons as a financial centre, settlement in Antwerp was 'hand-to-hand'.
15. Kellenbenz (1957 [1996], p. 134) gives more precise information on the evolution of the Amsterdam Exchange: 'The institution began as an open-air market in Warmoestreet, later moved for a while to New Bridge, which crosses the Damrak, then flourished in the "church square" near the Oude Kerk until the Amsterdam merchants built their own exchange building in 1611'. The Amsterdam exchange was fully open for business in 1613.
16. The identification of this early trade as 'futures' contracting is found in Gelderblom and Jonker (2005). This approach is at variance with the conventional view that futures trading began in Chicago in the nineteenth century, or the less conventional view that such trading began in the seventeenth-century Japanese rice market (West 2000; Schaede 1989).
17. Emery (1896, pp. 51–3) provides a number of references to late nineteenth-century German and French sources on options trading. The connection between German and English terminology is also discussed (p. 91). Courtadon (1982) examines option trading practices on the Paris exchange.
18. The acronym VOC is a reference to the English to Dutch translation of the Dutch East India Company, as the Verenigde Oostindische Compagnie.
19. In addition to share trading in Amsterdam, van Dillen et al. (2006) makes reference to trading in shares also occurring in Hamburg, Frankfurt, Middleburg, Cologne, Rouen and in other locations. However, there is no evidence that this trade was anything other than small-scale, occasional and generally unorganized (Barbour 1950, p. 76).
20. As shares were issued by specific chambers, trading was confined almost exclusively to those issued by the Amsterdam chamber. Even at later dates where trading in shares of other chambers emerged, shares of the Amsterdam chamber still demanded a substantial premium (for example Barbour 1950, p. 77).
21. The primary documentation associated with the Dutch Edict of 1610, which removed legal protection for 'windhandel' contracts, contains an important *memoir*, probably written by Isaac le Maire, which outlines arguments in favour of retaining short sales (van Dillen 1930; De Marchi and Harrison 1994; Gelderblom et al. 2010 [2009]). A number of arguments draw on the similarity of the trade in shares to the trade in goods: 'the authors proceed from free trade in goods (perfectly conventional from a common weal point of view), move on to the freedom to make forward purchases of commodities (accepted practice for at least several decades), and end with the freedom to trade in shares. This bundling, as well as the progression itself, may have been intended to persuade the reader that (all) share trading practices should unquestionably be regarded as no different in principle from trade in goods' (De Marchi and Harrison 1994, p. 55).
22. Though the actual recording of the transfer could be effected within the day, there were often delays associated with settlement if cash was not paid directly; for example the sale could be made by instalments and the transaction would require a contract to be drawn up. Problems could also arise in verifying the identity of the person transferring the shares and where bills of exchange were required for payment, for example if the seller was an offshore investor.
23. Wilson (1941, pp. 84–5) describes the options trade: 'A *prime à délivrer* (a call) was the option which A gave to B, obliging him to deliver on the following *rescontre* certain English securities – say £1000 East India shares – at an agreed price. If the speculation of the giver of the option was unsuccessful, he merely lost his option: if, on the other hand, the funds rose, he had the benefit of the rise. The *prime à recevoir* (a put) was the option given by A to B by which B was pledged to take from A on *rescontre* £1000 East India shares, say, at an agreed price. B became, in fact, a kind of insurance for A, obliged to make good to him the margin by which the funds might diminish in the interval.'
24. There was variable use of the terms to describe derivative security contracts. 'Time dealings' was used to refer to both forward and option contracts. Though 'time bargain' was occasionally used to refer to all types of time dealings, de la Vega and others use 'time bargain' to refer only to forward contracts. In

the terminology of the time, a time bargain was a usually a long-dated, transferable to arrive contract that did not involve the expectation of delivery. The confusion between the types of derivative security contracts appears in the US debate over 'anti-option' bills which were primarily aimed at curtailing futures and forward contract trading. The intricate dealings that were involved in the South Sea Bubble are discussed in various sources, including: Morgan and Thomas (1962, Ch. 2), Wilson (1941, Ch. 4), Hoppit (2002) and Shea (2007).

25. Mortimer makes no reference to the use of options in stockjobbing activities, giving some support to the position that Barnard's Act of 1734 was effective in deterring this activity. In contrast to Mortimer, another early source – Defoe (1719 [1850]) – makes no reference to forward trading, using examples which usually relate to cash transactions, for example using false rumours to influence the stock price, the idea being to buy low on negative rumours and selling high on positive rumours (pp. 139–40). However, it is not clear that Defoe had the best grasp of the financial transactions which were being done.
26. In Mortimer's time, the bulk of 'stock' being traded was British government securities, primarily term annuities and consols. The various legal restrictions on joint-stock issues introduced after the South Sea Bubble prevented new issues of shares until well into the nineteenth century. The bulk of available shares for trading were associated with the large companies formed prior to the bubble: the Bank of England, the British East Indies Company and the South Seas Company. The primary asset of these companies was, in turn, British government debt. Such 'stock' was typically purchased by instalment and, as a consequence, partially paid – 'light horse' – stock was a popular speculative vehicle as the 'margin' requirement was less.
27. A broker in this period was an intermediary or mutual agent who served as a witness, for a commission, to contracts between two parties. In London, legal brokers had to be licenced and sworn. While much of the commodity and joint stock business was conducted through brokers, dealing was not confined to sworn brokers and, at various times, many unlicenced dealers operated in the market.
28. The early history of options trading in England can be found in Morgan and Thomas (1962). An early discussion can be found in Duguid (1901). Barnard's Act was repealed in 1860.
29. The abuses associated with stockjobbing were due, at least partly, to the standard market practice of a significant settlement lag for purchases of joint stock. While there was a cash market conducted, often at or near the company transfer office, dealing for time had a legitimate basis in the practical difficulties associated with executing a stock transfer. This meant that when stock was sold for time, the short position had a considerable lead time to deliver the security. Trading involved establishing a price for future delivery of stock and paying a small deposit against the future delivery. In cases where the selling broker did have possession of the underlying stock when the transaction was initiated, there was little or no speculative element in the time bargain. However, this was not the case when the seller did not possess the stock. In addition, the purchaser for time did not usually have to take possession of the stock at delivery but, rather, could settle the difference between the agreed selling price and the stock price on the delivery date.
30. Michie (1999, p. 34) reports that the English national debt increased by about £500 million to £744.9 million between 1790 and 1815. Following Kaplan (2006) and Ferguson (1998), the substantial increase in the supply of debt available for issue and trade precipitated the creation of banking dynasties, most notably the House of Rothschild.
31. Cope (1978) takes a somewhat different view of these events.
32. Clews (1908 [1973]) claims that Little made and lost nine fortunes.
33. The search for rules to regulate financial trading could be found in various venues, not just Chicago. In addition to the discussion surrounding such trading in England associated with the Liverpool cotton contracts, such debates led to the attempt of Jules Regnault in France to create a financial science (Jovanovic 2006).
34. Of the various recent exchange mergers, in 1999, NYMEX merged with COMEX to form the New York Board of Trade. Markham and Harty (2008) give a detailed discussion of more recent mergers and developments.
35. The Senate debate included a vote on the George amendment which aimed to ban futures trading altogether. This amendment was prompted by the concern of southern members about the use of tax-to-destroy as a method of dealing with the anti-speculation arguments of the agrarians and Populists. This amendment was defeated by 51 to 19. However, as it turns out, the southern supporters of the George amendment held the balance in the House vote to suspend rules which lead to the defeat of the Hatch–Washburn bill.
36. Early US references to options often reflect a semantic confusion where 'options' refer to derivative securities in general, and not only to 'privileges'. Trades not settled for cash – that is, time contracts – were specified with a seller's or buyer's option to deliver. Such contracts did not have delivery as an option, as with 'privileges' and modern options contracts. Rather, the option in the contract

determined whether the buyer or seller would be able to initiate delivery, which could be made with proper notification any time during the life of the time contract. This 'American' option was in contrast to European practice where 'trading for account' dictated delivery on the expiration date, which was typically a regular *rescontre* settlement date. The various attempts in the late nineteenth century to pass 'anti-option' legislation were aimed at prohibiting trading of time contracts, as trading of privileges was relatively muted at that time.

37. Armstrong (1848, p. 9) reports: 'It is common observation that no sensible person will sell a privilege, and there are not many sold.' There were similar views regarding options trading in France (for example Preda 2006; Jovanovic 2006). Poitras (2009a) documents the increasing acceptance of options trading within a wider group of traders in the last quarter of the nineteenth century.
38. 'A pool is a temporary association of two or more individuals to act jointly in a security operation of a manipulative character. There is no inherent reason why manipulation should be carried out through the use of pools; many such manipulations have been carried on with great financial success by single operators, such as Drew, Little, Vanderbilt, Gould and Keene. During the 1920's, however, the pool developed a high degree of popularity. The possibility of combining capital, trading skill, experience and corporate connections into one cooperative venture appeared so attractive that it became the typical organization procedure of manipulators of that era. There was no particular size of the pool of the 1920's and early 1930's. The Radio pool, one of the largest, had about 70 members, the first Fox pool had 32, and the second 42. The profitable alcohol pool of 1933 had only eight participants' (Teweles and Bradley 1985, p. 269).
39. 'Stock Exchange Practices', Senate Report 1455, 73rd Congress, 2nd Sess., p. 63, quoted in Teweles and Bradley (1985).
40. Wolf (1982) provides background on the specific events that were associated with the CFTC options ban. Since the creation of the CFTC in 1974 to replace the Commodity Exchange Authority which had been part of the United States Department of Agriculture (USDA), changes to commodity futures and options regulations have usually been associated with the regular four-year reauthorization of the CFTC. For example, the 1982 reauthorization contained the Shad–Johnson Accord Index Act which specifies the authority of the SEC and CFTC for stock-related products. This Act gave the CFTC exclusive jurisdiction over stock index futures, while the SEC was given control over options on securities and currencies.

BIBLIOGRAPHY

Adams, C.F. and H. Adams (1871), *Chapters of Erie and Other Essays*, Boston, MA: James Osgood.

Alborn, T. (1998), *Conceiving Companies: Joint-Stock Politics in Victorian England*, London: Routledge.

Armstrong, W. (1848), *Stocks and Stock Jobbing in Wall Street, with Sketches of the Brokers and Fancy Stock*, New York: New York Publishing Company.

Barbour, V. (1950), *Capitalism in Amsterdam in the 17th Century*, Ann Arbor, MI: University of Michigan Press.

Buckley, H. (1924), 'Sir Thomas Gresham and the foreign exchanges', *Economic Journal*, **34**, 589–601.

Cardoso, J. (2006), 'Joseph de la Vega and the "Confusion de Confusiones"', in G. Poitras (ed.), *Pioneers of Financial Economics*, Vol. I, Cheltenham, UK and Northampton, MA, USA: Edward Elgar.

Clews, H. (1908), *Fifty Years in Wall Street*, New York: Irving Publishing, reprinted by Arno Press (1973).

Commodity Futures Trading Commission (CFTC) (2008), 'Staff report on commodity swap dealers and index traders with commission recommendations', September, Washington, DC.

Cope, S. (1978), 'The stock exchange revisited: a new look at the market in securities in London in the eighteenth century', *Economica*, **45**, 1–21.

Courtadon, G. (1982), 'A note on the premium market for the Paris stock exchange', *Journal of Banking and Finance*, **6**, 561–5.

Cowing, C. (1895), *Populists, Plungers, and Progressives: A Social History of Stock and Commodity Speculation, 1890–1936*, Princeton, NJ: Princeton University Press, reprinted 1965.

Cuillerier, I. and K. Fleitas (2008), 'Amaranth advisors and the FERC's regulatory authority', *Journal of Derivatives and Hedge Funds*, **14**, 70–77.

de la Vega, J. (1688), *Confusion de Confusiones*; reprinted in M. Fridson (ed.) (1996), op. cit.

De Marchi, N. and P. Harrison (1994), 'Trading "in the wind" and with guile: the troublesome matter of the short selling of shares in seventeenth-century Holland', in N. De Marchi and M. Morgan (eds), *Higgling: Transactors and their Markets in the History of Economics*, Annual Supplement to *History of Political Economy*, **26**.

De Marzo, P., M. Fishman and K. Hagerty (2005), 'Self-regulation and government oversight', *Review of Economic Studies*, **72**, 687–706.
de Pinto, Isaac (1771a), *An Essay on Circulation of Currency and Credit in Four Parts and a Letter on the Jealousy of Commerce*, transl. with annotations S. Baggs (1774), London; reprinted (1969) by Gregg International Publishers.
de Pinto, Isaac (1771b), *Jeu d'Actions en Hollande*, Amsterdam; reprinted (1969) by Gregg International Publishers.
de Roover, R. (1948), *Banking and Credit in Medieval Bruges*, Cambridge, MA: Harvard University Press.
de Roover, R. (1949), *Gresham on Foreign Exchange*, London: Harvard University Press.
de Roover, R. (1954), 'New interpretations in the history of banking', *Journal of World History*, **62**, 38–76.
Defoe, Daniel (1719), *The Anatomy of Exchange Alley or a System of Stockjobbing*; reprinted in J. Francis (1850), *Chronicles and Characters of the Stock Exchange*, 1st USA edition, Boston, MA: Crosby & Nichols.
Dickson, P. (1967), *The Financial Revolution in England*, New York: St Martin's Press.
Domowitz, I. and R. Lee (2001), 'On the road to Reg ATS: a critical history of the regulation of automated trading systems', *International Finance*, **4**, 279–302.
Duguid, C. (1901), *A History of the Stock Exchange*, series: The Stock Exchange in 1900, Centenary volume, London: G. Richards for the London Stock Exchange.
Eames, F. (1894), *The New York Stock Exchange*, New York: Greenwood Press reprint (1968).
Ehrenberg, R. (1928), *Capital and Finance in the Age of the Renaissance*, transl. H.M. Lucas, London: Jonathan Cape.
Einzig, P. (1964), *The History of Foreign Exchange*, 2nd edn, London: Macmillan.
Emery, H. (1896), *Speculation on the Stock and Produce Exchanges of the United States*, New York: Columbia University Press; reprinted (1968), AMS Press, New York.
Ferguson, Niall (1998), *The World's Banker: The History of the House of Rothschild*, London: Weidenfeld & Nicolson.
Forrester, R. (1931), 'Commodity exchanges in England', *Annals of the American Academy of Political and Social Sciences*, **155**, 196–207.
Franklin, C. and M. Colberg (1958), 'Puts and calls: a factual survey', *Journal of Finance*, **13**, 21–34.
Fridson, M. (ed.) (1996), *Extraordinary Popular Delusions and the Madness of Crowds; and, Confusion de Confusiones*, New York: Wiley.
Gehrig, T. and C. Fohlin (2006), 'Trading costs in early securities markets: the case of the Berlin Stock Exchange 1880–1910', *Review of Finance*, **10**, 587–612.
Geisst, C. (1997), *Wall Street, A History*, New York: Oxford University Press.
Gelderblom, O., A. de Jong and J. Jonker (2010), 'An Admiralty for Asia: business organization and the evolution of corporate governance in the Dutch Republic, 1590–1640', new version of paper presented to the Yale Conference on Shareholder Advocacy, 6–7 November 2009.
Gelderblom, O. and J. Jonker (2005), 'Amsterdam as the cradle of modern futures and options trading, 1550–1630', in W. Goetzmann and K. Rouwenhorst (eds), *The Origins of Value*, Oxford: Oxford University Press, pp. 189–205.
Gordon, J.S. (1999), *The Great Game, The Emergence of Wall Street as a World Power 1653–2000*, New York: Scribner.
Hafner, W. and H. Zimmermann (2009), *Vincenz Bronzin's Option Pricing Models: Exposition and Appraisal*, New York: Springer-Verlag.
Hicks, J.D. (1961), *The Populist Revolt: A History of the Farmers' Alliance and the People's Party*, Lincoln, NB: University of Nebraska Press.
Hieronymous, T. (1977), *The Economics of Futures Trading*, 2nd edn, New York: Commodity Research Bureau.
Hoppit, J. (2002), 'The myths of the South Sea Bubble', *Transactions of the Royal Historical Society*, **12**: 141–65.
Houghton, J. (1692–1703), *A Collection for Improvement of Husbandry and Trade*, London: Taylor, Hindmarsh, Clavell, Rogers & Brown; reprinted (1969), Farnborough: Gregg International Publishers.
Jovanovic, F. (2006), 'A nineteenth-century random walk: Jules Regnault and the origins of scientific financial economics', in G. Poitras (ed.), *Pioneers of Financial Economics*, Vol. I, Cheltenham, UK and Northampton, MA, USA: Edward Elgar, pp. 191–224.
Kairys, J. and N. Valerio (1997), 'The market for equity options in the 1870s', *Journal of Finance*, **52**, 1707–23.
Kaplan, H. (2006), *Nathan Mayer Rothschild and the Creation of a Dynasty: The Critical Years, 1806–1816*, Stanford, CA: Stanford University Press.
Kellenbenz, H. (1957), 'Introduction' to de la Vega *Confusion de Confusiones*; reprinted in M. Fridson (ed.) (1996), *Extraordinary Popular Delusions and the Madness of Crowds; and Confusion de Confusiones*, New York: Wiley, pp. vii–xxi.

Lee, R. (1998), *What is an Exchange?* Oxford, UK: Oxford University Press.
Lefèvre, E. (1923), *Reminiscences of a Stock Operator*, New York: Wiley (reprint 1994).
Lewin, C. (2003), *Pensions and Insurance before 1880: A Social History*, East Linton, Scotland: Tuckwell Press.
Lurie, J. (1972), 'Private associations, internal regulation and progressivism: the Chicago Board of Trade, 1880–1923, as a case study', *American Journal of Legal History*, **16**, 215–38.
Kumpan, C. (2006), 'Carrot and stick: the EU's response to new securities trading systems', *European Company and Financial Law Review*, **4**, 383–407.
Mahoney, P. (1997), 'The exchange as regulator', *Virginia Law Review*, **83**, 1453–500.
Malynes, G. (1622), *Consuetudo, vel Lex Mercatoria or the Ancient Law Merchant Divided into Three Parts According to the Essentiall Parts of Trafficke*, 1st edn, London: A. Islip; reprinted (1979), Norwood, NJ: Walter Johnson.
Markham, J. (1987), *The History of Commodity Futures Trading and Its Regulation*, New York: Praeger.
Markham, J. (2002), *A Financial History of the United States*, 3 vols, Armonk, NY: M.E. Sharpe.
Markham, J. and D. Harty (2008), 'For whom the bell tolls: the demise of exchange trading floors and the growth of ECNs', *Journal of Corporation Law*, **33**, 865–939.
Medbery, J. (1870), *Men and Mysteries of Wall Street*, New York: Greenwood Press reprint (1968).
Michie, R. (1986), 'The London and New York stock exchanges, 1850–1914', *Journal of Economic History*, **46**, 171–87.
Michie, R. (1999), *The London Stock Exchange: A History*, New York : Oxford University Press.
Morgan, V. and W. Thomas (1962), *The Stock Exchange*, New York: St Martins.
Mortimer, T. (1761), *Everyman his Own Broker; Or a Guide to Exchange Alley*, 2nd edn, London: S. Hooper; 13th edn published 1801.
Munro, J. (2000), 'English "Backwardness" and financial innovations in commerce with the low countries, 14th to 16th centuries', in P. Stabel, B. Blondé and A. Greve (eds), *International Trade in the Low Countries (14th–16th Centuries)*, Garant: Leuven-Apeldoorn, pp. 105–67.
Murphy, A. (1997), *John Law, Economic Theorist and Policy-Maker*, Oxford: Clarendon Press.
Neal, L. (1990), *The Rise of Financial Capitalism, International Capital Markets in the Age of Reason*, Cambridge: Cambridge University Press.
Neal, L. and L. Davis (2005), 'The evolution of the rules and regulations of the first emerging markets: the London, New York and Paris stock exchanges, 1792–1914', *Quarterly Review of Economics and Finance*, **45**, 296–311.
O'Sullivan, M. (2007), 'The expansion of the US stock market, 1885–1930: historical facts and theoretical fashions', *Enterprise and Society*, **8**, 489–542.
Parker, G. (1974), 'The emergence of modern finance in Europe 1500–1730', in C. Cipolla (ed.), *The Fontana Economic History of Europe*, Vol. 2, Glasgow: Collins, pp. 527–95.
Peri, G. (1638), *Il Negotiante*, Giacomo Hertz, Venice, last revised edition 1707.
Pirrong, C. (1995), 'The self-regulation of commodity exchanges: the case of market manipulation', *Journal of Law and Economics*, **38** (April), 141–206.
Pirrong, C. (1999), 'The organization of financial exchange markets: theory and evidence', *Journal of Financial Markets*, **2**, 329–57.
Pirrong, C. (2008), 'Clearing up misconceptions on clearing', *Regulation* (Fall), 22–8.
Poitras, G. (2000), *The Early History of Financial Economics, 1478–1776*, Cheltenham, UK and Northampton, MA, USA: Edward Elgar.
Poitras, G. (2002), *Risk Management, Speculation and Derivative Securities*, New York: Academic Press.
Poitras, G. (2009a), 'The early history of option contracts', in W. Hafner and H. Zimmermann (eds), *Vincenz Bronzin's Option Pricing Models: Exposition and Appraisal*, New York: Springer-Verlag, pp. 487–518.
Poitras, G. (2009b), 'From Antwerp to Chicago: the history of exchange traded derivative security contracts', *Revue d'Histoire des Sciences Humaines*, **20**, 11–50.
Preda, A. (2006), 'Rational investors, informative prices: the emergence of the "science of financial investments" and the random walk hypothesis', in G. Poitras (ed.), *Pioneers of Financial Economics*, Vol. I, Cheltenham, UK and Northampton, MA, USA: Edward Elgar, pp. 149–68.
Rajan, R. and L. Zingales (2003), 'The great reversals: the politics of financial development in the twentieth century', *Journal of Financial Economics*, **69**, 5–50.
Schaede, U. (1989), 'Forwards and futures in Tokugawa-period Japan', *Journal of Banking and Finance*, **13**, 487–513.
Shea, G. (2007), 'Understanding financial derivatives during the South Sea Bubble: the case of the South Sea subscription shares', *Oxford Economic Papers*, **59**, 73–104.
Tawney, R. (1925), 'Introduction', to *A Discourse Upon Usury* by T. Wilson (1572); reprinted (1962), London: Frank Cass (1962).
Taylor, C. (1917), *History of the Board of Trade of the City of Chicago*, Chicago, IL: Robert O. Law.

Teweles, J. and E. Bradley (1985), *The Stock Market*, 5th edn, New York: Wiley.
Todd, G. (1932), 'Some aspects of joint stock companies, 1844–1900', *Economic History Review*, **4**, 46–71.
Treptow, F. (2006), 'The economics of demutualization', PhD dissertation, University of Munich.
Unger, R. (1980), 'Dutch herring, technology and international trade in the seventeenth century', *Journal of Economic History*, **40** (June), 253–80.
van der Wee, H. (1977), 'Monetary, credit and banking systems', in E. Rich and C. Wilson (eds), *The Cambridge Economic History of Europe*, Vol. 5, London: Cambridge University Press, pp. 290–392.
van Dillen, J. (1927), 'Termijnhandel te Amsterdam in de 16de en 17de eeuw', *De Economist*, **76**, 503–23.
van Dillen, J. (1930), 'Isaac Le Maire en de handel in actien der Oost-Indische Compagnie', *Economisch-Historisch Jaarboek*, **16**, 1–165.
van Dillen, J., G. Poitras and A. Majithia (2006), 'Issac Le Maire and the early trading in Dutch East India Company shares', in G. Poitras (ed.), *Pioneers of Financial Economics*, Vol. I, Cheltenham, UK and Northampton, MA, USA: Edward Elgar, pp. 46–63.
van Houtte, J. (1966), 'The rise and decline of the market of Bruges', *Economic History Review*, **19**, 29–47.
Viaene, A. (2006), 'Les marchés à terme et conditionnels à la Bourse de Paris au XIXe siécle', in G. Gallais-Hamonno (ed.), *Le marché financier français au XIXè siècle: Aspects quantitatifs des acteurs et des instruments à la Bourse de Paris*, Vol. 2, Paris: Les Publications de la Sorbonne, pp. 571–600.
Weber, M. (1894), 'Stock and commodity exchanges', transl. S. Lestition (2000), *Theory and Society*, **29**, 305–38.
Weber, M. (1924), 'Commerce on the stock and commodity exchanges', transl. S. Lestition (2000), *Theory and Society*, **29**, 339–71.
West, M. (2000), 'Private Ordering at the World's First Futures Exchange', *Michigan Law Review*, **98**, 2574–615.
Williams, J. (1982), 'The origins of futures markets', *Agricultural History*, **56**, 306–25.
Wilson, C. (1941), *Anglo-Dutch Commerce and Finance in the Eighteenth Century*, reprinted (1966), London: Cambridge University Press.
Withers, H. (1910), *Stocks and Shares*, 2nd edn (1917), London: Smith, Elder and Co.
Wolf, A. (1982), 'Fundamentals of commodity options on futures', *Journal of Futures Markets*, **2**, 391–408.

4 Valuing equities in the UK and the US: fashions and trends

Janette Rutterford

INTRODUCTION

The dot.com boom and bust of the year 2000 made equity valuation a hot topic. How had share prices and intrinsic values got to be so far apart? Was it something to do with the way in which shares were valued? Unable to use book values, as high-tech firms had no tangible assets, with no earnings or dividend track record to go on, analysts turned either to multiples of turnover – they did have sales – or to gazing into a crystal ball and forecasting cash flows. These cash flow forecasts turned out to be on the optimistic side, assuming that each firm in the industry was going to be a winner. When investors realized that not everyone could monopolize market share, the valuation bubble burst.

More recently, in the credit crunch, the same thing happened. Analysts, this time bond analysts, thought they had cracked how to value collateralized mortgage obligations (CMOs). Using sophisticated methods – as sophisticated as discounted cash flow seemed in the 1960s – they valued highly complex instruments using complex models which, they tended to forget, had some pretty major assumptions built in. When, for example, the correlation coefficients they had assumed, or the credit ratings they had relied on, proved not to be the right ones, the market prices for CMOs moved very far away from their theoretical values.

This chapter looks at how investors have changed the way in which they value shares over time. The four key ways were book value, dividend and earnings yields, price–earnings ratios and discounted cash flow. The chapter explores an early dependence on book value, the assets to back the nominal value of the shares, and on dividend yields, with shares being valued as bonds, with a higher yield to reflect their more uncertain income. As firms became more profitable, dividends no longer represented the underlying earnings of firms. This was particularly true in the US, where firms did well out of the First World War and reinvested the majority of their earnings. Earnings yields and even price–earnings ratios were in common use in the Wall Street boom of the 1920s – with growth firms being allowed stratospheric price–earnings ratios – and after the Crash as static multiples of earnings which were no longer expected to grow.

In the UK, earnings were treated as a backdrop to dividends until the 1960s. A number of factors can explain this tardiness with respect to the US. First, UK firms had a historical tendency to pay out most of declared profits as earnings, so there was no big divide between earnings and dividends. Second, British firms did not experience the rapid growth that US firms did in the 1910s and 1920s. Third, profit and loss statements in the UK left a lot to be desired until the second half of the twentieth century. And finally, British taxation made it hard for investors to work out what earnings per share were, after corporate taxation and before personal taxation. It was much easier under the US tax system. As a result, it was not until the second half of the 1960s that the British adopted price–earnings ratios. Discounted cash flow, invented by actuaries and engineers in the nineteenth century, was recommended as a valuation method after the Second World War. But it was not until computers had made the calculations easy and the capital asset pricing model allowed easy estimation of the discount rate that both British and US corporate analysts began to concentrate on discounted cash flow valuation. Equity analysts, on the other hand, although they recognize discounted cash flow method as the most likely to give a good estimate of intrinsic value, have not let go of the relative valuation tools, price to book, dividend yield and the most popular price–earnings ratio.

INVESTORS AND MARKETS

I begin by looking at the types of investors and the kinds of securities they bought; in particular, new issues in the late nineteenth and early twentieth centuries. In Britain, equity investors originally consisted of wealthy[1] businessmen investing in companies with which they were personally connected (Maltby 1999, p. 34), although by the mid- to late nineteenth century increasingly efficient stock exchanges in both London and the provinces (in terms of trading stocks and shares), and improved access to financial information through rapid growth in financial periodicals, allowed other types of investor to emerge (Preda 2001; Vissink 1985).

By 1888, the *Statist* was able to identify four different types of shareholder, varying from the pure investor to the outright speculator. The *Statist*'s bona fide speculator and premium hunter were in shares for the short term, seeking to make capital gains on price movements. This still left two kinds of investor. First, the informed businessman, happy to receive a reasonable dividend from his investment in a company with which he was probably involved, as a director or customer (Maltby 1999, p. 35).[2] Such an investor looked to 'his security first and his interest next, and is content with four or five per cent when security is assured' (*Statist*, 14 July 1888, p. 42). Second, the greedy shareholder, often typified as 'the minister of religion, the shopkeeper's widow, the retired naval or military officer, the pensioned civilian' (*Statist*, 7 July 1888, p. 10), wants 7 or 8 per cent and thinks that 10 or 12 per cent is attainable, believing this to be 'tolerably safe' (*Statist*, 7 July 1888, p. 10). New issue prospectuses, such as those with flowery language, reports with maps attached to them, and of companies with figureheads on the boards of directors were, according to the *Statist*, designed to bamboozle investors.

In the US, early common stock investors were primarily bankers and industrialists. It was not until after the merger boom of 1897 to 1904 that common stocks began to be held by substantial numbers of investors (Baskin and Miranti 1997, p. 193; Davis 1966, p. 264).[3] The market was generally more speculative than in the UK, with: 'the stock exchange . . . a battleground for bulls and bears intent on locking horns at every available opportunity' (Geisst 1999, p. 101). Speculators dominated dividend seekers as share prices rose and fell dramatically during each market cycle, fuelled by share price manipulations and insider trading. Conservative investors bought bonds. Speculators or naive investors bought shares in the hope of amassing wealth as the industrialists and bankers had done. Capital gain was their goal.

In summary, then, while the emphasis of the American nineteenth-century investor was on domestic investments, primarily bonds, for their British counterparts, particularly in the second half of the nineteenth century, 'the world was their oyster' (Rutterford 2006).

New Issues

Nineteenth-century shares were mostly bought on issue, since new companies were coming to the market all the time. New issues could be divided, as could investors, into speculative and investment grade. The financial information available to investors was initially in the form of a prospectus, purely descriptive for speculative issues, and with some financial information for the investment-grade issues.

Speculative investments were typically in new companies, requiring investment capital to develop a good idea. By the 1860s, mines were the new speculation. For example, although the prospectus for the Cwm Dwyfor North Wales Copper & Silver Lead Mining Company, issued in 1868, contained the report of an 'expert' who claimed, 'I consider this a proper and safe investment for capitalists', the prospectus appealed fair and square to capital gain seekers by comparing the mine to one already traded on the stock market: 'The Great Laxey Lead and Copper mine at a cost of £4 per share on 15 000 shares is now saleable at from £19 to £24 per share' (Rothschild Archive: RAL XIII/230). Later in the century, the prospectus for the vastly oversubscribed Burma Ruby Mines issue of 1889, offered for subscription by N.M. Rothschild & Sons Limited, promised not dividends but only the capacity to 'yield a large amount of wealth'. This promise proved unfounded, as evidenced by the inclusion of shares in Burma Ruby mines in a (long) list of 'valueless shares' in the Estate of Sir Everard Hambro on his death in 1925 (London Guildhall Library: MS519219). Speculators bought in the hope of capital gain, guided by market psychology and, if lucky, by insider information.

Investment-grade shares, on the other hand, consisted mainly of existing companies coming to the market seeking funds to pay for industry consolidation[4] or to allow the vendor to realize part of his profits and provide funds for expansion. The 1886 prospectus for the highly profitable Arthur Guinness & Co. Limited gave as reason for the flotation the fact that the firm had attained enormous proportions and would doubtless grow still further, determining the 'present proprietor to seek some relief from the constant attention and strain which his position as sole owner unavoidably entails' (Rothschild Archive: RAL XIII/230).

Investment-grade companies typically made profits and were in a position to pay dividends from flotation. The standard approach to capitalizing these going concerns was to issue debentures and/or preference shares up to the balance sheet value excluding goodwill, and to issue ordinary shares to the vendors against goodwill. Any surplus money provided a small amount of working capital. This meant that those 'outsiders' wishing to invest in investment-grade limited liability companies were offered debentures or preference shares yielding a small premium over Consols rather than ordinary shares. In contrast, speculative companies tended to issue only ordinary shares, since they had no ongoing income out of which to pay debt interest or preference dividends.

I now turn to individual valuation methods, from book value, dividend and earnings yields to price–earnings ratios and, finally, discounted cash flow.

BOOK VALUE

Both British and American investors in shares were concerned with security of capital, which was deemed to provide backing for the market value: 'The value of an investment depends upon several circumstances: which are, the liability of the investment to depreciation in value, or to entire loss', and 'the annual return in the shape of rent, interest, dividend or other produce, which is obtained for the money invested' (Ward 1852, p. 5). Which took priority depended upon the risk aversion of the investor and their recent experiences. Ward, writing before limited liability became general, could assert: 'Many persons prefer security of capital to a large annual return for their investment' (Ward 1852, p. 1). Graham and Dodd, writing in the aftermath of the stock market crash of 1929, believed that: 'the typical investor was concerned primarily with the safety of principal and secondly in the continuance of income' (Graham and Dodd 1934, p. 52). Le Maistre, in the more optimistic mid-1920s, commented: 'the value of a going concern depends on its dividend paying capacity rather than on the book value of its assets'. Nevertheless, he devoted two chapters of his investment text to balance sheets and argued that success was broadly reflected therein (le Maistre 1926, p. 154). By this he meant that the potential investor could check to see whether his nominal investment was backed by real assets or, in US terminology, was 'watered stock'. It was considered of vital importance to investors in ordinary shares that the book value of their shares should be above par, particularly as, in Britain, new shares could not be issued below their nominal amount. If a company's assets depreciated in value, whether mines or plant and machinery, it was felt essential to create cash reserves out of any profits remaining after dividend payments. Reserves were also required to hedge against unforeseen contingencies: 'a wisely conducted company will always retain sufficient funds in hand to meet unforeseen emergencies' (Stacey 1923, p. 41).

In Britain, much attention was paid to the balance sheet. There were a number of reasons for this. First, from the 1840s onwards, a large number of journals and books were published on railway investments, which included detailed analyses of balance sheets, as, for example, *Ward's Treatise on Investments* (Ward, 1852, p. 172). How much to depreciate assets was discussed in a number of treatises, such as Samuel Laing's *On Deterioration of Railway Plant and on the Policy of Establishing a Reserve Fund* (Baskin and Miranti 1997, p. 144). Second, in Britain the profit and loss account, when provided, gave only limited financial information, being required to disclose only dividend payments to investors and transfers to reserves, until after the Second World War.[5] The profit figure was typically stated after (undisclosed) tax, depreciation and other expenses, and a sales figure was not provided. The balance sheet, on the other hand, did give some estimate of value in terms of fixed assets and stock in trade, although *Stacey* (1923, p. 23) warned that most assets in the balance sheet were at directors' valuation.

When looking at asset backing, tangibles such as property, plant and equipment were preferred to intangibles such as goodwill. In the new issues of the late nineteenth and early twentieth centuries, ordinary shares were often issued against goodwill with preference shares and debentures financing tangible assets. Brief balance sheets were provided in share prospectuses to highlight this fact. For example, in the prospectus for the issue of securities in Geo. Trollope & Sons, and Colls & Sons Limited, formed from the combination of two building businesses in 1904, the capital of the new company was to consist of £250 000 nominal in ordinary shares (taken by the vendors in part payment of the purchase price) and £200 000 of new money in the form of 5.5 per cent cumulative preference shares issued to the public. Of that £200 000, only £50 000 went to the company to provide working capital, the remainder going as cash payment to the vendors. The net assets of the company (including the £50 000 cash) were valued, in the usual course of business, at £286 000, thereby creating a large goodwill element in the initial balance sheet (Guildhall Library: MS19097).

As companies grew, undistributed profits and reserves could be used to write off goodwill. Le Maistre suggested that if goodwill represented more than one-quarter of the issued capital, a return on capital of 20 per cent should be required in order for a sum to be set aside each year to amortize goodwill as well as allowing for a 10–12 per cent dividend as a percentage of par value (le Maistre 1926, p. 230). However, he was more than happy with the concept of goodwill as applied to brand names such as Beecham's Pills and Veno's cough mixture. What investors had to worry about was goodwill created by overpayment for assets acquired when the company was set up, something which could not be recouped. Potential investors were urged to look carefully to see if the vendors had taken too much of the new money, leaving insufficient working capital with which to meet future business requirements (*Stacey* 1923, pp. 52–3).

British companies' balance sheets gradually became more opaque as far as estimates of share value were concerned. Hidden reserves, a tradition begun in the nineteenth century and challenged (unsuccessfully) in 1906 by shareholders in *Newton* v. *Birmingham Small Arms Company*, meant that asset values were often understated with respect to their market values. Shareholders were given no indication of the size of hidden reserves, nor were directors obliged to disclose them when asked (Maltby 2003, p. 27). Hidden reserves were deemed to be in the shareholders' best interests, allowing companies to provide what investors most desired: stable dividends and a stable share price (Young 1919, p. 44). Also, by the 1920s the trend towards amalgamations and global expansion of companies, begun in the late nineteenth century, had gained such momentum that the unconsolidated accounts provided by British holding companies were increasingly uninformative:

> their ramifications are often so vast and intricate that no one has any real knowledge of their position except a few directors and high officials. It is impossible for even an expert stockbroker to make a reasonable estimate of what such shares are worth, and to buy them is a pig in a poke. It may be a very good pig, but to buy it at a guesswork price is not business. (Caudwell 1930, p. 94)

Caudwell went on to give the example of Courtauld's American branch, known to be a major part of the Courtauld group but for which no accounts were published (Caudwell 1930, p. 101). Complaints multiplied (*Stacey* 1923; Withers 1930) but little was done until the Companies Act 1948.[6] This led commentators to conclude: 'too much attention should not be given to balance sheets' (Caudwell 1930, p. 101).

In the United States the issue of the relevance of book value, as companies grew, also concerned investors. Graham and Dodd (1934, p. 332) cited the case of F.W. Woolworth's, which started off public life in 1911 with $50 million of goodwill against $50 million nominal of share capital. By 1925, reserves had been used to write down the goodwill to a notional $1. An American, Ruskeyer, commented: 'it is a paradox of business that those concerns with a genuine goodwill, for reasons of conservatism, carry it at little or nothing among their assets, whereas those without real goodwill have an inflated item under that heading in the balance sheet' (Withers 1930, p. 57). However, American balance sheets were usually less opaque than those of their British counterparts. Consolidated accounts became the norm in the United States after a wave of amalgamations in 1897 to 1904 following antitrust legislation (Kobrak 2002, p. 4; Baskin and Miranti 1997, p. 194). Consolidated income statements of majors such as United States Steel gave revenues, expenses and taxation in more detail than did their British counterparts, partly due to the 'fair rate of return' concept applied to US utilities (Kobrak 2002, p. 8), allowing a more accurate picture of asset backing and profitability to be gained, although standards varied substantially between companies.[7] British companies, by comparison, gave limited financial data, concentrating on dividend payments and asset backing. All else was deemed superfluous. As the *Accountant* scathingly remarked as late as 1935, commenting on the 34-page accounts of Bethlehem Steel: 'It reminds us of that form of examination questions: say all that you can about . . .' (Maltby 2003, p. 21).

So, in the early twentieth century, estimating share value through book value, whilst of interest to investors on both sides of the Atlantic, was harder in the UK than in the US. The general lack of consolidation of company accounts meant that, prior to the 1948 Companies Act, British balance sheets failed to provide group, as opposed to company, book values. Those American companies, such as the conglomerates, which provided consolidated sets of accounts could be valued more easily using book value than could British companies. British analysts, such as those studying Courtauld above, could not even begin to make appropriate adjustments.

DIVIDEND YIELD AND EARNINGS YIELD

Dividend Yield

Speculators based their investment decision on impressions rather than hard facts. Investors had more to go on: for example, from the prospectus or the accounts of a company with a history, they could glean details of dividends already paid. They were able to estimate dividend per share, disclosed in the prospectus or accounts of a company with a history behind it, as a percentage of nominal value: and make, or be provided with, some estimate of the extent to which the dividend was covered by earnings.

From their inception, shares as securities were viewed as variants of bonds: 'A common stock is a bond which provides future payments indefinite in number and amount' (Preinreich 1936, p. 273). Dividends were the equivalent of bond interest, declared as a percentage of the nominal or par value of the shares. The par value of shares was equivalent to the par value of bonds. Although shares had no defined maturity date, neither did many government bonds; and, in any case, many companies in the nineteenth century lasted only a few years (Shannon 1954). This left the main perceived difference between bonds and shares as being that investors in the former were promised a regular fixed interest rate, whereas investors in the latter hoped for, but were not guaranteed, a higher dividend income.

Investors were clear as to the difference between dividends declared as a percentage of nominal value and their yield as a percentage of market value, or opportunity cost. For example, in a report to London investors by the Australian brokers, Lennon & Cape, describing the 14 shares listed on the Sydney Stock Exchange in 1861, the 'Rate of last dividend' and the 'Interest return' per annum were given in two separate columns of the report (Guildhall Library: MS18000, 1863, 973).

By the late nineteenth and early twentieth centuries, a number of benchmarks were used to analyse dividend yields. First, the dividend cover was of relevance. How protected was the dividend by earnings? For example: 'James Book & Co. (1915) offered preference shares covered five times by profits' (*The Economist*, 17 November 1928, p. 901).[8] Analysts adopted the same approach for equities and, quite early on, compared dividend yields with earnings yields, both as a percentage of nominal share capital. A broker's circular, designed for private circulation but inadvertently sent to all Guinness shareholders, was enthusiastic about the planned share placement, commenting: 'the dividend should therefore not be less than 18 per cent for this year and the earnings should reach 24 per cent' (Bailey 2003, 10).

Investors also considered the industry in which they were investing when assessing dividend yields.[9] Le Maistre, ex-Deputy Secretary to the Government of India Public Works Department and the author of a splendidly lucid text on investment, offered simple guidelines for investment in terms of appropriate dividend yield for different types of investment:

> The yield which investors as a whole are prepared to accept . . . as compared with the yield obtainable for Consols, naturally varies to a marked degree with different industries, but is fairly constant for each industry over a series of years, and naturally, the greater the risk, the higher the yield expected. (le Maistre 1926, p. 259)

According to le Maistre, dividend yields varied from 4.5 per cent to 5 per cent for well-established banks and insurance companies, through to 10 per cent plus a margin for mining shares, the margin being to replace capital, due to the finite life of the investment.

The dividend yield was also considered to be instrumental in putting a floor on share prices: 'In established securities, such as Imperial Tobacco or Shell, there is a point below which the market price is never likely to fall – that is, the point at which the investor buying is bound to be attracted by the dividend yield' (*The Economist*, 10 November 1928, p. 854).

As well as looking at bond yields and dividend yields at the individual security level, these were also compared at the market level to identify whether a market or sector was appropriately priced. In the UK, this comparator was usually considered to be the yield on Consols or, later, on long-term gilts: for example, the *Investors Chronicle* argued in 1949 that, if the differential between dividend yields and gilt yields became too small, there was an effective 'amber light on industrials' (*Investors Chronicle*, 1949, p. 73). An alternative comparison was with the yield on a fixed interest security issued by the same company or, in the US, a high-quality corporate bond index yield.[10]

I now turn to the differences in use of dividend and earnings yields between the UK and the US, concentrating on four aspects: dividend payout, compound growth, quality of accounts and taxation.

Dividend Payout

The percentage of earnings paid out as dividends, also called the dividend payout ratio, differed between British and American companies. In Britain, the thought process behind the income statement went as follows: to try to achieve a stable profit year on year, through the judicious use of hidden reserves, so as to allow a stable dividend pattern; to place most of the difference to depreciation or other disclosed reserves, and retain only a (small) residual balance as unappropriated profit. As well as pandering to the British investor's obsession for stability, 'Profits should not appear to fluctuate too violently in the interests of all concerned, with the exception perhaps of the merely temporary shareholder' (*Accountant*, 3 October 1925, quoted in Maltby 2003, p. 10). An additional impetus for this approach was provided by the tension between capitalists and workers: companies should be seen to be profitable enough to pay adequate dividends, but not too profitable. As the Labour MP, Ernest Bevin, remarked ominously: 'reserves .. are really the unpaid wages of industry' (Maltby 2003, p. 11).

In the US, the tradition was to pay out two-thirds of profits as dividend, leading to a more unstable dividend stream and allowing a build-up of large, notionally unappropriated profits.[11] 'First class American companies, on the whole, are conservative in their financial policy' (Caudwell 1930, p. 129). Graham and Dodd concurred:

> The typical English, French, or German company pays out practically all the earnings of each year, except those carried to reserves. Hence they do not build up large profit-and-loss surpluses, such as are common in the United States. Capital for expansion purposes is provided abroad not out of undistributed earnings but through the sale of additional stock. (Graham and Dodd 1934, p. 331)

Graham and Dodd argued that the British priority given to dividend policy stemmed in part from the requirement, included in the Companies Act 1929, that shareholders approve dividend payments at the annual meeting and that this carried 'an exceedingly valuable reminder to the management of its responsibilities, and to the owners of their rights, on this important question'. They contrasted this position with a lack of US shareholder control over dividend policy which, they claimed, '*fails* to produce the stable dividend rate which is its avowed purpose and the justification for the sacrifice it imposes' (Graham and Dodd 1934, p. 335).[12]

Compound Growth

One reason for the low dividend payouts in the US was the immense local US market protected by high tariffs, as well as rapid industrial progress in the US throughout the 1920s (Caudwell 1930, p. 123). The growth experienced by many US companies had led to increasing earnings diverging more and more from stable dividends. After the First World War, British companies were forced to come to terms with a strong pound, inflation and labour unrest. British investors after the First World War were grateful if dividends were maintained at pre-war levels. US firms, on the other hand, had benefited from the First World War in terms of increased demand for their goods; for example:

> old-time favourites such as General Electric and National Biscuit, and many others – e.g., American Can, Corn Products – that had been transformed from second-grade to well-entrenched enterprises by the prosperity of World War I. These [enterprises] formed the aristocratic group admiringly referred to as the 'blue chips'. (Graham et al. 1962, p. 410)

Fisher, in his 1930 text defending increased share price levels and, in particular, the New York Stock Exchange boom, explained that attitudes to earnings had changed during the 1920s. There were now expectations that earnings of American corporations would increase on account of technical progress within industry, that less risk was attached to those earnings than formerly (given a long-term rising trend), and also that earnings ploughed back instead of declared as dividends were accumulated at a compound rate of interest 'so to speak' (Fisher 1930, p. xxii). Dividend yields were no longer relevant in a world where dividends were maintained at 5 per cent, whilst earnings kept up to 10 per cent or even 25 per cent (Fisher 1930, p. 79).

This compound interest argument had been put forward in 1925 by Lawrence Smith, in his highly influential text, *Common Stocks as Long-Term Investments*. In this book, Smith reported the results of tests comparing the income and capital gains that could have been made on portfolios of ten different common stocks, relative to the returns on bonds or commercial paper, over a number of 20-year periods between 1866 and 1922. He showed that, regardless of whether an inflationary or deflationary environment had prevailed, equities revealed themselves to be a better investment than fixed-interest securities in terms of both income and capital gains. Smith explained this as being due to the effect of compound interest, at a rate of almost 2.5 per cent per annum, over the long term. He suggested that the source of this 2.5 per cent compound interest was threefold: population growth (since the 1820s, this had averaged over 2.4 per cent per annum); secular trend growth from the constantly accelerating speed of modern life; and the 'human factor'. This human factor referred to corporate managers, who were on the side of stockholders rather than bondholders, were increasingly professionalized, and returned a portion of earnings to surplus account to invest 'this increasing surplus in productive operation' (Smith 1925, p. 77). As Keynes put it, in his review of the book: 'there is an element of compound interest operating in favour of a sound industrial investment. Shares work out better than bonds by more than the difference between the apparent rates of interest on each' (Keynes 1925, p. 157). In other words, shares did better than their initial dividend yield suggested. Bonds did worse than the quoted bond yield, with high interest rates eroding their capital values, and inflation making the real worth of their depreciated capital even lower. By contrast: 'An investment in Common Stocks is an investment in real values' (Keynes 1925, p. 157).

Smith's empirical study triggered the realization, in the US, that earnings were not merely a cushion for dividends, but that undistributed profits also generated future, larger dividends and share price rises. Earnings were worthy of study in their own right and shares could be expected to rise in value over time, particularly in periods of growth and inflation. Wall Street was quick to switch to earnings as the primary factor employed when assessing investment values. As Graham and Dodd observed: 'Common stock values have come to depend exclusively upon the earnings exhibit' (Graham and Dodd 1934, p. 350). Keynes also took these lessons to heart, returning to the insurance companies with which he was involved to recommend an increase in the percentage of investment funds devoted to shares (Scott 2002, p. 82). However, he was not optimistic that the results would be quite so impressive when returns on British securities were studied:[13]

> I have the impression that it might not turn out quite so favourably to ordinary shares, partly because our businesses have, for obvious reasons, not gone ahead at quite the same pace, and partly because American industrial concerns may have been rather more conservative than ours in the division of profits. (Keynes 1925, p. 158)

In other words, Keynes recognized that differences in dividend payout policy and in profits growth between American and British companies could explain valuation differences. Indeed, despite Keynes's acceptance of the relevance of earnings to share valuation, his misgivings prevailed. The British attachment to dividend yield proved hard to give up. Dowrie and Fuller were able to comment in their 1950 US investment text:

> the dividend rate was at one time accepted as the dominant factor in the valuation of all but the most highly speculative shares and to a large extent this emphasis has continued in the security markets of other nations. (Dowrie and Fuller 1950, p. 504)

Quality of Accounts

Another factor in the different emphasis between the UK and the US on dividends and earnings was the quality of accounts. In the UK, the content of the income statement was very limited, the dividend payment being the key disclosure and the profit figure given as an afterthought, designed mainly to provide cover for the dividend. Turnover figures did not have to be disclosed until as late as 1976 in the UK (Toms and Wilson 2003), with companies arguing that their competitors could misuse this information. As far as the balance sheet was concerned, the failure to make consolidated accounts compulsory until 1948 meant that the true book value of all subsidiaries' assets could often not be estimated. Thus, it was difficult to estimate profit ratios such as return on sales or return on assets, with any confidence. In the US, by contrast, companies, particularly the railroads and the major monopolies such as US Steel, provided detailed accounts from the early 1900s. The emphasis in these accounts was sales less costs, leaving earnings available to the different classes of investor clear to the analyst. Sales and earnings could be tracked from year to year, without the hidden reserves so beloved of British company directors. British investors looked to the dividend as the only trustworthy number in the accounts. American investors were able to gain extra information from the company's earnings figure.

Taxation

Another influence was tax. In the US, companies and individuals were taxed separately. This system allowed companies to report earnings after corporate taxes, taking no account of individual income tax or capital gains tax. The concept of 'net earnings' was clear to all. In the UK, the company did not exist as a separate taxable entity until the introduction of a corporate tax in 1965. Companies paid income tax on behalf of investors, who might then be liable for additional tax, according to their individual income. This made it difficult to estimate income tax after 'company' tax but before 'investor' tax. May, in a paper attempting to compare American and European equity values, commented:

> From the British point of view, American company profits are subjected to double taxation, the corpus of company profits not being a separate taxable entity in England. Hence to make British earnings comparable with those of other countries, we show them before tax. (May 1939, p. 736)

In practice, this meant that is was possible for US companies, but not for their UK counterparts, to estimate earnings after corporate tax and before personal income tax.

In summary, the continued British preference for dividend yield as a key valuation, compared with the move by US investors in favour of earnings, can be attributed to a number of differences between their respective environments. One difference was to do with dividend payout policy; in the UK, earnings were mostly paid out as dividends, making earnings a cushion for dividends rather than, as in the US, a separate element in the income statement. A second difference was the difficulty British investors had in determining the true earnings figure from the accounts, due to the unconsolidated nature of accounts and a lack of a sales figure hampering profit analysis; in the US, by contrast, the major companies provided detailed income statements and consolidated balance sheets. A third difference can be explained by differences in British and US growth rates. British companies failed to grow dramatically in the post-First World War period. Profits were viewed as cyclical, reverting to a long-term mean, whereas in the US, Smith and Fisher highlighted the long-term growth trend in earnings of many American companies from the First World War to the Depression of the 1930s. A final difference was to do with the British taxation system which made it more complex than in the US to identify corporate earnings after corporate tax but before personal income tax.

Earnings Yield

In the UK, the emphasis on dividends, backed by earnings and assets, as a means of appraising shares lasted through to the 1950s and 1960s:

> The British investor is interested first and foremost in employing his funds so that he gets a good yield. He is far-sighted about this; he does not fall into the simple trap of owning shares with high immediate yields but he goes for the securities which are likely, in his opinion, to give him a good return on his money next year or the year after that. (*Investors Chronicle*, 27 October 1951, p. 994)

Dividend yield was also a major determinant of share value in the US but only up to the mid-1920s. Graham and Dodd offered evidence for this when they argued that increased dividends led to increased share prices, regardless of the pattern of earnings over time. They cited the relative share price performance of two railroad stocks, Atchison and Union Pacific, where the more liberal dividend policy of Union Pacific between 1915 and 1924 caused a greater share price increase than for Atchison, despite the fact that the latter had the greater earnings per share during that period and the greater book value (Graham and Dodd 1934, p. 336). Graham and Dodd maintained that retained earnings were of little value to the investors; they critiqued companies such as United States Steel as being singularly ineffective in using their large accumulated surplus to any good effect (Graham and Dodd 1934, p. 329).

Most American investors, however, had by the mid-1920s turned their attention from dividends to earnings for the purpose of valuing all types of common stock. For example, a Rowe & Pitman broker's circular from August 1928, titled 'Aviation Shares', reveals the differences in approach to valuation of American and British companies. The two American companies covered, United Aircraft & Transport Corporation and Curtiss-Wright Corporation, were discussed in the context of earnings relative to share price and relative to assets. For example:

> It is estimated that the earnings of Curtiss-Wright, Keystone & Curtiss-Robertson, which have net assets of \$31 810 000, for this year will amount to about \$8 600 000 which is equivalent to more than \$1 per share on 6 500 000 shares of common stock, after paying \$2 per share on 1 000 000 class A. These figures do not include possible earnings from the flying services and airport companies which have net assets of \$46 650 000. The present price of Curtiss-Wright common shares is 28¾. (Barings archive, MS203276/6, p. 2)

In comparison, the analysis of the five British aviation shares centred, as usual, on dividend yield, as supported by earnings and assets:

> The dividend yield on Rolls Royce is naturally low (at 4%), seeing that the Company earns nearly twice the amount of its dividend rate and that its net assets amount to nearly 40/- per share (compared with a 51/3 share price) without including its holding in Rolls-Royce of America which has never been shown on the balance sheet as an asset. (Barings archive, MS203276/6, p. 4)

PE RATIOS

Intrinsic Value

In the US, in the 1930s, historically low share prices after the Crash of 1929 encouraged American authors of investment texts to put forward methods of estimating intrinsic value for individual shares for use in determining which stocks to buy.[14] Graham and Dodd defined intrinsic value to be 'that value which is justified by the facts' as distinct from 'market quotations established by artificial manipulation or distorted by psychological excesses' (Graham and Dodd 1934, p. 17). They acknowledged that market values could deviate from intrinsic values, but believed that these two values would converge for 'shares in which the popular interest is keen enough to promise a fairly swift response to value elements which he [the analyst] is the first to recognise' (Graham and Dodd 1934, p. 22).

The search for intrinsic value was greater in the US than in the UK, partly due to the cynicism shown by British economists such as Keynes,[15] and partly due to the fact that Wall Street experienced a greater fall in 1929 than did the London Stock Exchange. In London, share prices had recovered their 1929 levels in nominal terms by 1934. In the US, this did not happen until 1953 (Shiller 2001). Graham and Dodd believed that there were plenty of opportunities in the depressed markets of the 1930s and 1940s to buy shares with an intrinsic value well above their market price. To estimate intrinsic value,

Graham and Dodd preferred to look at earnings rather than dividends. They also, as did other Americans, capitalized those earnings. Thus, the rather ad hoc British comparison of dividend yields across securities was transformed into a share valuation methodology. By capitalizing earnings, Americans could compare the intrinsic value with the market value, and estimate by how much, in value terms, the share was cheap or dear. A yardstick of ten times earnings was the accepted standard of valuation (Graham and Dodd 1934, p. 451). Dowrie and Fuller confirmed the existence of the ten times earnings rule of thumb, saying that this allowed corporations to pay 6 to 7 per cent as dividends. Nevertheless, by 1950, they considered a maximum multiple of 15 appropriate for the 'soundest and most stable stock, without the adoption of a speculative attitude', but referred in shocked tones to financial journalists who had suggested a characteristic multiple for the General Electric Company of 40 (Dowrie and Fuller 1950, p. 514).

Value versus Growth

The argument as to the appropriate earnings multiple boiled down to one issue: were firms essentially stable, meaning that they exhibited 'resistance to change and hence greater dependability for the results shown in the past' (Graham and Dodd, 1934, 38), or were they on an upward earnings trend, warranting higher capitalization multiples or more complex valuation metrics, the rosier their future prospects? The British were very much of the stability school. They believed that markets went up and down but that steadiness of dividends and earnings was paramount. It was foolhardy to value shares on expected growth:

> A new system of valuing shares has come into fashion. We used to calculate the yield on them according to the dividend paid. Then we proceeded to the much more scientific and correct system (if we are not quite certain that profits have not been overstated) of valuing them, not by the dividend paid, but by the rate of profit earned . . . But from this quite sensible step, another one, which takes valuation into the realm of dreams was easy – the step which values shares not by what the company is earning, but by what it may be expected, or hoped, to be going to earn some day. (Withers 1930, pp. 142–3)

In the US, those of the 'stability' or 'value' school (Graham and Dodd 1934; Dowrie and Fuller 1950; Evans and Barnett 1940) argued for constant earnings capitalization multiples that took average historic earnings into account. For example, as late as 1962, Graham et al. (1962, pp. 510–11), after 'long and prayerful thought', came up with the formula of dividing the ten-year average earnings by twice the high grade bond yield to determine a central market value, around which the price would oscillate. Until the mid-1950s, they had the advantage of showing that, in the long run, markets did indeed oscillate around a long-run average; the Standard & Poor's index did not recover its 1929 peak value until 1953. Post-First World War growth seemed a temporary aberration in a century-long analysis.

Those of the 'growth' school[16] argued that historic average earnings were not an indicator of future potential. The most recent earnings were a better indicator of the future than a long-run historic average. Graham and Dodd gave a tongue-in-cheek analysis of the typical Wall Street method of analysing earnings during the boom years of the 1920s:

> 1. Find out what the stock is earning. (This usually means the earnings per share as shown in the last report.)
> 2. Multiply these per-share earnings by some suitable 'coefficient of quality' which will reflect:
>   a. The dividend rate and record.
>   b. The standing of the company – its size, reputation, financial position and prospects.
>   c. The type of business (e.g. an electric light company will sell at a higher multiple of earnings than a baking company).
>   d. The temper of the general market. (Bull market multipliers are larger than those used in bear markets.)
>
> The foregoing may be summarised in the following formula: Price = earnings per share x quality coefficient. (Graham and Dodd 1934, p. 351)

This quality coefficient or earnings capitalization multiple became known as the price–earnings ratio or P/E multiple.

Graham and Dodd's cynicism stemmed from the high P/E ratios achieved on some stocks during the 1920s boom years. For example, General Electric Company traded on a P/E multiple of 95 in 1930 (Dowrie and Fuller 1950, p. 500). Graham and Dodd believed that investors had lost sight of intrinsic value and were blindly following Smith's recommendation of buying a diversified portfolio of industrials that would, as in the past, outperform bonds. Smith had provided no valuation metric, so there was no idea of a cheap or dear price. Any price for 'blue chip' industrials was the right price. Although not yet formally articulated as a 'hypothesis', investors in the 1920s essentially believed in the efficiency of stock markets. There was no need to determine a share's intrinsic value; the market price was the fair price for the share, whatever that might be. As Fisher argued: 'We are in a dynamic world where the old conception of any fixed ratio of earnings to prices of stocks as a proper ratio must yield to the demands of the shifting scales of industrial effort', while 'New and promising inventions explain high P/E ratios' (Fisher 1930, p. 90). Thus was born the new era of investment theory, 'conspicuously reticent on the mathematical side' (Graham and Dodd 1934, p. 314).

In the UK, investors continued to think of intrinsic value in terms of dividend yields backed by earnings right up to the 1960s. Although consolidated accounts were produced from the mid-1930s on by some companies, and generally required by the 1948 Companies Act, UK analysts did not switch to P/E ratios until 1965, when corporation tax finally allowed the separation of corporate and personal taxes. By 1966, *The Economist* was using P/E ratios with aplomb: 'Holders of Jaguar A shares can reflect on a P/E ratio of under 8, the best in the industry' (*The Economist*, 12 February 1966, p. 648). Prospective P/Es were also calculated, not on the most recent earnings but those expected for the year to come. *The Economist* found that: 'at 19/3d, Viyella's P/E ratio on this year's likely profits is around 25' (*The Economist*, 14 September 1968, p. 76), while the new issue of Copydex was discussed in the context of its prospective P/E ratio (*The Economist*, 14 September 1968, p. 78). Only a few years before, new issues had still been priced, in Britain, on prospective dividend yield.[17]

Both value and growth schools used the P/E ratio as a key valuation metric. Value investors such as Graham and Dodd used the P/E ratio to show how the intrinsic values of low P/E shares were above their market values. Proponents of the growth school argued that high P/E was a sign of future growth and encouraged investors to buy high P/E stocks in the expectation of profiting from that future growth. By the late 1960s, the P/E ratio had become, and is still, the most common valuation metric on both sides of the Atlantic. However, today it is generally accepted that the best method, in theory, for determining intrinsic value is discounted cash flow.

DISCOUNTED CASH FLOW

Estimating the present value of all future dividends (for the shareholder) or of all future operating cash flows (for the corporate acquirer) is now taught in all major investment and finance text books (for example Damadoran 2006; Brealey and Myers 2003; Copeland et al. 2000), and is used in many, if not all, broking firms as the theoretically appropriate method for determining intrinsic value. And yet, discounted cash flow as a valuation methodology has been very slow to become accepted, in both the UK and the US. In this section, I look at when discounted cash flow was first conceived, and then discuss why it took so long to be implemented in practice.

The concept of the intrinsic value of a share being the present value of all the future dividends first emerged in the mid-nineteenth century. There were two separate literatures: that of actuaries, engineers and land valuers, developing discount tables to value shares or assets according to mathematical formulae; and the economists, academics and practitioners who came to this approach via interest rates and opportunity cost of funds. In the UK, Armstrong, a mining engineer, used discounted cash flow to value mine leases and, indeed, mining companies for flotation (Pitts 2001). Sutton (1882) prepared the first textbook for the Institute of Actuaries, including a section on varying annuities.[18] Todhunter (1901), an actuary, and Guild (1931), an American academic practitioner, both developed models of share prices assuming constant growth rates in perpetuities, Todhunter considering an infinite dividend stream growing at a constant rate, and Guild capitalizing a finite constant growth stream and the terminal value being the present value of a future P/E multiple.

The application of discounted cash flow to share valuation acquired some impetus in the US immediately prior to the Second World War. Preinreich (1936) developed a model in which earnings were expected to grow over a finite period on an expanded capital base and argued that only discounted cash flow techniques could value such growth firms correctly. Williams, generally credited with popularizing the dividend valuation model, wrote his PhD on this topic whilst at Harvard University; the thesis was published as *The Theory of Investment Value* in 1938. In the Preface, he defined investment value (his equivalent of intrinsic value) as: ‘the present worth of future dividends, of practical importance to every investor because it is the *critical* value above which he cannot go on buying or holding, without added risk’ (Williams 1938, p. viii). In the book, he provided potential investors with ‘algebraic budgets’ using estimates concerning future growth, earnings and the capital structure of a company. However, the economist Fisher had already considered share values in present value terms (1907, 1930) and used this framework to try to explain rising prices in the 1920s:

> Since every stock price represents a discounted value of the future dividends and earnings of that stock, there are four reasons that may justify a rise in the price level of stocks:
>
> 1. Because the earnings are continually plowed-back into business instead of being declared in dividends, this plowing-back resulting in an accumulation at compound interest, so to speak;

2. Because the expected earnings will increase on account of technical progress within the industry;
3. Because less risk is believed to attach to those earnings than formerly;
4. Because the 'basis' by which the discounting has been made is lowered. (Fisher 1930, p. xxii)

In practice, the early use of the dividend valuation model was limited to simplistic growth assumptions or even no growth at all. Williams (1938) estimated a 'true' value for the common stock of General Motors Corporation. Assuming that the earnings of common stock could be expected to flatten out and fluctuate narrowly around $3.52, and a dividend distribution of 83.5 per cent of earnings (past performance, somewhat modified), he estimated 'normal' dividends of $2.90 which, capitalized at 5.25 per cent, gave an investment value of $55.25 (Williams 1938, pp. 395–408).

Multiples, according to Preinreich, were only appropriate in a stable world:

> the time-honoured method of appraising a security through the simple process of dividing the annual earnings by the desired rate of return leads to an acceptable result only in the case of a bond or a share of stock in a corporation which has reached the limit of expansion. (Preinreich 1936, p. 274)

Despite these developments, multiples continued to be the dominant valuation approach, although taking expected earnings and dividends into account, rather than relying on historic averages. Where forecasts were available, prospective ratios were used, as for example in pricing new issues, or future average expected earnings estimated as input into a 'normalized' or trend P/E. This did not really solve the problem of valuing companies with varying growth rates. One difficulty was obtaining tables of dividends showing different growth rates for different periods. Economists Clendenin and Van Greave (1954) produced a set of discount tables for valuing growth shares in the *Journal of Finance*; Durand (1957) and Gordon (1962) popularized the formula for infinite growth at a constant rate, sometimes referred to as 'Gordon's growth model'.

By the late 1960s, the 'nifty fifty' US stock market boom was in full swing. Companies such as IBM were forecast to have stratospheric future growth. The hunt was on for how to use growth valuation models in practice. Bauman (1963) published more detailed tables in a monograph entitled *Estimating the Present Value of Common Stocks by the Variable Rate Method.* Written at the height of the stock market boom, it attempted to help investors puzzled by large gains being achievable from highly rated stocks becoming even more highly rated, on a P/E basis, whereas there were 'only modest profits from well-entrenched high quality companies bought at prices between 12 and 16 times current earnings' (Bauman 1963, Preface). Bauman argued that the present value of future dividends approach would only now begin to 'revolutionize investment thinking' for three main reasons: electronic computers, recently developed, would allow present value tables to be used to value individual stocks; the increasingly divergent growth rates of dividends and earnings had reduced the relevance of P/E ratios and dividend yields as valuation metrics;[19] and the fact that common stocks had become more popular with institutional investors meant that there were more investors 'able and willing to use sophisticated and elaborate analytical techniques, including the present value approach, in arriving at investment decisions' (Bauman 1963, Preface).

The valuation approach of considering shares to be worth the present value of their future dividend stream did not supplant the simpler metrics. This was partly because of the difficulty of forecasting the numbers to put into the formulae: 'Increasing emphasis on earning power correspondingly increases the roughness of any calculation of intrinsic value, because estimation of earning power must place great emphasis on future expectations and in consequence is particularly dependent on intangible, qualitative forces' (Dowrie and Fuller 1950, 269–70). It was also partly due to the fact that choices of discount rate were arbitrary.[20] The present value approach was also blamed for overpricing 'growth stocks'. Graham et al. argued that 'no clear-cut arithmetic sets a limit to the present value of a constantly increasing earnings power. Such values could become "worth" any value set upon them by the market' (1962, 409). Worse: 'Our view is that in many of these cases the valuation process itself has given a speculative character to the purchase of these shares' (Graham et al. 1962, 58). Just as in the late 1990s, choice of valuation methodology appeared to influence the estimated intrinsic values and market prices of growth stocks.

The discounted cash flow model failed really to take off in the US until the 1980s and 1990s and the most recent stock market boom. The application of the capital asset pricing model, postulated in the 1960s (Sharpe 1964; Lintner 1965), allowed analysts to estimate an appropriate risk-adjusted discount rate for each share's discounted cash flow valuation, replacing the ad hoc approach used by Bauman (1963) and others. And yet, most equity analysts continued to use the P/E ratio. There are a number of reasons for this. First, the number of companies to be analysed by each analyst far exceeded the number of projects analysed by any one company. Forecasting cash flows for each company being analysed was too time-consuming a process. Second, the market crash of 1974 gave reason to the 'value' school once more, giving ratios another lease of life. Third, the dividend valuation model is highly sensitive to the dividend input: the more highly valued the share and the lower the dividend yield, the more sensitive the model is to small changes in estimates. Only when corporate financiers introduced the approach of valuing companies at the operating level and not the dividend level was this problem resolved (Copeland et al. 1990). Finally, as in the era of 'nifty fifty stocks', the share valuations of the late 1990s could not be explained by ratios. New sectors such as the Internet spawned companies with no balance sheets or earnings to speak of. Analysts were forced to turn to forecasting cash flows, and to assume high growth rates, to be able to determine values close to market prices. This trend was an international one. But it is still the case that although corporate finance analysts prefer discounted cash flow, equity analysts remain wedded to market multiples, be they price to book ratios, dividend yields or P/E ratios.

CONCLUSION

This chapter has traced the history of equity valuation techniques from the late nineteenth century to the late twentieth century. I have shown how investors initially tried to value shares using book value, and dividend yield using bond valuation techniques applied to riskier equities. They looked for asset backing and a dividend yield higher than that for bonds, which came ahead of shares in the queue for income.

The chapter has highlighted how US analysts switched from dividend yield to earnings yield and the P/E ratio much earlier than in the UK, due to a traditionally lower payout ratio and high profits during and after the First World War. Edgar Laurence Smith, writing in 1925, showed how an equity portfolio would have easily outperformed a bond portfolio in the early twentieth century due to the miracle of compound growth; that is, the miracle of reinvested earnings. Investors began to value shares using price-earnings ratios, with growth firms valued at stratospheric multiples in the boom of the late 1920s, and P/E ratios of over 100 deemed acceptable for the new high-tech industries. *Plus ça change*. British analysts lagged behind, treating earnings as a backdrop to dividends, partly due to higher dividend payout ratios, partly due to poor disclosure in profit and loss accounts, partly due to complex taxation making earnings after corporate tax difficult to calculate and partly because British firms had less profits to analyse.

Discounted cash flow was recommended as early as the 1930s for equity valuation but was slow to come in as it required computer technology which was not commonly available until the 1980s. I can remember trying to value a bond's cash flows using a computer the size of a room, when working at an investment bank in the 1970s. But even though discounted cash flow is the methodology taught in universities and used by equity analysts, the old-fashioned methods – which offer relative values rather than intrinsic values – are still the most commonly used.

NOTES

1. Investors required wealth since the high individual nominal value of shares (perhaps £100) excluded less wealthy investors from acquiring them (Jefferys 1954). Later issues of shares with nominal values of 5 shillings (25p) or even 1 shilling (5p) (in the boom year of 1927 (Thomas 1978, p. 33)) put ordinary share investment within the reach of a greater number of individuals.
2. For example, the Geo. Trollope & Colls issue of 1899 gave preferential treatment to applications from their customers, and the 1913 issue for shares in Claudius Ash Sons & Co. Limited, merchants and manufacturers of mineral teeth and dental materials, offered preferential treatment to members of the dental profession. The 1928 placing of Solignum shares was initiated by writing to the customers asking for expressions of interest (London Guildhall Library: MS18000, 1899, 1913, 1928).
3. For example, between 1910 and 1920, the number of shareholders in United States Steel increased from 22 000 to 104 000 and, for American Telephone & Telegraph, from 35 000 to 120 000 (Sturgis 1924, p. vi).
4. For example, the Thames Iron Works & Shipbuilding & Engineering Company was floated in 1899, the year in which it acquired John Penn & Sons.
5. For further discussion of the provision of profit and loss accounts and balance sheets by English companies in the nineteenth and twentieth centuries, see Rutterford (2011), especially Appendix I.
6. The 1929 Companies Act required information to be given on investments in subsidiaries and amounts due to and from them. Also, goodwill had to be separately stated (Edwards 1989, pp. 134–6).
7. For example, Graham and Dodd (1934, 43–4) criticized over half the 'important enterprises' of the United States for failing to disclose, separately, sales, net earnings, depreciation, interest charges, non-operating income, income taxes, dividends paid and surplus adjustments, with Pocohontas Fuel Company providing no income statement at all.
8. Although the 'times covered' method was condemned as 'thoroughly objectionable' by Graham and Dodd (1934, p. 106), and criticized much later by the *Investors' Chronicle* (1949, p. 21).
9. This industry approach began with railroads, but was soon extended to bank shares, insurance company shares, mines and utilities, as well as industrials. For an early example, see Ward (1852).
10. Although Smith (1925) in his comparison of US common stock returns and bond returns also used short-term commercial paper as a benchmark. Raynes (1928, 1937) in comparable studies on UK data used equivalent corporate fixed interest securities from the same companies as the ordinary shares chosen.

11. Graham et al. (1962, p. 482) cite an average of roughly two-thirds as the norm between 1871 and 1930.
12. However, allowing for reserves, the dividend policy of British firms does not seem to have differed too much in practice from that of their US counterparts.
13. Although studies by Raynes (1928) (updated in 1937) found that ordinary shares did outperform the bonds from the same industrial companies when looking at the 25-year period to 31 March 1927.
14. These texts were aimed at university students who were future entrants to the burgeoning security analysis industry, professionalized by the creation of the Chartered Financial Analysts and their journal, the *Financial Analysts' Journal.*
15. Keynes compared the stock market to a beauty contest and to a casino. He believed that stock market prices were influenced more by speculative factors than by the real worth of assets (Andersen 1983–84, p. 282), and that fair value analysis was a waste of time for all but a subset of stocks (Poitras 2002, p. 15).
16. The 'stability' and 'growth' schools still live on under the more modern pseudonyms of 'value' and 'growth'.
17. Although certain sectors, such as banks and utilities, continued to be valued in terms of dividend yield (Barker 1999).
18. Soldofsky (1966), in a survey of share valuation models, cites Sutton as the first source of varying annuity tables. Faulhaber and Baumol (1988) refer to the work of a German forester, Faustmann (1849), in which he applied present value theory to optimizing the value of forestry land.
19. Graham et al. (1962, p. 18) had been reluctant to admit that the falling dividend payout ratio, observable from the 1940s onwards, was not a temporary phenomenon.
20. For example, in the numerous articles published in the *Financial Analysts' Journal* and *The Journal of Finance* in the 1950s, discount rates of between 5 and 9 per cent were used, with little reason given

BIBLIOGRAPHY

Primary Sources

Rothschild Archive, New Court, St. Swithin's Lane, London. Prospectuses, 1858–1916 (XIII/230).
Guildhall Library, Manuscripts Section, Aldermanbury, London. Applications for Listing (MS18000).

Secondary Sources

Andersen, T.A. (1983–84), 'Some implications of the efficient capital market hypothesis', *Journal of Post Keynesian Economics*, **6**, 281–94.

Bailey, D. (2003), *Hichens, Harrison & Co. plc: 1808–2003*, London: Hichens, Harrison & Co.

Barker, R. (1999), 'Survey and market-based evidence of industry-dependence in analysts' preferences between the dividend yield and price-earnings ratio valuation models', *Journal of Business Finance and Accounting*, **26** (3–4), 393–418.

Baskin, J.B. and P.J. Miranti Jr. (1997), *A History of Corporate Finance*, Cambridge: Cambridge University Press.

Bauman, W.S. (1963), *Estimating the Present Value of Common Stocks by the Variable Rate Method*, Research Monograph 61, Ann Arbour, MI: Bureau of Business Research, Graduate School of Business Administration, University of Michigan.

Blakey, G.G. (1994), *The Post-War History of the London Stock Market*, Didcot: Management Books.

Brealey, R.A. and S.C. Myers (2003), *Principles of Corporate Finance*, 6th edn, New York: McGraw-Hill.

Caudwell, F.W.H. (1930), *A Practical Guide to Investment*, London: Effingham-Wilson.

Clendenin, J.C. and M. Van Greave (1954), 'Growth and common stock values', *Journal of Finance*, **9** (4), 365–76.

Copeland, T., T. Koller and J. Murrin (2000), *Valuation: Measuring and Managing the Value of Companies*, 3rd edn, New York: John Wiley & Sons.

Damadoran, A. (2006), *Damadoran on Valuation*, 2nd edn, New York: John Wiley & Sons.

Davis, L. (1996), 'The capital markets and industrial concentration: the US and UK, a comparative study', *Economic History Review*, Second Series, XIX(2): 255–72.

Dowrie, G.W. and D.R. Fuller (1950), *Investments*, New York: John Wiley & Sons.

Durand, D. (1957), *Bank Stock Prices and the Bank Capital Problem*, New York: National Bureau of Economic Research.

Edwards, J.R. (1989), *A History of Financial Accounting*, London: Routledge.
Evans, G.H. and G.E. Barnett (1940), *Principles of Investment*, Boston, MA: Houghton Mifflin Company.
Faulhaber, G.R. and W.J. Baumol (1988), 'Economists as innovators: practical products of theoretical research', *Journal of Economic Literature*, **26**, 577–600.
Faustmann, M. (1849), 'Martin Faustmann and the evolution of discounted cash flow', *Commonwealth Forestry Institute Paper*, Oxford: University of Oxford, reprinted 1968.
Fisher, I. (1907), *The Rate of Interest*, New York: Macmillan.
Fisher, I. (1930), *The Stock Market Crash and After*, New York: Macmillan.
Geisst, C.R. (1999), *Wall Street*, New York: Oxford University Press.
Gordon, M.S. (1962), *The Investment, Financing and Valuation of the Corporation*, Homewood, IL: Irwin.
Graham, B. and D.L. Dodd (1934), *Security Analysis*, New York: McGraw-Hill.
Graham, B., D.L. Dodd and S. Cottle (1962), *Security Analysis: Principles and Techniques*, New York: McGraw-Hill.
Guild, S.E. (1931), *Stock Growth and Discount Tables*, Boston, MA: Financial Publishing Company.
Investors Chronicle (1949), *Practical Investment*, London: Eyre & Spottiswoode.
Jefferys, B. (1954), 'The denomination and character of shares 1855–1885', in E.M. Carus-Wilson (ed.), *Essays in Economic History*, London: Edward Arnold, pp. 344–57.
Keynes, J.M. (1925), 'An American study of shares versus bonds as permanent investments: book review', *The Nation and The Athenaeum, Supplement*, 157–8.
Kobrak, C. (2002), 'Notes on the equity revolution and accounting systems: a comparison of Germany and the United States', Conference Paper, European Business History Conference, Helsinki, August.
le Maistre, G.H. (1926), *Investments for All: Their Importance, Selection and Management*, London: John Murray.
Lintner, J. (1965), 'Security prices, risk, and maximal gains from diversification', *Journal of Finance*, December, 587–615.
Maltby, J. (1999), '"A sort of guide, philosopher and friend": the rise of the professional auditor in Britain', *Accounting, Business and Financial History*, **9** (1), 29–50.
Maltby, J. (2003), '"We do not share the troubles of our trans-atlantic cousins": the statutory framework for accounting in the UK and the US in the inter-war period', Working Paper, University of Sheffield.
May, A.W. (1939), 'American and European valuation of equity capital: a comparison', *American Economic Review*, **29** (4), 734–45.
Pitts, M.V. (2001), 'In praise of the "other" William Armstrong: a nineteenth century British engineer and early management consultant', *Accounting History*, **6** (2), 33–58.
Poitras, G. (2002), 'The philosophy of investment', *Journal of Post Keynesian Economics*, **25**, 105–21.
Preda, A. (2001), 'The rise of the popular investor: financial knowledge and investing in England and France, 1840–1880', *Sociological Quarterly*, **42** (2), 205–32.
Preinreich, G. (1936), 'The fair value and yield of common stock', *Accounting Review*, **11**, 130–41.
Raynes, H.E. (1928), 'The place of ordinary stocks and shares (as distinct from fixed interest bearing securities) in the investment of life assurance funds', *Journal of the Institute of Actuaries*, **59**, 21–35.
Raynes, H.E. (1937), 'Equities and fixed interest stocks during twenty-five years', *Journal of the Institute of Actuaries*, **68**, 483–507.
Rutterford, J.M. (2006), '"The world was their oyster": investment diversification pre-World War I', in J.M. Rutterford, M. Upton and D. Kodwani (eds), *Financial Strategy*, Chichester: Wiley Press, pp. 5–24.
Rutterford, J.M. (2011), '"Propositions put forward by quite honest men": company prospectuses and their contents, 1856 to 1940', *Business History*, **53** (6), 866–99.
Scott, P. (2002), '"Towards the 'cult of the equity'?" Insurance companies and the interwar capital market', *Economic History Review*, **55** (1), 78–104.
Sharpe, W.F. (1964), 'Capital asset prices: a theory of market equilibrium under conditions of risk', *Journal of Finance*, September, 425–42.
Shannon, H.A. (1954), 'The limited companies of 1866–1883', in E.M. Carus-Wilson (ed.), *Essays in Economic History*, London: Edward Arnold, pp. 380–415.
Shiller, R.J. (2001), *Irrational Exuberance*, Princeton: Princeton University Press.
Smith, E.L. (1925), *Common Stocks as Long-Term Investments*, New York, USA and London, UK: Macmillan.
Soldofsky, R.M. (1966), 'A note on the history of bond tables and stock valuation models', *The Journal of Finance*, **21**, 103–10.
Stacey's Guide to Stock Exchange Investment (1923), London: Basing Syndicate.
Sturgis, H.S. (1924), *Investment: A New Profession*, New York: Macmillan.
Sutton, W. (1882), *Institute of Actuaries' Text Book of the Principles of Interest, Life Annuities and Assurances, Part I, Interest Including Annuities Certain*, London: Layton.
Thomas, W.A. (1978), *The Finance of British Industry 1918–1976*, London: Methuen.

Todhunter, R. (1901), *The Institute of Actuaries Text-Book on Compound Interest and Annuities*, London: Layton.
Toms, S. and J.F. Wilson (2003), '"Scale, scope and accountability: towards a new paradigm of British business history', *Business History*, **45**(4); 1–24.
Vissink, H.G.A. (1985), *Economic and Financial Reporting in England and the Netherlands: A Comparative Study over the Period 1850 to 1914*, Assen/Maastricht: Van Gorcum.
Ward, R.A. (1852), *A Treatise on Investments*, 2nd edn, London.
Williams, J.B. (1938), *The Theory of Investment Value*, Cambridge, MA: Harvard University Press.
Withers, H. (1930), *The Quicksands of the City and a Way Through for Investors*, London: Jonathan Cape.
Young, T.E. (1919), *A Plain Guide to Investment and Finance*, London: Macdonald & Evans.

5 The evolution of the managed funds industry: investment trusts in nineteenth-century Britain

Elaine Hutson

INTRODUCTION

The managed funds industry has a long and chequered history. The pooling of securities to form investment funds can be traced to France in the late eighteenth century, when vehicles comprising life annuities issued by the French government were traded on the Paris bourse (Taylor 1962; Velde and Weir 1992; Poitras 2011). The first investment fund with an explicit diversification requirement was the Eendragt Maakt Magt ('Unity Creates Strength'), founded in Holland in 1774 (Rouwenhorst 2005). Another early diversified fund was the Société Générale des Pay-Bas pour favoriser l'Industrie Nationale, which was created in Brussels in 1822 (Cassis 1990). However, it is the British funds of the late nineteenth and early twentieth centuries that are the direct antecedents of the modern managed funds industry.

The managed funds industry in nineteenth-century Britain grew out of an investment environment that saw declining government bond rates and an immense expansion of the range of risky securities available. A series of speculative manias and panics in the first half of the nineteenth century made the concept of diversification appealing to a burgeoning middle class who wanted to protect their capital at the same time as preserving living standards in a climate of falling interest rates, but did not have sufficient funds to diversify efficiently on their own. The first British fund – the Foreign & Colonial Government Trust[1] – was established in 1868. Listed on the London Stock Exchange, this fund paid a fixed dividend, and diversification was assured via a requirement in the Foreign & Colonial's prospectus that no more than 10 per cent of the fund could be invested in the securities of any one issuer.

In this chapter, I focus on the early years of the British investment trust industry, from its inception in 1868 until the fallout from the Barings crisis in the 1890s. I begin with a brief history of the British investment trust industry during this period, then discuss the forces that contributed to the industry's genesis and growth. Next, I detail the features of the early trusts, and demonstrate the remarkable similarity of the Foreign & Colonial Government Trust to the Eendragt Maakt Mag, founded almost a century earlier. While many of the early investment trusts were well managed, some were not, and I discuss some of the scams that abounded, particularly during the speculative stock market boom in the late 1880s.

A BRIEF HISTORY

The founders of the Foreign & Colonial Government Trust were Samuel Laing, James Thompson Mackenzie and Philip Rose. These men were well known and well respected in London business and society. Samuel Laing was a businessman, lawyer and member of parliament, and is particularly known for his involvement in the financing and management of the early railway companies. Philip Rose was Disraeli's lawyer and advisor. The Chairman was Lord Westbury, a barrister, member of parliament and former Lord Chancellor. The Foreign & Colonial Government Trust proved popular, and over the next few years the founders launched four more 'issues', which were essentially separate trusts under the same management. This fund still exists as the Foreign & Colonial Investment Trust.[2]

While London remained the main centre for trust development, several investment trusts were established during the nineteenth century in Scotland. The First Scottish American Investment Trust was founded in 1873 by merchant Robert Fleming in the then wealthy Scottish city of Dundee. Having discovered the investment potential of the United States during a visit a few years earlier, Fleming's trusts specialized in American securities, particularly railroad bonds. The prospectus for the First Scottish American Investment Trust specified a capital raising of £150 000, but the response from potential investors was so great that this was increased to £300 000 (Fowler 1928, p. 345). The trust started out with 30 stocks, each comprising no more than 7 per cent of the portfolio (Burton and Corner 1968, p. 20).

By 1875, there were 23 (London-listed) trusts with a total market capitalization of £32 131 640, which was 0.6 per cent of the market value of the London Stock Exchange (Scratchley 1875, p. 8). The trusts had faced their first major challenge in the form of default in many of their constituent securities. The years 1873–76 saw a severe recession and the end of the American Civil War, and numerous foreign governments and railroad companies defaulted on their bonds. Several securities held by the fourth issue of the Foreign & Colonial Government Trust were in default – chief among them the bonds of the war-ravaged southern US states: the Alabama 8 percents, the City of Mobile (Alabama) 8 percents, the Louisiana 8 percents, the Louisiana 6 percents and the Spanish 3 percents. The American Investment Trust, formed in March 1873 and specializing in railroad bonds, suffered from defaults on the bonds of:

> the Detroit and Milwaukee, the Gilman, Clinton, and Springfield, Missouri, Kansas, and Texas, and Mobile and Montgomery railroads, and upon the shares of the Michigan Central railroad company, and from only one half-year's interest having been received upon the Canada Southern, Toledo, Peoria and Warsaw, and Toledo, Wabash and Western railroad companies. (Scratchley 1875, 25)

Despite these and other defaults, in 1875 all of the trusts paid their dividends and expenses in full (Scratchley 1875, pp. 21–33). But the recession worsened, and in 1876 several trusts defaulted or partially defaulted. These included the Governments & Guaranteed Securities Permanent Trust, which a group of shareholders tried to have wound up, eventually taking legal action against the trustees in 1879 (Walker 1940, p. 348). The legal case that resulted threw up a second major challenge to the industry within a few years of the first. Following the Companies Acts of 1856 and 1862 which gave equityholders limited liability, a period of speculative mania followed by panic left the limited liability company with a severely dented reputation. According to *The Economist*, the reason most of the early funds were established as trusts rather than companies was 'an evident attempt to avoid the now unpopular name of company' (cited in Walker 1940, p. 341). The judgment in the Governments & Guaranteed Securities Permanent Trust case decreed that the trust was illegal, being an 'association of more than twenty persons for the acquisition of gain' (Stutchbury 1964, p. 2). Most of the investment trusts responded by incorporating. The Submarine Cables Trust, however, refused to incorporate, and after an order for it to be wound up, the trustees appealed and the original judgment against the Governments & Guaranteed Securities Permanent Trust was reversed (Fowler 1928, 349). By that time, however, all of the other trusts had converted to companies, and the Submarine Cables Trust was the only fund to remain a trust. The term 'investment trust', however, continued to be used by the industry.

Investment trusts experienced a boom during the late 1880s, and in 1888 the London Stock Exchange established a separate official list for investment trusts (Steiner 1929, p. 25). Estimates of the extent of the boom differ. Burton and Corner (1968) suggest that at the end of 1886 there were 28, and that between 1887 and 1890, 70 new funds were formed, giving a total of nearly 100 by 1890. Burton and Corner (1968) admit, however, that some of these were probably not pure investment trusts, and may have been mixtures of holding, finance and investment companies. Cassis (1990) suggests that there were only 12 trusts quoted on the London Stock Exchange in 1886, with a nominal paid-up capital of £5 million. He concurs, however, with Burton and Corner on an additional 70 having been formed by 1890, giving a total paid-up capital of £50 million.

The Barings crisis of 1890 pricked the speculative stock market bubble of the late 1880s, and with it the boom in investment trusts. The trusts holding South American securities were the first to encounter trouble (Burton and Corner 1968, p. 35). As the crisis turned into a major economic downturn, and as the United States followed Britain into recession in 1893, all of the trusts were adversely affected to a greater or lesser degree. Dividends were suspended and stock values slumped. Those that had been long established (having purchased their portfolio securities before the late 1880s boom) were the least effected, but even some of the more respectable trusts saw their equity entirely wiped out. Quoting *The Economist* from May 1896, Rutterford (2009) states that the average fall in the investment funds' stock prices in the years after the Barings crisis was 35 per cent, including the total loss of some of the 'more speculative' investment trusts. Among the best trusts, only seven had a value greater than the issue price (Steiner 1929, p. 29). Others were liquidated or merged. In the fallout, it became clear that several trusts had been near-fraudulently managed, engaging in several high-risk activities other than fund management, and fleecing stockholders in the process. I will give some examples of these trusts in the section 'Scams and Profiteering'.

GENESIS AND GROWTH

In his book *On Average Investment Trusts* (1875), Arthur Scratchley, who was a lawyer and an actuary, begins with a section entitled 'Origin of trust associations'. In this he warns against the evils of speculation, and strongly advocates investment trusts on the basis that they offer investors the benefits of diversification. In the next section of his book, Scratchley liberally quotes the 'opinions of public writers and others'. It is clear that these early British funds were marketed to smaller investors as an alternative to the standard investment vehicle of the day – consols (British government bonds) – and that the founders of these funds had a good understanding of risk as well as the benefits of diversification. A Mr Ray, who was an 'experienced manager of an important Trust', advocates investment trusts as a better alternative to government bonds for smaller investors. It is worth quoting this passage in full:

> Many persons believe that 3 per cent. stock in the English Funds is the best of all investments, yet they seek to obtain a larger interest. The great principle involved is *how to obtain a high rate of interest with the utmost possible security*. There are many people to whom the profitable investment of their small capital is of vital importance. They may be, and many are, entirely dependent on the interest; in such cases 3 per cent from Consols would be a meagre pittance, insufficient even for support, and many a heart would be gladdened if an increased interest could be obtained and the capital remain safe. It should be borne in mind, however, that if investments bearing a high rate of interest are touched at all, it should be on a system to divide and sub-divide them so as to secure an average. It is obvious that people with a small amount to invest cannot secure the advantages of high interest and that safety which is afforded by a combination of various securities, and it is questionable whether investors of anything under £10 000 can secure equal advantages to those offered by the principle of cooperation in investments carried out by trusts and companies established for that purpose. (Scratchely 1875, pp. 3–4)

This passage hints at two related explanations for why the first trusts appeared when they did – during the second half of the 1860s. The first relates to falling yields in the government bond market, and a trend that had been apparent from the 1820s for investors to seek higher yields in order to maintain their living standards. A second, related factor is that a series of speculative manias and subsequent panics during the first half of the century – particularly in foreign markets – led investors to search for a way to earn higher returns while minimizing the chance of loss of both capital and income.

In the early 1800s, consols yielded between 4 and 5 per cent. For most of the nineteenth century, the consol yield trended downward, and by the early 1890s it was close to 2 per cent. A series of debt conversions began in 1822 with the replacement of the 'navy five percents' with bonds paying 4 per cent (Steiner, 1929, p. 18). Four years later, a 4 per cent consol issue was converted to bonds paying 3.5 per cent. The converted 'navy fives' were again converted to 3.5 per cent in 1830 (Morgan and Thomas 1962, p. 115). These conversions would have substantially reduced the incomes of people relying on the interest from government bonds for their living expenses. Consider the plight of a widow with an endowment of £5000 invested in the 'navy fives'. Her income would have fallen from £250 in 1820 to £175 in 1830 – a reduction of £75 or 30 per cent. This would have necessitated either substantial retrenchment, or alternatively have sent the suffering widow in quest of a higher-yielding investment.

Several economic historians have at least partly attributed several periods of speculative mania and panic between the 1820s and the 1860s to investors seeking higher returns in order to retain the living standards that they enjoyed before the government bond conversions (Steiner 1929; Morgan and Thomas 1962; Kindleberger 1993, 1996). In the 1820s and 1830s, the mania was for foreign government bonds as well as company stocks, while the boom of 1845 and the subsequent panic of 1847 was the first of the railroad bubbles. During the 1860s, following the passage of the Companies Acts, a boom in registration of limited liability companies was followed by a panic in 1866 (Morgan and Thomas 1962, p. 131). The early investment trusts appeared after an unprecedented four decades of speculative manias and panics, and only two years after the first crash in the stocks of limited liability companies. This was not a new phenomenon; according to Kindleberger (1993, p. 160), the debt conversion in 1717 contributed to the South Sea Bubble. The genesis of the Eendragt Maakt Magt seems to have been similar; its formation in 1774 was preceded by the financial crisis of 1772–73 (Rouwenhorst 2005).

The period of greatest growth in investment trusts in the late 1880s coincided with the biggest debt conversion of the nineteenth century. Falling yields during the late 1870s and 1880s allowed the British government to convert almost all of its long-term debt from 3 per cent to 2.75 per cent, and by 1903 it was 2.5 per cent (Morgan and Thomas 1962, p. 116; Burton and Corner 1968, p. 29). Kindleberger (1993) suggests that the conversion in 1887 fed speculative mania for stocks of the late 1880s; the exponential growth in investment trusts from 1887 to 1890 accompanied the stock market boom.

TYPICAL FEATURES OF THE EARLY TRUSTS

The Foreign & Colonial Government Trust had many features in common with the Eendragt Maakt Magt.[3] These features are summarized in Table 5.1. Both funds used a fee system that will be familiar with investors today, comprising a subscription fee and an annual management fee. They charged similar management fees (0.25 and 0.20 per cent), but investors in the British fund paid an up-front fee of five times the fee charged to investors in the Dutch fund – 2.5 per cent (that is, £2 10s per £100 of stock) compared to 0.5 per cent. Most of the early British trusts were 'fixed' in the sense that they paid a fixed dividend, they had a limited life, and the composition of the portfolio was set at inception and could be changed only in exceptional circumstances. The Foreign & Colonial and the Eendragt Maakt Magt both promised a fixed dividend – 6 per cent and 4 per cent respectively – and both were planned to have fixed lives, of 24 and 25 years respectively. These periods were calculated on the basis that by the end of 24 or 25 years all of the share certificates would have been redeemed, after which time any remaining funds would be distributed to investors; in the case of the Foreign & Colonial Government Trust, investors were issued with 'reversion coupons' which gave them entitlement pro rata to any remaining funds. A major difference between the two funds, however, was that while the Foreign & Colonial's investment portfolio was fixed for the life of the trust, this does not appear to have been the case for the Eendragt Maakt Magt, although the latter's complex diversification requirement would in practice have allowed the managers little discretion to rebalance the portfolio.

Both funds had explicit diversification requirements. The Eendragt Maakt Magt's was more complex than the Foreign & Colonial's, and resulted in portfolio comprising a large range of securities from a variety of issuers (no more than two or three from one particular issuer), whereas the Foreign & Colonial simply promised to invest no more than 10 per cent of the portfolio in the securities of any one government. Both were

Table 5.1 Main features of the Foreign & Colonial Government Trust and the Eendragt Maakt Magt

	Foreign & Colonial Government Trust	Eendragt Maakt Magt
Up-front fee	2.50%	0.50%
Management fee	0.25%	0.20%
Dividend promised	Fixed 6%	Fixed 4%
Anticipated life	24 years (maximum)	25 years
Constituent investments	Foreign government bonds	Foreign bonds and plantation loans
Diversification requirement	The portfolio was to contain not more than 10% in the stock of any one government	The portfolio was divided into 20 classes; each class was to consist of at least 20 to 25 securities, with no more than 2 or 3 of a particular security
Extent of discretion to rebalance the portfolio	Portfolio composition could be changed only in exceptional circumstances	Tightly restricted due to detailed diversification requirement
Tradable?	Yes	Yes
Information on constituent bonds made public?	Yes	Yes
Early redemption by lottery?	Yes	Yes

Notes: This table provides the main features of the Foreign & Colonial Government Trust and the Eendragt Maakt Magt, as detailed in their prospectuses. The information is drawn from Scratchley (1875) and Rouwenhorst (2005) respectively.

tradable, being listed on the Amsterdam (Eendragt Maakt Magt) and London (Foreign & Colonial Government Trust) stock exchanges. Interestingly, both funds published lists of their constituent securities, with the Eendragt Maakt Magt printing a list of them in the share documentation, and the Foreign & Colonial naming the issuing governments in its prospectus.

A remarkable feature of both funds was early redemption by lottery. While the actual method of lottery was not made clear in the Foreign & Colonial Government Trust's prospectus, the Eendragt Maakt Magt's prospectus explains the rather complex lottery process in detail. These lotteries would have been a bonanza for the early redeemers, particularly if the shares had been issued at a discount. This was the case for the Foreign & Colonial's shares; their par value was £100, but they were issued at £85. If an investor's shares were picked for redemption at £100 after a year, for example, they would have earned the £6 coupon plus a capital gain of £15, giving an annual return (on the £85 outlay) of 25 per cent. It is reported in Scratchley (1875, p. 18) that by 1875, of the Foreign & Colonial's 5883 certificates issued, 1745 had been redeemed at a cost of £174 500. The early redeemers had in total received a premium of £26 175 in addition to the interest earned over the seven-year holding period.

Lotteries were a common feature of early securities issues during this period; there is in fact a long history of their use in financial markets (Rouwenhorst 2005; Kindleberger 1993). Gambling was very much part of upper-class culture in the seventeenth to nineteenth centuries, and Kindleberger (1993, p. 175) argues that this filtered down to the emerging middle class:

> Gambling was close to a requirement. An aristocratic attribute to take risks and not to be concerned with mundane safety – values summed up in such slogans as 'never take cover' or 'never count the change' – spread ultimately to the middle classes. Being the major borrowers of the time, 'governments pandered to the gambling instinct (or acquired trait) with lottery loans and tontines'. (Kindleberger 1993, p. 175)

It is perhaps the case that in order to compete with government securities and possibly direct investment in foreign government and other bonds, promoters of investment funds felt it necessary to include lottery-like features.

Most of the early British trusts had features similar to the Foreign & Colonial. The trust deeds limited the holding of any one security to between 3 and 10 per cent of the portfolio, and the benefits of diversification (or 'averaging' as it was then called), particularly for small investors, were the main selling points used by trust promoters. The trusts had fixed dividends, and like the Foreign & Colonial they tended to be fixed in portfolio composition. The Scottish trusts were an exception, but even in Robert Fleming's trusts there was little portfolio turnover; Fleming 'always insisted on a most careful and thorough investigation before making a purchase' (Gilbert 1939, p. 16). This feature of the early funds, however, was relaxed over time. By the late 1880s and into the 1890s, investment trusts were being more actively managed, and managers were increasingly reluctant to reveal the composition of their portfolios. This was a major shortcoming of the industry, and it was widely criticized, particularly during the boom of the 1880s when *The Economist* labelled such funds 'blind pools' (Burton and Corner 1968, p. 30). Another feature that changed over time was the trusts' limited life; most investment funds formed after the legal challenges of the late 1870s were established as perpetual.

Scratchley (1875) provides data and in some cases other information on all the investment trusts that existed at the time, including such features as capital raised, par value of the shares, promised interest and issue price. Following the launch of the Foreign & Colonial in 1868, several others followed: the Submarine Cables Trust in 1871, three issues of the Government Stock Investment Company in 1872 and 1873, and the Share Investment Trust and the Governments & Guaranteed Securities Trust in 1872. In 1873, nine new trusts appeared, and five were created in 1874. Several features of the funds formed after 1872 – particularly those related to capital structure – diverged substantially from the very prudent model of the Foreign & Colonial. Although we cannot be certain that Scratchley provided full information on each trust, it appears that leverage became standard in funds initiated from 1873. Leverage was initially obtained via preference shares, but debentures soon emerged in the capital structures of the trusts. Many funds issued a range of securities, including ordinary shares (sometimes called deferred shares), preference shares and debentures. Fund managers of the time well understood the effect of leverage on returns to shareholders (Burton and Corner 1968, p. 49). The Share Investment Trust was the first to use leverage. This trust issued what would be known today as a 'stapled' security. Each £100 subscribed gave the investor a preference share certificate promising a fixed coupon of 6 per cent, and a 'deferred' certificate that gave the holder entitlement to 'surplus income' (Walker 1940, p. 346).

SCAMS AND PROFITEERING

Although many nineteenth century investment trusts were prudently and respectably managed, others were not. This is particularly the case for the funds established during the boom years of the late 1880s, many of which appear to have been established as fraudulent operations (Cassis 1990). This would hardly have been unusual in London in the late nineteenth century, as White (2007) colourfully describes:

> Insurance and banking frauds, crooked stock-jobbers, wild international speculations in gold and diamond mines, and reckless gambles in domestic company fluctuations, all fuelled City money fever till the century's end. As one critic complained in 1894, 'We are overrun with rotten limited liability companies, flooded with swindling "bucket shops", crashes and collapses rain upon us, and the "promoter" and the "guinea-pig" still and ever enjoy impunity'. (White 2007, p. 169)

For investment trust promoters wanting to enrich themselves at the expense of shareholders, the method of choice was the 'founder's share'.[4] Founders' shares were issued to trust founders and other hangers-on, supposedly in return for preliminary expenses and underwriting. Dividends were paid on founders' shares after preference and ordinary shareholders received their agreed dividend payment, and were linked to 'profit' rather than to the par value of the share.

The Railway Share Trust Company, established in April 1873, was an early issuer of founders' shares, and it was also highly levered. Of a total capital of £2000200, £1 million comprised 'A' (ordinary) shares, and £1 million in 'B' (preference) shares. The remaining £200 of capital comprised 200 founders' shares with a par value of £1. This trust had a sister company, formed a month earlier in March 1873 – the Railway Debenture Trust Company. This was probably the first to issue founders' shares, and its leverage was impressive: the prospectus allowed for the issue of debentures of up to five times the value of subscribed ordinary capital. The ordinary shareholders of this fund actually bore even more risk than this leverage implies, because the ordinary shares were only partly paid. But the founders' shares were, of course, fully paid and the prospectus granted founders 10 per cent of the profits in every year in which not less than 6 per cent was declared on the ordinary paid-up capital. The founders of the Railway Debenture Trust Company profited substantially in the two years after its formation. The founders received £3500 (a return of 1650 per cent) in each year (Scratchley 1875).

Abuses relating to founders' shares reached their zenith in the late 1880s. *The Economist* (14 June 1890) describes the returns to founders in the Trustees, Executors & Securities Insurance Corporation in 1889: the holders of £1000 of founders' shares earned £84000, or 8300 per cent. In another example, the Commercial Union Brewery Investment Corporation in 1889 granted founders a dividend of £9435 on 200 £1 fully paid shares (*The Economist*, 12 July 1890) – an annual return of over 4600 per cent.

These colossal returns were partly the result of leverage. Given that dividends were paid to founders after preference and ordinary shareholders received their fixed dividends, the use of founders' shares encouraged additional revenue-raising and risk-taking, and founders and managers undertook all sorts of activities unrelated to trust management. These included:

> acting as trustees or executors; hiring safes and acting as custodians of valuables; investing in securities; making advances on security of real estate; dealing in securities, land and mortgages, bills, promissory notes . . . issuing shares on commission; promoting new companies and acting as underwriters of new capital issues. (Burton and Corner 1968, p. 30)

The worst abuses saw trusts becoming involved in equity raisings – the initial public offerings (IPOs) of new companies. The conflict of interest is obvious: if an IPO was not fully subscribed, unsold shares of (usually) doubtful worth could simply be absorbed by the trust. *The Economist* (15 March 1890) estimated that at least 90 per cent of the profit of the Trustees, Executors, & Securities Insurance Corporation was earned from company promotions and underwriting. These sorts of practices had in fact been going on, but perhaps not so brazenly, for more than 25 years. Scratchley (1875, p. 28) notes that the Railway Share Trust Company – which, as discussed above, was a pioneer of founders' shares – 'made the larger part of its profits from "commissions and other business," and not merely from investing the funds entrusted to it'.

The Economist warned of the conflicts of interest that resulted in supernormal profits for holders of founders' shares in three named investment trusts:

> Of course we do not suggest that there is anything improper in these gentlemen or anybody else taking founders' shares, but we hardly appreciate the frame of mind which reconciles the holding of such shares with the occupation of the fiduciary position of a director. In our view, a company director should have no rights, except to be paid his fees, which are not shared by the general body of proprietors. And, apart from that consideration, it is quite obvious that the joint stock principle could not be carried out successfully if it were subjected to *such a process of milking* as the three companies referred to, where the founders or their representatives, for an investment of £1,400 have received, or expect to receive, a million and a half sterling. (*The Economist* 3 May 1890).

After the Barings crisis and the subsequent collapse in financial markets, the £10 ordinary shares of Trustees, Executors, & Securities Insurance Corporation were trading at minus £2. The negative value is explained by the fact that the £10 par value was partly paid. The company had called the £7 unpaid portion of the share in order to repay debenture holders, and shareholders were willing to pay £2 to be relieved of this commitment (Burton and Corner 1968, p. 36).

By the turn of the century, a smaller, more conservatively managed investment trust industry emerged from the crisis of the 1890s. Of the estimated 100 investment trust companies that existed in 1890, 50 had been liquidated or merged by the 1920s, 30 of which had disappeared before the end of the 1890s (Burton and Corner 1968, p. 42). In 1903 the remaining trusts had a total capital value of £60 to £70 million, which was approximately 1 per cent of the market capitalization of the London Stock Exchange (Burton and Corner 1968, p. 45). It was due to these well-managed surviving funds, as well as to the fact that the benefits of diversification were well established, that the industry overcame the tarnished reputation it temporarily acquired after the revelations of profiteering during the late 1880s.

NOTES

1. In 1863, two collective investment vehicles were established in London: the International Financial Society and the London Financial Association. These organizations raised capital via public subscription and on-lent mostly to railroad companies. Being undiversified, they were not considered to be true investment trusts (Grayson 1928; Steiner 1929).
2. http://www.fandc.com/new/it/Default.aspx?id=78413.
3. The information on these two funds is drawn largely from Scratchley (1875) and Rouwenhorst (2005).
4. Echoes of the founders' share were subsequently to be found in the capital structures of several of the less respectable United States trusts during the 1920s; see Flynn (1930).

BIBLIOGRAPHY

Burton, H. and D.C. Corner (1968), *Investment and Unit Trusts in Britain and America*, London: Elek Books.
Cassis, Y. (1990), 'The emergence of a new financial institution: investment trusts in Britain 1870–1939', in J.J. Van Helten and Y. Cassis (eds), *Capitalism in a Mature Economy: Financial Institutions, Capital Exports and British Industry, 1870–1939*, Aldershot, UK and Brookfield, VT, USA: Edward Elgar, pp. 139–58.
Flynn, J.T. (1930), *Investment Trusts Gone Wrong*, New York: New Republic.
Fowler, J.F. (1928), *American Investment Trusts*, New York: Harper & Bros.
Gilbert, J.C. (1939), *A History of Investment Trusts in Dundee 1873–1938*, London: P.S. King.
Grayson, T.J. (1928), *Investment Trusts: Their Origin, Development and Operation*, New York: John Wiley & Sons.
Kindleberger, C.P. (1993), *A Financial History of Western Europe*, 2nd edn, Oxford: Oxford University Press.
Kindleberger, C.P. (1996), *Manias, Panics and Crashes*, 3rd edn, London: John Wiley & Sons.
Morgan, E.V. and W.A. Thomas (1962), *The Stock Exchange: Its History and Functions*, London: Elek Books.
Poitras, G. (2011), *Valuation of Equity Securities: History, Theory and Application*, Singapore and London: World Scientific.
Rouwenhorst, K.G. (2005), 'The origins of mutual funds', in W.N. Goetzmann and K.G. Rouwenhorst (eds), *The Origins of Value: The Financial Innovations that Created Modern Capital Markets*, Oxford: Oxford University Press.
Rutterford, J. (2009), 'Learning from one another's mistakes: investment trusts in the UK and the US, 1868–1940', *Financial History Review*, **16** (2), 157–81.
Scott, P. (2002), 'Towards the "cult of equity"? Insurance companies and the interwar capital market', *Economic History Review*, **55** (1), 78–104.
Scratchley, A. (1875), *On Average Investment Trusts*, London: Shaw & Sons.
Steiner, W.H. (1929), *Investment Trusts, American Experience*, New York: Adelphi Co.
Stutchbury, O.P. (1964), *The Management of Unit Trusts*, London: Thomas Skinner & Co.
Taylor, G.V. (1962), 'The Paris bourse on the eve of the revolution, 1781–1789', *American Historical Review*, **67** (4), 951–77.
Velde, F.R. and D.R. Weir (1992), 'The financial market and government debt policy in France, 1746–1793', *Journal of Economic History*, **52** (1), 1–39.
Walker, C.H. (1940), 'Unincorporated investment trusts in the nineteenth century', *Economic History (Supplement of The Economic Journal)*, **4** (15), 341–55.
White, J. (2007), *London in the Nineteenth Century*, London: Jonathan Cape.

PART II

STUDIES OF CURRENT STOCK MARKET GLOBALIZATION

6 The social closure of the stock exchange

Alexandru Preda

INTRODUCTION

The aim of this chapter is to discuss stock exchanges from a sociological point of view, as fundamental institutions of modern societies. The focus here will be on social closure – that is, on the processes through which institutional control mechanisms are set in place. These mechanisms contribute to providing stock exchanges with a distinct institutional identity, while integrating them within the social fabric. The steps I will undertake here are the following: first, I discuss the notion of social institution in relationship to those of control and identity. Second, I provide a brief overview of how the sociological literature – especially foundational works from the nineteenth century – have conceptualized stock exchanges. Third, I discuss the mechanisms of social control set in place by stock exchanges, especially during the nineteenth century. I investigate here the role of informational technologies as intrinsic to these mechanisms. Finally, I examine contemporary aspects of the social closure of stock exchanges. In light of the transformations that stock exchanges have gone through during the last decades or so, this may seem puzzling: the technologization, the shifts in the ownership structure, the emergence of alternative trading platforms seem to have weakened the stock exchange as a social institution, and so hence to have made social closure superfluous. I will argue that matters are more complex than that. And now, on to the first step: why is it important to discuss the social closure of stock exchanges?

SOCIAL INSTITUTIONS AND CLOSURE

What is a social institution, and what do we mean when we say that stock exchanges are institutions of modern societies? And what do we mean by the social closure of this institution? Note here the claim that stock exchanges are social institutions, and not merely economic institutions. This means that their relevance goes beyond a set of allocation functions: their impact on society is not reducible to the distribution of available resources, or to providing liquidity to firms and entrepreneurs. It means that stock exchanges have a political and cultural relevance as well. Stock exchanges are connected to other institutions: they are subject to external constraints; they have intra-institutional commitments, or face pressures coming from other institutions, among others. One solution would be to say that institutions are sets of formal rules of behaviour, together with sets of expectations about how these rules should be followed, or performed in everyday activities. Such sets would cover functional domains of society (see Abbott 2009, p. 404). This kind of definition, however, has several problems: first, not all rules are formal. In many situations, informal rules and understandings play a more important role than formal ones, not to mention that formality and informality can sometimes be at odds with each other. Second, we need to explain what makes such rules resilient: how is it possible that members of an institution follow them? And how can institutions change?

All these issues, and many more, have brought to attention at least two kinds of factors relevant for understanding how institutions work: the first kind is provided by informal elements such as customs and shared beliefs (for example Nee 2005, p. 55). The second is provided by the web of personal relationships supporting mutual obligations, partly codified and partly not, and having a rule-like force (Mohr and White 2008, p. 488). These obligations, which are concretized in everyday actions, constrain actors in a much more efficient way than abstract rules. Thus, from a sociological point of view, institutions are conceived as having a dual aspect, cultural and relational (Mohr and White 2008, p. 492; DiMaggio and Powell 1991, p. 65). The cultural aspect is understood as meaning, as shared beliefs or as values, while the relational aspect is provided by the social networks and groups within which patterns of meaning are produced and circulated. While the term 'meaning' is admittedly somewhat vague, we can specify it as consisting in the symbols with the help of which two sets of experiences are ordered (Geertz 1973, p. 49): on the one hand, experiences within the group, and on the other hand, the ways in which external observers experience group activities. These symbols are not abstract, but concrete and material: among others, they are incorporated in the artifacts enabling observers to experience group activities.

These arguments have at least the following consequences: social groups and networks evolving or consolidating into institutions will set up mechanisms of control which are intrinsic with respect to their identity (White 2008, p. 20). Institutions will then perpetuate these control mechanisms, upgrade and adapt them in response to external pressures, as well as to internal changes. This means that such groups will seek to establish and control the ways in which they perceive and define themselves, as well as the ways in which they are perceived by external observers. Mechanisms of control will also contribute to the legitimacy of groups and networks within society at large. There are several ways for achieving control: one would be to control access to group activities, by controlling the spatial, temporal and social means for participating into these activities. One can set up operating hours, for instance, or pick up a specific space where activities unfold, or set up criteria for group membership such as wealth, education or personal recommendations. Mostly, groups will use a mix of all these criteria for controlling access. Another mechanism would be to control the symbolic and social arrangements through which external observers can access these activities. Of course, one could argue here that external observers can directly access such activities by simply looking at what the group is doing. The notion of control, as required by the group's identity, however, would preclude this: the group in question would not allow uncontrolled direct observation, but would rather provide the mechanisms through which outside observers can do this. Such mechanisms can consist in journalistic or fictional representations of group activities, or of the outcomes thereof. Representations do not necessarily have to be stories: a statistical table or a balance sheet is also a means of observing what a company is doing, for instance.

Closure and control over a group or a network's identity can often have at least two kinds of consequences: first, subordinated groups emerge as part of institutional consolidation. If we look at the medical and legal professions, for instance, we can see that subordinated groups (nurses, legal aides) emerge in processes of institutionalization, through which (medical or legal) organizations acquire legitimacy (Abbott 1988, p. 72). Second, groups performing similar activities can emerge outside the institutionalization process but in relationship to it: such external groups can resist control attempts while seeking access to activity tools controlled by the institutional group, or they can try and develop alternative tools for their activities. Conflicts can emerge around attempts to secure institutional identities.

One effect of institutional closure is the emergence of status groups, based on symbols of prestige: control mechanisms entail internal and external differentiations among groups, differentiations which are expressed not only in terms of income and access to activities, but also in terms of how group members are socially perceived and ranked. Status is characterized by the 'social appreciation of "honor", related to common group characteristics' (Weber 1972 [1921], p. 534). These common characteristics are expressed not only in relational terms (who knows whom) and economic resources (for example income), but also in the symbolic terms of social prestige. Differentiation among intra-institutional groups, as well as between internal and external ones, takes the form of social hierarchies, where prestige and honour play a prominent role. Moreover, institutional groups will emphasize prestige not only as a trust-building instrument, but also as a more general feature of their social standing.

It follows from the above arguments that closure and control are intrinsic features of how social institutions work. This means that stock exchanges, in the process of their institutionalization, will set up social mechanisms for achieving closure, mechanisms leading among others to the emergence of both subordinated and external groups. Understanding these mechanisms is relevant not only with respect to how exchanges as institutions become legitimate features of modern societies, but also with respect to the arrangements for conducting transactions and for setting prices. Moreover, understanding the technological evolution of modern stock exchanges – which is so crucial with respect to contemporary developments – requires understanding of how technology (and especially price-recording technology) works as a control mechanism. Without the processes of social closure set in motion in the late eighteenth and early nineteenth centuries, the technological set-up of modern financial markets would probably be a different one. In the following, I discuss how stock exchanges have been conceptualized in the sociological literature, in relation to issues of closure and control. Afterwards, I will go step by step through the features of closure presented above and detail how they were constituted in London, New York and Paris.

SOCIOLOGICAL APPROACHES TO CLOSURE AND STOCK EXCHANGES

The focus on this section is primarily on how classic sociology authors from the nineteenth century, such as Karl Marx and Max Weber, perceived the institution of the stock exchange and how they placed it within their respective theoretical systems. That during the nineteenth century stock exchanges become objects of theoretical attention outside the domain of economics is relevant for their status in society. During the previous century, the overwhelming majority of writings on the stock exchange consisted of pamphlets, satires and moral tracts. One cannot dismiss these so easily, since they indicate how broader audiences saw the financial transactions: namely, in moral and negative terms. If we look at how writers of the nineteenth century treat finance, however, we can see that the genre of the satire is not dominant any more (which does not mean that satires disappear). Generally speaking, we can distinguish among several genres: one is that of financial journalism (see Poovey 2008); another is that of the investment manual; yet another is that of the social-philosophical treatise which, while using historical elements or not, integrates the analysis of stock exchanges into a broader explanatory system for modern societies. It is this latter genre which concerns me here.

Among late-nineteenth-century sociologists, probably the one who was most aware of the role of the stock exchange as a social institution was Max Weber. Karl Marx, whose thinking influenced Weber, paid more attention to financial markets in the third volume of *Das Kapital* (Marx 1964 [1894]). While he initially considered financial speculation as an atavistic manifestation of the primitive accumulation of capital, Marx came to revise his position in later, posthumously published writings. He saw financial capital (which he called credit capital) as being autonomous with respect to the industrial capital required by the manufacturing industries. Industrial overproduction, together with the autonomous reproduction of capital, leads to a migration of capital from the sphere of production into that of financial speculation, as well as to a loose coupling between the latter and the need to finance industrial production. At the same time, savings have to be transformed into capital, and this happens by attracting them into the sphere of finance and by putting them to work in financial transactions (see also Preda 2009, pp. 36–7). Thus, while he did not deal directly with the institution of the stock exchange, Marx was well aware of the social importance of financial markets, which he did not relegate to the role of providing financing for industrial production. In the Marxian perspective, financial markets appear as an expression of mature capitalism, and are only loosely coupled to the sphere of production. Since one of their major roles is to transform savings into capital, their legitimacy is crucial. If financial markets were not perceived as a legitimate social institution, savers would not repeatedly put their money into this process. Thus, the institutional aspect of markets, which goes beyond their allocation functions, is ascribed a prominent role.

Max Weber, by contrast, was concerned not only with the more abstract role of financial capital, but also with that of the stock exchange as a social institution. In 1894, he published two popular essays about the stock exchange, which apppeared in a series directed at a broader public (Weber 2000a [1894], 2000b [1894]). Additionally, he dealt extensively with stock exchanges and financial markets in *Economy and Society* (Weber 1972 [1921]). Weber noticed from the outset that stock exchanges have the character of 'gentlemen's clubs' and of 'plutocratic organizations' (Weber 2000a [1894], pp. 326, 333). This closure required controls over membership and access, as well as an emphasis on honour and reputation. The latter provide the basis on which stock exchanges are integrated into society. Weber saw the honour system and the mechanisms of social control as important for instituting a system of norms and obligations which have to be respected by the members of these institutions. Control of access, for instance, was important because it limited the possibilities of manipulation. In the same way, the participation of national, large-scale capital holders to financial transactions is important for the national economy, if only because it controls and limits competition coming from foreign capital (Weber 2000a [1894], p. 333).

Since stock exchanges are the sites where national financial capital competes with foreign capital, they are not only economic, but also political institutions. Necessarily, the state must intervene in the ways they work. Exchanges also forge ties with other political institutions and thus become even more integrated in the social fabric. This process of social integration is accompanied by a deepening and differentiation of the knowledge and expertise required by participation in financial transactions. This differentiation necessitates a strengthening of reputation and honourability as mechanisms of social control and, argues Weber (2000a [1894], p. 334), on modern exchanges formal organization and closure should go even deeper than it was the case in his time in Germany.

This emphasis on stock exchanges as important social institutions anchored in closure and control can be explained, among others, by the way in which Weber conceives their social role as opposed to their economic functions. While exchanges may fulfil allocation functions, this is not the only thing that they do: financial transactions, and stock exchanges with them, deepen reciprocal dependency among social actors: they create, in Weber's words, a system of reciprocal tributary obligations (Weber 2000a [1894], pp. 315, 320) which, while different from the personal obligations of pre-modern societies, contribute to stabilizing the social fabric.

What Weber's analysis (and to a lesser extent Marx's as well) emphasizes is that stock exchanges as institutions cannot be exclusively seen in terms of economic functions, but need to be taken into account under their social aspects as well. Moreover, what Weber's emphasis on honour and prestige intimates is that these aspects play a significant role with respect to how the economic functions of the stock exchange are performed. Honour and prestige are influenced by how observers perceive the activities of the stock exchanges, and by the ways in which these activities can be accessed. Access, in turn, is tied to issues of closure and control. I will turn now to discussing how control mechanisms were set in place on nineteenth-century stock exchanges, and how these shaped their institutional features.

THE SOCIAL CLOSURE OF MODERN STOCK EXCHANGES

When discussing the emergence of stock exchanges as modern institutions, and the role played by closure in this process, we need to take into account at least two elements: first, the legal status of stock exchange transactions; second, the social organization of the stock exchanges until the dawn of the eighteenth century.

Stock exchange transactions did not take the form of written, legally endorsed contracts. Transactions on the trading floor were conducted by means of oral exchanges and of hand signs; until very recently, this was the norm (Zaloom 2006, pp. 8–9). An example of how transactions were conducted is provided by Caitlin Zaloom's ethnography of the Chicago Board of Trade in the late 1990s: clerks monitored the traders' signals and scribbled down transactions on slips of paper; they handed the slips to runners, who brought them to the back office, where they were recorded by other clerks (Zaloom 2006, p. 60). At least as important as the social organization of transactions was the fact that during the eighteenth and nineteenth centuries financial transactions were not legally acknowledged as commercial contracts. This happened only in the early twentieth century in both London and New York, and only after a series of high-profile court cases (see

Preda 2009, pp. 61–2; Wachtel 2003, p. 27). The Paris Bourse constitutes an important exception here: in Paris, the transactions on the Bourse were legally acknowledged as commercial contracts since 1724, when a royal decree instituted control mechanisms for participating in transactions. According to contemporary observers, however, Paris had not only the official, state-endorsed and controlled Bourse, but also an unofficial one, the coulisse, with a much higher volume of transactions (Vidal 1910; Walker 2001). The transactions of the coulisse were not legally acknowledged as commercial contracts, while those of the Bourse were.

The centuries-long absence of a legal definition of stock exchange transactions as commercial contracts raises the question of how their legitimacy was understood by the public at large (including investors). During the eighteenth century, this was indeed a problematic issue, related among others to the lack of control mechanisms. In London and New York, financial transactions were conducted in coffeehouses and open places (streets and gardens): access was free for all persons who were interested in trading and had the necessary disposable income. Many of these places had a bad social reputation, being associated with disreputable trades or with violence. Of course, the practice of sending agents to trade on one's behalf was widespread enough, especially in cases where the principal did not want to reveal their identity, for strategic reasons, but also for reasons of prestige. Moreover, there were no mechanisms of controlling who could be a broker and who could not, so that the brokerage of financial securities was a side activity for people of different professions. Transactions could take place at different times of the day. Parallel transactions in the same security, at different prices, were common. While lists of securities existed and were circulated (Neal 1990), nobody could tell how the printed prices had been obtained, by whom, at what time of the day, and from which transactions.

This lack of social controls made possible the direct observation of financial transactions: everybody could go and see close up how financial trading was conducted; brokers and traders had a bad press in eighteenth century pamphlets and their social reputation was quite low (for example Bowen 1986). Generally, the legitimacy of financial transactions was questioned not only by educated casual observers and pamphleteers, but also by economists such as Adam Smith (see Preda 2009, pp. 32–3). Against this background, a process of social enclosure was started, characterized by the introduction of control mechanisms with regard to space, time, membership and price lists. While the state played a central role in the creation of financial markets in the late seventeenth century (Carruthers 1996), in France (and to a much lesser extent in Britain) it has also played a role in setting up control mechanisms. In New York and London, however, the autoformation of group monopolies is much more significant in the institutionalization of control mechanisms and of closure.

In Britain, at the end of the seventeenth century, an Act of Parliament (1697) granted brokers a ten-year monopoly over transactions, requiring a large deposit and a membership fee. After its expiration, these control mechanisms disappeared. In France, however, a royal edict from 1724 set up the broad conditions under which the Paris Bourse was to work for the next centuries: the number of official brokers was set at 60; membership conditions were established along criteria of wealth, religion, residency, citizenship and social status. Transaction hours were established, and so was the place where these could take place. The close-up access of the public was forbidden. The erection of a dedicated building in the early nineteenth century reinforces these control mechanisms.

While in France the state played a dominant role, in London and New York monopolistic appropriation of control was the primary mechanism through which stock exchanges were institutionalized. Groups of brokers seized control over space, by renting a coffeehouse and demanding an access fee. In parallel, these groups organized themselves as private clubs, and instituted yearly membership fees, as well as membership criteria according to wealth, religion and social status (for example Michie 1999, p. 34; Poitras 2000, p. 297; Hennessy 2001, p. 16). The organizational form of private clubs allowed these groups to acquire the buildings where financial transactions were conducted, a move which reinforced their control of access. This closure was accompanied by instituting transaction times, limiting visitors' access to the premises, and instituting internal governance boards. In parallel, codes of conduct were set up, which regulated not only the conditions of membership, but also the ways in which brokers had to conduct themselves on the premises of the exchange (with a heavy emphasis on honour), the manner in which transactions had to be conducted, and the penalties for bad (social) behaviour. On the New York Stock Exchange, for instance, trading was ritualized: brokers had assigned chairs and had to wear formal attire during trading hours. While defaulting on contracts was discouraged by means going from public humiliation to exclusion, it did not mean that defaults or non-execution of contracts did not happen. The internal rules set by the governance board of the exchanges were regarded by courts of law as having binding power in such cases. These rules, however, could hardly work without appeal to an honour system (that is, brokers enjoying social prestige and honourability) which included control of social behaviour as well.

One effect of these mechanisms of control was that stock exchange membership became a very expensive affair: while seat prices fluctuated according to economic conditions, they continually increased over the nineteenth century (for example Davis et al. 2005, p. 4). Seats on the stock exchange were legally considered the ownership of stockbrokers: they could be sold with the agreement of the governance board; corporations, for instance, were not permitted to own seats on the New York Stock Exchange. Internal control over membership and over the activities of stockbrokers also had the effect of making external regulatory interventions difficult: as long as the stock exchange had the status of a private association or club, there was little legal basis for intervening in its activities. This is why, among others, brokers of the New York Stock Exchange (NYSE) were forbidden to advertise their services by mail: this could be easily construed as interstate commerce, opening the door to federal regulation. Brokers of the NYSE were also forbidden to hold membership in other exchanges; brokerage houses, however, circumvented this interdiction by employing members of several exchanges: while no single person could be a member on several exchanges, people working for the same brokerage could hold different memberships, and this arrangement facilitated the circulation of information across institutional boundaries.

The control and closure mechanisms set in place in the institutionalization of stock exchanges had a series of consequences: first, internal subordinated groups emerged. An instance of these is provided by clerks who, while being inferior in status to brokers, nevertheless had to fulfil social criteria such as guarantees of honourability. Second, the legitimacy of brokers included their public representation as a status group, characterized by honour and prestige. Such public representations were included in books and newspaper articles representing stock exchanges as honourable institutions, but also in tourist guides and in the brokers' own literary production: some of the latter dabbled in poetry, published books on sports, and generally engaged actively in representing the institution and its members as being endowed with social prestige. At least as important is the fact that such a status group could now select its own customers: brokers imposed minimum sizes for transaction orders, to the effect that only wealthy individuals could afford their services.

The social closure of stock exchanges had another important effect, namely the emergence of parallel transaction systems, which tried to escape or circumvent the control efforts of the former. In France, early in the eighteenth century, the state created the status group of official stockbrokers, who were quasi civil servants and inherited their seats. But, in addition to the Bourse, the French state tolerated an alternative system, the coulisse: unofficial brokers, or coulissiers, traded securities in the neighbourhood of the Paris Bourse. Their transactions were not legally recognized as commercial contracts, yet, according to observers of that time, the transactions volume of the coulisse greatly exceeded that of the Bourse. In New York, the constitution of the Stock Exchange governed by its Regular Board did not prevent financial transactions from being made in the street, on what came to be known as the Curb Exchange. While the Regular Board set limited trading hours, financial transactions continued in the evening in the lobbies of Manhattan hotels. One form of resisting attempts at control was the refusal to move indoors: until the 1920s, the street traders and brokers refused to move into a building of their own (see Preda 2009, p. 67).

Control of access, time, place and membership had to be completed by control of price lists: after all, prices and volumes were key information for investors. While price lists existed in England during the eighteenth century, none was designated as official, since there was no institutional body to claim such authority. What is more, several quotation lists existed, but they did not make clear where the price information came from, when and how it was obtained. As parallel transactions in the same security took place in the street, it was difficult to exclude the possibility that several prices existed for one and the same security. After the creation of stock exchanges, however, the governing bodies had the power to publish and circulate official quotation lists, and to decide which securities should be included on these lists. While official lists were published and circulated under the institutional authority of stock exchanges, they could not stop unofficial brokers producing their own lists. An important aspect of closure and control, which deserves a separate, lengthier treatment, was thus control over price data: who owned and controlled the information about prices, as well as the technology of collecting and distributing prices?

All in all, closure and control – as expressed in the control of space, time, membership and price lists – are intrinsic to the long process of institution-building, a process in which transactions in financial securities morph from a disreputable activity conducted in the street into a socially reputable and entirely honourable activity, one which is significant for the national economy.

CLOSURE, CONTROL AND PRICE DATA

Controlling access to stock exchange as an institution means controlling the most important kind of data used and circulated by it, namely price and volume. These, however, are not independent of their material support, of the technologies employed in producing and circulating them, or of the ways in which these technologies are used. Moreover, it matters whether such technologies are real-time or not: that is, are the prices being recorded and circulated as they happen or are they recorded only later – and if so, how much later? Additionally, the circulation of price information – essential for attracting investors – raises the issues of their legal status: is price data owned by anybody, and if so, by whom?

Up to the late 1860s, brokers on the New York Stock Exchange employed a system of courier boys to circulate paper slips with transaction data to brokerage offices (see Downey 2002, p. 65). Not all data were accurately recorded, and many slips got lost. Starting in 1868, official price lists of the NYSE included closing prices, which were then reprinted in newspapers, but these prices were not necessarily reliable (Preda 2009, p. 122). Among others, the uncertainty of their source (who was the broker providing them), typographical errors and forgeries made price lists unreliable. Additionally, street transactions ran parallel to those of the NYSE, at prices which were not included in the official lists.

In 1867, Edward Callahan, an engineer, introduced a new machine on the New York Stock Exchange, called the stock ticker. This was a telegraph which printed numbers and letters on a paper strip, instead of printing the dots and dashes of the Morse code. It was cheaper to operate, because it made a second (expensive) Morse operator superfluous. Ticker machines were installed on the floor of the stock exchange, and telegraph lines were laid, connecting brokerage offices with the floor of the NYSE. The ticker printed a flow of price and volume data, together with abbreviations of securities names. The data were arranged in two lines on the ticker tape. Investors situated in brokerage offices could now observe transactions on the floor of the NYSE as they happened; while delays still existed, especially in periods of intensive transactions, the time taken was much less than to circulate price lists printed in newspapers. During the last decades of the nineteenth century, the stock ticker spread outside New York City: while ticker services were expensive (brokerage office rented the machines), this was nonetheless a success (Preda 2008, p. 230).

The introduction of a medium which could record and circulate data as they were produced raised several questions. First, who controlled access to this data? Second, what was their legal status: who owned them? Third, who could interpret the data in an authoritative fashion? Control and closure of the stock exchange would have been incomplete if such an important element were to be left out. Alongside official brokerages, which were NYSE members, a vast number of unofficial brokerages existed, with different degrees of reputability and financial muscle (Hochfelder 2006). They were of course interested in getting access to the stock ticker data, in the same way in which stock exchanges were interested in preventing them from doing so. Conflicts over control were almost preprogrammed. Some unofficial brokerages went so far as to instal fake tickers in their offices, or tapped into the wires of official brokerages. The boards of stock exchanges, on their part, were bent on destroying or banning tickers from their floors on several occasions (Wyckoff 1972, p. 33).

The second of the above questions was answered in 1905, in a high-profile case which was brought before the US Supreme Court (198US 236): *Chicago Board of Trade* v. *Christie Grain and Stock Co.* In this case, a bucket shop (unofficial brokerage office) from

Chicago had tapped the wires of the Chicago Board of Trade in order to obtain ticker prices, and used them in trading options (a type of transaction which was illegal). Among others, the Supreme Court upheld the position of the Chicago Board of the Trade, that it owned the price data. This, in turn, reinforced the control of the exchange: as owners of the data, stock exchanges could not only transform them into a commodity, but also select the users entitled to have access to them.

The data generated by the use of tickers also created a new kind of problem: the challenge to explain price variations happening in the absence of any (political) events which could be taken as causal factors. Moreover, the ticker data were different in nature from price list data (more price variations were recorded, and more accurately than before); they required interpretation, and interpretation in turn required specific skills. In the same way in which reading the ticker data required concentration and attention, interpreting it required particular skills such as the ability to recognize patterns of repetition. Interpretation, in turn, which could be not only a means of bringing in more clients, but also a source of prestige and authority, could not be left uncontrolled.

Around the turn of the twentieth century, a group of brokers turned to a more systematic gathering, processing and interpretation of price and volume data generated by the ticker. They switched from brokerage to analytical activities, and began producing newsletters, articles and magazines dedicated to the analysis of price movements. They also produced diagrams of price variations, and claimed to be able to forecast future price movements from the history of price variations (see Preda 2007). Several factors contributed to this development. Data compilation and statistics did not enjoy much prestige in brokerage houses, sometimes being relegated to low-status clerks. Differentiating analysis from brokerage contributed to elevating the status of statistics. Moreover, while official members of the New York Stock Exchange, for instance, were forbidden to advertise by mail, analysts were not. By moving into analysis and circulating their opinions more freely, former brokers could contribute to building an audience which followed price movements. Additionally, brokerages could not prevent some of their members moving into the interpretation of price movements and taking their skills with them. They could however build alliances, and consolidate control over price data by controlling their interpretation as well.

Price data analysis, in the form of chartism, took off in the 1920s and 1930s, when analyst firms became an established part of the market landscape. Analysts invented their own tradition of thought; they used endorsements from known speculators in order to persuade the public that chart analysis was a useful instrument in understanding and forecasting price movements. The consolidation of control of the interpretation of prices went hand in hand with control over the recording and distribution of price data; both were part of the consolidation of stock exchanges as institutions.

Going back to the issue of social closure, its features and role in institution-building, the following can be argued: social closure includes jurisdictional elements, such as a group establishing monopolistic claims over a body of knowledge (see Abbott 1988). In the case of the stock exchange, this happens both with stockbrokers and with analysts. Additionally, though, groups establish spatio-temporal controls, as well as controls over membership, over the ownership of price data, its circulation and distribution. These controls are not grounded in knowledge-based jurisdictional claims, but in claims of social honourability and prestige. Control and closure mean here not simply establishing barriers; they mean establishing specific ways of accessing, observing and participating in financial transactions on the stock exchange. Closure thus includes the specific observational modes through which the public gets access to the stock exchange.

SOCIAL CLOSURE AND TECHNOLOGICAL DEVELOPMENT

Since the introduction of the stock ticker in 1867, stock exchanges have been through a continuous process of technological development. Contemporary exchanges rely heavily on technology for data recording and for trading. This latter has shifted from the old-fashioned floors and pits to electronic platforms. Indeed, many stock exchanges, if not a majority of them, have completely abandoned floor trading and have merged with electronic communication networks. The recent media prominence of trading algorithms, or robots, is just one aspect of how heavily dependent on technology contemporary stock exchanges are. At the same time, the public access to trading is easier than ever before: while this access is of course dependent on disposable income, and requires a minimum of knowledge, it suffices to have a laptop computer and broadband access in order to open a trading account with an electronic brokerage house. Control barriers such as minimum order size, or brokerage fees, are considerably lower than a couple of decades ago. Does all this mean that social closure plays a lesser role nowadays than during the last two centuries, or that it has disappeared altogether?

The argument made in the previous sections was that social closure is achieved, among other means, by instituting control mechanisms over access to activities, including observational access, as well as jurisdictional claims over a specialized body of knowledge. Based on this, it cannot be argued that social closure has disappeared, or that it plays a lesser role than in the previous centuries. First of all, one cannot for instance argue that mechanisms of spatio-temporal control – so important during the nineteenth century – have disappeared. They have changed shape, in accordance with technological developments. In contemporary electronic markets, the issue of spatial control is not expressed any more as who can directly observe floor transactions or not, but as who can place their computer servers closest to those of the stock exchange, thus reducing data latency. In a way similar to that in which during the nineteenth century access to the trading floor became the object of internal and external regulations, newer developments indicate that server placement becomes not only a source of revenue (through renting space in the data warehouses of the stock exchange), but also a regulatory issue. Regulatory proposals formulated by the Commodity Futures Trading Commission, together with the Securities & Exchange Commission in the aftermath of the 'flash crash' from 6 May 2010, suggested ensuring equal access to collocation services or barring third-party vendors from such locations (US Commodity Futures Trading Commission and SEC 2010, p. 9).

The technological differentiation of electronic trading platforms has also engendered new forms of closure and control. Whereas in earlier times participants to transactions were selected by minimum order sizes and brokerage commissions, within the contemporary landscape of electronic trading not all platforms are available in equal measure to all participants: alternative trading systems such as the Better Alternative Trading System

(BATS) are open to institutional traders, not retail ones. Dark pools are over-the-counter, cross-network systems that do not reveal trading information to the outside. Control over information has probably become one of the major features of the closure of modern financial exchanges. At the same time, even in the era of electronic trading, the access of a broader public to financial transactions is not devoid of control mechanisms. These are expressed, among others, in the organization of electronic brokerage houses, which provide retail traders with access.

One aspect of social closure discussed above is the jurisdiction over expertise: that is, the monopolization of the body of knowledge required by participation to financial transactions, and the institutionalization of control mechanisms. One instance of this institutionalization is the transformation of traders and analysts into professional groups, a transformation which includes the emergence of professional associations, conferences, education and training, as well as recruitment and certification procedures. This institutionalization has been accompanied by internal differentiation and specialization: the emergence and consolidation of different categories of analysts, the consolidation of their authority, and the effects of their coverage on price volatility (see Zuckerman 1999) are consequences of this process. The authority of analysts, for instance, has been subject to public and regulatory scrutiny during the recent financial crises, and regulatory controls have been set in place (Swedberg 2005). Nevertheless, their institutionalization and status as a professional group has been not diminished, but rather reinforced by regulators.

CONCLUSION

My argument here has been that stock exchanges should not be understood as only fulfilling a restricted set of economic functions, but as social institutions. Institution-building and consolidation includes setting up mechanisms of control which regulate observation and participation. Control means selection criteria for accessing the activities in question not only as a participant, but as an observer as well. Control also means social closure, as a prerequisite for constructing an image of honour and reputability, which in turn confers legitimacy upon the institution of the stock exchange. Instating controls is not devoid of conflicts and frictions; and in many cases, tensions among vested interest groups arise in this process. Groups can fight over legal definitions, or over escaping controls or circumventing them. Controls also include jurisdiction over a particular body of knowledge, as well as differentiation and professionalization processes in relationship to this knowledge.

Throughout the nineteenth century, the consolidation of the stock exchange as an institution is characterized by such processes of setting in place mechanisms of control over institutional identity. Control of space and time, of membership, and of observational access is accompanied by the public emphasis on prestige and honourability, on the respectability of stock exchanges and of their members. At least two types of conflict go hand in hand with instituting these mechanisms: conflicts over access to data and observational technologies (including here data recording); and conflicts over marginality. The first type includes conflicts over the legal status of price data, as well as repeated attempts to prevent outsiders accessing data recording technologies, or to keep such technologies away from the trading floor. The second type includes struggles to escape institutional controls, among other means by the refusal to move indoors, or by processes of internal differentiation between brokers and analysts.

The continued technologization of stock exchanges throughout the twentieth century, a process which continues into the twenty-first century, does not mean that mechanisms of control and closure disappear. The disappearance of trading floors, for instance, does not imply that spatial controls have entirely lost relevance. Hotly debated issues such as collocation and low latency data, and the regulatory measures linked to them, indicate that the problem of instituting spatial and temporal controls is still very much with us, only in a different form. While technology changes the shape of financial markets and the ways in which they work, this does not mean that it diminishes social closure, or that it abolishes all controls. All in all, stock exchanges have evolved technologically, but this does not mean that nowadays they are less of a social institution; quite the contrary. What has happened is that in the process of their technologization stock exchanges have evolved into global institutions, while retaining strong links to states and to transnational political institutions (such as European Union governance bodies). This means that closure and control will continue to play a significant role for the ways in which they work. However, the concrete ways in which closure will work will not be that of the twentieth century any more.

REFERENCES

Abbott, Andrew (1988), *The System of Professions: An Essay on the Division of Expert Labor*, Chicago, IL: University of Chicago Press.

Abbott, Andrew (2009), 'Organizations and the Chicago School', in Paul S. Adler (ed.), *The Oxford Handbook of Sociology and Organization Studies*, Oxford: Oxford University Press, pp. 399–420.

Bowen, H.V. (1986), 'The pests of human society: stockbrokers, jobbers, and speculators in mid-eighteenth century Britain,' *History*, **78**: 38–53.

Carruthers, Bruce (1996), *City of Capital: Politics and Markets in the English Financial Revolution*, Princeton, NJ: Princeton University Press.

Davis, Lance E., Larry Neal and Eugene N. White (2005), 'The highest price ever: the great NYSE seat sale of 1928–1929 and capacity constraints', Cambridge, MA: NBER Working Paper 11556.

DiMaggio, Paul J. and Walter W. Powell (1991), 'The iron cage revisited: institutional isomorphism and collective rationality', in Walter W. Powell and Paul J. DiMaggio (eds), *The New Institutionalism in Organizational Analysis*, Chicago, IL: University of Chicago Press, pp. 63–82.

Downey, Gregory J. (2002), *Telegraph Messenger Boys: Labor, Technology, and Geography, 1850–1950*, New York: Routledge.

Geertz, Clifford (1973), *The Interpretation of Cultures*, New York: Basic Books.

Hennessy, Elizabeth (2001), *Coffee House to Cyber Market: 200 Years of the London Stock Exchange*, London: Ebury.

Hochfelder, David (2006), '"Where the common people could speculate", The ticker, bucket shops, and the origins of popular participation in financial markets, 1880–1920', *Journal of American History*, **93** (2), 335–58.

Marx, Karl (1964 [1894]), *Das Kapital. Kritik der politischen Ökonomie. Dritter Band, Buch III. Der Gesamtprozeß der kapitalistischen Produktion*, Berlin: Dietz.

Michie, Ranald (1999), *The London Stock Exchange: A History*, Oxford: Oxford University Press.

Mohr, John W. and Harrison White (2008), 'How to model an institution', *Theory and Society*, **37**, 485–512.

Neal, Larry (1990), *The Rise of Financial Capitalism. International Capital Markets in the Age of Reason*, Cambridge: Cambridge University Press.

Nee, Victor (2005), 'The new institutionalisms in economics and sociology', in Neil J. Smelser and Richard Swedberg (eds), *The Handbook of Economic Sociology*, 2nd edn, New York and Princeton, NJ: Russell Sage Foundation and Princeton University Press, pp. 49–74.

Poitras, Geoffrey (2000), *The Early History of Financial Economics, 1478–1776: From Commercial Arithmetic to Life Annuities and Joint Stocks*, Cheltenham, UK and Northampton, MA, USA: Edward Elgar.
Poovey, Mary (2008), *Genres of the Credit Economy: Mediating Value in Eighteenth and Nineteenth Century Britain*, Chicago, IL: University of Chicago Press.
Preda, Alex (2007), 'Where do analysts come from? The case of financial chartism', in Michel Callon, Yuval Millo and Fabian Muniesa (eds), *Market Devices*, Oxford: Blackwell, pp. 40–64.
Preda, Alex (2008), 'Technology, agency, and financial price data', in Trevor Pinch and Richard Swedberg (eds), *Living in a Material World. Economic Sociology Meets Science and Technology Studies*, Cambridge, MA: MIT Press, pp. 217–52.
Preda, Alex (2009), *Framing Finance. The Boundaries of Markets and Modern Capitalism*, Chicago, IL: University of Chicago Press.
Swedberg, Richard (2005), 'Conflicts of interest in the US brokerage industry', in Karin Knorr Cetina and Alex Preda (eds), *The Sociology of Financial Markets*, Oxford: Oxford University Press, pp. 187–206.
US Commodity Futures Trading Commission and SEC (2010), 'Preliminary findings regarding the market events of May 6, 2010. Report of the Staffs of the CFTC and SEC to the Joint Advisory Committee on Emerging Regulatory Issues', Washington, DC: CFTC and SEC.
Vidal, E. (1910), *The History and Methods of the Paris Bourse*, Washington, DC: Government Printing Office.
Wachtel, Howard (2003), *Street of Dreams: Boulevard of Broken Hearts. Wall Street's First Century*, London: Pluto Press.
Walker, Donald (2001), 'A factual account of the functioning of the 19th century Paris bourse', *European Journal for the History of Economic Thought*, **8** (2), 186–207.
Weber, Max (2000a [1894]), 'Stock and commodity exchanges', *Theory and Society*, **29,** 305–38.
Weber, Max (2000b [1894]), 'Commerce on the stock and commodity exchanges', *Theory and Society*, **29,** 339–71.
Weber, Max (1972 [1921]), *Wirtschaft und Gesellschaft*, Tübingen: Mohr.
White, Harrison (2008), *Identity and Control: How Social Formations Emerge*, 2nd edn, Princeton, NJ: Princeton University Press.
Wyckoff, Peter (1972), *Wall Street and the Stock Markets. A Chronology (1644–1971)*, Philadelphia, PA: Chilton.
Zaloom, Caitlin (2006), *Out of the Pit: Traders and Technology from Chicago to London*, Chicago, IL: University of Chicago Press.
Zuckerman, Ezra (1999), 'The categorical imperative: securities analysts and the illegitimacy discount', *American Journal of Sociology*, **104** (5), 1398–438.

7 Demutualization and the globalization of stock markets

Giovanna Zanotti

INTRODUCTION

Contemporary stock exchanges are the result of a long transformation process that started in January 1993 when the Stockholm Stock Exchange changed its structure from a cooperative owned by members into a for-profit company with ownership opened to outsiders. Before this date, stock exchanges were characterized by the identity of owners and traders who formed a cooperative with a limited number of members. Exchanges were not managed for profit but for the benefit of the members. Decisions were taken in the form of one vote for each member. In some other cases, for example in some European countries, exchanges were under government control. Starting from the final decade of the twentieth century, exchanges radically changed their governance. In the new governance structure, the identity between members and owners has been eliminated, the exchange is run for profit and the decisions are taken on a one share, one vote basis. Furthermore, until 1998 there were no publicly traded exchanges. In 1998 the Australian Stock Exchange first decided to go public and to list its shares. This process is known as demutualization and it is considered to be one of the major changes that has occurred in global capital markets in the last decades. Table 7.1 gives a summary of the demutualization process up to the demutualization of the New York Stock Exchange in 2006 and of the major stock exchanges that were involved in the process.

In this chapter, the determinants and the implications of demutualization are examined. The following section is dedicated to differences in stock exchange governance models. Next, a definition of demutualization is given, and the determinants of demutualization are reviewed. Finally, empirical research on demutualization is analysed.

GOVERNANCE MODELS FOR STOCK EXCHANGES

Stock exchanges can be organized following different governance models. Two elements characterize and distinguish each model: the ownership structure and the goals pursued. Based on these two elements, the financial literature has identified five corporate governance structures for exchanges:

1. the non-profit organization;
2. the cooperative model;
3. the for-profit organization;
4. the public model;
5. the hybrid model.

Table 7.1 Demutualization and listing of stock exchanges, 1993–2006

	Demutualization	Listing
Stockholm Stock Exchange	1993	OMX
Helsinki Stock Exchange	1995	OMX
Copenhagen Stock Exchange	1996	OMX
Amsterdam Stock Exchange	1997	Euronext 2000
Italian Stock Exchange	1997	LSE
Australian Stock Exchange	1998	1998
Singapore Stock Exchange	1999	2000
Athens Stock Exchange	1999	2000
Hong Kong Stock Exchange	2000	2000
Paris Bourse	2000	Euronext 2000
Deutsche Borse	2000	2001
Toronto Stock Exchange	2000	TSX 2002
London Stock Exchange	2000	2001
Sydney Stock Exchange	2000	2002
Oslo Stock Exchange	2001	2002
Philippines Stock Exchange	2001	2003
NASDAQ	2001	2002
Bourse Madrid	2001	2006
Tokyo Stock Exchange	2001	Not listed
Osaka Stock Exchange	2001	2004
Swiss Exchange	2002	Not listed
New Zealand Stock Exchange	2003	2003
Bourse Malaysia	2004	2005

The main characteristic of a non-profit model is that any profit or surplus generated by the exchange cannot be distributed. The income of these exchanges derives mainly from the fee charged for providing services to the clients or owners. The organization is controlled by and run for the interests of consumers. The final objective of non-profit exchanges is to provide customers with all services needed efficiently and at low cost.

The cooperative or mutual model is built around the idea of membership. Cooperatives offer their services only to members, and membership is usually limited to agents that are interested in and make use of the cooperative services. Voting rights are assigned only to members and decisions are taken on the one head, one vote principle. The goal of the cooperative is the maximization of the member-consumer surplus. Any profit is distributed to the members in the form, for example, of a reduction of the fees paid for accessing the services. The non-profit model and the cooperative model are similar. The difference is that non-profit companies are prevented from distributing profits in cash, which cooperatives are allowed to do. In practice most cooperatives are run not for profit.

For-profit companies are allowed to distribute profits to their equity holders in the form of dividends. For-profit companies do not have restrictions on customers (everybody can buy the company services if interested) and owners (everybody can buy the equities and receive profits in the form of dividends). The ownership, the membership and the use of the services are completely separate. The final objective of a for-profit company is profit maximization.

In public models, the government owns part of the exchange. Public exchanges can operate on a non-profit or a for-profit basis and their primary goal is to pursue the objectives defined by the government. They do not focus on short-term profits but aim for different objectives such as long-term market development and investors' education.

Hybrid models combine elements of previous models. For example, in public–private exchanges the ownership of the government and of private investors is combined and the institution pursues public goals as well as private investors' interests. Another example of a hybrid model is an exchange owned by users and investors that is run in the interest of both categories of agent. Final users will be guided by a final objective that is cost-efficiency, while final investors will look for profit maximization.

Traditionally stock exchanges have been organized as member-owned cooperatives. Three reasons could explain why stock exchanges were traditionally organized as mutual cooperatives. The first reason is historical. Prior to the twentieth century, the cooperative form of enterprise was very common. Not only stock exchanges but also insurance companies, savings banks and other organizations were organized as cooperatives. Furthermore stock exchanges were often created as 'member clubs'. Brokers that used to meet at Jonathan's coffeehouse to buy and sell securities created the London Stock Exchange (LSE) in 1773. The original brokers become the owners and the users of the exchange, and as long as they could, they ran it in their interests. The second possible explanation of the prevalence of cooperatives as a governance model for stock exchanges is the homogeneity of the members. Hansmann (1988) has shown that when firm employees are highly homogenous the cooperative model can help to reduce contracting costs and is the most efficient form of control. Shleifer and Vishny (1997) and Hart and Moore (1998) arrive at the same conclusion: cooperative structures are economically efficient when members are homogeneous. Users of services of traditional exchanges were 'homogeneous agents'. They all were local traders, interested in transmitting their orders at the lowest cost. They had the same preferences and goals. The cooperative structure worked efficiently. Finally Macey and O'Hara (1999) explain the prevalence of the cooperative structure by making reference to the 'nature of the exchange product' and to the 'relationship investment' between listing firms and exchanges. Exchanges provide companies with sets of services (listing, monitoring and liquidity) but at the same time companies provide exchanges with the shares to trade. This creates a non-diversifiable investment in the relationship between exchanges and companies and makes the cooperative structure, which ensures companies participation in the governing of the enterprise, the most appropriate governance structure.

Other reasons can explain why some stock exchanges were under government control. This happened in countries where the trading volumes were not large enough to justify the costs of the creation and maintenance of an exchange. In these circumstances, the government offered issuers an alternative to the traditional banking system by creating the exchange. In government-owned exchanges the services offered (listing, trading and liquidity) were considered 'public goods' to be guaranteed to all interested investors. Government-owned exchanges were often operating as a monopoly, with final objectives fixed by government itself. Some of these stock exchanges, after a while, started to generate enough trading volumes and fees to become private companies.

Starting from the 1990s the governance of stock exchanges changed significantly and rapidly and an increasing number of exchanges demutualized. But what exactly is 'demutualization' and what can explain the emergence of private companies as the dominant model for stock exchange ownership structure?

DEMUTUALIZATION DEFINITION

There is no unique definition of demutualization. Demutualization can be defined as: 'the change in legal status of the Exchange from a mutual association with one vote per member (and possibly consensus-based decision making) into a company limited by shares, with one vote per share (with majority-based decision making)' Akhtar (2002).

Steil (2002) defines an exchange as demutualized when it is characterized by a separation of ownership and membership and there is the possibility for outsiders to buy the exchange's shares. According to Steil, an exchange is demutualized when members are free to sell their shares to non-members. Governance structures where shares were held almost exclusively by members and could not be sold without the approval of the Exchange Supervisory Board, such as that of Deutsche Borse and Paris Bourse before their initial public offering (IPOs), could not be considered fully demutualized according to Steil's definition, even if managed for profit. This definition of demutualization underlines the separation between ownership and membership that determines a change in the incentive structure of the exchange.

Based on the above definitions, demutualization is characterized by two key elements: a change in the ownership structure, and a change in the final objective. A stock is then demutualized when it is no longer owned only by users, but also by outside investors looking for profit maximization.

Demutualization is usually a gradual transformation and takes place in stages with different results (Treptow 2006). The first stage involves the transformation of the cooperative exchange into a joint-stock company, often without any change in ownership. In this stage seats are transformed into shares. Then the exchange starts to be run as a for-profit organization. At the third stage a percentage of the shares might be sold to investors other than original members (listed companies, institutional investors) in an initial private placement. Finally the exchange goes public, shares are listed and all investors can buy and sell shares. The stock exchange becomes a listed company (Figure 7.1).

In the case of public-owned exchanges the first step toward demutualization was privatization. Shares of privatized companied were, usually, at first bought by financial

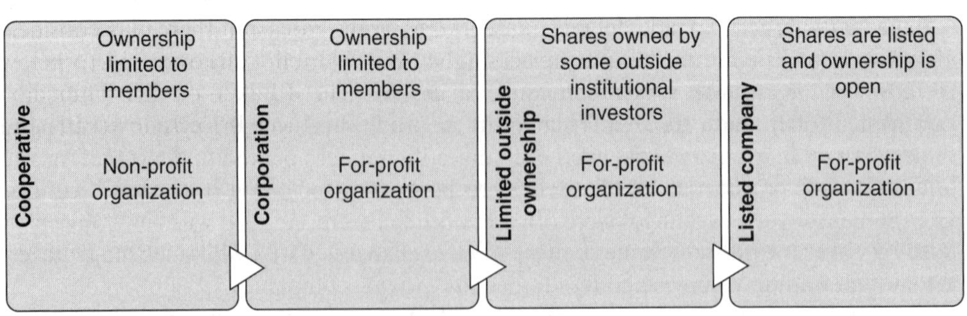

Figure 7.1 The process of demutualization: an example

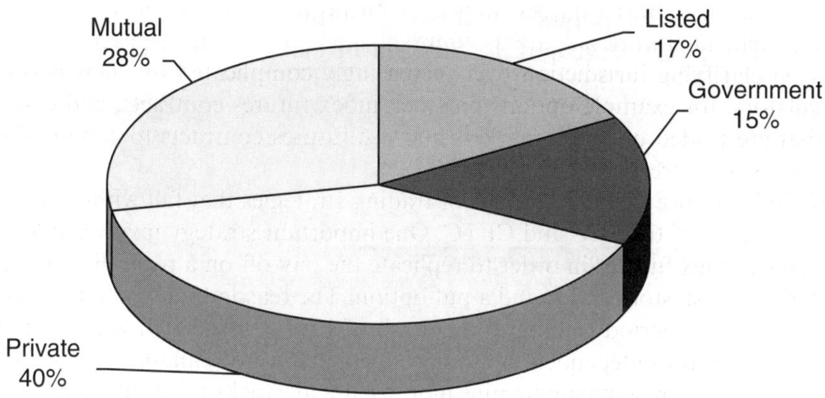

Source: World Federation of Stock Exchanges.

Figure 7.2 The governance of exchanges, 2007 (by number)

intermediaries or other exchange members. As a consequence of demutualization, an increasing numbers of exchanges are now for-profit private or listed companies.

In a study conducted in 2007, the World Federation of Exchanges classifies 90 exchanges according to four models (Figure 7.2):

1. Twenty-five mutual exchanges (27.8 per cent).
2. Thirty-six private companies (40 per cent).
3. Fifteen listed exchanges (16.7 per cent).
4. Fourteen government-owned exchanges (15.6 per cent)..

In mutual exchanges control and trading rights are combined. They are run not for profit and the originated surpluses are retained by the exchange or distributed to members in form of reduced fees. Mutual control remains relevant in South America and Africa. Among developed countries, the last exchange to retain the mutual structure was the American Stock Exchange (AMEX) that was a mutual organization until 2008 when it was acquired by the New York Stock Exchange (NYSE) Euronext group. All major exchanges in developed countries today are demutualized.

Exchanges organized as private companies are characterized by having a separation of the control of the exchange and the right to trade. Control and ownership are separated even if original members often remain the dominant owners. Limitations can exist on the transfer of shares to non-member shareholders or on the size of the holding by any single shareholder. Financial institutions have usually a high representation in the board composition of these exchanges. They can be run for profit (16 exchanges of the sample) or not for profit (20 exchanges). Private company exchanges are found in developed countries (for example the Swiss Stock Exchange) and in emerging markets as well (Budapest Stock Exchange).

Listed exchanges have offered their shares to a wide range of investors through an IPO. All major stock exchanges – the NYSE, Euronext, London Stock Exchange (LSE), Deutsche Borse are just a few examples – have listed shares. Listed exchanges are concentrated in

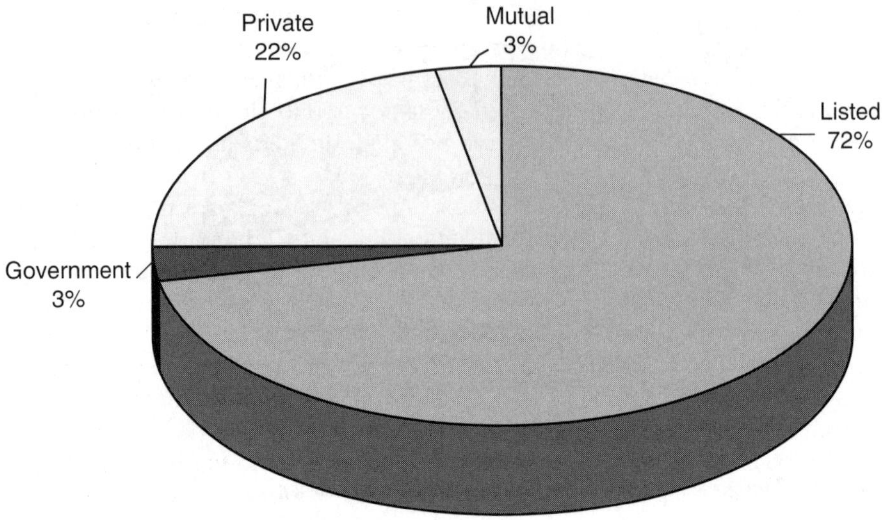

Source: World Federation of Stock Exchanges.

Figure 7.3 The governance of exchanges, 2007 (by equity turnover)

Europe and in North America. Bursa Malaysia, Panama and Philippines are some example of listed stocks in emerging markets. All listed exchanges are run for profit.

Government-controlled exchanges are, at least in part, controlled by the government that also has a representation on the board. They are typically non-profit institutions and are declining in Europe but still common in Middle Eastern countries. The most important example of this type of exchange is the Saudi Arabia Stock Exchange (Figure 7.2).

Figure 7.2 changes significantly if the equity turnover[1] of the exchange is considered (Figure 7.3). Listed exchanges include the largest exchanges and in 2005 represented 72 per cent of the total equity turnover. Private exchanges represented 22 per cent, and the remaining 6 per cent was shared between government and mutual exchanges. The percentage of listed exchanges further increased if we consider that after 2007 other exchanges listed their shares (the Spanish Stock Exchange and the South African Stock Exchange in 2006, the Brazilian Stock Exchange in 2007, the Mexican Stock Exchange in 2008) or became part of a listed group (in 2007 Borsa Italiana became part of the London Stock Exchange).

THE DETERMINANTS OF DEMUTUALIZATION

Different motivations can explain why, at a certain point, the for-profit model emerged as the most common model for exchanges. The most natural explanation is that that the for-profit model is more efficient. If this hypothesis is accepted – that is, that stock exchanges changed their status into for-profit companies to increase efficiency – we still have to explain why this emerged as an issue starting from the 1990s. Technological development with its consequences for competition is considered to be a very important driver of demutualization. Increased heterogeneity of traders is another factor explaining why exchanges moved towards for-profit organization. Capital-raising, management incentives, illiquidity, changes in regulations and the increased number of alliances are other reasons that can explain the success of private for-profit companies. In this section, the determinants of demutualization are examined.

Efficiency

For many years stock exchanges operated in a poor competitive environment, due to protectionist policies pursued by national authorities and the preferences of stock exchange operators. Exchanges were managed as monopolies, in the interest of members with limited attention to efficiency. Demutualization turned stock exchanges into private companies. In a competitive market, private organizations have one unique objective: profit maximization. As a consequence, there are strong incentives to exploit any inefficiency and to act in the interests of the whole exchange and not only of members. This implies that shareholders will support any innovation, any technological change, as long as this is perceived as being able to increase the demand for the services offered by the exchange and to increase market competitiveness.

Stock exchanges organized as cooperatives and non-profit organizations are not prevented from profit-maximizing. Such exchanges can also exploit inefficiencies and try to increase profits. But several factors can explain why incentives to reduce inefficiencies are lower for cooperative exchanges. First, cooperatives are managed in the members' interests. Innovations and change are undertaken when able to reduce the costs and increase the benefits for the members, but not necessarily for all the exchange participants. Cooperative members will thwart any project that may be in the exchange's interest but can significantly reduce their personal business. The opposition of members worried about losing part of their business delayed, in some exchanges, the switch from a dealer–market-maker trading floor system to electronic trading. The interests of members kept the exchange entrenched in an obsolete structure. The second reason that can explain why cooperatives do not always have the incentive to eliminate inefficiency is that they are prevented from distributing profits. As a consequence members participate only indirectly, in the form of fee reduction or improved quality of the services, to inefficiency reduction.

Also, government-owned structures could in theory exploit inefficiencies and maximize profits. However government-owned institutions are often characterized by multiple objectives: promoting education and assisting long-term development of the capital market are just a few examples. Furthermore political intervention, bureaucratic inertia and protectionist policies can reduce the search for efficiency in government-owned exchanges.

But if demutualization was driven by the search for higher efficiency, what can explain why increasing efficiency became such an issue starting from the 1990s?

Competition

For a long period in their history exchanges operated in a monopoly environment. Organizations operating in a monopoly do not have incentives to try to exploit inefficiencies. They can easily pass inefficiencies to customers, increasing the cost of the services. Shareholders of private profit-maximizing companies, in a monopoly, will try to use the market power to their advantage, acting anti-competitively in order to increase profits as much as possible. As underlined by Lee (2002) cooperatives have some advantages over for-profit companies in the context of low competition. Cooperative owners are also cooperative members and consumers, and will be prevented from increasing prices too much or acting in a non-competitive way. This can explain why for a long time mutual cooperatives were the dominant model for stock exchanges. But this holds if all the users and members are homogeneous. This is not true if some group tries to act anti-competitively to gain an advantage. For example the controlling group can choose to reduce the fees they pay at the expense of other users, or they can block technology changes that are not in their interest. So when competition is low and members are homogeneous, cooperatives can be an optimal governance model.

But if competition increases it becomes more difficult for existing members to protect their 'market share' and their inefficiencies. Initial members will try to limit the access of new users and to limit competition if this is perceived as a threat to them. But if some others members are in favour of opening up the market, they will act to remove barriers. This happened, for example, when traditional members tried to restrict the access of foreign financial institutions to their local market. Shareholders of private for-profit companies will instead support competition if they believe that this will enhance the attractiveness and the performance of the exchange. Competition will force them to stop acting anti-competitively (as in the monopoly situation) and to maximize profits through inefficiency reduction and quality improvement. According to Aggarwal (2002) increased global competition was the main driver of stock demutualization. This can explain why the first to demutualize were the Nordic exchanges, small but highly open and facing increasing competition from other exchanges, mainly London. So, when exchanges were operating as monopolies and member-traders were homogeneous, cooperatives were a good governance model. Competition gave profit-maximizing institutions strong incentives to reduce inefficiency. Increased member heterogeneity, a consequence of globalization and of the increased number of services and products offered by exchanges, made the decision process of cooperatives complicated and led larger members to act to remove the one head, one vote system.

Technology

According to Domowitz and Steil (1999), Schmiedel (2001) and Steil (2002, 2003), demutualization was driven by technology changes and the introduction of automation in trading systems. Traditional exchanges had a physical location (the trading floor) where traders met to negotiate. Access to the trading floor had to be limited to avoid overcrowding. Traders that wanted to be members of the exchange had to pay a fee for membership. To get buy and sell orders executed on the trading floor, other traders had to pay members of the exchange. In this context, as underlined by Steil (2002), the 'trading system' was nothing but a set of rules governing the way transactions were concluded on the floor. Exchanges without the member-traders were nothing but empty boxes. The presence of traders gave a value to the exchange. As a natural consequence member-traders ran exchanges. The introduction of automated trading totally changed the way to execute orders. Orders started to be placed and executed on computers located in every part of the world. Physical presence was eliminated. Limited access was no longer an issue: computers gave the possibility of trading simultaneously a large amount of orders. The value of the exchange today is no longer given by the presence of traders but derives from the automated trading system. The efficiency of the trading system and its capability to attract an increasing amount of orders gives value to the exchange. The owners of the trading system can sell access to it on a for-profit base.

Technology development has also allowed the creation of new alternative trading systems able to compete with traditional exchanges in attracting new trading. In 1993, alternative trading systems accounted for 13 per cent of the volume of NASDAQ and for 1.4 per cent of the volume of the NYSE. In 2000 they attracted 30 per cent of the total share volume of NASDAQ and 3 per cent of the NYSE (Aggarwal and Dahiya 2006). The growing importance of alternative trading systems forced traditional exchanges to pursue cost reduction and to adopt more efficient trading systems. But efficient trading systems are costly to develop and the exchange business model started to be characterized by high upfront costs.

Traditional members that derived profit from intermediating non-member orders tried to stop technological changes that were expected to reduce the demand for their intermediation services even when the change was in the interest of the whole exchange. But finally competition from other systems forced them to accept the change. Market-makers in London tried to resist and blocked the adoption of electronic trading systems until the mid-1990s. The same happened with members of the New York Stock Exchange.

Automation of the trading system has several advantages: increased reliability of execution, instantaneous match of orders, reduced transaction costs and increased efficiency. Furthermore automation has made competition intense and global. Investors are no longer limited to their local market but are free to negotiate orders in the market that provides the highest liquidity, the highest reliability of execution and the lowest fees. To keep business, exchanges have to offer quality and low-cost services. Technology reduced the production and distribution costs of trading and created more integrated and competitive markets. Technology forced exchanges to form alliances and to merge in order to reach the critical mass needed to develop efficient trading systems. This has been one of the most important drivers of stock market globalization and of stock exchange consolidation. The cost of developing a new trading system is very high but once developed the marginal costs of adding new members is very low. Economies of scale in developing and managing an efficient trading system are one reason that can explain the mergers between the London Stock Exchange and Borsa Italiana and between the NYSE and Euronext.

Small and medium-sized regional exchanges operating in competitive environments were the first to be affected by the technology development. Their volumes of trading started to migrate towards larger and more efficient exchanges. To counteract this trend they had to move towards more efficient corporate governance structures or to merge with larger exchanges. This can explain why small and medium-sized exchanges were the first to demutualize.

Increased Heterogeneity

Cooperatives act in the interest of members. If members are homogenous they all have the same interests and give the same value and priority to a given objective. But if members are heterogeneous and their preferences diverge, then the cooperative structure can lead to conflict of interests between members with different goals. Since in cooperatives voting rights are widely dispersed, the decision process can become very difficult. Members have to arrive at a decision starting from different objectives. Each member will try to maximize their own interest and the decision process can lead to inefficient choices that are in the interest of some of the exchange members but not all. Private for-profit companies instead have one single goal (profit maximization), clearly defined, accepted by all participants and easily measurable. If the exchange is listed, shareholders not accepting the goal can sell their shares. All decisions are taken based on profit maximization.

The increased heterogeneity of traders is one of the reasons that could explain why in the 1990s cooperatives' members started to look at the for-profit model as the 'optimal' model. Several factors increased the diversity of market participants. One factor was the internalization and globalization of securities trading. Large international banks and local players became members of the same market. Local players and large international banks had different incentives to maintain barriers to outside ownership. For international banks, the opening of the ownership and the transformation into a private company with a voting system based on the number of shares owned was a way to increase control over the exchange. For local players, demutualization was a threat to the services they offered and to their market power. Locals tried to limit changes. International banks fostered changes aimed at increasing their market power. It was the pressure of large international banks that forced Amsterdam and London to shift to automated trading.

Another factor that has increased the heterogeneity of members has been the increased number of securities and services offered by exchanges. As a consequence, some members focused only on some of the services and others started playing an active role in different services. The two groups ended up with different objectives.

With the development of capital markets and of the exchanges, size also became a source of heterogeneity. For example, one of the reasons that delayed the adoption of an electronic trading system for the NYSE is considered to be the different size of floor brokers and smaller specialists occupying 464 of the 1366 seats available, 'two dollar' brokers holding another 317 seats and big Wall Street institutions having the remaining 575 seats. Small and medium-sized brokers were interested in protecting their market share and tried to defer the adoption of the automatic trading system as much as possible against the interest of large banks. The cooperative system based on the one head, one vote system gave greater power to small brokers.

Two theoretical papers investigate how heterogeneity can impact upon the governance of exchanges. Hart and Moore (1998) compare a cooperative where decisions are taken on the one head, one vote basis with an exchange owned by outsiders that maximizes profits. The one head, one vote system is identified as a cause of inefficiency and conflict of interest in cooperatives with heterogeneous members and different objectives. In this case the voter who ensures the simple majority takes a key role. If this voter bases his decision on personal interests and not on the overall interest of the exchange, inefficiencies arise. Decisions might be based on personal interest more than on the general interest. Outside owners of private companies instead maximize profits and take decisions that are coherent with this goal.

Pirrong (1999, 2000) examines the impact of member diversity on governance structure and arrives at the opposite conclusion: higher heterogeneity makes the non-profit structure optimal. When member diversity increases, the cooperative model becomes more efficient. As explained by Steil (2002), the differences between Hart and Moore and Pirrong can be explained by the hypothesis underlying the two models. Hart and Moore hypothesize that in traditional exchanges run as cooperatives, profits are equally shared between members. They also hypothesize that for-profit exchanges are characterized by separation of ownership and membership. Pirrong does not allow for profit distribution in the case of cooperatives. For Pirrong, exchange profits are distributed to members but there is no separation between owners and members. So the for-profit version of the Pirrong exchange is very similar to the cooperative structure of Hart and Moore. Another difference in the two models is related to the source of heterogeneity. For Hart and Moore, members differ only in relation to the quantity of services that they demand. For Pirrong, members also differ on efficiency and this allows Pirrong to conclude that low-cost members force high-cost members not to extract too much surplus, otherwise the low-cost member will threaten to leave the exchange. This explains why cooperative structures are more efficient when heterogeneity increases. However, the Pirrong version of a for-profit exchange (not allowing separation of ownership and membership) is more similar to traditional exchanges than to the new for-profit organizations. Deutsche Borse and Paris Borse prior to their IPOs in 2001 can be considered similar to the for-profit exchanges for Pirrong. Borsa Italiana prior to the merger with LSE is another example. Both models are based on strong assumptions that are not readily applicable to reality.

Raising of Capital

The need of exchanges to access capital beyond the membership base to finance growth and implement technological developments can be considered another factor contributing to demutualization. Capital availability in cooperatives is limited to member capital. Companies open to outside investors have easier access to new funds. This is particularly relevant if the exchange is listed. As pointed out by Steil (2002), however, most exchanges have had no immediate need for fresh capital after demutualization so that, empirically, raising capital has not been a significant driver of demutualization. More recently Ramos (2006a) finds that stock exchanges demutualized to raise capital and to finance future strategic alliances.

Management Incentives

Another reason to explain the growing importance of the for-profit model for exchanges is that they offer the strongest incentives to increase and to monitor management performance. For-profit companies have a unique goal, profit maximization, which is measurable and to which management compensation can be linked. Cooperatives, government-controlled exchanges and hybrid models have multiple objectives and it is very difficult to measure the consistency of management performance with different goals. So managers can try to justify not producing desirable results as the consequence of having to compromise between different goals. Management of private companies has a unique objective to: maximize profits. Managers are hired for that and are judged based on their ability to reach that goal. In case of listed exchanges, managers are also subject to market discipline. If the stock exchange underperforms, it may be subject to a hostile takeover and the management may be replaced. Their compensation can be directly linked to the performance of the exchange shares and their success can be easily measured. This will further increase managerial incentives to deliver acceptable performance. Other governance models are not subject to the same market discipline and managers have less incentive to exploit inefficiency. When competition increases, exchanges move towards for-profit companies to give managers the strongest incentives to exploit inefficiency.

Strategic Alliances and Partnership

The governance structure can also influence the ability of stock exchanges to pursue alliances, partnership and acquisitions. Listed exchanges have a currency (the price of their stock) to use, in addition to cash, to complete alliances and other corporate operations. Cooperatives cannot use publicly issued shares to complete corporate acquisitions. They have to pay in cash the costs of any corporate alliance. This will increase the opportunity cost of making any alliance or acquisition. Technology improvement, increased competition and globalization forced exchanges to find alliances and to merge. Mergers generate economies of scale. Central services and common facilities can be shared between exchanges and this reduces fixed costs. Mergers and alliances can be considered a way to face competition, and the transformation of seats into shares reduces the amount of cash needed. Several exchanges decided to merge after demutualization. The Helsinki Stock Exchange merged with the Stockholm Stock Exchange after demutualization. The Paris Bourse, Amsterdam and Brussels stock exchanges merged after demutualization to create Euronext.

Illiquidity

Cooperatives and non-profit organizations often do not allow for distribution of profit. In the case of cooperatives, some profit can be recognized by members in terms of better access to the services offered or an increase in the quality of the services. But to have access to the appreciation of their initial investment, members of the cooperatives have to leave member status by selling seats. Owners of listed exchanges can capitalize their initial investment by selling their shares to other investors. So they will support any investment they perceive as able to increase the value of the exchange. Cooperative members may be reluctant to invest in new projects that generate returns to which they do not have immediate access. As a consequence, costly investments aimed at increasing the value of the exchange are less likely in cooperatives than in for-profit companies. Cooperatives may be subject to underinvestment problems. The illiquidity of the initial investment can also create conflicts of interest when members are diverse. Large and small members can perceive the costs and the benefits of a new investment very differently. If there are a few large members originating the majority of the business and a significant number of small companies providing only a small portion of the business, and the voting system is based on one head, one vote, then the small members are critical in the decision process. They can delay good investment because their perceived benefits are limited and they cannot take full advantage of the increased value of the exchange. In for-profit companies, shareholders can participate in the increased value of the exchange through the increase in the share price. In some cases, small members decided to support demutualization in order to receive stock in the demutualized exchange that could be sold in the market to receive a return from their investment.

Homogenization of Regulations

Another important driver of demutualization for European exchanges was the approval of European Directives aimed to harmonize regulations and to create a single market for financial products. The objective of the 93/22/CEE Directive, known as the Investment Service Directive (ISD), was the creation of a single market of financial services in Europe. This Directive defined the principle of mutual recognition and home-country control. Based on this principle each national European stock exchange should offer unlimited access to intermediaries authorized in other European stock exchanges. National barriers on trading in Europe had to be eliminated. Financial institutions performing the same activity should be regulated in the same way all around Europe. The harmonization of regulations increased competition between European exchanges, forcing them towards a search for higher efficiency.

Also in other countries, the change in regulation can be considered as an important driver of increased competition and demutualization. National authorities wanted to protect their national exchanges but progressively started to eliminate barriers to competition. This happened in all major developed countries, especially in Europe and the United States. The initial protectionism had helped exchanges to grow and to acquire enough trading volume to compete in the international arena without the protection of national authorities.

THE LISTING OF STOCK EXCHANGES

Once demutualized, exchanges became public companies with their own securities listed on a market. The main reason to list a stock exchange is considered to be the possibility to collect resources. Such resources are needed to grow autonomously, or to negotiate alliances with other stock exchanges from a stronger position or to take over a competitor. Listing the exchange has several advantages, and some negative effects as well. A first advantage of listing is that it allows direct access to investors and to funding opportunities. For listed exchanges it becomes easier to collect the resources needed to carry out programmes of investment in new technologies. A second advantage is that an assessment of the exchange's market value is always available. Managers are assigned the goal of pursuing strategies able to increase the market value of the stock exchange for shareholders. They can be judged and remunerated with compensation schemes linked to the share performance. Managers also know that if they act in their own interests and this causes a reduction in the value of the exchange, they can be subject to hostile takeovers. This should give them the maximum incentive to avoid inefficiencies, to maximize the value of the exchange and to act in the interests of shareholders.

The drawbacks of being listed include the threat of hostile takeover: the control of the exchange becomes 'purchasable'. The initial listing process also has a cost, and maintaining listing has several costs, for example listing fees and transparency costs. Finally, listed exchanges may focus too much on short-term performance and it may become difficult to pursue medium- and long-term investments without providing proper justification to shareholders.

EMPIRICAL EVIDENCE ON THE PERFORMANCE OF DEMUTUALIZED EXCHANGES

Empirical research has investigated whether listing allowed stock exchanges to increase their efficiency and performances. Schmiedel (2002) finds a positive relation between demutualization and cost efficiency, but Schmiedel (2002) finds cooperatives to be more productive. Krishnamurti et al. (2003) analyse 40 stocks traded both on an Indian demutualized exchange and on an Indian exchange that was not demutualized, and find that the demutualized exchange offered lower transaction costs. Mendiola and O'Hara (2004) analyse how eight stock exchanges[2] performed in the year following the demutualization. Based on their results, exchanges shares overperform both the stocks traded on their markets and the IPOs listed in the same year. The stock exchange IPOs exhibited first-day positive returns and continued to perform well in the months or years after the listing. The overperformance is positively linked to the percentage of shares sold to outside investors. Mendiola and O'Hara (2004) explain the long-run performance of these exchanges as a consequence of the change in the corporate governance. Serifsoy (2005) uses the same sample as Schmiedel but with a longer time frame, and finds evidence that after demutualization exchanges increase in efficiency but not in productivity. Serifsoy (2008) compares efficiency and productivity of exchanges with different governance structures (for example, mutual exchanges and demutualized but customer-owned and publicly listed exchanges) by employing a panel data set of 28 stock exchanges for the years 1999 to 2003. The analysis shows that demutualized exchanges are more technologically efficient but exhibit lower productivity growth than mutual exchanges. Making reference to the difference between demutualized but customer-owned and publicly listed exchanges, there seems to be no evidence that the latter are more efficient or have a higher productivity rate than the former.

Treptow and Wagner (2005) empirically analyse a different issue: the determinants of demutualization. They start from the consideration that members of an exchange will support demutualization only when they perceive that maintaining the old ownership structure will lead to a reduction of demand for exchange services and, as a consequence, reduce profits. They hypothesize that members of small exchanges should vote for demutualization earlier than members of large exchanges. The second factor Treptow and Wagner analyse is the degree of competition. Exchanges that are not subject to competition should have less incentive to change the governance structure of the exchange. The third factor considered is the number of equity issuers. If demutualization increases efficiency and reduces costs (as argued for example by Steil) then equity issuers will try to force the exchange to demutualize. But demutualization could be delayed by the government or by the regulatory authorities when the 'economic importance of the exchange' is very high. Finally, the degree of openness of an economy should increase the propensity to demutualize. The empirical analysis was performed on a sample of 49 exchanges analysed in the period 1995–2003. The results obtained show that small economies with a high degree of competition are more likely to demutualize. This relation increases when the economic importance of the exchange declines. The number of equity issuers has a positive and significant relation with the propensity to demutualize. Owners of large exchanges seem to be more open to demutualization.

Aggarwal and Dahiya (2006) measure the performance of listed exchanges taking into consideration different performance measures. First they consider the first-day return. Empirical studies in the financial literature have demonstrated a significant positive return on the first trading day (the 'IPO under pricing'). Aggarwal and Dahiya provide further results consistent with the literature. Only four of the 20 exchanges analysed had a negative first-day return. The median first-day return was 17.3 per cent, with some cases of very significant performance (Osaka Stock Exchange + 150 per cent). In the long term, the performance is also positive and shares of exchanges outperformed their market index in a period of 3–4 years after the IPO. Aggarwal and Dahiya also estimate some measures of operating performances, arriving at the conclusion that in 2004 most exchanges performed well with a median operating margin equal to 33.8 per cent. The median annual growth rate for the five years following the IPO for the 20 exchanges was equal to 10 per cent for sales and 19 per cent for operating income. Another interesting feature is the absence of debt. Listed exchanges are characterized by a median debt to total asset ratio equal to 0.4 per cent.

Ramos (2006b) investigates why exchanges go public. According to Ramos stock exchanges are more likely to demutualize when they are established in democratic countries with higher corporate governance standards, and when they face strong competition or need to raise capital. Small and younger exchanges are less likely to go public due to the high fixed costs required to start their business (Ritter 1987). There may also be an adverse selection problem (Chemmanur and Fulghieri 1999). Less liquid, riskier exchanges worried about their reputation are more likely to demutualize. The IPO literature also demonstrates that companies go public because owners want to diversify their risk (Pagano et al. 1998) and that going public improves reputation. Finally the IPO literature (Brau and Fawcett 2006; Roell 1996) finds that companies go public to raise capital. Testing this hypothesis on a sample of 109 exchanges, Ramos (2006a) finds that traditional hypotheses common to the traditional IPO literature are not supported in case of stock exchanges: larger, riskier and older exchanges are not more likely to go public. Stock exchanges go public to raise capital and to finance mergers and alliances. Results indicate that merging seems to be a strong motivation for stock exchanges to demutualize and that competition forced exchanges to look for alliances and to demutualize. Ramos (2006a) finds a significant statistical coefficient when testing the hypothesis that stock exchanges went public to facilitate future acquisitions.

Otchere and Abou-Zied (2008) investigate the performance of the Australian Stock Exchange (ASX) after the IPO. They find that the ASX has significantly overperformed the stock index and a control group of companies. The stock exchange profitability ratios increased after the demutualization, a result that holds after controlling for the Australian rate of growth. They also prove that after demutualization the number of foreign investors on the ASX increased and the bid–ask spread narrowed most for small companies. They conclude that not only was demutualization and listing able to enhance the value of the exchange for its shareholders, but it was also beneficial for the stock market. Islam (2010) analyses 11 demutualized stock exchanges during the period 1996–2008 and finds that demutualization increases exchange financial performance, size and liquidity, and lowers the level of debt. Exchanges with relatively large size, low debt and high value of trade are more likely to demutualize. Islam concludes that demutualization enhances the value of the exchange.

CONCLUSIONS

Demutualization is the process that since the 1990s has transformed stock exchanges from mutually owned cooperatives into private for-profit companies. The for-profit model has several benefits compared to other models. Profit maximization becomes the unique goal of the exchange and this introduces a strong incentive to reduce inefficiencies and to increase exchange value. The objective of the exchange is easily measurable and widely accepted. Managers are subject to market discipline and have more incentive to perform well. Decisions are simplified and guided by a common goal. Finally, shares of the exchange can be used to pay for alliances and acquisitions, and to reward shareholders bringing business to the institution. On the other side, cooperatives tend to promote the customers' interests at the expense of other agents' interests. However, cooperatives often have multiple objectives, making it difficult to evaluate and reconcile them. The decision process can be very difficult and the members may not have an incentive to reduce inefficiency when they perceive this as a potential reduction of their business.

The cooperative structure can be considered an optimal governance model when competition is low and when members have homogeneous preferences. Government-owned exchanges have the same limits as cooperatives but they also face the problem of political interference and bureaucracy. So government-owned institutions can be considered optimal models only when the private sector is not yet sufficiently developed or when the private sector is not credible. Empirical research has demonstrated that demutualization increases stock exchange performance. The fact that an increasing number of exchanges has been demutualized can be considered as a further proof that the for-profit listed model is an efficient governance structure in increasingly globalized markets.

NOTES

1. Exchanges are classified into five size groups based on the total equity turnover of 2005 as reported by the World Federation Exchange. Very small exchanges are characterized by an annual turnover below US$5 billion. Small exchanges have an equity turnover between US$5 billion and US$50 billion. Medium exchanges are in the range of US$50 billion to US$200 billion. Large exchanges have an annual turnover between US$200 billion and US$1 trillion. And very large exchanges are defined has having an annual equity turnover higher then US$1 trillion. Ten of the 90 exchanges of the sample are very large and their

percentage on equity turnover is 84 per cent. The 12 large exchanges cover 12 per cent of the equity turnover. Fifteen exchanges are classified as medium and they offer 3 per cent of the total turnover. The remaining 1 per cent are small (19) and very small (34) exchanges.
2. Singapore Stock Exchange, Athens Stock Exchange, Deutsche Borse, Euronext, Toronto Stock Exchange, Australian Stock Exchange, Hong Kong Stock Exchange, London Stock Exchange and NASDAQ.

BIBLIOGRAPHY

Aggarwal, Reena (2002), 'Demutualization and corporate governance of stock exchanges', *Journal of Applied Corporate Finance*, **15**, 105–13.

Aggarwal, Reena and S. Dahiya (2006), 'Demutualization and public offerings of financial exchanges', *Journal of Applied Corporate Finance*, **18** (3), 96–106.

Akhtar, Shamshad (2002), *Demutualization of Stock Exchanges*, Manila, Philippines: Asian Development Bank.

Brau, James C. and Stanley E. Fawcett (2006), 'Initial public offerings: an analysis of theory and practice', *Journal of Finance*, **61** (1), 399–436.

Chemmanur, Thomas and Paolo Fulghieri (1999), 'A theory of the going public decision', *Review of Financial Studies*, **12**, 249–79.

Domowitz, I. and B. Steil (1999), 'Automation, trading costs, and the structure of the securities trading industry', in R.E. Litan and A.M. Santomero (eds), *Brookings-Wharton Papers on Financial Services 1999*, Washington, DC: Brookings Institution Press, pp. 33–81.

Hansmann, H.B. (1988), 'Ownership of the firm', *Journal of Law, Economics and Organization*, **4** (2), 267–304.

Hart, Oliver and Jonh Moore (1996), 'The governance of exchanges: members' cooperatives versus outside ownership', *Oxford Review Economic Policy*, **12**, 53–69.

Hart, Oliver and John Moore (1998), 'Cooperatives vs. outside ownership', NBER Working Paper No. 6421.

Islam, Azzam (2010), 'Stock exchange demutualization and performance', *Global Finance Journal*, **21** (2), 211–22.

Krishnamurti, Chandrasekhar, John M. Sequeira and Fu Fangjian (2003), 'Stock exchange, governance and market quality', *Journal of Banking and Finance*, **27** (9), 1859–78.

Lee, Ruben (2002), 'The future of securities exchanges', The Fifth Annual Conference of the Brookings-Wharton Papers on Financial Services.

Macey, Jonathan R. and Maureen O'Hara (1999), 'Globalisation, exchange governance and the future of exchanges', Brookings-Wharton Papers on Financial Services.

Mendiola, Alfredo and Maureen O'Hara (2004), 'Taking stock in the stock markets: the changing governance of exchanges', working paper.

Otchere, Isaac and Khaled Abou-Zied (2008), 'Stock exchange demutualization, self-listing and performance: the case of the Australian Stock Exchange', *Journal of Banking and Finance*, **32** (4), 512–25.

Pagano, Marco, Fabio Panetta and Luigi Zingales (1998), 'Why do companies go public? An empirical analysis', *Journal of Finance*, **53** (1), 27–64.

Pirrong, Craig (1999), 'The organization of financial exchanges markets: theory and evidence', *Journal of Financial Markets*, **2**, 329–57.

Pirrong, Craig (2000), 'A positive theory of financial exchange organization', *Journal of Law and Economics*, **2**, 437–71.

Ramos, Sofia B. (2006a), 'Stylized facts about stock exchanges: empirical evidence', working paper.

Ramos, Sofia B. (2006b), 'Why do stock exchanges demutualize and go public?' working paper, Swiss Finance Institute.

Ritter, Jay R. (1987), 'The costs of going public', *Journal of Financial Economics*, **19**, 269–81.

Roëll, Ailsa (1996), 'The decision to go public: an overview', *European Economic Review*, **40**, 1071–81.

Schmiedel, H. (2001), 'Technological development and concentration of stock exchanges in Europe', Bank of Finland Discussion Paper No. 21.

Schmiedel, H. (2002), 'Total factor productivity growth in European stock exchanges: a non-parametric frontier approach', Bank of Finland Discussion Paper No. 11.

Serifsoy, B. (2005), 'Demutualization, outsider ownership, and stock exchange performance: empirical evidence', Goethe University Frankfurt Working Paper Series: Finance and Accounting.

Serifsoy, B. (2008), 'Demutualization, outsider ownership, and stock exchange performance: empirical evidence', *Economics of Governance*, **9** (4), 305–39.

Shleifer, A. and R.W. Vishny (1997), 'A survey of corporate governance', *Journal of Finance*, **52**, 737–83.

Steil, Benn (2002), 'Changes in the ownership and governance of securities exchanges: causes and consequences',

Brooking-Wharton Papers on Financial Services, http://www.fese.be/initiatives/other_reports/brookings_wharton_2002.pdf
Steil, Benn (2003), 'Comment letter on NYSE governance to Special Committee on Governance of the NYSE', 1 July.
Treptow, Felix (2006), *The Economics of Demutualization: An Empirical Analysis of the Securities Exchange Industry*, Innovation und Entrepreneurship series, Munich: Deutscher Universitäts-Verlag, Gabler Edition Wissenschaft.
Treptow, Felix and Stefan Wagner (2005), 'Stock exchanges and issuers: a changing relationship', *Quarterly Journal of Economic Research*, **74** (4), 125–39.

8 How stock exchange mergers and acquisitions affect competitors' shareholder value: global evidence

Iftekhar Hasan, Heiko Schmiedel and Liang Song

INTRODUCTION

Stock exchange mergers and acquisitions (M&As) have recently become a growing trend due to capital market globalization, the innovation of technology and stock exchange demutualization (Hasan et al. 2003; Knowledge@Wharton 2006). For instance, the NYSE Group and Euronext merged and became the first transatlantic equities market, NYSE Euronext. Furthermore, NYSE's competitor, NASDAQ, recently bought the Nordic stock exchange operator OMX. Global exchange integrations such as these may create more competition and increase the efficiency of capital flows (US Securities and Exchange Commission 2007).

The existing literature has investigated the effects of stock exchange M&As from several dimensions including stock liquidity (Nielsson 2009; Hasan et al. 2010; Francis et al. 2010; Hasan and Schmiedel 2004). However, many parties, including investors, firms and financial intermediaries, and the overall economy, are involved and affected by such an analysis (Nielsson 2009). Therefore, the existing literature concerning the effects of stock exchange M&As is selective and incomplete in its coverage. In this chapter, we examine how stock exchange M&As affect their competitors' shareholder value in order to provide additional insight into the influence of stock exchange M&As.

Specifically, we focus on 63 stock exchanges involved in 63 M&As between 2000 and 2007 and investigate their public competitors' short-run share price responses. We define that two stock exchanges are competitors if they are both located in the same continent or region. We find that when one stock exchange is merged with another, its competitor significantly loses shareholder value. When the stock exchange is involved in a horizontal (cross-region) transaction its competitor loses more value than if it were involved in a vertical (within-region) one. When the stock exchange is merged with another stock exchange in a country that has a more developed stock market or higher governance, it will hurt its competitors' shareholder value more.

This study makes several contributions to the literature. First, after stock exchanges are demutualized and merged with other stock exchanges, it is important to question whether these integration events create or destroy shareholder value. However, although more and more stock exchanges are going public, most stock exchanges are still not traded publicly and cannot provide necessary stock price data. By focusing on the share price response of non-public stock exchanges' public competitors, we can overcome this problem and examine how non-public stock exchanges M&As affect shareholder value from another aspect. Second, the competitors' M&A activities will significantly influence the stock exchange's market share and further its revenues. Thus, this chapter can also guide outside investors to value stock exchange shares in response to their competitors' integration activities.

The remainder of the chapter is organized as follows: the next section presents the related literature and develops our hypotheses. We then describe the sample and provide descriptive statistics. Empirical tests and results are presented in the following section. We conclude with an overview of the findings of the chapter.

RELATED LITERATURE AND HYPOTHESIS DEVELOPMENT

The existing literature has demonstrated the benefit of stock exchange M&As. For example, Hasan and Malkamäki (2001) found that economies of scale and scope exist among the stock exchanges. Nielsson (2009) demonstrated that stock trading liquidity significantly increased after the Euronext stock exchange mergers. More importantly, Arnold et al. (1999) found that the merging of US regional stock exchanges attracted market share and led to narrower bid–ask spreads. Thus, shareholders of stock exchanges benefit from the synergy gains that occur with M&As and the stock exchanges' competitors will lose market share. We summarize the related hypotheses as follows:

Hypothesis 1: The competitor's stock price response to the announcement of a stock exchange M&A activity is negative.

Stock exchange M&A deals can be classified as two types. Specifically, the deal is a horizontal integration if the stock exchange integrates with another exchange that has a similar business model and a vertical integration otherwise. M&As between two partners with the same business models enable stock exchanges better to acquire knowledge, skills and governance mechanisms from partner exchanges than vertical deals (Tasi 2001; Anand and Khanna 2000; Dessein 2005; Gomes-Casseres et al. 2006). The existing literature (for example Serifsoy 2007) has shown that exchanges that diversify into related activities are less efficient than exchanges that remain focused on the cash market. In addition, horizontal M&As can enhance the stock exchange's market power in its own country or other countries and put more market pressure on its competitors. Based on these arguments, we hypothesize that:

Hypothesis 2: If the stock exchanges' integration activities are horizontal, its competitor loses more shareholder value.

Stock exchange M&A deals can also be classified as cross-region and within-region. The formation of a global exchange is an important driver for many stock exchange M&As. Thus, we expect that cross-region integration activities can put more market pressure on stock exchange competitors because they can attract more outsider investors. Additionally, the learning effect is more pronounced when the partner stock exchange is located in another region. Thus, the synergy gain in cross-region deals should be much larger and should attract more market share from the stock exchange's competitors. Our hypothesis can be formalized as follows:

Hypothesis 3: If the stock exchanges' integration activities are cross-region, its competitor loses more shareholder value.

In cross-region deals, the difference in stock market development and investor protection between the partnering country and the sample exchange's country might also influence its competitor's shareholder value. The more developed a stock market is, the more liquidity it can provide. Thus, when the partnering stock exchange is located in a country with a more developed stock market, there should be more synergy gain for the sample stock exchange because of the increased access to liquidity. Krishnamurti et al. (2003) argue that small and medium-sized investors would be attracted to the exchange scoring higher on these variables: use of technology, internal control systems, transparency and investor protection. Thus, shareholders of such stock exchanges would benefit from increased revenue due to increased trading volumes and initial public offerings (IPOs); as such, their competitors would lose shareholder value. Similarly, the stock exchange with relatively low governance standards may benefit from the governance transfer effect in the process of the consolidation. Specifically, the low-governance stock exchange learns how to govern its firms more effectively from the partnering exchange (Tasi 2001; Anand and Khanna 2000; Dessein 2005; Gomes-Casseres et al. 2006). Thus, when the partnering stock exchange is located in a country with higher investor protection, there should be more synergy gain for the sample stock exchange from increased governance effects and in the future put more market pressure on its competitors. In our chapter, we hypothesize that:

Hypothesis 4: If the stock exchange is merged with another stock exchange in a country with better market development, its competitor loses more shareholder value.

Hypothesis 5: If the stock exchange is merged with another stock exchange in a country with better governance, its competitor loses more shareholder value.

DATA

Sample Description

To construct our final sample, we first collected stock exchange M&A announcement data from 2000 to 2007 from a series of sources, including newsletters and press releases from the World Federation of Exchanges and the European Federation of Securities Exchanges, the Internet, press archives and ad hoc announcements of individual stock exchanges. From these sources, we obtained 63 completed M&A deals.

Panel A of Table 8.1 presents the stock exchange M&A events categorized by year of announcement. As shown in Table 8.1, the number of stock exchange M&As is not evenly distributed over the 2000–2007 sample period. The largest number of announcements of M&As in one year is 14 in 2006, followed by 11 in both 2002 and 2007. Panel B shows that 68.25 per cent of total stock exchange M&As are horizontal and 63.49 per cent are cross-region. Panel C presents the M&A events by type of technological integration and shows that complete system integration dominates our sample.

Table 8.1 Announcements of stock exchange M&As

Panel A: Annual distribution of stock exchange integration activities		
Year of announcement	Number of announcements	Percentage of total
2000	7	11.11
2001	11	17.46
2002	7	11.11
2003	3	4.76
2004	7	11.11
2005	3	4.76
2006	14	22.22
2007	11	17.46
Total	63	100
Panel B: Distribution of stock exchange integration activities by type		
Type of integration activities	Number of announcements	Percentage of total
Horizontal	43	68.25
Vertical	20	31.75
Cross-region	40	63.49
Within-region	23	36.51
Panel C: Distribution of stock exchange integration activities by type of technological integration		
Type of technological integration	Number of announcements	Percentage of total
Outsourcing	2	3.17
Common access	2	3.17
Common systems	8	12.70
Common operation	4	6.35
Complete system integration	35	55.56
Other type of integration	12	19.05

Note: This table presents the sample distributions by year and type of integrations.

To examine the share price reaction, we included 14 public stock exchanges with stock price data available in Datastream. As shown in Table 8.2, these public stock exchanges are located in different regions such as North America, South America, Asia Pacific and Europe, and are all large stock exchanges.

For each stock exchange in our 63 stock exchange M&A deals, we matched one public stock exchange competitor using the following procedure. First, the corresponding public stock exchange competitor needed to be located in the same region as our sample exchange. If there was more than one public stock exchange that was located in the same region as our sample exchange, we selected the public stock exchange that did not have M&A and alliance activities around the event window of our sample stock exchange. There were several stock exchanges from the Middle East and North African regions. We were unable to find public stock exchange competitors from these regions and so we excluded them from our sample. Our final event study sample included 63 stock

Table 8.2 List of public stock exchanges

No.	Public stock exchange company name	The country location of its headquarters	The region of its headquarters	Stock exchange in which its stock is listed	Market value at the end of 2007 ($ million)
1	Australian Securities Exchange	Australia	Asia Pacific	Australian Securities Exchange	9058.76
2	Chicago Board of Trade	United States	North America	New York Stock Exchange	12 021.10
3	Chicago Mercantile Exchange	United States	North America	NASDAQ	36 524.01
4	Deutsche Boerse	Germany	Europe	Frankfurt Stock Exchange	20 126.72
5	Euronext	France	Europe	Paris Bourse	2326.04
6	Hong Kong Stock Exchange	Hong Kong (China)	Asia Pacific	Hong Kong Stock Exchange	15 262.42
7	London Stock Exchange	United Kingdom	Europe	London Stock Exchange	10 981.25
8	NASDAQ	United States	North America	NASDAQ	5631.27
9	New York Stock Exchange	United States	North America	New York Stock Exchange	23 259.04
10	OMX Exchanges	Sweden	Europe	Stockholm Exchange	4872.95
11	Osaka Securities Exchange	Japan	Asia Pacific	Osaka Securities Exchange	1263.40
12	São Paulo Stock Exchange	Brazil	South America	São Paulo Stock Exchange	16.26
13	Singapore Exchange	Singapore	Asia Pacific	Singapore Exchange	9934.95
14	TSX Group	Canada	North America	Toronto Exchange	3533.05

Note: This table describes 14 public stock exchange companies used in our sample, the country and the region in which their headquarters are located, the stock exchanges in which they are listed and their market value at the end of 2007.

exchanges (39 in Europe, 10 in North America, 3 in South America and 17 in the Asia-Pacific region) and 116 event observations.

Variable Definition and Summary Statistics

In our regression specification, we included a series of deal characteristics as follows. The variable *Cross_Region* is a dummy variable, which is equal to 1 when the deal is a cross-region transaction, and is otherwise 0. The dummy variable *Horizontal* equals 1 when the deal is a horizontal transaction and 0 otherwise. *Technological_Integration_Dummies* is a series of dummy variables to indicate the type of technological integration (outsourcing, common access, common systems, common operations, complete system integration, and other types of integration).

We also controlled for a series of exchange characteristics, which were measured at the fiscal year-end prior to the integration announcement. We obtained the data from Worldscope and defined the variable *Log (Total_Assets)* as the natural logarithm of total assets. The variable *Tobin's Q* is defined as the ratio of market value of assets over book value of assets. The variable *Leverage* is defined as total liabilities divided by total assets, while the variable *Cash_Flow* is equal to operating income before depreciation minus interest expenses minus income taxes minus capital expenditures, scaled by total assets.

We employed the natural logarithm of GDP per capita (*Log(GDP_Per_Capita)*) and the natural logarithm of GDP growth (*Log(GDP_Growth)*) to control for the countries' macroeconomic conditions, which are from the World Development Indicator database. We also constructed two dummy variables: *Same_Language*, which equals 1 when two partnering stock exchanges' countries share the same language reported in atlas and zero otherwise; and *Same_Legal_System*, which equals 1 when two partnering stock exchanges' countries share the same legal origin as reported in La Porta et al. (1998), and zero otherwise. To measure the difference in stock market development between the partnering stock exchange country and the sample stock exchange's country, we constructed the difference of three variables from the World Development Indicators: market capitalization of listed stock scaled by gross domestic product (GDP), stock traded turnover ratio, and total value of stock traded scaled by GDP (*Difference_Market_To_GDP*, *Difference_Turnover* and *Difference_Stock_Trade_To_GDP*). We took the country-level indices on shareholder rights and accounting standards, and the efficiency of the legal system, from La Porta et al. (1998). We then used the product of the shareholder rights index and the efficiency of the legal system to construct the index of shareholder protection. The differences of the corresponding indices (shareholder protection index and accounting standards) between the partner stock exchanges' country and the sample stock exchange's country (*Difference Shareholder Protection* and *Difference Accounting Standards*) provide an indication of the difference in investor protection between the partnering stock exchanges' countries.

Table 8.3 presents the summary statistics. Financial variables are Winsorized at the 1st and 99th percentiles to avoid the effect of outliers. The summary statistics of these variables are consistent with what has been reported in the existing literature.

TESTS AND RESULTS

Event Study Findings

We conducted a standard event study to measure the competitor's stock price response associated with the announcement of stock exchange M&As. The model is specified as:

$$r_{it} = \alpha_i + \beta_{1,i} r_{m,jt} + \varepsilon_{it} \tag{8.1}$$

where i is the exchange competitor index, j is the exchange country market index, t represents a one-day period time index and $r_{i,t}$ represents the daily rates of return. These

Table 8.3 Summary statistics

Variable	Obs	Mean	Std. Dev.	Min	Max
Panel A: Exchange performance measures					
Competitor's CAR[−1,1] (%)	116	−1.02	0.37	−6.52	4.23
Panel B: Deal characteristics					
Horizontal_Integration	63	0.63	0.48	0.00	1.00
Cross_Region	63	0.68	0.47	0.00	1.00
Panel D: Exchange characteristics					
Total_Assets ($ millions)	116	7125.01	11356.04	45.76	68467.36
Cash_Flow	116	0.10	0.11	0.03	0.37
Leverage	116	0.45	0.18	0.41	0.76
Tobin's Q	116	2.98	2.24	1.04	8.47
Panel E: Difference in language and legal system					
GDP_Per_Capita ($)	116	23256.26	7378.03	998.35	36478.03
GDP_Growth (%)	116	2.89	2.53	−2.21	10.36
Panel F: Macroeconomic development					
Same_Language	116	0.51	0.27	0.00	1.00
Same_Legal_System	116	0.29	0.26	0.00	1.00
Panel G: Difference in capital market development					
Difference_Market_To_GDP (%)	116	0.05	0.69	−2.35	2.56
Difference_Turn_Over (%)	116	0.13	0.61	−1.75	1.67
Difference_Stock_Trade_To_GDP (%)	116	0.19	0.89	−2.32	1.99
Panel H: Difference in country-level governance					
Difference_Shareholder_Protection	116	1.59	20.90	−40.00	48.00
Difference_Accounting_Standards	116	2.78	11.25	−20.00	56.00

Note: This table presents the summary statistics. Performance measures and exchange characteristics are Winsorized at the 1st and 99th percentiles. Variable definitions are given in Appendix Table A8.1.

variables are calculated for all stocks in our sample using Datastream's total return index (RI), which includes dividends as well as price changes. $r_{m,jt}$ is defined as domestic market return. The announcement day is day zero, the estimation period for the market model estimate begins on day −150 and ends on day −31.

We constructed a standardized parametric test statistic to determine whether the mean abnormal return is significantly different than zero.[1] We also reported the results of Wilcoxon signed-rank tests. As shown in Table 8.4, the stock exchange competitor's three-day cumulative abnormal return is a statistically significant −1.85 per cent (Z-statistic = −3.35) for stock exchange M&As. The non-parametric tests confirm these findings. This evidence suggests that if a stock exchange is involved with an M&A deal, its competitor loses significant shareholder value.

We further classified our sample into different groups to examine patterns in the sub-samples. As shown in Table 8.4, the stock exchange competitor's three-day cumulative abnormal return was a statistically significant −2.08 per cent (Z-statistic = −3.64) for

Table 8.4 Competitors' cumulative return [−1, 1] around announcement of stock exchange M&A in full and subsample

Event type	Number of observations	Competitor's CAR[−1,1] (%)	Z-statistic	Proportion of negative value (sign test) (%)
M&A	63	−1.85	−3.35***	75**
Cross-region M&A	40	−2.08	−3.64***	78**
Within-region M&A	23	−1.78	−3.13***	71**
Horizontal M&A	43	−1.99	−2.98***	79**
Vertical M&A	20	−1.66	−3.11***	81**

Note: This table presents the results of the event study in full and subsamples. *, ** and *** stand for significance at the 10%, 5% and 1% levels.

cross-region stock exchange M&As. The stock exchange competitor's three-day cumulative abnormal returns for within-region integration events were a little bit lower, but still significant. This evidence may suggest that if the stock exchange is involved in a cross-region M&A deal instead of a within-region deal, its competitor loses more shareholder value. The non-parametric tests (sign tests) confirm these findings. Table 8.4 also shows that if the stock exchange is involved in a horizontal M&A deal instead of a vertical one, its competitor may lose more shareholder value.

Cross-Sectional Analysis

Methodology and results

In this section, we examine the cross-sectional differences in the stock exchange competitor's short-run abnormal returns for the stock exchange M&A announcements using regression analysis. The model specification is as follows:

$$\begin{aligned} \textit{Competitor's CAR[1,1]} &= \alpha_i + \beta_1 \textit{ Deal Characteristics} + \beta_2 \textit{Exchange Charactistics} \\ &\quad + \beta_3 \textit{ Macro Development} + \beta_4 \textit{ Other Control Variables} + \varepsilon \end{aligned} \tag{8.2}$$

where the dependent variable *Competitor's CAR[−1, 1]* is the stock exchange competitor's three-day announcement abnormal return. The deal characteristics include the variables *Horizontal_Integration* and *Cross_Region*. The exchange characteristics include *Log(Total_Assets)*, *Tobin's Q*, *Leverage* and *Cash_Flow*. The other control variables include *Log(GDP_Per_Capital)*, *Log(GDP_Growth)*, *Technological_Integration_Dummies*, *Same_Language* and *Same_Legal_System*. Country and year fixed effects were also included in our estimation.

As shown in Table 8.5, if the stock exchange is involved in a horizontal M&A deal instead of a vertical one, its competitor loses more shareholder value. We also found that if the stock exchange is involved with a cross-region M&A deal instead of a within-region deal, its competitor loses more shareholder value. These results are not only statistically significant, but are also economically significant. Based on the results shown in column (1), the stock exchange competitor's three-day cumulative abnormal return if the

Table 8.5 Cross-sectional analysis of CARs upon announcement

Dependent variable	Competitor's CAR[−1,1]		
	(1)	(2)	(3)
Deal characteristics			
Horizontal_Integration	−0.310**	−0.324*	−0.301*
	(−2.269)	(−1.901)	(−1.903)
Cross_Region	−0.325**	−0.321***	−0.331***
	(−2.078)	(−3.672)	(−3.901)
Exchange characteristics			
Log (Total_Assets)		0.623	0.123***
		(0.801)	(4.314)
Tobin's Q		−0.351	−0.132
		(−0.892)	(−0.101)
Leverage		1.356	0.361
		(1.014)	(0.078)
Cash_Flow		−0.041	−0.054
		(−0.302)	(−1.013)
Macroeconomic variables			
Log(GDP_Per_Capita)			−1.011
			(−0.892)
Log(GDP_Growth)			0.516
			(0.367)
Control for			
Technological_Integration_Dummies	Yes	Yes	Yes
Same_Language	Yes	Yes	Yes
Same_Legal_System	Yes	Yes	Yes
Country effect	Yes	Yes	Yes
Year effect	Yes	Yes	Yes
Adjusted R-squared	0.15	0.18	0.21
No. of observations	116	116	116

Note: The dependent variable is the stock exchange competitor's three-day cumulative abnormal return (CAR) in percentage points. Variable definitions are given in Appendix Table A8.1. In brackets are t-statistics based on standard errors adjusted for heteroskedasticity and country clustering. *, ** and *** stand for significance at the 10%, 5% and 1% level respectively.

stock exchange was involved in a horizontal M&A deal was on average 0.310 per cent higher than that if the stock exchange was involved with a vertical M&A deal. The stock exchange competitor's three-day cumulative abnormal return if the stock exchange was involved in a cross-region M&A deal was on average 0.325 per cent higher than that if the stock exchange was involved in a within-region M&A deal.

Market development

In cross-region deals, the difference in stock market development between two partnering countries might also influence a stock exchanges competitor's shareholder value.

Table 8.6 Cross-sectional analysis of CARs upon announcement controlling for the difference in capital market development

Dependent variable	Competitor's CAR[−1,1]		
	(1)	(2)	(3)
Deal characteristics			
Horizontal_Integration	−0.324*	−0.361*	−0.367*
	(−1.901)	(−1.878)	(−1.971)
Cross_Region	−0.314***	−0.341***	−0.325***
	(−3.891)	(−3.901)	(−3.999)
Difference in capital market development			
Difference_Market_To_GDP	−0.173***		
	(−4.012)		
Difference_Turnover		−0.160***	
		(−4.103)	
Difference_Stock_Trade_To_GDP			−0.067***
			(−4.001)
Control for			
Exchange characteristics	Yes	Yes	Yes
Macroeconomic variables	Yes	Yes	Yes
Technological_Integration_Dummies	Yes	Yes	Yes
Same_Language	Yes	Yes	Yes
Same_Legal_System	Yes	Yes	Yes
Country effect	Yes	Yes	Yes
Year effect	Yes	Yes	Yes
Adjusted R-squared	0.21	0.22	0.21
No. of observations	116	116	116

Note: The dependent variable is the stock exchange competitor's three-day cumulative abnormal return (CAR) in percentage points. Variable definitions are given in Appendix Table A8.1. In brackets are t-statistics based on standard errors adjusted for heteroskedasticity and country clustering. *, ** and *** stand for significance at the 10%, 5% and 1% level respectively.

If a stock exchange is merged with another stock exchange in a country with a more developed stock market, it will put more market pressure on its competitors. In this subsection, we attempt to test this empirically.

Specifically, we added another term (*Difference_Market_To_GDP, Difference_Turnover* or *Difference_Stock_Trade_To_GDP*) to the regression, respectively. As shown in Table 8.6, our main results still hold. The coefficients of the variables *Difference_Market_To_GDP, Difference_Turnover* or *Difference_Stock_Trade_To_GDP* were significantly negative. One percentage of change in the variable *Difference_Market_To_GDP* led to a 0.173 per cent decline of the stock exchanges competitor's three-day cumulative abnormal return. These results suggest that if a stock exchange is merged with another stock exchange in a country with a more developed stock market, it will hurt its competitors' shareholder value.

Table 8.7 Cross-sectional analysis of CARs upon announcement controlling for the difference in governance

Dependent variable	Competitor's CAR[−1,1]	
	(1)	(2)
Deal characteristics		
Horizontal	−0.324***	−0.412***
	(−3.999)	(−4.013)
Cross_Region	−0.312***	−0.302***
	(−5.001)	(−4.012)
Difference in capital market development		
Difference_Turnover	−0.035***	−0.036***
	(−3.992)	(−3.783)
Difference in governance		
Difference_Shareholder_Protection	−0.021***	
	(−3.903)	
Difference_Accounting_Standards		−0.102***
		(−2.981)
Control for		
Exchange characteristics	Yes	Yes
Macroeconomic variables	Yes	Yes
Technological_Integration_Dummies	Yes	Yes
Same_Language	Yes	Yes
Same_Legal_System	Yes	Yes
Country effect	Yes	Yes
Year effect	Yes	Yes
Adjusted R-squared	0.23	0.25
No. of observations	116	116

Note: The dependent variable is the stock exchange competitor's three-day cumulative abnormal return (CAR) in percentage points. Variable definitions are given in Appendix Table A8.1. In brackets are t-statistics based on standard errors adjusted for heteroskedasticity and country clustering. *, ** and *** stand for significance at the 10%, 5% and 1% level respectively.

Governance

Similarly, the difference in governance that occurs within two partnering stock exchanges' countries might also influence the shareholder value of the stock exchanges' competitor. If the stock exchange is merged with another stock exchange in the country with higher governance, it will help the stock exchange to improve its corporate governance and put more market pressure on its competitors. In this subsection, we attempt to test this theory empirically.

Specifically, we added another term (*Difference_Shareholder_Protection* or *Difference_Accounting_Standards*) to the regression. As shown in Table 8.7, our main results still held. The coefficients of the variables *Difference_Shareholder_Protection* and *Difference_Accounting_Standards* were significantly negative. These results are not only statistically significant but are also economically significant. For instance, one percentage point change in the variable *Difference_Shareholder_Protection* decreased the stock exchange competitor's three-day cumulative abnormal return by 0.021 per cent. These results suggest that if a stock exchange is merged with another stock exchange in a country with higher governance, it will help the stock exchange improve its corporate governance and hurt its competitors' shareholder value.

Robustness Tests

To ensure that our results are robust, we examined another model specification as follows:

1. Because we conducted the event study in a multi-country context, we extended the market model by adding a US market return term to equation (8.1) in order to calculate abnormal return.
2. We used different event windows, that is, [−2, 2] and [−3, 3], to calculate abnormal return.
3. We used different estimation windows, that is, [−120, 30] and [−150, 40], to calculate abnormal return.

Using these different regression specifications, we still found qualitatively similar results. Although these results are not reported, they can be made available upon request.

SUMMARY AND CONCLUSIONS

In this chapter, we matched 63 stock exchanges involved in 63 M&As between 2000 and 2007 to a public stock exchange in the same region and investigated these public stock exchanges' short-run share price responses. We found that when one stock exchange is merged with another, its competitor loses significant shareholder value. When a stock exchange is involved in a horizontal (cross-region) transaction instead of a vertical (within-region) one, its competitor loses more shareholder value. If a stock exchange is merged with another stock exchange in a country with a more developed stock market or with higher governance, it will hurt its competitors' shareholder value.

Recently, more and more stock exchanges are going public; however, many stock exchanges are still not being traded publicly. By focusing on the share price response of a non-public stock exchange's public competitor, this chapter examines how these non-public stock exchange M&As affect shareholder value from another aspect. Furthermore, the competitors' M&A activities will significantly influence the stock exchange's market share and further its revenues. Thus, this chapter can be a guide for outside investors to value stock exchange shares in response to their competitors' integration activities.

NOTE

1. A detailed description of the test statistics and their calculation can been seen in Mackinlay (1997).

REFERENCES

Anand, B.N. and T. Khanna (2000), 'Do firms fearn to create value? The case of alliances', *Strategic Management Journal*, **21**, 295–315.

Arnold, T., P. Hersch, J.H. Mulherin and J. Netter (1999), 'Merging markets', *Journal of Finance*, **52**, 655–81.

Dessein, W. (2005), 'Information and control in ventures and alliances', *Journal of Finance*, **65** (5), 2513–49.

Francis, B., I. Hasan, H. Schmiedel, Y.W. Fang and L. Song (2010), 'Network of stock exchanges: what creates liquidity?' Working Paper, Rensselaer Polytechnic Institute.

Gomes-Casseres, B., J. Hagedoorn and A.B. Jaffe (2006), 'Do alliances promote knowledge flows?' *Journal of Financial Economics*, **80**, 5–33.

Hasan, I. and M. Malkamäki (2001), 'Are expansions cost effective for stock exchanges? A global perspective', *Journal of Banking and Finance*, **25**, 2339–66.

Hasan, I., M. Malkamäki and H. Schmiedel (2003), 'Technology, productivity and stock exchanges: a global experience', *Journal of Banking and Finance*, **27**, 1743–73.

Hasan, I. and H. Schmiedel (2004), 'Does network add value? Evidence from the stock exchange', *International Review of Financial Analysis*, **13**, 601–19.

Hasan, I., H. Schmiedel and L. Song (2010), 'Growth strategies and value creation: what works best for stock exchanges?' Working Paper, European Central Bank and Bank of Finland.

Knowledge@Wharton (2006), 'LSE, NYSE, OMX, NASDAQ, Euronext . . . Why stock exchanges are scrambling to consolidate', written statement, http://knowledge.wharton.upenn.edu/article.cfm?articleid=1428.

Krishnamurti, C., J.M. Sequeira and F. Fangjian (2003), 'Stock exchange governance and market quality', *Journal of Banking and Finance*, **27**, 1859–78.

La Porta, R., F. Lopez-de-Silanes, A. Shleifer and R. Vishny (1998), 'Law and finance', *Journal of Political Economy*, **54**, 471–517.

Mackinlay, A.C. (1997), 'Event studies in economics and finance', *Journal of Economic Literature*, **35** (1), 13–39.

Nielsson, U. (2009), 'Stock exchange merger and liquidity: the case of Euronext', *Journal of Financial Markets*, **12** (2), 229–67.

Serifsoy, B. (2007), 'Stock excange business models and their operative performance', *Journal of Banking and Finance*, **31**, 2978 3012.

Tasi, W. (2001), 'Knowledge transfer in intraorganizational networks: effects of network position and absorptive capacity on business unit innovation and performance', *Academy of Management Journal*, **44** (5), 996–1004.

US Securities and Exchange Commission (2007), 'A global view: examining cross-border exchange mergers', written statement.

APPENDIX

Table A8.1 Definitions of the variables

Variables	Description
Exchange performance measures	
Competitor's CAR [−1, 1]	The stock exchange competitor's three-day cumulative abnormal return (in percentage points) calculated using the market model as shown in equation (8.1)
Deal characteristics	
Intergration_Type	It is equal to 3 if the deal is an M&A, 2 if the deal is a joint venture, and 1 if the deal is a non-equity alliance
Horizontal_Integration	It equals 1 if the deal is a horizontal transaction, otherwise 0
Cross_Region	It is equal to 1 if the deal is a cross-region transaction, otherwise 0
Technological_ Integration_Dummies	Dummy variables to indicate the various types of technological integration including outsourcing, common access, common systems, common operations, complete system integration, and other type of integration
Exchange characteristics	
Total_Assets	The stock exchange's total assets
Cash_Flow	Operating income before depreciation minus interest expenses minus income taxes minus capital expenditures, scaled by total assets
Leverage	Total liabilities scaled by total assets
Tobin's Q	Market value of assets over book value of assets
Macroeconomic development variables	
GDP_Per_Capita	GDP per capita
GDP_Growth	Annual GDP growth
Difference in language and legal environment	
Same_Language	It equals one when two partnering stock exchanges' countries share the same language and zero otherwise
Same_Legal_System	It equals one when two partnering stock exchanges' countries share the same legal origin and zero otherwise
Difference in capital market development	
Difference_Market_ To_GDP	The difference in the market capitalization of listed stock scaled by GDP between the partner stock exchange's country and the sample stock exchange's country
Difference_Turnover	The difference in the stock traded turnover ratio between the partner stock exchange's country and the sample stock exchange's country
Difference_Stock_ Trade_To_GDP	The difference in the total value of stock traded scaled by GDP between the partner stock exchange's country and the sample stock exchange's country
Difference in governance	
Difference_Share_ Holder_Protection	The difference in the shareholder protection index (the product of the shareholder rights index and the efficiency of the legal system) between the partner stock exchange's country and the sample stock exchange's country
Difference_Accounting_ Standard	The difference in accounting standard index between the partner stock exchange's country and the sample stock exchange's country

9 Cross-listing and the evolution of global stock market liquidity

Manuela Geranio

Debate on cross-listing began back in the 1970s, but is still alive and kicking. The globalization of capital markets, combined with the recent consolidation wave among stock exchanges, has encouraged growing competition among major listing centres to capture companies choosing to raise capital through equity issues beyond their home markets. Indeed, a company that cross-lists its shares can get listed on one or more equity markets besides the domestic one. The most common case of cross-listing is that of a secondary listing, which is where the main market remains the firm's home market, while the secondary market is more likely a US exchange (or some other global financial hub). More rarely, in the case of a primary listing, the foreign market becomes the only stock exchange where the company's shares will be admitted and traded.

Typically, a company facilitates the negotiations of its shares in a foreign country by issuing depositary receipts (DRs or ADRs[1]). A depository receipt represents ownership in the shares of a foreign stock, according to a specified ratio, and is denominated in local currency (that is, dollars in the US). DR programmes' complexity and costs vary, according to the aims of the issue (that is, trading only or also collecting new funds) and the targeted investors (institutional investors only or the general public). For instance, in the US, the easiest and least costly channel is the over-the-counter (OTC) segment, for which Level I ADRs are issued and traded on the OTC Bulletin Board or Pink Sheets. Institutional investors can be targeted by private placements (Regulation S/Rule 144a), but official listings on main exchanges require Level II or Level III ADRs (the latest being required in the case of issuance of new shares).

A large part of cross-listing literature focuses on DRs, as they play a crucial role in international listing. In particular, the majority of papers refer to official listed programmes (that is, ADRs levels II and III) as they study the scrutinizing role played by listing authorities and equity market supervisory institutions. In the following section I provide a review of related theories and empirical findings. Such review will be precipitated by a picture of the cross-listing market in the last decade, in order to appreciate better the past evolution of studies and new emerging perspectives.

A CURRENT PICTURE OF CROSS-LISTING ACTIVITY

Figure 9.1 reports on the evolution in the number of domestic and foreign listed companies in world equity markets between 2000 and 2009 (data from the World Federation of Exchanges). Since the beginning of this period the total amount has grown. Total listed companies increased from 31 802 to 45 358. Among them, foreign listed companies

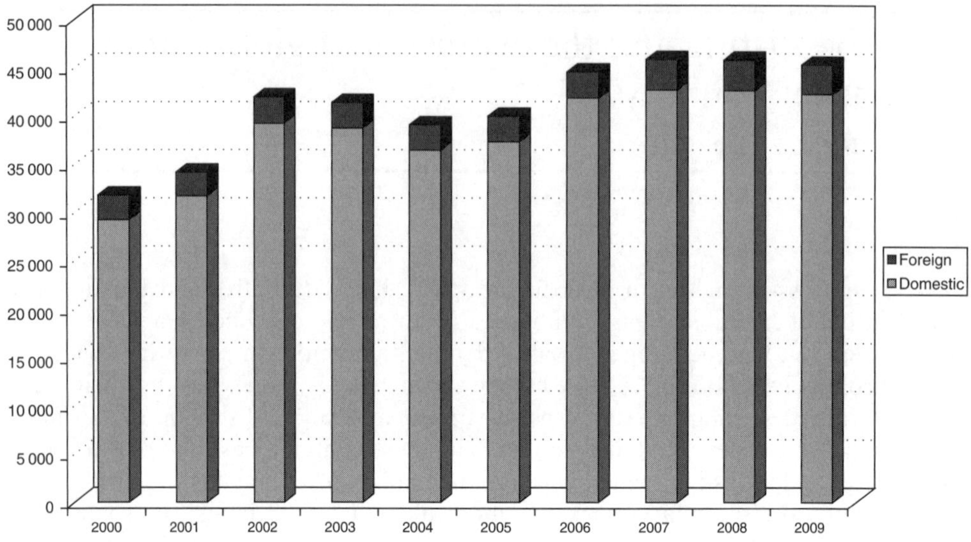

Figure 9.1 *Number of domestic and foreign listed companies on world markets*

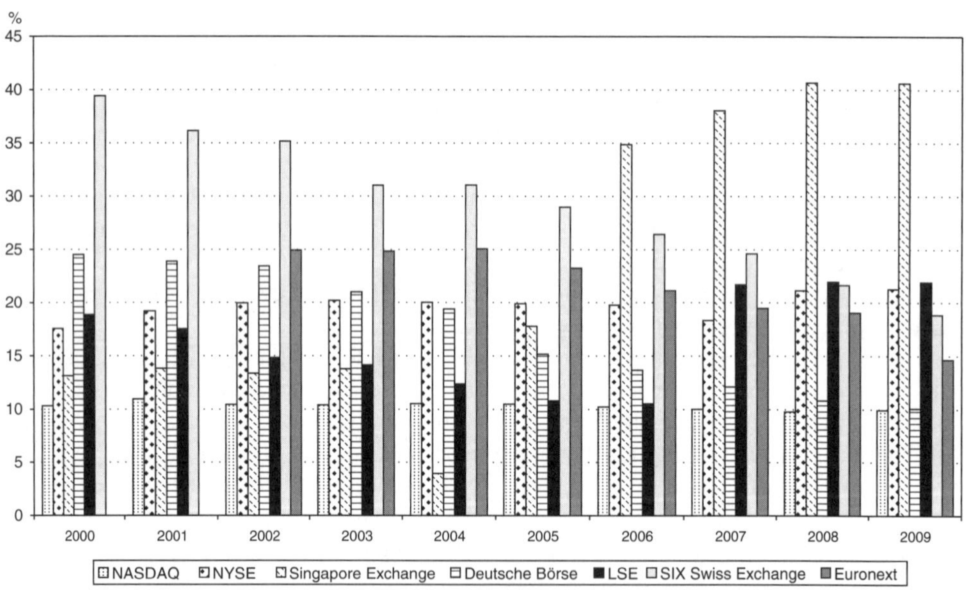

Figure 9.2 *Percentage weight of foreign firms on major stock exchanges*

increased in absolute terms from 2544 to 3095 but their relative weight on total amount decreased from 9 per cent to 7 per cent.

Figure 9.2 reports the percentage weight represented by foreign firms in the major markets since 2000. At the beginning of the decade, the Swiss market appeared as the most internationalized, as nearly 40 per cent of listed companies were foreign-based.

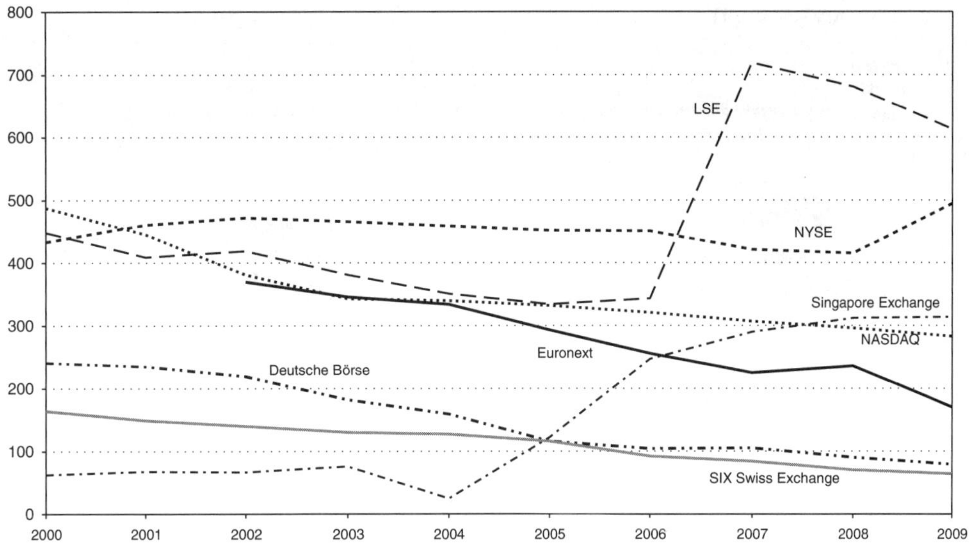

Figure 9.3 Number of foreign listed companies on selected stock exchanges

However, this proportion was halved by 2009. An opposite trend characterized the Singapore Stock Exchange in 2009, where the proportion of foreign-listed companies increased from 13 per cent to 41 per cent. Foreign company relevance at NASDAQ was quite stable at 10 per cent, while the proportion slightly increased at the New York Stock Exchange (NYSE), reaching 21 per cent by the end of 2009. Similarly, London Stock Exchange (LSE) registered companies had a weighting of 22 per cent foreign companies at the end of 2009, which is up from 2005 when the percentage was down to 11 per cent. The weight of foreign companies on other European exchanges halved on average from 25 per cent to 13 per cent from 2002 to 2009.

As for the most attractive markets, Figure 9.3 shows that during 2005, the London Stock Exchange overtook NYSE in terms of the number of listed companies. The increase of foreign firms listing in London was a consequence of the launch of the Alternative Investment Market (AIM) in 1995, a lighter requisites exchange devoted to attracting smaller companies. Overall, in 2000 to 2009 the NYSE slightly increased its number of foreign companies while NASDAQ lost foreign participants. Similarly, all main European markets saw a reduction in the number of foreign listed companies. Among Asian markets, the Singapore Exchange saw a very significant increase in the number of listed companies, thanks in particular to the high number of IPOs by Chinese firms.

In terms of the country of origin of foreign listed firms, the pattern changed significantly over the decade to 2010. Figure 9.4 compares the geographical breakdown of firms that cross-listed in 2000 and in the period 2008–10[2] at the NYSE and the LSE (data were retrieved from the Bank of New York Mellon database). In both cases, cross-listings from firms based in more developed countries (that is, Continental Europe and the UK) diminished, while ADRs programmes from emerging countries increased. In the US, North Asian countries (China in particular) increased their

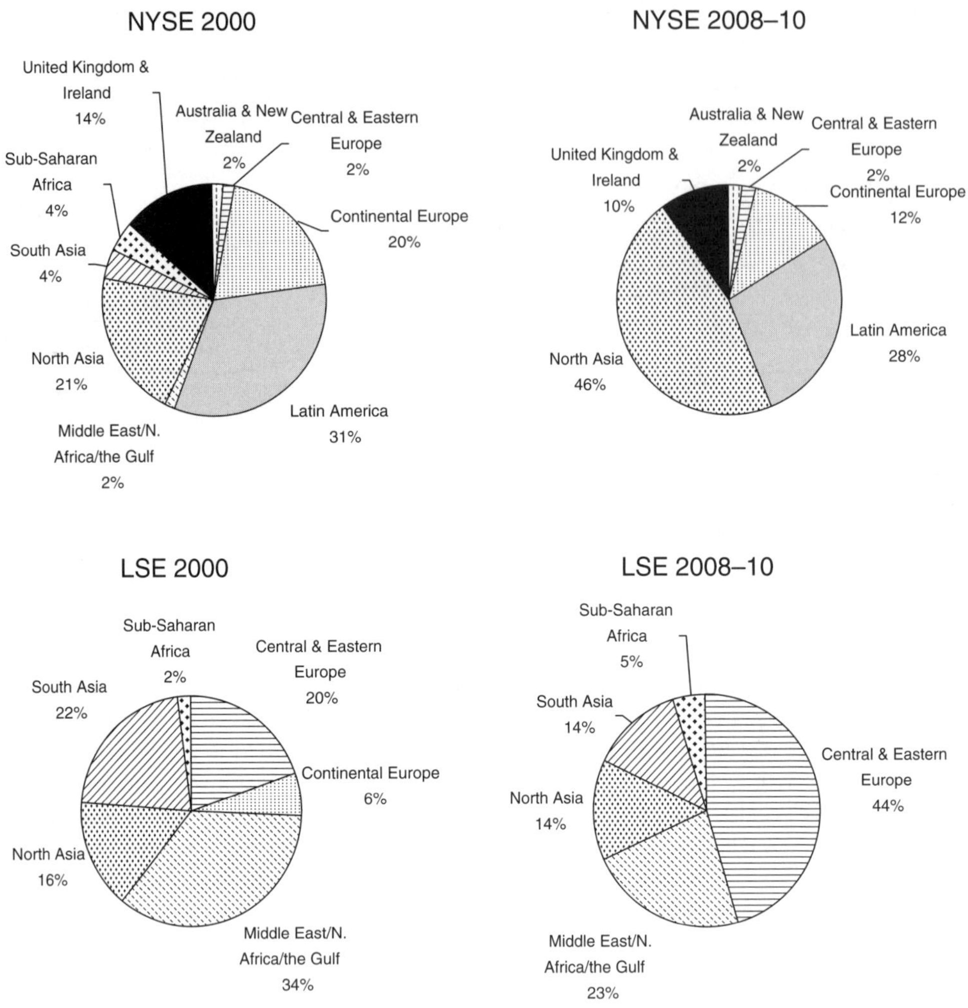

Figure 9.4 Geographical breakdown of cross-listed firms

presence, while Eastern European countries (especially Russia) did the same in the UK.

The basic trends described here showed that the international listing market is changing its shape. Such evidence can be useful to understand better how the academic debate on this topic has evolved over the past few years, as well as which issues remain to be addressed.

LITERATURE REVIEW

Parallel to the increasing number of DR programmes and growing investor interest, substantial research has been conducted on the subject during the 1990s and 2000s.

Up to the early 1990s, researchers focused primarily on topics such as the valuation and liquidity effects of the cross-listing decision, the impact of listing on a company's global risk exposure and the cost of equity capital (see Karolyi 1998). The changing patterns of ADRs markets and, in particular, the surge of emerging-countries issuers shifted the debate on the effective advantages that a company seeks through cross-listing. In a thought-provoking article by Stulz (1999), the cost of capital reduction obtained by ADR issuers was claimed not on market segmentation, as it used to be, but rather on the exposure of a foreign listed firm to a better corporate governance system. Cross-listing began to be seen as a way through which firms incorporated in countries with poor legal systems could bond themselves to the enforcement of stricter securities laws and regulators. Since then, the bonding hypothesis has obtained large support by scholars, as reported by Karolyi (2006) and more recently by Ferris et al. (2009). Nonetheless, traditional theories on ADRs were not completely dismissed by empirical evidence. The slowdown in cross-listings within the US that has been occurring since 2002, that is, right after the introduction of the Sarbanes-Oxley Act (SOX), questioned the corporate governance argument and inspired further research aimed at comparing the competitiveness of different markets for foreign shares. Today, scholars agree that the reasons for listing abroad might vary consistently over time and across countries and firms. Companies opting to list their shares abroad are driven by more than one single reason at a time. Consequently, empirical research supports a variety of reasons for cross-listing. Most recent papers on the topic have focused their attention on multimarket trading, liquidity and arbitrage (Gagnon and Karolyi 2010a).

TRADITIONAL EXPLANATION FOR CROSS-LISTING

Conventional wisdom theories (see Karolyi 1998, 2006) justify cross-listing deals with barriers to investment capital. If markets are segmented and investors are discouraged from investing overseas, a company can get listed in investors' home market in order to provide it with diversification and to obtain a reduction in the cost of capital. Furthermore, cross-listing can benefit companies by increasing the liquidity of their shares. Additionally, market impact and potential arbitrage opportunities will arise as new DRs issues are placed.

Market Segmentation Hypothesis

This hypothesis argues that most benefits of cross-listing arise from circumventing or mitigating the effects of investment barriers that segment capital markets across national boundaries. Early studies related to the subject were conducted by Errunza and Losq (1985), who investigated the pricing implications of a 'mildly segmented' international market structure, and by Alexander et al. (1987). Errunza and Losq document that 'ineligible securities' (when a group of investors is restricted from investing in them) demand a bigger risk premium, while 'eligible ones' are priced as if there were no segmentation. Such models suggest that lowering the barriers would lead to a lower risk premium and a lower cost of capital because of risk-sharing across investors from more countries. It can also be explained in terms of demand and supply: restricted investors support demand for the ineligible securities, which show low levels of correlation with eligible ones and have no substitutes, while barriers put constraints on supply, forcing the price to rise; when those barriers decrease, thanks to market integration processes (which could be DR programmes), then supply rises and the correlation increases. Accordingly, the valuation gain depends on the degree to which the home country is integrated in the world market. Foerster and Karolyi (2000) showed that the long-run performance of DRs, over a benchmark of global equity offerings, is positive and significant particularly when the issuer comes from a country with low accounting standards.

Investor Recognition Hypothesis

This hypothesis is based on Merton's (1987) modification of the capital asset pricing model (CAPM). One of the model's main assumptions is removed, allowing for information asymmetries, while it is hypothesized that investors typically prefer to invest in firms that they know more about. Consequently, when a company gets its shares listed on a market, such as in the US, its visibility and name recognition increase, expanding both in theory and in practice its shareholders base relative to its domestic listed peers. Since in the model the expected rate of return on a stock is negatively related to the size of a firm's investor base, the effect is a positive post-cross-listing performance. Lang et al. (2004) investigated the relation between cross-listing in the US and the information environment of non-US firms, finding that cross-listing on a US exchange involves greater analyst coverage and increased forecast accuracy, resulting in a generally better valuation. Sarkissian and Schill (2008) and Ammer et al. (2005) demonstrated that US investors prefer to invest more in better-known foreign companies and companies that they are more familiar with, both culturally and from a trading point of view; this suggests that the effect of the 'investor recognition hypothesis' would be stronger in the case of these companies' cross-listings rather than those of their lesser-known peers. Baker et al. (2002) showed that listing on the NYSE brings more analyst coverage and media attention compared to listing on the LSE. This theory is also coherent with the results reported by Foerster and Karolyi (1999), which associated a better price impact – meaning stronger in the short run and less negative in the long run – for those companies raising equity compared to non-capital-raising comparables.

Business Strategy Hypothesis

This hypothesis suggests that listing on the US market may be part of a company's strategy, implying either financial considerations, business ones, or both. One of the implications is that the cross-listing decision is based on a cost–benefit analysis that is firm-specific and therefore likely to vary across companies. In 2001, Bancel and Mittoo surveyed the costs and benefits of foreign listing expected by managers of European cross-listed companies. Increased visibility, prestige and image as well as growth in shareholder base were perceived as major benefits, while investor relations, expenses and legal fees were perceived as major costs. The majority of managers perceived positive net benefits. Such positive perceptions were associated with firms that after cross-listing experienced an increase in trading volumes, and that had domestic financial disclosure requirements similar to the cross-listing country ones. Pagano et al. (2002) argued that cross-listing in the US sends a signal to the market that a company has become a global player, while the operation reinforces its competitive position in the industry, strengthening its reputation with stakeholders. Lins et al. (2005) found that that greater access to external capital markets was one of the most important reasons to justify cross-listing in the US. Empirically, such benefit is particularly strong for emerging-market firms and less relevant for more developed-market firms.

Liquidity Impact

A fourth traditional area of investigation concerns the impact of cross-listing on shares' liquidity. Typically, stocks experience an increase in total trading volume and a decrease in home market spreads, due in large part to the competition from the new market. Foerster and Karolyi (1998) confirmed such effects on a sample of Canadian stocks listed in the US. Similar results were obtained by Foerster and George (1995), Chan et al. (1996) and Smith and Sofianos (1997) in studies on bid–ask spreads, price volatility and trading volumes in shares of firms cross-listed on US markets.

As reported in a market survey by Mittoo (1992), superior liquidity provided by overseas exchanges is also one of the goals indicated by managers of companies planning to list abroad. Higher liquidity resulting from international listing also has implications for management monitoring, as pointed out by Stulz (1999). First, with greater liquidity, the market for a firm's equity becomes more efficient in the sense that it more quickly and more accurately reflects information about the firm. This makes the firm's stock price more informative and hence more useful in monitoring management. Second, greater liquidity makes it easier for active investors not only to accumulate positions in a stock but also to sell these positions.

Market Reaction to Cross-Listing

Although findings are not always clear and consistent with each other, the literature has associated cross-listing on US exchanges with a positive market reaction in terms of stock value. Past event studies bring us to the following conclusion: share prices have an initial positive reaction, while post-listing performances up to one year are generally negative, although they vary depending on market and company-specific factors (Miller 1999; Doukas and Switzer 2000). This kind of behaviour is stronger when foreign firms cross-list on Anglo-Saxon exchanges, and almost insignificant in other cases (Lau et al. 1994). Looking for explanatory variables, some studies analysed changes in company risk exposure and required returns while other studies focused more on liquidity aspects. A recent study by Roosenboom and Van Dijk (2009) cited the following explanations for ADR price behaviour: the overcoming of investment barriers erected by market segmentation; increased liquidity thanks to deeper capital markets; greater information disclosure due to more stringent requirements, as well as enhanced media attention, greater analyst coverage and improved forecast accuracy; and higher standards of corporate governance thanks to an environment that has higher standards for minority shareholders' protection. The same paper also recalls the main disadvantages in deciding to cross-list: increased pressure on executives due to closer public scrutiny; increased reporting and disclosure requirements; additional scrutiny by analysts in advanced market economies; additional listing fees.

Bris et al. (2009) compared the impact on prices of two alternative ways through which foreign firm shares could be exchanged at the London Stock Exchange. Indeed, up until 2004, foreign firms could be exchanged in the LSE under two distinct programmes: admission to trading and official listing. The first was initiated by a market maker dealer without the firm's involvement. The second commenced with the explicit firm decision to cross-list on the LSE and satisfy its disclosure and monitoring requirements. An event study around the listing trading dates documented positive and significant valuation effects for cross-listed firms, and positive but statistically insignificant valuation effects for firms admitted to trading. A cross-sectional analysis of the abnormal returns showed that the documented valuation benefit of cross-listing on the LSE is robust to the inclusion of proxies for liquidity, ease of access to capital, and investor protection. This same paper also documented that firms from emerging markets, which are potentially more segmented, do not enjoy higher abnormal returns than do firms from developed countries. These results are considered consistent with the positive valuation effects suggested by the information-based motives for cross-listing and provide very limited support for the market segmentation and liquidity hypotheses.

ALTERNATIVE RESEARCH APPROACHES ON CROSS-LISTING

The partially changed landscape for cross-listing in the 2000s motivated the development of new research approaches to explain the main advantages of overseas listing. The slowdown in the pace of new international cross-listing combined with the increased cross-border capital flows[3] and the changing pattern of cross-listed firms, which frequently have originated from emerging countries, were all signals that the market for ADRs has evolved and changed since its 'golden age' in the 1990s.[4]

Incentives for most developed countries firms to cross-list have decreased. On the one hand the aggregation among major developed stock exchanges (that is, NYSE–Euronext, NASDAQ–OMX, LSE–Borsa Italiana) reduced differentiation in listing requirements and also decreased cross-listing intentions from more developed countries (after the NYSE–Euronext agreement, why should a French company list at NYSE?[5]). Moreover the introduction of the Sarbanes–Oxley Act (SOX) in 2002 raised costs and burdens for companies listed in the US, thus diminishing the appetite for cross-listing. On the other hand, the evolution of trading systems has also changed the global playing field for broker-dealers, as it has reduced the communication barriers that once separated the markets. The consolidation of trading platforms of regulated exchanges reduced trading costs and encouraged more brokerage firms to become trading members of both exchanges (that is, NYSE and Euronext). Furthermore, the recent abolition of concentration rules in many European countries[6] encouraged major broker-dealers to launch new global trading platforms, which allowed investors to buy and sell foreign securities, often operating in their local currency.

Here follows a summary of different theories about cross-listing benefits developed to cope with this changed landscape.

The Bonding Hypothesis

This hypothesis argues that cross-listing benefits derive from enhanced investor protection and reduced agency costs of controlling shareholders when the firm is bound to the enforcement of stricter securities laws and regulators (the typical example being that of an emerging-country company bonding to US laws and Securities and Exchange Commission monitoring). This so-called 'bonding argument' has encouraged a growth in academic literature, including Coffee (1999, 2002) and Stulz (1999) among the field's pioneers. In particular are Coffee's research focus on the 'legal bonding' instruments associated with listing in the US: disclosure and monitoring performed by the Securities and Exchange Commission (SEC), availability to investors of effective and low-cost legal action (that is, class actions), and commitment provided to the exchange by the firm to provide financial information according to General Accepted Accounting Principles (GAAP) and SEC requirements. In his 1999 article, Stulz maintained that the cost of capital reduction obtained by ADR issuers could be explained by the exposure of the listed foreign firms to a better system of corporate governance rather than by the market segmentation argument.

Both Coffee (2002) and Stulz (1999) underlined the role of the 'reputational bonding' that results from listing in the US. Indeed, the foreign issuer is exposed to the scrutiny of 'reputational intermediaries', including US underwriters, auditors, debt rating agencies, securities analysts and the stock exchange itself.

In the following years, many authors enhanced the bonding argument and reported favourable empirical evidence. Reese and Weisbach (2002) found that subsequent to cross-listing on the US markets, firms from civil law countries issued most of their new equity outside of the US. In contrast, equity issuance for English common law firms tends to be inside the US. The authors concluded that common law firms cross-list in the US in order to tap into US capital markets, whereas civil law firms cross-list for bonding purposes which allows them to raise more equity, both in their home market and around the world.

According to Doidge et al. (2004), firms from non-US countries bind themselves to the US legal system by cross-listing on stock exchanges in order to finance their growth opportunities and therefore gain a valuation premium compared to their domestic-listed peers. In this sense, the bonding hypothesis implies a higher performance for firms that raise capital following the US listing, signalling realization of these growth opportunities. The hypothesis predicts higher valuation effects for firms with a poor quality of investor protection as well.

Halling et al. (2008) analysed trading volume locations for shares cross-listed in the US. The fraction of trading that occurs in the US tends to be larger for companies from countries that are geographically close to the US and feature low financial development and poor insider trading protection. For companies based in developed countries, trading volume in the US is larger if the company is small, volatile and technology-oriented, though this does not apply to emerging-country firms. The domestic turnover rate increases in the cross-listing year and remains higher for firms based in developed markets, but not for emerging-market firms. Domestic trading volume actually declines for companies from countries with poor enforcement of insider trading regulation, thus supporting the bonding hypothesis.

Abdallah and Goergen (2008) studied a sample of 175 companies that cross-listed on 19 different stock exchanges during the period 1990–2000, arguing that the control structure is a determinant of the cross-listing location. More precisely, such a decision is likely to be influenced by the existence of large private benefits of control. If the controlling shareholder has large private benefits of control, he may prevent the firm from cross-listing on a common law market as the better shareholder protection in this type of market will limit his benefits. Second, high-risk companies may cross-list on a market with good shareholder protection as such a market has better diversification potential. Third, as countries with good shareholder protection tend to have more developed stock markets, they are more likely to attract firms with substantial financing needs. Fourth, firms wanting to increase the liquidity of their stock will prefer to cross-list on a market with better shareholder protection than their home market. Finally, firms may bond themselves to protect their minority shareholders by cross-listing on a market with better shareholder protection. Results confirm that firms with concentrated control, that have a higher level of risk and those with more pronounced financing needs cross-list on a market with better investor protection. Such evidence supports the bonding hypothesis, as firms from markets with weak shareholder protection tend to cross-list on markets with significantly higher shareholder protection.

Doidge (2004) tested the hypothesis that the private benefits of control decrease when foreign firms cross-list their shares in the US. Indeed, controlling shareholders can use a US listing to bond themselves in order to assure minority shareholders that they are less likely to be exploited. The evidence supports the bonding hypothesis, as foreign firms that cross-list on US exchanges register voting premiums that are 43 per cent lower than non-US firms that do not cross-list. Such difference is larger for firms from countries that provide poor protection to minority investors.

More recently, Doidge et al. (2009a) studied the role played by private benefit of control in the cross-listing decision. US securities laws and, to a lesser extent, market scrutiny represent severe constraints to the extraction of private benefits by controlling shareholders. An empirical study covering 4000 companies from 31 countries found support for the hypothesis that high private benefits of control reduce the probability for a firm to cross-list in the US.

Lel and Miller (2008) examined the ability to identify and remove poorly performing chief executive officers (CEOs) by cross-listed firms to test the effectiveness of US investor protections in improving corporate governance of such firms. Firms from weak investor protection regimes that are cross-listed on a major US exchange are more likely to terminate poorly performing CEOs than non-cross-listed firms. Cross-listings on exchanges that do not require the adoption of the most stringent investor protections (OTC, private placements and London listings) are not associated with a higher propensity to shed poorly performing CEOs. These results provide direct support for the bonding hypothesis.

In their paper, Ferris et al. (2009) reviewed the extensive empirical literature recently produced on cross-listing and related changes in corporate governance. They concluded that empirical evidence strongly supports the legal bonding hypothesis as an explanation of the cross-listing decision, while the empirical support for reputational bonding is lower. They also underlined that growth opportunities and the need for external capital emerged in the empirical research as critical factors in a firm's decision to list abroad.

Literature production was also extensive among authors who reported evidence against the bonding argument. Witmer (2006) examined cross-listed stocks that delisted in the US. Smaller firms with a lower percentage of turnover in the US were more likely to delist. These results were interpreted as being consistent with the liquidity hypothesis and with Merton's awareness hypothesis. NASDAQ-listed firms were more likely to delist, which was consistent with the bonding and signalling hypotheses. However, firms were also more likely to cross-delist if they are from countries with poorer investor protection or if they are listed in the post-Sarbanes–Oxley period. These findings are opposite to the predictions of the bonding hypothesis. They are more supportive of the 'avoiding hypothesis', whereby the added costs of US regulations seem to deter these firms from maintaining a US listing. Finally, the author found an average negative return of approximately 5 per cent around the delisting announcement. This negative return was mitigated if the stock had a low proportion of turnover in the US, which also supported the liquidity and bonding hypotheses.

Siegel (2005) questioned the validity of the legal bonding hypothesis by reporting evidence on the scarce effectiveness of SEC enforcement policy against cross-listed foreign firms. Detailed evidence from Mexico showed that US law enforcement neither deterred nor punished insiders who collectively took billions of dollars from their firms. The study found moreover that the SEC has rarely been able to enforce US securities laws against any US-listed foreign firm. Similarly, the effectiveness of legal actions promoted by minority shareholders to enforce the securities laws against cross-listed foreign firms was historically poor due to institutional obstacles. The author concluded that reputational bonding instead of legal bonding better explains the success of cross-listings.

King and Segal (2004) also supported the view that reputational bonding is what matters, as opposed to legal bonding. By studying Canadian firms that cross-listed in the US they found that positive effects on market valuation were obtained only by companies that developed active trading in the US. Indeed, a large amount of trading on the US market involves higher coverage by analysts and intermediaries. As a consequence, trading volumes is viewed as a proxy for the degree to which a foreign firm has been successful in bonding its reputation to the US markets.

Bris et al. (2007) explored the differential effects of cross-listing on prices and separated the different sources of the benefits of cross-listing. These sources include market segmentation, liquidity and the bonding of controlling shareholders to lower expropriation of firm resources. Results showed that even though the market segmentation and bonding effects were both statistically significant, the economic significance of segmentation was more than double that of bonding. The authors commented on the reduced willingness of firms to list in the US by using two arguments. On the one hand, Sarbanes–Oxley has increased the cost of adopting better governance while its benefits are not substantial. On the other hand, market segmentation has decreased significantly in recent years.

Similarly, Roosenboom and van Djik (2009) gave evidence for the fact that market reactions to cross-listings differ across destination markets and, as such, their explanatory causes might differ too. By analysing 526 cross-listings from 44 different countries on eight major stock exchanges, the authors documented significant announcement returns of 1.3 per cent on average for cross-listings on US exchanges, 1.1 per cent on the London Stock Exchange, 0.6 per cent on exchanges in continental Europe, and 0.5 per cent (not significant) on the Tokyo Stock Exchange. Moreover, they tested which hypothesis could better explain such differences; they found that improved disclosure and bonding theory better explained the cross-listings effects on US exchanges, while overcoming segmentation and bonding were associated with higher announcement returns on the London Stock Exchange. The evidence was mixed for continental European exchanges and Tokyo.

Sarkissian and Schill (2008) tested whether foreign equity listings were associated with permanent valuation gains and examined how market and firm characteristics influence any valuation effects. Using a global sample of 1676 listings placed in 25 countries, the authors found that much of the valuation gains to overseas listings were not permanent. Such a transitory nature of valuation gains holds for both average US listings and average first-time firm listings. Little evidence of permanent effect emerged on returns for firms that listed abroad, even for firms' listings in markets that were more liquid, provided better legal protection or had a larger shareholder base.

Competition among Markets and SOX Impact

The reduction in the number of cross-listing programmes towards the US registered in the first years of the new millennium, combined with the introduction of the SOX in 2002, inspired new contributions to discuss the change in the attractiveness of US markets.

Doidge et al. (2009b) compared the determinants and consequences of cross-listings on the New York and London stock exchanges from 1990 to 2005. The aims of the study were to evaluate the relative benefits of the New York and London exchange listings and to assess whether these relative benefits changed over time, particularly after the introduction of the Sarbanes–Oxley Act in 2002 and the parallel surge of AIM in London. Empirical results showed that cross-listings have been falling on both the US exchanges as well as on the Main Market in London, but such declines are explained by changes in firm characteristics rather than by changes in the benefits of cross-listing. Investigating the 'cross-listing premium' (that is, the valuation differential between listed and non-listed firms) from 1990 to 2005, the authors found a significant and permanent premium for US exchange listings, while no premium for listings on London's Main Market was found for any year. Confirming previous results by Reese and Weisbach (2002), firms that list in the US increase their capital-raising activity at home and abroad while a London listing has no such impact. The authors concluded that their results were consistent with the bonding hypothesis on governance benefits for foreign firms listing in New York. These benefits have not been seriously eroded by the SOX and cannot be replicated through a London listing (indeed, in London foreign issuers are granted a lighter regime in terms of requisites and shareholders' rights protection).

Marosi and Massoud (2008) reported different evidence on the capability of US markets to attract foreign companies by looking at the increasing number of foreign firms exiting US capital markets. By studying 148 delistings of foreign companies from US markets which occurred between 1990 and 2006, they examined the reasons underlying this trend. One of their main findings was that the passage of the Sarbanes–Oxley Act has reduced the net benefits of a US listing and registration, particularly for smaller foreign firms with lower trading volume and stronger insider control.

Doidge et al. (2010) examined the recent increase in the number of foreign firms leaving US markets. They concluded that foreign firms terminated their SEC registration because they no longer required outside funds to finance growth opportunities, while they found no evidence that the introduction of the SOX affected the deregistration decision. Deregistering firms' insiders benefit from greater discretion to consume private benefits without having to raise higher-cost funds. Foreign firms with more agency problems have worse stock-price reactions to the adoption of Rule 12h-6 in 2007, which made deregistration easier, than those firms more adversely affected by the compliance costs of the SOX. Stock-price reactions to deregistration announcements are negative, but less so under Rule 12h-6, and more so for firms that raise fewer funds externally.

Litvak (2007) studied the impact of the SOX on cross-listed companies by using a natural experiment. Indeed, the SOX applies to some cross-listed firms (those listed on level 2 or 3), but not to others (listed on level 1 or 4). By comparing reactions of SOX-exposed foreign firms to reactions of otherwise similar SOX-unexposed foreign firms, investor beliefs about the costs and benefits of the SOX were tested. Results reported that stock prices of foreign firms subject to the SOX declined significantly, compared to cross-listed firms not subject to the SOX and to non-cross-listed firms, during key announcements indicating that the Act would fully apply to cross-listed issuers. In cross-sectional tests, high-disclosing firms and firms from high-disclosing countries experienced the strongest declines, while faster-growing companies experienced weaker declines. This evidence is consistent with the view that investors expected the Sarbanes–Oxley Act to have a net negative effect on cross-listed foreign companies, with high-disclosing companies suffering larger net costs, and faster-growing companies from poorly governed countries suffering smaller costs.

ADR Programmes from Emerging Countries

The increasing flow of ADR programmes launched by emerging countries' firms stimulated another area of research. Chung (2006) studied the relationship between firm liquidity and the level of protection provided to investors. The analysis involved 204 ADR programmes from 29 countries listed on both the NYSE and NASDAQ. Results confirmed that there were wider bid–ask spreads amongst the ADRs from countries with weak investor protection. Such effects proved to be stronger during financial crisis periods, such as the case of the Asian crisis in the late 1990s.

Silva and Chavez (2008) analysed liquidity costs for stocks and ADRs listed in the US from the four main Latin American markets (Argentina, Brazil, Chile and Mexico). Latin America has been one of the most important contributors to the growth of the NYSE ADR market. By 2001, the value of ADRs trading at the NYSE represented more than 80 per cent of total trading in the home markets of Argentina, Chile and Mexico, and 56 per cent of that in Brazil. The results indicated that there were differences in liquidity costs across countries, with Brazilian firms bearing on average higher liquidity costs. Local firms that were cross-listed presented, on average, a liquidity cost advantage over non-cross-listed ones. However, this improvement was not uniform across all firms, as country and size effects influenced the results. In particular, liquidity costs were lower in the ADR market than in the local market in the case of large firms, while the opposite occurred for small firms. Thus, the liquidity benefits of cross-listing internationally can neither be generalized across firm size and country of origin, nor used as an additional argument to explain the price premium of cross-listed firms.

Impact of Multimarket Trading and Liquidity

The circumstance that the share of a cross-listed firm can be traded on multiple markets might have relevant consequences on the price discovery process and share liquidity. The increased availability of intraday trading data combined with important improvements in the econometric methodology recently led some scholars to deepen the research in this field, adding to the traditional contributions on ADRs' liquidity (see below).

Gagnon and Karolyi (2009) investigated the dynamics of returns and trading volume of 556 foreign stocks cross-listed on US markets. Evidence indicated that stocks characterized by a lower degree of information asymmetry tended to experience return reversals in one market following high-volume days in the other market, and that stocks associated with a higher degree of information asymmetry tended to exhibit weaker reversals, or even continuations, in one market following unusually high-volume days in the other market.

In another paper (Gagnon and Karolyi 2010b), the same authors investigated arbitrage opportunities for a sample of 506 US cross-listed stocks from 35 different countries. The average deviation from price parity that they found was quite small (4.9 basis points) but showed large dispersion in the sample. Price deviation changes were positively related to proxies for holding costs that could impede arbitrage, even after controlling for transactions costs and foreign investment restrictions.

CONCLUSIONS AND FURTHER ISSUES

The wide literature on international listing is still attracting contributions nowadays. Traditional and more recent research streams offer both valid and complementary explanations of such a complex and fascinating topic in finance. Nonetheless, there are some areas of study that still need to be developed, particularly in light of the changing environment for cross-listing markets. Some of these areas of concern are the growth of cross-listing venues alternative to the US markets, the consolidation of stock exchanges and the impact of technology on trading.

The majority of contributions in the ADR literature focus on cross-listing onto US stock markets. Indeed, the NYSE and NASDAQ have always been among the most preferred exchanges to cross-list. Furthermore, other stock markets such as London, Tokyo and, more recently, Singapore are also attracting larger numbers of foreign firms. Research on non-US markets is quite limited. Filling such a gap could lead to a more complete understanding of the impact of cross-listing on firm value.

The recent wave of consolidation among US and some European stock exchanges largely reduced incentives for European firms to cross-list in the US. At the same time, a common framework and reduced trading costs encouraged more US brokerage firms to become trading members of EU exchanges. From an academic point of view, it would be interesting to assess the impact of such industry trends on liquidity and price discovery for traded shares.

Other structural changes are at work in equity markets, as a consequence of the development of technology and proprietary trading systems. Many banks and traders have developed proprietary tools to facilitate the trading and management of cross-listed shares. The market impact of such new trading channels represents a third promising area for further research on cross-listed shares.

NOTES

1. American depositary receipts (ADRs) are DRs issued and traded on the US markets. Because of their historical importance and the high volumes traded, often the term ADR is used to refer to DRs in general, including instruments that trade on other international major stock exchanges.
2. I chose to compare one single year (2000) with a triennium (2008–10) as the flows of cross-listing firms strongly reduced in later years. Cross-listings at the NYSE were 117 in 2000 and 51 in 2008–10, while at the LSE they were 52 in 2000 and 23 in 2008–10.
3. According to IMF-CPIS data, at the end of 2007, global portfolio investments amounted to $39.9 trillion with a compound annual growth rate (CAGR) during the period 2001–07 of 21.1 per cent. Equity accounted for 43 per cent and debt for 57 per cent.
4. According to Coffee (2002), in 1990, 352 depository receipt programmes from 24 countries were in effect in the United States, but by 1999 this number had grown to 1800 programmes from 78 countries. The combined market capitalization of these companies exceeded $6 trillion at the end of 1999.
5. One of the explicit aims of the NYSE–Euronext merger was to attract listings of companies that would otherwise not list in the US because of, among other reasons, the US's stricter regulatory arm after the Sarbanes–Oxley Act in 2002.
6. As implied by the Markets in Financial Instruments Directive (MiFID) since 2007.

REFERENCES

Abdallah, W. and M. Goergen (2008), 'Does corporate control determine cross listing location?' *Journal of Corporate Finance*, **14**, 183–9.

Alexander, G., C. Eun and S. Janakiramanan (1987), 'Asset pricing and dual listing on foreign capital markets: a note', *Journal of Finance*, **42**, 151–8.

Ammer, J.M., S. Holland, D. Smith and F. Warnock (2005), 'Look at me now: what attracts US shareholders?' Board of Governors of the Federal Reserve System International Finance Discussion Paper No. 815, available at http://ssrn.com/abstract=556208.

Baker, H., J. Nofsinger and D. Weaver (2002), 'International cross-listing and visibility', *Journal of Financial and Quantitative Analysis*, **37**, 495–521.

Bancel, F. and U.R. Mittoo (2001), 'European managerial perceptions of the net benefits of foreign stock listings', *European Financial Management*, **7** (2), 213–36.

Bris, A., S. Cantale, E. Hrnjic and G.P. Nishiotis (2009), 'The value of information in cross-listing', available at http://ssrn.com/abstract=972049.

Bris, A., S. Cantale and G. Nishiotis (2007), 'A breakdown of the valuation effects of international cross-listing', *European Financial Management*, **13** (3), 298–530.

Chan, K.C., W. Fong, B.C. Kho and R.M. Stulz (1996), 'Information, trading and stock returns: lessons from dually-listed securities', *Journal of Banking and Finance*, **20** (1), 1161–87.

Chung, H. (2006), 'Investor protection and the liquidity of cross-listed securities: evidence from the ADR market', *Journal of Banking and Finance*, **30**, 1485–505.

Coffee, J. (1999), 'The future as history: the prospects for global convergence in corporate governance and its implications', *Northwestern University Law Review*, **93**, 641–708.

Coffee, J. (2002), 'Racing towards the top? The impact of cross-listings and stock market competition on international corporate governance', *Columbia Law Review*, **102**, 1757–831.

Doidge, C. (2004), 'US cross-listings and the private benefits of control: evidence from dual-class firms', *Journal of Financial Economics*, **72**, 519–53.

Doidge, C., G.A. Karolyi, K. Lins, D.P. Miller and R.M. Stulz (2009a), 'Private benefits of control, ownership and the cross-listing decision', *Journal of Finance*, **64**, 425–66.

Doidge, C., G.A. Karolyi and R.M. Stulz (2004), 'Why are foreign firms that are listed in the US worth more?' *Journal of Financial Economics*, **71**, 205–38.
Doidge, C., G.A. Karolyi and R.M. Stulz (2009b), 'Has New York become less competitive than London in global markets? Evaluating foreign listing choices over time', *Journal of Financial Economics*, **91**, 253–77.
Doidge, C., G.A. Karolyi and R.M. Stulz (2010), 'Why do foreign firms leave US equity markets?' *Journal of Finance*, **65**, 1507–53.
Doukas, J. and L. Switzer (2000), 'Common stock returns and international listing announcements: conditional tests of the mild segmentation hypothesis', *Journal of Banking and Finance*, **24** (3), 471–501.
Errunza, V. and E. Losq (1985), 'International asset pricing under mild segmentation: theory and test', *Journal of Finance*, **40**, 105–24.
Ferris, S.P., A.K. Kim and G. Noronha (2009), 'The effect of cross-listing on corporate governance: a review of the international evidence', *Corporate Governance: An International Review*, **17** (3), 338–52.
Foerster, S. and G.A. Karolyi (1998), 'Multimarket trading and liquidity: a transaction data analysis of Canada–US interlistings', *Journal of International Financial Markets, Institutions and Money*, **8**, 393–412.
Foerster, S.R. and G.A. Karolyi (1999), 'The effects of market segmentation and investor recognition on asset prices: evidence from foreign stocks listing in the US', *Journal of Finance*, **54**, 981–1014.
Foerster, S.R. and G.A. Karolyi (2000), 'The long-run performance of global equity offerings', *Journal of Financial and Quantitative Analysis*, **35**, 499–528.
Forster, M.M. and T.J. George (1995), 'Trading hours, information flow and international crosslisting', *International Review of Financial Analysis*, **4**, 19–34.
Gagnon, L. and G.A. Karolyi (2009), 'Information, trading volume, and international stock return comovements: evidence from cross-listed stocks', *Journal of Financial and Quantitative Analysis*, **44** (4), 953–86.
Gagnon, L. and G.A. Karolyi (2010a), 'Multi-market trading and arbitrage', *Journal of Financial Economics*, **97**, 53–80.
Gagnon, L. and G.A. Karolyi (2010b), 'Do international cross listings still matter?' Johnson School Research Paper Series n. 32.
Halling, M., M. Pagano, O. Randl and J. Zechner (2008), 'Where is the market? Evidence from cross-listings in the United States', *Review of Financial Studies*, **21** (2), 725–61.
Karolyi, G.A. (1998, 'Why do companies list shares abroad? A survey of the evidence and its managerial implications', *Financial Markets, Institutions and Instruments*, **7** (1), 1–60.
Karolyi, G.A. (2006), 'The world of cross listings and cross listings of the world', *Review of Finance*, **10,** 99–152.
King, M. and D. Segal (2004), 'International cross-listing and the bonding hypothesis', Bank of Canada Working Paper, 2004–17.
Lang, M., K. Lins and D.P. Miller (2004), 'Concentrated control, analyst following and valuation: do analysts matter most when investors are protected least?' *Journal of Accounting Research*, **42**, 581–623.
Lau, S., D. Diltz and V. Apilado (1994), 'Valuation effects of international stock exchange listings', *Journal of Banking and Finance*, **18**, 743–55.
Lel, U. and D.P. Miller (2008), 'International cross-listing, firm performance and top management turnover: a test of the bonding hypothesis', *Journal of Finance*, **63**, 1897–937.
Lins, K., D. Strickland and M. Zenner (2005), 'Do non-US firms issue equity on US stock exchanges to relax capital constraints?' *Journal of Financial and Quantitative Analysis*, **40**, 109–33.
Litvak, K. (2007), 'The effect of the Sarbanes–Oxley Act on non-US companies cross-listed in the US', *Journal of Corporate Finance*, **13**, 195–228.
Marosi, A. and N. Massoud (2008), '"You can enter but you cannot leave . . .": US securities markets and foreign firms', *Journal of Finance*, **63** (5), 2477–506.
Merton, R.C. (1987), 'Presidential address: a simple model of capital market equilibrium with incomplete information', *Journal of Finance*, **42**, 483–510.
Miller, D.P. (1999), 'The market reaction to international cross-listing: evidence from depositary receipts', *Journal of Financial Economics*, **51**, 103–23.
Mittoo, U. (1992), 'Managerial perceptions of the net benefits of foreign listing; Canadian evidence', *Journal of International Financial Management and Accounting*, **4**, 40–62.
Pagano, M., A.A. Roell and J. Zechner (2002), 'The geography of equity listing: why do companies list abroad?' *Journal of Finance*, **57**, 2651–94.
Reese, W.A.J. and M.S. Weisbach (2002), 'Protection of minority shareholder interests, cross-listings in the United States, and subsequent equity offerings', *Journal of Financial Economics*, **66**, 65–104.
Roosenboom, P. and M.A. Van Dijk (2009), 'The market reaction to cross-listings: does the destination matter?' *Journal of Banking and Finance*, **33**, 1898–908.
Sarkissian S. and M.J. Schill (2008), 'Are there permanent evaluation gains to overseas listing?' *Review of Financial Studies*, **22** (1), 371–412.
Siegel, J. (2005), 'Can foreign firms bond themselves effectively by submitting to US law?' *Journal of Financial Economics*, **75** (2), 319–60.

Silva, A.C. and G.A. Chavez (2008), 'Cross-listing and liquidity in emerging market stocks', *Journal of Banking and Finance*, **32**, 420–33.
Smith, K. and G. Sofianos (1997), 'The impact of a NYSE listing on the global trading of non-US stocks', Working Paper 97-02, New York Stock Exchange, New York.
Stulz, R.M. (1999), 'Globalization, corporate finance, and the cost of capital', *Journal of Applied Corporate Finance*, **12**, 8–25.
Witmer, Jonathan L. (2006), 'Why do firms cross-(de)list? An examination of the determinants and effects of cross-delisting', Working Paper, Bank of Canada.

PART III

EVALUATING STOCK MARKET GLOBALIZATION

10 Latin American stock markets: recent history and prospects[1]

Augusto de la Torre and Sergio L. Schmukler

INTRODUCTION

Back in the early 1990s, economists and policy-makers had high expectations about the prospects for domestic capital market development in emerging economies and, particularly, in Latin America. Unfortunately, they are now faced with mixed results. Though many still hope for securities markets to develop, the reality is that equity and corporate bond markets in many emerging economies remain highly illiquid and segmented, with trading and capitalization concentrated on a few firms. Stock markets in many developing countries have seen listings and liquidity decrease, as a growing number of firms have cross-listed and raised capital in international financial centers such as New York and London. Debt tends to be concentrated at the short end of the maturity spectrum and denominated in foreign currency, exposing countries to maturity and currency risks, though this trend started to revert somewhat in the mid-2000s. Moreover, government debt has crowded out corporate bond markets in many countries, at least until recently.

The state of capital markets looks particularly poor when considering the many efforts already undertaken to improve the macroeconomic environment and reform the institutions believed to foster financial development. In the case of Latin America, the results appear even more discouraging in light of the better evolution of capital markets in East Asia and their rapid growth in developed economies (especially in international financial centers). This disappointing performance has made conventional policy recommendations for capital market development questionable, at best. Policy-makers are left without clear guidance on how to revise the reform agenda and many of them do not envision a bright future for domestic capital markets.

The failure to develop deep and efficient capital markets may have important consequences, as growing empirical evidence suggests that financial development is not just correlated with a healthy economy, but actually causes economic growth and has a positive impact on poverty alleviation and income distribution as well.[2] Therefore, a better understanding of the drivers of capital market development and the reasons for the perceived failure of the reform efforts in many emerging economies can provide useful guidance to policy-makers.

In this chapter we briefly review the recent evolution of stock markets, and capital markets more generally, in Latin America and other regions. Furthermore, we link this evolution to the financial globalization process. Finally, we discuss some policy lessons.

EVOLUTION AND GLOBALIZATION OF STOCK MARKETS

The developments in domestic stock markets over the 1990s and 2000s, as well as their prospects, would be difficult to understand without considering the trends in global capital markets. Studying how international capital markets have evolved not only provides a benchmark to assess the performance of domestic markets, but also helps us to understand to what degree local developments are the result of changes in international capital markets.

An important message from the analysis is that financial globalization has expanded to such a degree that it has become difficult to ignore. Moreover, many new developments have taken place over the late 2000s, bringing about significant changes to capital markets in both developed and developing nations. However, despite the perception of widespread financial globalization, the international financial system is far from being perfectly integrated and there is evidence of persistent capital market segmentation both across and within countries.[3]

Main Developments in International Capital Markets

Capital markets in developed countries have grown substantially over recent decades, experiencing a large boom in the 1990s. As part of this process, companies raised more capital in bond and equity markets, while both retail and institutional investors increased their participation in capital markets. Financial markets experienced such a development that by 2004 the combined credit to the private sector by financial institutions, stock market capitalization, and private bonds outstanding reached an average of over 260 percent of gross domestic product (GDP) for G-7 countries, compared to about 100 percent in 1975.

The development of capital markets in rich countries has been accompanied by an increasing financial integration across nations. This globalization is not new. International capital flows have existed for a long time.[4] In fact, according to some measures, the extent of global capital mobility and capital flows 100 years ago is comparable to today's level. At that time, however, only a few countries and sectors participated in financial globalization. Capital flows tended to follow migration and were generally directed towards supporting trade flows. For the most part, capital flows took the form of bond flows and were of a long-term nature. Plus, the international system was dominated by the gold standard, with gold backing national currencies.

The advent of the First World War represented the first blow to this wave of financial globalization, which was followed by a period of instability and crises, ultimately leading to the Great Depression and the Second World War. After these events, governments reversed financial globalization, imposing capital controls to regain monetary policy autonomy. This depressed capital flows, which reached very low levels during the 1950s and 1960s. The international system was then dominated by the Bretton Woods arrangement of fixed but adjustable exchange rates, limited capital mobility, and autonomous monetary policies. The 1970s witnessed the beginning of a new era in the international financial system. As a result of the oil shock and the break-up of the Bretton Woods system, a new wave of globalization began. With the disintegration of the Bretton Woods arrangement of fixed exchange rates, countries were able to open up to greater capital mobility while keeping the autonomy of their monetary policies.

While globalization at the beginning of the twentieth century mainly entailed flows from rich countries (mostly the United Kingdom) to emerging economies, most of the action in the more recent globalization phase has taken place among developed economies. In this phase, capital flows across developed countries have increased sharply. At the same time, capital market activity has concentrated in few large international financial centers, mainly in Frankfurt, London, New York, and Tokyo.

Developing Countries and the Globalization Process

While most of the capital market development and globalization portrayed above have taken place in financial centers and in developed economies, developing countries have also been affected by the same underlying trends and were able to participate to some extent in these processes. The global trends affected developing countries in at least two ways. First, new capital became available in international financial markets, with developing countries trying to attract it to their domestic markets. Second, developing countries tried to emulate the increasing use of capital markets that characterized developed economies by implementing several reforms.

The efforts to attract international capital to developing countries were in part a result of the increased availability of liquidity in global markets, which led to booms in capital flows. New capital became available following the oil shock of 1973, which provided international banks with fresh funds to invest in developing countries. These funds were used mainly to finance public debt in the form of syndicated loans. The capital flows of the 1970s and early 1980s led to the debt crisis that started in Mexico in 1982. To solve this crisis, Brady Bonds were created, leading to the subsequent development of sovereign bond markets in emerging economies.

The recent wave of capital flows differs in at least two ways from the 1976–82 period of capital inflows: first, in terms of magnitude; and second, in terms of flow composition. Capital flows to emerging economies during the 1990s peaked in 1997, reaching nearly US$340 billion, decreasing sharply in the following years as a consequence of the financial crises in East Asia and Russia. Since then, capital flows have recovered, experiencing strong growth and reaching about US$412 billion in 2004. The composition of capital flows to developing countries has also changed significantly. The importance of official flows more than halved, with private capital flows becoming the major source of capital for a large number of countries. The nature of private capital flows has also changed markedly. Foreign direct investment (FDI) has grown continuously since the early 1990s. Mergers and acquisitions (M&As) were the most important source of this increase, especially those resulting from the privatization of state-owned companies. Portfolio flows also became important.

A salient feature of the recent wave of financial globalization has been the internationalization of financial services, that is, the use of international financial intermediaries by local issuers and investors. This internationalization has been achieved through two main channels. The first channel is an increased presence of international financial intermediaries in local markets. Along with capital flows, international financial institutions have begun to operate in developing countries. The second channel involves the use of international financial intermediaries and markets located outside the country, by local issuers and investors. One example of the latter channel is the listing and trading of shares in major world stock exchanges, mostly in the form of depositary receipts.[5]

Developing countries have tried different ways to attract the new capital available in international markets. One has been financial liberalization, which mostly took place in the late 1980s and early 1990s in developing countries, some years after developed countries had liberalized their financial systems. As part of the liberalization process, governments and firms actively raised capital in international financial markets and foreigners were allowed to invest in domestic markets. Financial liberalization also implied that international financial institutions were allowed to enter developing countries, purchasing local banks and establishing local branches or subsidiaries. Another way to attract foreign capital has been through privatization processes, initiated by Chile and the UK and then followed by most countries. Privatization proceeds were substantial; in developing countries, they climbed from US$2.6 billion in 1988 to US$66.6 billion in 1997. Furthermore, as several privatizations were conducted through public offerings on local stock exchanges, the process also had a direct impact on domestic stock market capitalization and trading. As mentioned above, the boom in equity flows and FDI is to a large extent explained by cross-border acquisitions of state-owned enterprises. Finally, developing countries tried to improve the climate for capital to flow in by pursuing macroeconomic stabilization, better business environments, and stronger economic fundamentals.

Besides these efforts to attract foreign capital, developing countries also tried to emulate the performance of capital markets in developed economies by implementing a series of reforms thought to foster domestic securities markets development. These reforms had their own logic and are easy to understand in the context of globalization.

At the early stages, the reforms had primarily a development focus. The main idea was that capital markets would provide relatively cheap financing, mobilizing savings efficiently to their most productive use and offering investors attractive investment opportunities. The intention of fostering capital markets squared well with the global trend of moving towards a market-oriented system and emulating the functioning of capital markets in developed economies. Among other things, capital markets would exert competition on domestic banking systems, which in many developing countries charged high intermediation spreads. After the East Asian crisis of 1997–98, some regarded the development of local capital markets as a way to make the financial systems of developing countries more stable.[6] The rationale was that financial markets, and especially bond markets, could be the 'spare tires' of the system, sustaining finance when the 'main tires' (banks) were flattened by a crisis. Moreover, changes in asset prices could help to absorb shocks. Additionally, instruments increasingly denominated in local currency and of longer duration, in addition to a broader derivatives market, could help to reduce systemic risk.

The idea of reforming the financial system led to a barrage of reforms, which can be grouped into first- and second-generation reforms. First-generation reforms focused on building a solid foundation for capital market development; second-generation reforms tried to increase market activity and liquidity, broaden investor participation, and expand the universe of instruments traded.

Apart from the liberalization and privatization mentioned above, reform efforts were complemented in a number of cases by structural pension system reforms, shifting from public defined-benefit systems to private defined-contribution ones. Among other things, the new pension systems were expected to boost the availability of long-term finance for the private sector. Chile was the first country to adopt this system in 1981 and many other countries implemented similar reforms over the 1990s.[7]

Enticed by their potential benefits, governments also approved new legislation aimed at creating the proper market infrastructure and institutions for capital markets to flourish. In particular, countries created domestic securities and exchange commissions, considerably developed the regulatory and supervisory framework, and took important strides towards establishing and improving the basic environment for market operations. The latter included new policies related to centralized exchanges, securities clearance and settlement systems, custody arrangements, and varying degrees of improvements in accounting and disclosure standards. More recently, new laws and regulations intended to protect creditors and investors – including improvements in the general legal framework and property rights, minority shareholders rights, bankruptcy laws, and insider trading regulations – have enhanced this infrastructure.

Main Developments in Domestic Stock Markets

Although capital markets in many developed countries have witnessed a boom during the 1990s and 2000s, the picture is more mixed when focusing on developing countries, with wide heterogeneity across nations.[8] Some countries experienced growth of their domestic stock markets, but in most cases this growth was not as significant as that witnessed by industrialized nations. Other countries experienced an actual deterioration of their domestic stock markets. Noticeable differences arise when comparing the development of domestic capital markets across regions. Among emerging economies, capital markets in East Asia have developed relatively well. On the other hand, markets in Latin America have lagged behind, characterized by delistings and illiquidity.

The contrast between the large number of policy initiatives and reforms and the dismal performance of capital markets raises several questions. Is there a lack of relation between fundamentals and capital market development? To what extent have capital markets responded to reforms? Were the reforms misconceived? Were expectations too optimistic? Are other factors affecting domestic stock markets and driving out the impact of reforms? Is more time needed to see the full fruits of reforms? Does the reform agenda need to be rethought? These are difficult questions to answer, but the analysis in the rest of this chapter will help to shed light on these issues.

POLICY IMPLICATIONS

The evidence suggests that the state of securities markets in many emerging economies, and especially in Latin America, is disheartening. Despite the intense reform effort of the 1990s and 2000s, local capital markets in most emerging economies remain underdeveloped. Although some developing countries have experienced growth of their domestic markets, this growth in most cases has not been as significant as that witnessed by industrialized nations. Other countries experienced an actual deterioration of their capital markets, as a growing number of firms have cross-listed and raised capital in international financial centers. In the case of Latin America, the results appear even more discouraging given the intensity of reform efforts in the region and the better evolution of capital markets in East Asia and their rapid growth in developed economies. Furthermore, the evidence summarized in de la Torre and Schmukler (2006) shows that capital markets in Latin America are below what can be expected after controlling for several factors found to affect capital market development, including income levels, economic size, macroeconomic policies, and legal and institutional development. The evidence also shows that the relation between globalization and domestic market development is complex, and in many cases differs from what was expected at the beginning of the reform process. In particular, our results indicate that improvements in fundamentals and capital market reforms lead to a higher share of activity in international financial markets.

Drawing policy implications for the reform agenda from the foregoing evidence is not as simple a task as is often believed. Assessing the evidence is a process that, by nature, involves significant resort to judgment calls. There is thus ample scope for differing – yet reasonable – explanations for the gap between expectations and outcomes. This section aims at providing a flavor of the range of perspectives on this question by identifying three typological views. The first two views are general characterizations of two different diagnoses that have emerged repeatedly in the debate. The third view is essentially our re-evaluation of the first two views, based on how we interpret the available evidence. While each of the three views emphasizes distinct aspects of the evidence, reaching different diagnoses and drawing different lessons, they are not necessarily incompatible.

The first view, encapsulated in the message, 'be patient and redouble the efforts', contends that past reforms were essentially right, that the reforms needed in the future are mostly known, and that reforms – especially second-generation ones – have long gestation periods before producing visible dividends. It thus recommends letting market discipline work, while forging ahead patiently with further reform implementation efforts. The second view, encapsulated in the message, 'get the sequence right', draws attention to problems that arise when some reforms are implemented ahead of others. Its central prescription is that key preconditions should be met – including the achievement of a minimum institutional strength – before fully liberalizing domestic financial markets and allowing free international capital mobility.

Despite their important contributions and insights, we argue that these two views do not properly address some relevant aspects of the evidence. We thus propose a third view, which arises from the identification of some of the shortcomings of the previous two views. This third view can be encapsulated in the message, 'revisit basic issues and reshape expectations'. It contends that perhaps the most questionable aspect of the first two views is their implicit assumption that domestic capital market development in emerging economies should be measured against the benchmark of capital markets in industrialized countries. Indeed, for the first two views, the reform path may be long and difficult, but the expected outcome is, in most cases, only one – to look increasingly like a mini Wall Street. But it is difficult to accept this premise given the evidence, which suggests that certain characteristics of emerging markets in general, and Latin American countries in particular, have traditionally not been fully considered in the analysis and policy debate. These characteristics include small economic size, limits to risk diversification, presence of weak currencies, prevalence of systemic risk, and the impact of financial globalization, among others. The third view thus invites a serious analysis of the implications of these characteristics, in particular for the reform agenda going forward. The implications are paramount, as we illustrate in de la Torre and Schmukler (2006) by discussing in some detail issues pertaining to the interaction of capital market liquidity and risk diversification, with economic size, globalization, and segmentation of access.

The third view therefore calls for a more varied reform agenda, as a one-size-fits-all approach is destined to fail. The third view emphasizes that a key step in designing country-specific reforms should be a determination of whether the emerging economy in question can sustain an active domestic market for private sector equity securities. It also argues that, ultimately, any reform agenda for capital markets needs to be couched within a broader vision of financial development for emerging markets in the context of international financial integration.

CONCLUSIONS

Our work yields important lessons for the debate on the future of stock markets – and capital markets more generally – in emerging economies, and those in Latin America in particular. Three main messages stand out from the analysis.

First, it is very difficult to understand where domestic capital markets stand today without analyzing them in the context of globalization. For many countries, a significant part of the capital market activity takes place abroad. Domestic capital market development and internationalization are closely related; therefore any evaluation of capital markets that just focuses on domestic markets is likely to have severe limitations.

The increasing use of international capital markets is having both positive and negative effects on domestic markets. In terms of positive effects, the financing obtained by firms and governments in international markets has traditionally tended to be of a longer-term nature than that obtained in domestic markets. Also, when firms go to international capital markets, they become more transparent, providing domestic investors with better investment opportunities. As governments and the largest firms obtain financing abroad, there is a potential for a 'crowding-in' effect, increasing the domestic financing for other issuers. Aside from these positive effects of internationalization on domestic markets, there are also some negative ones. For instance, the listing of large local firms in international markets can have a negative impact on domestic market trading and liquidity, as trading activity might migrate abroad. Moreover, financing in international markets is volatile, with the risk premium increasing substantially during crisis periods. Foreign bond financing tends to be denominated in foreign currency, exposing issuers to currency risk. These factors have led many to link financial globalization with crises.

One important feature of the current globalization process is that it is characterized by segmentation across countries and firms. This is relevant because if countries and companies benefit from access to foreign capital, only a small group of countries and firms are the ones reaping most of the benefits. For example, while net private capital flows to developing countries have increased during the 2000s, private capital does not flow to all countries equally. Some countries tend to receive large inflows, while other countries receive little foreign capital. And within those developing countries that do receive capital flows, not all agents are equally able to reap, at least directly, the benefits of financial globalization. In particular, the evidence suggests that the largest companies are the ones most able to tap international financial markets. This segmentation might increase the gap between those countries and firms that are able to internationalize, and the rest.

The second big message from the study is that expectations about the reform process and policy options need to be revisited. This view contrasts with the other explanations as to why capital market reforms did not work as expected. Those explanations argue either that reforms need more time to produce the expected effects or that the sequencing of reforms was incorrect. Here, we claim that the reform process did not take into consideration important aspects related to the nature of globalization and emerging economies.

According to the evidence, capital market reforms and improvements in fundamentals have indeed had a positive impact on domestic capital markets. But this process has also helped countries to obtain financing in international capital markets, sometimes at the expense of domestic market development. Barring attempts to isolate countries from the international financial system, future policies will need to take into account the effects of globalization on capital markets. Future policies might also aim at trying to integrate the rest of the economy with the international system. To the extent that full integration is not possible, future policies might need to consider ways in which globalization can have positive spillover effects on all sectors of the economy, including those that are not directly linked to the international financial system.

Capital market development policies need to take into account the intrinsic characteristics of developing countries (such as small size, illiquid markets, lack of risk diversification, presence of weak currencies, and prevalence of systemic risk), and how these features limit the scope for developing deep domestic capital markets. These limitations are difficult to overcome by the reform process. In other words, even if countries carry out all the necessary reforms, they might not obtain the domestic capital market development that many expected in the early 1990s.

The third big message from this study is that although securities markets in Latin America have grown substantially since 1990, capital markets in the region remain underdeveloped when compared to markets in industrial and East Asian countries. Furthermore, the evidence also shows that there is a shortfall in domestic stock market activity in the region after controlling for many factors, including per capita income, macroeconomic policies, and measures of the legal and institutional environment. In other words, Latin American countries have lower domestic stock market development than countries with similar fundamentals and policies in other regions. Although there are different possible explanations as to why Latin America has performed worse, it is difficult to reach a definite answer with the available evidence. Future work is necessary to shed more light on this issue.

Our conclusions do not lead to simple policy recommendations. On the contrary, the evidence from our work opens a new array of questions that might prompt future policy discussions. In this sense, the contribution of our study is to raise new issues that cannot be easily ignored when designing new policies.

NOTES

1. This chapter is based on the first chapter of the book by the same authors, de la Torre and Schmukler (2006). We thank Jose Azar and Francisco Ceballos for excellent assistance.

2. The literature on the finance–growth nexus is vast. Reviews of this literature can be found in a variety of forms to suit all sorts of different tastes. A comprehensive review is found in Levine (2005). Rajan and Zingales (2001, 2003), by contrast, provide shorter reviews in less technical language. Caprio and Honohan (2001) offer an excellent rendition that emphasizes the World Bank contributions to the empirical literature.
3. French and Poterba (1991) and Tesar and Werner (1995) present evidence of home bias in international investment. Several papers have also found that investors exhibit a preference for larger, geographically and culturally closer firms, both within and across countries (see, for example, Coval and Moskovitz 1999; Grinblatt and Keloharju 2001; Huberman 2001).
4. Eichengreen and Sussman (2000) offer a millennium perspective.
5. There are different ways to 'list' domestic stocks in international financial markets. A traditional way is to cross-list the shares on another exchange. European companies tend to use this method of internationalization most often. A very popular way to internationalize among emerging market firms has been through depositary receipts, called American depositary receipts (ADRs) or global depositary receipts (GDRs). These are foreign currency-denominated derivative instruments, issued by international banks like the Bank of New York or Citibank, representing home securities held with a local custodian. Trading in DRs in US exchanges has expanded from US$75 billion in 1990 to US$1 trillion in 2005, and there were more than 1900 sponsored ADR programs in 2006, issued by firms from 73 countries. DR programs grow or shrink depending on demand, since the issuance of DRs and the conversion back to the underlying shares only involves a small transaction cost. See Levy Yeyati et al. (2009).
6. See, for example, Greenspan (1999), Herring and Chatusripitak (2001), IFC (2001) and Batten and Kim (2001).
7. The evidence from Chile suggests that pension reform can have a significant impact on capital market development and economic growth. See Corbo and Schmidt-Hebbel (2003).
8. Note that this heterogeneity also extends to developed countries.

REFERENCES

Batten, J. and Y. Kim (2001), 'Expanding long-term financing through bond market development: a post-crisis policy task', in K. Yun-Hwan (ed.), *Government Bond Market Development in Asia*, Manila: Asian Development Bank, pp. 5–48.

Caprio, G. and P. Honohan (2001), *Finance for Growth: Policy Choices in a Volatile World*, New York: Oxford University Press, and Washington, DC: World Bank.

Corbo, V. and K. Schmidt-Hebbel (2003), 'Efectos Macroeconómicos de la Reforma de Pensiones en Chile', presented at the Conference on 'Reformas a los Sistemas de Pensiones: Sus Efectos y Retos', organized by the International Federation of Pension Funds Administrators, 10–11 July, Panama.

Coval, J. and T. Moskovitz (1999), 'Home bias at home: local equity preference in domestic portfolios', *Journal of Finance*, **54**, 2045–73.

de la Torre, A. and S. Schmukler (2006), *Emerging Capital Markets and Globalization: The Latin American Experience*, Palo Alto, CA: Stanford University Press and Washington, DC: World Bank.

Eichengreen, B. and N. Sussman (2000), 'The international monetary system in the very long run', *World Economic Outlook Supporting Studies*, April.

French, K.R. and J.M. Poterba (1991), 'Investor diversification and international equity markets', *American Economic Review*, **81** (2), 222–6.

Greenspan, A. (1999), 'Do efficient financial markets contribute to financial crises?' Financial Markets Conference of the Federal Reserve Bank of Atlanta, Sea Island, GA, USA.

Grinblatt, M. and M. Keloharju (2001), 'How distance, language, and culture influence stockholdings and trades', *Journal of Finance*, **56** (3), 1053–74.

Herring, R. and N. Chatusripitak (2001), 'The case of the missing market: the bond market and why it matters for financial development', Wharton Financial Institutions Center Working Paper, University of Pennsylvania.

Huberman, G. (2001), 'Familiarity breeds investment', *Review of Financial Studies*, **14** (3), 659–80.

International Finance Corporation (IFC) (2001), *Building Local Bond Markets: An Asian Perspective*, Alison Harwood (ed.), Washington, DC: World Bank.

Levine, R. (2005), 'Finance and growth', in P. Aghion and S. Durlauf (eds), *Handbook of Economic Growth*, Amsterdam: Elsevier Press, pp. 865–934.

Levy Yeyati, E., S. Schmukler and N. van Horen (2009), 'International financial integration through the law of one price', *Journal of Financial Intermediation*, **18**, 432–63.

Rajan, R. and L. Zingales (2001), 'Financial systems, industrial structure, and growth', *Oxford Review of Economic Policy*, **17** (4), 467–82.
Rajan, R. and L. Zingales (2003), *Saving Capitalism from the Capitalists*, New York: Crown Business Division of Random House.
Tesar, L. and I. Werner (1995), 'Home bias and high turnover', *Journal of International Money and Finance*, **14** (4), 467–92.

11 What happened on 6 May 2010? Anatomy of the flash crash

Geoffrey Poitras

> [R]emarkably fast-growing IT-driven ECNs, MTFs, and other off-exchange trading facilities are giving rise to noticeable issues such as market fragmentation, regulatory discrepancies between markets and free-riding on the self-regulatory functions of incumbent exchanges in the EU and US. In the near future, this trend is also likely to affect Japanese stock markets. The 'flash crash' that occurred in the US in May 2010 is an example of a phenomenon arising from these factors. (Atsushi Saito, President and Chief Executive Officer, Tokyo Stock Exchange Group)

Despite being a key element in capitalist society, much activity in the stock market happens outside the glare of public scrutiny. In turn, regulation of the stock market is predominantly civil, with criminal sanctions reserved only for the most egregious actions. In the US, the federal stock market regulator, the Securities and Exchange Commission (SEC), is only empowered to impose civil penalties. Criminal prosecution falls within the purview of the Justice Department. Similarly, important instances of historical regulation, such as the seventeenth-century Dutch ban on *in blanco* short selling or the eighteenth-century English ban on trading of privileges (see Poitras, Chapter 3 in this volume), did not involve criminal sanction. Rather, legislation removed the protection of the courts for those involved in such trading. Despite various bans and restrictions, 'prohibited' trading continued. Where sanctions associated with trading restrictions are particularly prohibitive, then trading shifts to alternative jurisdictions, for example hedge funds domiciled in overshore tax havens use a master–feeder fund structure to avoid public filing requirements in the US. The collapse of the Madoff hedge fund Ponzi scheme in 2008 illustrates that lack of transparency in stock market dealings continues to the present.

In this opaque milieu of stock market trading, periodic market failures provide situations where the light of public scrutiny reveals detailed information on market activities not regularly available. The bulk of stock market history is compiled from: regular reports of trading by self-regulatory entities, such as the exchanges; legislatively and administratively mandated reports by government regulators; and the numerous books, pamphlets, periodicals, newspapers and other literature produced by and for market participants. Of these primary sources, the various commissions, government reports and related publications generated by infrequent market failures have been invaluable. Under the public pressure produced by market disruption, information about trading activities that would typically be considered proprietary is revealed. The annals of stock market history are replete with examples of invaluable information from such events, from Isaac Le Maire's 'Memorandum to the Lord Advocate' in January 1609 (Jonker 2009) to the 'Findings regarding the market events of May 6, 2010' by the staffs of the SEC and Commodity Future Trading Commission (CFTC) in September 2010 (SEC 2010a). Combined with information obtained from regular public filings by the exchanges and selected companies, SEC (2010a, 2010b) provides a robust description of the US stock market landscape at the end of the first decade of the twenty-first century.

WHAT HAPPENED ON 6 MAY 2010?

A quick sketch of events is provided in SEC (2010a, p. 1):

> On May 6, 2010, the prices of many US-based equity products experienced an extraordinarily rapid decline and recovery. That afternoon, major equity indices in both the futures and securities markets, each already down over 4% from their prior-day close, suddenly plummeted a further 5–6% in a matter of minutes before rebounding almost as quickly.
>
> Many of the almost 8000 individual equity securities and exchange traded funds ('ETFs') traded that day suffered similar price declines and reversals within a short period of time, falling 5%, 10% or even 15% before recovering most, if not all, of their losses. However, some equities experienced even more severe price moves, both up and down. Over 20 000 trades across more than 300 securities were executed at prices more than 60% away from their values just moments before. Moreover, many of these trades were executed at prices of a penny or less, or as high as $100 000, before prices of those securities returned to their 'pre-crash' levels.
>
> By the end of the day, major futures and equities indices 'recovered' to close at losses of about 3% from the prior day.

Though SEC (2010a) is at pains to avoid the terminology, the stock market events of 6 May 2010 are generally referred to as the 'flash crash'. This euphemism arises from the perceived importance of high-frequency traders in precipitating the disturbing but brief breakdown in the basic price discovery process for certain stocks, for example Kirilenko et al. (2010).

Immediate concern about the flash crash in Congress was expressed by: the Senate Committee on Banking, Housing, and Urban Affairs; the Senate Committee on Agriculture, Nutrition and Forestry; and the House Committee on Financial Services. These committees specifically requested that the staffs of the SEC and CFTC produce a report relating to 'the business transactions or market positions of any person that is necessary for a complete and accurate description of the May 6 crash and its causes' (SEC 2010a). The result was two reports. A 'Preliminary Findings' report delivered 18 May 2010 to the Joint Advisory Committee on Emerging Regulatory Issues (JAC) (SEC 2010b) and a final 'Findings' report also delivered to the JAC on 30 September 2010 (SEC 2010a). Armed with the power of Congress to provide impetus to the investigation, SEC (2010b, 2010a) provides unprecedented insights into the workings of the electronic US stock market of the twenty-first century. Historic institutional changes in the stock market have been precipitated by a technological revolution in trading. The changes go beyond exchange demutualization and the demise of the exchange trading floor.

In addition to depth of useful data about the stock market trading landscape, SEC (2010a) also reveals the approach of regulators to understanding the changes under way. In particular, the flash crash involved the fragmentation of market liquidity undermining the basic price discovery process for certain stocks. While SEC (2010a) and (2010b) provide a detailed and helpful description of current trading practices on modern electronic trading networks, it is apparent that 'market participants' are in charge of the trading process. Regulators reacted to the 6 May events in the stock market by continuing the reversal of Bush-era stock market liberalization rule changes that began following the stock market collapse of 2008–09, for example the price limit-triggered short sale price test rule (SEC 2010c). The previous rules had been introduced to facilitate the activities of large stock market participants, including but not limited to high-frequency traders. In particular, starting with Reg ATS in 1998, impediments to rapid execution of two-sided trades – such as market circuit breakers, programme trading restrictions and the up-tick rule for short sales – were progressively eliminated to facilitate activities such as high-frequency trading. The regulatory reaction to the flash crash was to introduce a single stock circuit breaker rule. Despite claims that 'the staffs of the CFTC and the SEC are working together with the markets' (SEC 2010a, p. 6), the regulatory confusion created by having two regulators, the SEC and the CFTC, is more than apparent. Faced with a wide range in public opinion, the regulators are having considerable difficulty in determining what happened and, as a consequence, finding appropriate regulatory adjustments.

Based on SEC (2010a), there is much in the flash crash to digest. Measures of 'buy-side' and 'sell-side' 'market liquidity' are employed together with classifications for traders, such as 'fundamental sellers' and 'fundamental buyers', defined as: 'as market participants who are trading to accumulate or reduce a net long or short position. Reasons for fundamental buying and selling include gaining long-term exposure to a market as well as hedging already existing exposures in related markets' (SEC 2010a, p. 2). The operative event that triggered the flash crash happened at 2.32 p.m. when: 'a large fundamental trader (a mutual fund complex) initiated a sell program to sell a total of 75 000 E-Mini [S&P 500 futures] contracts (valued at approximately $4.1 billion) as a hedge to an existing equity position'. From this point, SEC (2010a) traces the process by which this trade was absorbed by the stock market. Other than noting that 'only two single-day sell programs of equal or larger size – one of which was by the same large fundamental trader – were executed in the E-Mini in the 12 months prior to May 6', little attention is paid to the decision process of the large fundamental seller that generated this trade. No substantive mention is made of centuries of regulatory oversight required to deal with disruptive short speculative trades in the stock market.

The flash crash involved two interrelated liquidity events: one in the deep market for E-mini index futures and the Standard & Poor's S&P 500 index ETF (SPY); and, another in the market for individual stocks. The E-mini liquidity event ended almost as abruptly as it started (SEC 2010a, p. 4):

> At 2.45.28 p.m., trading on the E-Mini was paused for five seconds when the Chicago Mercantile Exchange ('CME') Stop Logic Functionality was triggered in order to prevent a cascade of further price declines. In that short period of time, sell-side pressure in the E-Mini was partly alleviated and buy-side interest increased. When trading resumed at 2.45.33 p.m., prices stabilized and shortly thereafter, the E-Mini began to recover, followed by the SPY.
>
> The Sell Algorithm continued to execute the sell program until about 2.51 p.m. as the prices were rapidly rising in both the E-Mini and SPY.

However, the flash crash did not end with recovery in the E-mini and SPY prices around 2.45 (SEC 2010a, p. 5):

> Even though after 2.45 p.m. prices in the E-Mini and SPY were recovering from their severe declines, sell orders placed for some individual securities and ETFs (including many retail stop-loss orders, triggered by declines in prices of those securities) found reduced buying interest, which led to further price declines in those securities.

The flash crash involving individual securities did not end until around 3.00 p.m. with implications primarily for retail investors (SEC 2010a, p. 6):

> during the 20 minute period between 2.40 p.m. and 3.00 p.m., over 20000 trades (many based on retail-customer orders) across more than 300 separate securities, including many ETFs, were executed at prices 60% or more away from their 2.40 p.m. prices. After the market closed, the exchanges and FINRA met and jointly agreed to cancel (or break) all such trades under their respective 'clearly erroneous' trade rules.[1]

While SEC (2010a) observed that 'severe dislocations in many securities were fleeting', such a conclusion masks the serious potential problems that the flash crash represents.

HISTORICAL ANTECEDENTS OF THE FLASH CRASH

Referencing the events of 6 May 2010 as 'the flash crash' aims to connect the activities of high-frequency traders with the disruption of the stock market price discovery function on that date. However, such an interpretation is misguided. This conclusion can be illustrated historically by considering events surrounding a decidedly similar liquidity event: the stock market crash of 1987. Similarities appear despite a considerable difference in the trading milieu. Though the crash of 1987 did have a technological aspect, a more dramatic revolution in communications and trading technology was still on the horizon. High-frequency trading strategies were not available, though various 'programmed' trading strategies had progressively been introduced during the decade prior to the 1987 crash. There were also a variety of practical and legal restrictions limiting trading in stock index futures and options. Stock index ETFs did not appear until the early 1990s. Despite these differences, the primary regulatory resolution is similar in both events: the use of pricing circuit breakers (for example NYSE Rule 80B, 'Trading halts due to extraordinary market volatility'). In the case of the flash crash, this solution involved a reworking of the rules to allow the imposition of five-minute circuit breakers on prices for individual stocks, and not just circuit breakers associated with the market index values implemented following the 1987 crash.

The causes of the stock market crash of October 19–20 1987 have been debated ad nauseum. The analysis includes: reports by the exchanges, for example the CME and the New York Stock Exchange (NYSE); the regulators, for example reports by the SEC, the Government Accountability Office, the CFTC and the Brady Commission; and academic studies, for example Macey et al. (1989), Edwards (1988) and Tosini (1988). For sheer attention and regulatory impact, the crash of 1987 is the 'disaster of disasters' compared to the flash crash. Significant incremental reforms were made to market practices, ranging from the introduction of trading circuit breakers triggered by large market moves to rules impacting upon the capitalization of specialists on the NYSE trading floor. Physical hardware changes were also made to the execution system for processing orders on the NYSE. Another fallout from the crash was the drastically reduced use of stock markets for dynamic portfolio insurance trading strategies designed to achieve replication of an untraded put option pay-off. From the early 1980s to the crash of 1987, such schemes had been actively promoted to institutional investors by a number of the leading investment banks and finance academics, including Fischer Black and Mark Rubinstein.[2]

In retrospect, the crash of 1987 still has many lessons for the present, if only these lessons could be adequately understood. As with the flash crash, analysis of the crash by regulators has the flavour of an apology for the current method of oversight. Tosini (1988, p. 35), a director at the CFTC at the time of the crash, is an excellent example: 'there are many profound, complex and far-reaching issues before the CFTC, as well as other federal agencies and the Congress, concerning stock market and derivative market activities and performance during October . . . the call for "further research" has hardly ever been more timely'. The various reports made some key observations, for example the Brady Report (Presidential Task Force on Market Mechanisms 1988) recognized that the markets for stocks, stock options and stock index futures were actually one integrated market, 'linked by financial instruments, trading strategies, market participants and clearing and credit mechanisms'. Despite this integration, the regulatory and institutional structure which was designed for separated markets was unable to deal with 'intermarket' pressures. The Brady Commission recommended a number of reforms designed to provide for a more integrated approach to market oversight. These recommendations did little to change the conflicting mandates of regulators overseeing activity in the stock market.

Both the crash of 1987 and the flash crash speak directly to the problems raised by the systemic change in financial markets brought on by the historical resurgence in speculative exchange trading of equity derivatives. Various events have since been replayed because some lessons were not fully understood. This happened because analysis of the crashes, on the whole, focused on the specific events that occurred during the crash and did not adequately distinguish between the singularity and the commonality of the specific events. Poitras (2002, pp. 52–8) details the chain of events in the crash of 1987. As measured by the Dow Jones Industrial Average (DJIA), the US equity market had achieved a peak of 2722 in August of 1987. Price–earnings (P/E) ratios for the S&P 500 were averaging 23, relatively high considering the potential for negative market sentiment. In modern parlance, the equity market was due for a correction. On Wednesday 15 October 1987 there was a news release reporting an unexpectedly large US trade deficit, banks raised prime rates and there was considerable downward pressure on equity prices. The S&P 500 fell from over 314 to below 306. Despite a calming statement by Treasury Secretary Baker on the Thursday, the S&P 500 fell again to 298. When some negative Producer Price Index (PPI) and industrial production numbers hit the market at the open on Friday, the stage was set. Significantly, even though things were gloomy, none of this was a shadow of events about to unfold. This leads to a key observation about the crash: it was an severe event that was not associated with a correspondingly severe negative information inflow to the market.

The crash actually started on Friday 17 October 1987. In the face of the somewhat negative sentiment, the DJIA fell a record 108 points. The S&P 500 started the day at

298 and fell to around 282. These were significant market moves that, all things considered, may have presented some buying opportunities. Over the weekend, there was some chatter about a dispute between the US and Germany over interest rates, leading to speculation that the US might let the dollar fall, an event which would be negative for US equities. There was the usual carry-over on foreign markets, such as Tokyo and Australia, though the wave of intense selling had not yet hit international markets. The New York market opening was confronted with rumours in the news that the US had attacked Iranian oil platforms in the Persian Gulf, which almost surely added to the rush of sell orders. At the open the DJIA was down 67 points. The S&P 500 futures contract on the CME fell 18 points at the open. At a time when 100 million share volumes were uncommonly large, the NYSE processed 50 million shares in the first half hour. Despite the market turbulence, a 10 a.m. meeting of NYSE officials and major brokerage houses did not feel a trading halt was needed.

The sequence of events which was to follow was structured around two institutional procedures. The first concerns the method of executing stocks on the NYSE. Historically, stocks trades on the NYSE involved a floor broker for a member firm having to walk the order to an NYSE trading post for that stock, and execute the trade directly with the specialist or with another broker using open outcry. At the time of the 1987 crash, this was still the case for block trades involving 10000 or more shares. This manual method of trading was inefficient and costly for trades involving large bundles of stocks which have to be sold at once. Such trades were being done not only by index arbitragers, but also by a wide range of market participants. To improve market performance for these traders, the NYSE introduced the Designated Order Turnaround (DOT) in 1976. This system permitted the computerized execution of small trades. Effectively, brokers with member firms could enter trades into a computerized order system, permitting trades to be entered in brokers' offices. Upon receiving the order, the DOT system would automatically route the trade to the appropriate NYSE specialist, where it would be executed. The whole process could be completed in a matter of minutes.

The success of the DOT system led to a new and improved version, the Super-Dot, being implemented in 1984. This new DOT system further enhanced execution times and access. This remarkable progress in information technology created its own demand from a growing legion of program traders. This category includes a range of trading strategies, including portfolio insurance and index arbitrage. Program traders could enter the exact weights for a portfolio of stocks which could be executed simultaneously by computer entry. Prior DOT execution risk in such strategies was an important deterrent. Yet, the interaction between the progress in information technology and the trading of newly introduced financial engineering products was not well understood at the time and, as illustrated in the flash crash, continues to the present. Hints of the crash of October 1987 were observed on 11–12 September 1986 and on 23 January 1987 when 'excessive' stock market volatility was observed. These preliminary tremors attracted some attention, and efforts were made to track the activities of program traders through the DOT system. A poll by NYSE of specialists and floor traders found that, almost without exception, program trading was done through the DOT. On average, in the year leading up to the crash, DOT orders from program traders were found to average around 18 per cent of all DOT trades with over 28 per cent of all orders on 19 October 1987 being due to program traders.

In addition to the DOT, the other essential institutional feature to consider in evaluating the crash of 1987 is the short sale rule, for example Macey et al. (1989). More precisely, from 1938 until 2004, Section 10(a) of the Securities Exchange Act regulated short sales of stocks registered on a national securities exchange. The rule has historical roots in the concentrated short selling that precipitated the market break of 1937. The SEC adopted Rule 10(a)-1 in 1938 to restrict short selling in a declining market. More precisely, Rule 10(a)-1 prohibited short selling of securities, except when the short sale either takes place above the last sale price of that security; or, at the last price, if that price is above the preceding price. The idea is that the rule prevents excessive and accelerating downward pressure on prices during a market downturn and provides preferential treatment for traders that are long stock and want to exit positions. However, there is no such rule on futures markets. As such, dynamic portfolio insurance strategies could be implemented by shorting stock index futures, instead of attempting to short the underlying stocks in the cash market. In addition, the single-digit percentage margins on futures contracts were only a small fraction of the 50 per cent margins on stocks.[3]

These substantive differences across cash and derivative security markets for stocks can be attributed to regulatory competition between the CFTC, which regulates commodity futures contracts and futures exchanges, and the SEC, which regulates stock markets and stock exchanges. The effects of this competition continue to the present.[4] The roots of this two-regulator system can be traced to Depression era reforms which were well suited to markets where commodities were traded separately from trading of financial securities. Along with the Securities Act (1933) and the Securities Exchange Act (1934) to deal with stock market reform, the Grain Futures Act (1922) was amended and renamed the Commodity Exchange Act (CEA) (1936). With various amendments and updates over the years, the CEA is still the centrepiece of US commodities regulation. The CEA (1936) extended the government's control of futures trading considerably: authority over speculative limits was established; registration requirements were imposed on floor brokers and futures commission merchants; cheating, fraud and market manipulation were made specific criminal offences; and restrictions were imposed on options trading. For more than seven decades, the CEA has provided a successful model for sustainable speculative exchange trading of commodities.

By 1974, the growth in both volume of trade and the number of new contracts (over which the CEA gave little effective control to regulators) brought a thorough reform. The CEA was amended to include the Commodity Futures Trading Act which forms the basis of current US government commodities regulation. The CEA (1974) empowered the Commodity Futures Trading Commission (CFTC). This marks a technical beginning to the competition between the futures industry, centred in Chicago and regulated by the CFTC, and the stock markets, centred in New York and regulated by the SEC. The CFTC is an 'independent' five-member commission appointed by the president, with authority to regulate all US futures trading and exchange activity. Included in the CFTC's mandate was the right to approve both the introduction of new contracts and changes in exchange bylaws. Together with these powers, the CFTC also has considerable emergency authority, for example assessment of large civil fines, and cease and desist orders. In 1978, several amendments were made to the Act dealing with the issue of jurisdiction. In opposition to the position of both the SEC and the US Treasury, the

CFTC was given exclusive jurisdiction over all future contracts, including the newly emerging financial futures contracts. Subsequent and ongoing legislative action has focused on clarifying jurisdiction over increasingly complicated overlaps between the two regulators, for example options on stock index futures contracts, and commodity ETFs that are traded on stock markets and use futures contracts to capture the commodity price exposure.

Portfolio insurance includes a range of trading strategies that fall within the overlapping jurisdictions of the SEC and CFTC. One important strategy involves dynamically trading stock index futures in order to replicate the pay-off on a portfolio composed of the underlying cash stock index and a put option. The reason that dynamic trading was so attractive in the period leading to the crash of 1987 is associated with the relatively limited array of path-independent option products that were available. Exchange traded option maturities were a maximum nine months, not all stocks had traded options, index options were relatively illiquid and the over-the-counter (OTC) market lacked sufficient liquidity to provide options with the exercise price variation and longer-term maturity dates that many institutional investors desired. Even though absence of arbitrage requires that cash-and-carry arbitrage conditions apply to the spot and futures markets, the sheer volume of trading on 19 October meant that a wide spread between the stock index futures and the underlying cash market stock index was seemingly inevitable. What emerged was much worse: an information technology breakdown. The rush of sell orders effectively crashed the DOT system. At 11.45 a.m. the ticker was approximately one hour behind and a number of stocks had yet to open because of the lack of an orderly market. By 2 p.m. volume had reached 400 million. The final numbers for 19 October were 603 million shares traded, with a drop of 508 points (23 per cent) on the Dow and 80.75 points on the S&P 500, a loss of nearly 30 per cent. At the bell the ticker was approximately 130 minutes behind.

This slaughter on the stock exchanges led to a flurry of overnight activities. As the US market collapse spread overseas, there were complete or almost complete trading halts on the Tokyo and Hong Kong stock exchanges. There was an unprecedented drop on the London FT Index. The opening of the New York market was preceded by reassuring statements and actions from the Federal Reserve Board (FRB), major banks were lowering prime rates and the NYSE shut down the DOT system to prevent the execution of program trades. A temporary and partial trading halt was implemented just after 11 a.m. as the market approached 180 on the S&P futures, while the cash market was trading just below 220. This seemed to spell the end of the crash. Prices recovered and by 2 p.m. the spread between cash and futures narrowed close to normal levels, though the spread did widen as the close approached. At the end of the day, the DJIA was up 102 points on a volume of 608 million shares. Due to actions taken to combat the crash, there was strong recovery of the dollar and a decline in interest rates. The low prices combined with the sudden brightening of the economic picture led to a buying spree, both in the US and offshore. By the close Thursday 20 October the market had recovered about half of what was lost on Monday.

The crash of 1987 was an unprecedented security market event. It exposed serious weaknesses in a regulatory system that was designed to fight the battles arising from old technology. Problems originated from an inability to assess and structure the rapid changes in the stock market. This was a debacle which was created by a well-intentioned need to innovate, to improve portfolio management of large financial institutions and investment companies. As it turns out, the portfolio insurance programs based on dynamic trading were generally unable to deliver the protection which was claimed *ex ante*. The situation for which the insurance was most important, the protection of losses in the event of a market collapse, led to preconditions which prevented the outcome from being achieved. The programs could only get so big and it was not possible for more than a small fraction of market participants to pursue successfully such dynamic trading strategies. In addition, there are numerous untold stories of other strategies, such as delta hedging by option traders, which also contributed to the crash. Undoubtedly, such traders also contributed to the selling via both the DOT and floor trading which only added to the downward pressure on prices.

HIGH-FREQUENCY TRADING AND THE FLASH CRASH

SEC (2010a) identifies an unusually large (75 000 = \$4.1 billion in equity value) short trade in the E-mini contract by a mutual fund complex as the proximate cause of the liquidity event that produced the flash crash.[5] No further is information is given about the identity of the trader or the reason for engaging in the large short trade. As a reaction to the negative market sentiment that preceded this trade on 6 May, it is possible that the trade was a crude attempt at 'legitimate hedging activity':

> By 2.30 p.m., the S&P 500 volatility index ('VIX') was up 22.5 percent from the opening level, yields of ten-year Treasuries fell as investors engaged in a 'flight to quality,' and selling pressure had pushed the Dow Jones Industrial Average ('DJIA') down about 2.5 per cent [*sic*].

There is evidence that the same mutual fund complex had placed one similar-sized trade in the previous year that was subsequently closed in a single day, but no further information is given about the motivation for these trades. Such a pattern of trading is not consistent with execution of a dynamic portfolio insurance strategy. Consistent with the arguments supporting short selling in SEC (2010c), there is implicit acceptance by SEC (2010a) of short seller rights to engage in 'legitimate hedging activity'. However, in the absence of any further information, the short trades by the 'large mutual fund complex' would appear to be yet another instance of aggressive and disruptive short side speculative exchange trading (for example see Poitras, Chapter 3 in this volume).[6]

Given the implicit assumption of SEC (2010a) that such aggressive short trading is acceptable, attention focuses on the trading mechanics of the failure to provide sufficient stock market liquidity to clear the trade. The trade was submitted at a time of the day when the circuit breakers in the cash market that were in place at the time would not be triggered. Consistent with typical trading activity (SEC 2010a, p. 3) sell pressure was initially absorbed by:

- high frequency traders ('HFTs') and other intermediaries in the futures market;
- fundamental buyers in the futures market; and
- cross-market arbitrageurs who transferred this sell pressure to the equities markets by opportunistically buying E-Mini contracts and simultaneously selling products like SPY, or selling individual equities in the S&P 500 Index.

The role of some HFTs as high-tech 'scalpers' is apparent in the stock market process of transforming the large speculative E-mini short trade:

> HFTs accumulated a net long position of about 3300 contracts. However, between 2.41 p.m. and 2.44 p.m., HFTs aggressively sold about 2000 E-Mini contracts in order to reduce their temporary long positions. At the same time, HFTs traded nearly 140000 E-Mini contracts or over 33% of the total trading volume. This is consistent with the HFTs' typical practice of trading a very large number of contracts, but not accumulating an aggregate inventory beyond three to four thousand contracts in either direction.

As such, attributing the crash to scalping activities by HFTs is misguided. However, HFTs are involved in a much wider range of activities than high-tech scalping. The key factors producing the crash are to be found elsewhere.

As with the crash of 1987, the flash crash is yet another instance where speculative trading of stocks using futures exchanges conflicts with the stability of the price discovery process in the cash market for stocks. More precisely, pricing stability in the cash market for stocks has historically depended on the speculative hypothecation demand (leveraged purchases using margin and other sources of borrowing) being offset with speculative cash market short selling (using borrowed securities that will be later repurchased and returned to the lender). The availability of stock for lending on the short sale provides an effective limit on speculative short selling. Stock index futures contracts do not face such a physical constraint. Cross-market arbitrage trading is the transmission mechanism that translates the speculative short selling in the futures market into the cash market. The implication of this in the flash crash is apparent in the following:

> In the four-and-one-half minutes from 2.41 p.m. through 2.45.27 p.m., prices of the E-Mini had fallen by more than 5% and prices of SPY suffered a decline of over 6%. According to interviews with cross-market trading firms, at this time they were purchasing the E-Mini and selling either SPY, baskets of individual securities, or other index products.

While the E-mini and the SPY recovered quickly from the temporary liquidity shortage, it was cross-market arbitraging using less liquid stocks and, especially, ETFs that created the 20000 broken trades, with retail investors on one side of the bulk of these trades – more than two-thirds of these broken trades were ETFs.

Despite avoiding reference to a 'flash crash', SEC (2010a, II.2.d, pp. 45–8) does provide a useful, if incomplete, examination of 'Equity-based high frequency traders' activities on 6 May. The problems confronting stock market regulators addressing disruptive trading behaviour is apparent in the description (p. 45): 'HFTs are proprietary trading firms'. In effect, the precise trading strategies used by these firms are outside the purview of the regulator. However, there is sufficient information to provide a general functional description:

> HFTs are proprietary trading firms that use high speed systems to monitor market data and submit large numbers of orders to the markets. HFTs utilize quantitative and algorithmic methodologies to maximize the speed of their market access and trading strategies. Some HFTs are hybrids, acting as both proprietary traders and as market makers. In addition, some HFT strategies may take 'delta-neutral' approaches to the market (ending each trading day in a flat position), while others are not delta-neutral and sometimes acquire net long and net short positions.

The recognition that HFT strategies can involve both proprietary trading and market making is a decided improvement over SEC (2010b) where a functional definition for proprietary HFT firms focuses on market making:

> (1) the use of high-speed and sophisticated computer programs for generating, routing, and executing orders; (2) use of co-location services and individual data feeds offered by exchanges and others to minimize network and other types of latencies; (3) very short time-frames for establishing and liquidating positions; (4) the submission of numerous orders that are cancelled shortly after submission; and (5) ending the trading day in as close to a flat position as possible (that is, not carrying significant, unhedged positions overnight)

The definitional transition from the 'Preliminary report' of May 18 to the 'Final report' of 30 September reflects learning on the part of the regulator precipitated by the congressional authority given to investigate the market disruption of 6 May. However, even armed with such authority, not all activities of proprietary HFT trading firms were exposed to the glare of public scrutiny.

The primary data sources for the SEC (2010a) examination of proprietary HFT trading were: minute-by-minute FINRA Equity Trade Journal data covering less than half of aggregate stock market volume; 15-minute interval data covering trading on all major US stock exchanges by executing broker-dealers; and direct interviews with HFT firms that were 'identified by FINRA as either engaging in high frequency trading strategies (such as electronic market making or statistical arbitrage), or providing trading access to other HFT firms' (p. 45). Significantly, the 'audit trail data' provided by FINRA only:

> includes trades reported by NASDAQ, reported to the NASDAQ TRF, and the ADF. It does not include trades executed on any other exchanges, including the NYSE, NYSE Arca, and BATS, or reported to any other exchange's trade reporting facility. Accordingly, the data encompasses less than half of the trading volume during the most volatile period on May 6. Moreover, HFTs generally are understood to be less active in the OTC market than in exchange markets.

In effect, even backed with the power of Congressional investigative authority, SEC (2010a) is unable to obtain even half the information on the trading activities of participants central to stock market activity during a crucial time period. This sustains a conclusion (SEC 2010a, p. 7):

> the events of May 6 clearly demonstrate the importance of data in today's world of fully-automated trading strategies and systems. This is further complicated by the many sources of data that must be aggregated in order to form a complete picture of the markets upon which decisions to trade can be based. Varied data conventions, differing methods of communication, the sheer volume of quotes, orders, and trades produced each second, and even inherent time lags based on the laws of physics add yet more complexity.

This conclusion begs the question: if the data are so important, why is SEC (2010a) only able to obtain less than half the minute-by-minute trading activity of the 'proprietary HFT trading firms' that may have been the source of transmitting disruptive short speculations into the broader stock market?

Despite these limitations, SEC (2010a) is able to obtain remarkable results about trading activities of 'proprietary trading firms' using HFT methods. In the end, 12 HFTs, responsible for 46 per cent of the trades on the FINRA Equity Trade Journal, were identified and interviewed for SEC (2010a, p. 45):

> Of the HFTs we interviewed, we did not find uniformity in response to market conditions on May 6. Although some HFTs exited the market for reasons similar to other market participants, such as the triggering of their internal risk parameters due to rapid price moves and subsequent data-integrity concerns, other HFTs continued to trade actively. Among those HFTs that continued to trade, motivations varied, but were in part based on whether they thought their algorithms would be able to operate successfully (profitably) under the extreme market conditions observed that afternoon.

Further breakdown of HFT activities based on closer examination of the FINRA audit trail is illuminating:

> we found that 6 of the 12 HFTs scaled back their trading during some point after the broad indices hit their lows at about 2.45 p.m. Two HFTs largely stopped trading at about 2.47 p.m. and remained inactive through the rest of the day. Four other HFTs appear to have each significantly curtailed trading for a short period of time, ranging from as little as one minute (from 2.46 p.m. to 2.47 p.m.) to as long as 21 minutes (from 2.57 p.m. to 3.18 p.m.).

It seems that some of the purely 'market-making' HFTs stopped market-making, leaving proprietary HFTs to dominate the trading results during the most important time period.

> [A]ggregate trading activity of these 12 HFTs picked up just after 2.30 p.m. and increased significantly during the period in which the broad indices were rapidly declining from 2.43 p.m. through 2.46 p.m. . . . HFT trading activity during those three minutes increased by over 250% for NYSE Arca-listed securities, which we note are predominately ETFs.

Recalling that more than two-thirds of broken trades were in ETFs, SEC (2010a, p. 47) draws the following conclusion from the FINRA audit trail:

> The data suggests that for at least the period from 2.00 p.m. through 2.40 p.m. on May 6, HFTs were relatively more active in ETFs (listed primarily on NYSE Arca) than corporate stocks (listed primarily on NYSE and NASDAQ). Furthermore, their reduced participation in NYSE Arca-securities with broken trades reveals that they too were part of the general withdrawal of liquidity seen in those products.

The final significant result from the FINRA data was: 'HFTs were primarily sellers of securities on May 6.'

Because the flash crash was a 'downside' liquidity event, SEC (2010a, pp. 47–8) also:

> examined a data set obtained from the largest public quoting markets on May 6 – each of the equities exchanges and Direct Edge (EDGA and EDGX). This data included total dollar volume on those markets across all securities by 15-minute increments, and was further categorized according to liquidity-taking and liquidity-providing buys and sells.

This 15-minute interval data covers a different range of stock trading activity where identification of specific HFT firms was not directly possible, though the executing broker-dealer was identified. To address this problem:

> Specific participant data was also provided for each executing broker-dealer that was among the top 20 aggressive sellers on each market during the rapid price decline on May 6. From this list of aggressive sellers, we aggregated data for 17 executing broker-dealers that appear to be primarily associated with HFT firms in order to compare trading patterns of these firms with the rest of the market.

For the six business days prior to 6 May: 'these 17 HFTs averaged 43.8% of total dollar volume on the public quoting markets'. Closer examination of this trading data provides the 'smoking gun' of the flash crash:

> As a percentage of total market dollar volume, the activity for these 17 HFT firms increased in the period from 2.00 p.m. through 2.45 p.m. to a high of 50.3%, before sharply falling to 36.6% in the period from 2.46 through 3.00 p.m. This pattern is consistent with some HFT firms reducing or pausing trading during that time. Notably, the 17 HFT firms escalated their aggressive selling more significantly (reaching a total of $9.3 billion) than any other category of trading during the rapid price decline in the period ending 2:45 p.m.

The associated conclusion is: 'In general . . . it appears that the 17 HFT firms traded with the price trend on May 6 and, on both an absolute and net basis, removed significant buy liquidity from the public quoting markets during the downturn'. Less kind words could classify the net activities of these proprietary HFT firms as 'predatory' or 'abusive' short selling.

THE FLASH CRASH AND THE SEC MARKET INITIATIVES

The years following the introduction of Regulation ATS in 1998 have witnessed changes in the stock market regulatory environment rivalling the sweeping changes of the Depression era. In 2005, these changes culminated in Regulation NMS and Regulation SHO. Regulation ATS: 'increased competition with traditional exchanges by establishing a regulatory framework for alternative trading systems (ATSs) to trade listed securities without registering as exchanges' (Kramer and Corcoran 2010, p. 295). In turn, by giving trade-through protection to automated quotations but not manual quotations, Regulation NMS facilitated the transition to electronic trading, further encouraging the development of high-frequency trading strategies and the dispersion of trading activity across a variety of market trading platforms. The passage of amendments to Regulation SHO in July 2007 that eliminated the price test for short sales – both Rule 10(a)-1 for exchange listed securities and the related NASDAQ bid test rule – marks the last of the major stock market liberalization initiatives by the SEC. The fallout from the financial collapse of 2008–09 has precipitated a process of retrenchment that includes the introduction of Rule 201 of Regulation SHO which reinstates a form of short sale price tests, and the introduction of single stock circuit breakers in response to the flash crash.

Crashes represent severe downside disruptions in the price discovery process. The aftermath of the discontinuous fall in prices inevitably leads to intense focus on the activities of stock market short sellers. While there were crash elements in the financial collapse of 2008–09, the systemic problems in the stock market were more pronounced and the downside movement in prices more ongoing. Release No. 34-61595 'Amendments to Regulation SHO' (SEC 2010c) is the regulatory response to the relatively unrestricted short selling during the time period associated with the financial collapse. Being prepared so soon after the implementation of Regulation SHO amendment in 2007, SEC (2010c) is a historical curiosity. The stock market regulator is being forced by events to backtrack on a substantive market structure initiative. As is evident in the tone of the discussion in SEC (2010a, esp. II.D), the implementation of Regulation SHO in 2007 was well founded in empirical evidence and regulatory procedure. The regulatory change did not restore Rule 10(a)-1 that applied to all stocks. Instead, Rule 201 only imposes the price test on individual stocks experiencing price declines greater than a fixed value. Significantly, Rule 201(d) provides important exceptions for intermarket arbitrage that undermine the ability to address the disruptive aspects of short selling.[7]

It is difficult to be critical of market structure and liberalization initiatives by the SEC. Some type of regulatory change was needed in response to changes in trading technology. It is natural and expected for the SEC actively to involve those players directly involved at the centre of stock market trading: large broker dealers, specialized trading firms and the exchanges and other self-regulatory organizations. Public comment periods and advisory panels are typically dominated by contributions from these players and the rule-making process dictates that careful consideration be given to such input. It is difficult enough to balance the often disparate views of these players. As a consequence, formulation of regulatory rules that protect the activities of 'proprietary trading firms' is not surprising, even if such rules lead to destabilizing outcomes. Rules that impinge on the profitability of large broker-dealers or require significant changes in market trading practices are likely to face fierce resistance. As with the crash of 1987, the flash crash illustrates that the problem of large players driving the process of regulatory change is exacerbated where the trading firms are operating in both cash and futures markets and subject to the differing regulators.

For centuries, intermarket arbitrage has been an important source of profitability for dealers in financial markets. In medieval times, Venetian and Florentine bankers arbitraged exchange rates across fairs in different geographical locations. Intermarket arbitrage in the stock market achieved modern characteristics during the nineteenth century. There was 'shunting' between London and the regional stock exchanges and 'arbitraging' between London and foreign markets (for example Michie 1986; Haupt 1870). The introduction of trading in stock index futures contracts and other derivatives created another opportunity for intermarket arbitrage, in this case between the cash and futures markets. While this variant of intermarket arbitrage was novel for the stock market, such trading is well developed in the commodity markets where the liquidity provided by speculative exchange trading enhances the stability of the price discovery process. Previous to the severe restrictions on trading time contracts and other derivative securities imposed during Depression-era stock market reforms, such trading was conducted in the same venue as cash market trading.

Sustainable speculative exchange trading of commodity futures contracts depends on characteristics of the underlying cash market. The history of futures trading is replete with examples of contracts that were introduced and failed due to lack of connection with the cash market. For example, the first interest rate futures contracts, the Government National Mortgage Association (GNMA) and GMNA II, failed due to difficulties in arbitraging the cash and futures markets. The relationship between futures prices for different delivery dates and between futures prices and spot prices varies with each commodity depending on the specifics of the associated short and long cash-and-carry arbitrages.[8] As a group, financial futures have prices that are tightly bound by the short and long arbitrages. In contrast, various physical commodities have a marked difference between the short and long arbitrages due to limitations on the ability to short sell the spot commodity. In addition, arbitrages for physical commodities are impacted upon by considerations of storability, seasonality and other factors affecting the convenience yield. As a consequence, over time physical commodities can exhibit both backwardation and contango in the term structure of futures prices due to factors other than the relationship between the pecuniary carry cost and carry return, which determine the term structure for financial futures prices.

For financial futures, ease of short arbitrage execution depends on the availability of the spot commodity for short selling. Eurodollars futures have the desirable characteristic that both the spot commodity and the borrowing instrument are the same, funds are both borrowed and lent in the eurodollar deposit market. Similarly, currency futures involve borrowing and lending in the eurocurrency deposit market. Other financial futures involve different markets for the cash market borrowing and lending involved in the notional arbitrage. For example, the notional short arbitrage in T-bond futures involves borrowing a deliverable T-bond that is sold in the cash market using a term repurchase agreement (RP), with a simultaneous long position established in T-bond futures to reacquire the T-bond to deliver on the short, using the funds from the maturing RP. The notional short arbitrage in stock index futures involves borrowing the stock index ETF, selling in the cash market and investing the proceeds in the broker call loan market, simultaneously taking a long position in stock index futures – using the funds from the maturing broker call loan to settle the delivery on the future purchase that returns the index ETF to the lender on the short.[9]

Notional arbitrages are theoretical constructs that assume, for example, simultaneous transactions. Actual execution of the arbitrage can differ. Ultimately, arbitragers will chose the trading strategy that produces the most profit. For financial futures, this involves minimizing transaction costs and execution time. In the stock market, the SEC market structure initiatives have created a windfall for the large proprietary trading firms engaged in intermarket arbitrage. Even in Rule 201 on short sale price test restrictions, Rule 201(d) provides specific exemptions for certain domestic and international arbitrage transactions. Maintaining arbitrage equality between cash and futures prices has become a hallmark of SEC policy, particularly in the period since Regulation ATS. The domination of 'proprietary HFT firms' in intermarket arbitrage of stock index futures contracts is more than apparent in SEC (2010a). The activities of these firms provide an almost instantaneous conduit for uncollateralized speculative short sales in the futures market to be transmitted into the cash market. The futures short is only secured by the margin deposit ensuring marking to market requirements are met.

The actual cash and carry arbitrage for stock futures is impacted by the necessity of allowing sales of stock by traders not in possession of the stock at the time it is being sold. For example, such provisions are essential to market makers where the objective is to balance long and short cash positions by the end of the trading day. Recognizing that the proprietary trading desks of broker-dealers can be involved in arbitrage activity, there is a subtle difference between such intermarket arbitrage short selling and the naked short selling prohibited by Regulation SHO. A 'naked' short sale arises when: 'the seller does not borrow or arrange to borrow the securities in time to make delivery to the buyer within the standard three day settlement period. As a result, the seller fails to deliver securities to the buyer when delivery is due; this is known as a "failure to deliver"'.[10] This leads to the concept of 'threshold securities' specified in Regulation SHO where short selling is curtailed in a stock which exceeds the threshold for allowable failures to deliver in a given time frame. Yet, through the exemptions provided for intermarket arbitrage, a de facto naked short sale can be placed using stock index futures contracts. The collateral constraint imposed in the cash market is the responsibility of the intermarket arbitrage firm, the stock market traders best able to avoid 'failure to deliver' sanctions.

The removal of short sale price test restrictions in July 2007 exposed the weakness of the collateral constraint on the unrestricted cash market short selling associated with speculative exchange trading of futures contracts. The SEC has chosen to deal with these difficulties using an evolution of circuit breaker rules and restricted price tests that complicate but do not substantively restrict intermarket arbitrage activity. In the absence of restrictions on leveraged purchasing of stock, including long purchases in the futures market and with borrowed funds in the cash market, there is an understandable reluctance to impose overly stringent restrictions on short selling. Disruptions to the price discovery process from leveraged stock purchases often precipitate the predatory short selling that characterizes market crashes. Balancing of long and short speculative demands along the time path is needed to ensure accurate price discovery. In the absence of intermarket arbitrage transmitting stock index futures speculation into the cash market, the supply of collateral available for short sales (that is, stock available for lending) provides an effective mechanism for achieving this balance. Because leveraged margin purchases at broker-dealers are eligible sources of short sale collateral, increases in leveraged speculation simultaneously increase the ability to do collateralized short sales.

It is a commonplace to observe that the evolution of the stock market embodied in the SEC market structure and liberalization initiatives was precipitated by the revolution in trading and communications technology. Despite the potential and realized benefits of these technological advances, no attention was given to the over two-century-old tradition of the three-day settlement lag that facilitates various facets of disruptive short selling. In the middle of the nineteenth century, three-day settlement was considered to be the shortest time practical to affect the delivery of the stock certificate. Market makers that had sold a security not owned at the time of sale needed the time to locate stock for delivery. With the trading technology of modern markets, a system of accounting for collateral available for short sales is not only possible but necessary. Instead of potentially ineffective and inefficient circuit breakers and price tests, a requirement that all short sales on a given trading day locate collateral by the opening of business for the next trading day is not only feasible but desirable. More stringently, short sales could be required to locate collateral prior to the trade.

Cash market short selling based on collateral available for lending is the convention in commodity markets. For example, in the gold market central banks often lend to short sellers charging a short sale fee that depends on market conditions. Tightening collateral requirements on short selling in the stock market would provide an increased incentive for firms to locate stock needed for the short sale. Instead of a market characterized by firms specializing in locating stocks to avoid failure to deliver, technological advances could permit the creation of collateral depositories that would provide access to stock available for lending to short sellers for a nominal fee. Periods of heighten leveraged purchases would provide simultaneous increases in collateral available for short sales. Similarly, collateral constraints in periods of excessive short selling would result in increased costs for increasingly limited collateral. Most importantly, the intermarket arbitrage trading that transmits unconstrained short selling with futures to the cash market would be dampened by the collateral constraint. As a consequence, stock index futures prices would not mirror cash market prices as closely. Instead, futures prices would be impacted by the costs of collateral. Excessive short futures selling would cause futures to sell at a discount to cash, increasing the incentive to purchase in the futures market and reducing the generation of short sales in the cash market. Similarly, excessive long futures purchases would result in leveraged purchases of stock increasing the supply of collateral available for short selling in the cash market.

CONCLUSION

Like other stock market crashes, the brief flash crash of 6 May 2010 involved a severe downside disruption in the price discovery process. The aftermath of any such discontinuous fall in prices inevitably leads to intense focus on the activities of stock market short sellers. The regulatory response to the flash crash, SEC (2010a, 2010b), provides a fascinating glimpse into the stock market at the end of the first decade of the twenty-first century. Combined with the amendments to Regulation SHO introduced to address short selling during the financial collapse of 2008–09, the SEC has opted to employ a combination of single stock circuit breakers and restricted price tests to deal with disruptive short selling. While such restrictions on short selling are a decided improvement over unrestricted short selling, this chapter argues that the most effective route to dealing with disruptive short selling originating from futures markets is to tighten significantly the requirements associated with locating stock available for short sale. From the beginning of trade in stocks in the early seventeenth century, the *in blanco* sale of stock has met with regulatory restrictions. Only in the last few decades has the progress of technology instilled the modern hubris that such restrictions are unnecessary.

NOTES

1. FINRA is the Financial Industry Regulatory Authority, the largest independent self-regulatory authority for securities firms doing business in the United States. FINRA oversees nearly 4580 brokerage firms, about 162 850 branch offices and approximately 630 695 registered securities representatives. FINRA is involved with: registering and educating industry participants; examining securities firms; writing and enforcement of rules and ensuring compliance with federal securities laws; information and education for the investing public; providing trade reporting and other activities for the securities industry; and administration of a dispute resolution forum for investors and registered firms. FINRA performs market regulation functions under contract for the major US stock markets, including the NYSE, NYSE Arca, NYSE Amex, NASDAQ and the International Securities Exchange. FINRA has approximately 3000 employees located in Washington, DC and New York, with an additional 20 regional offices. More information can be found at http://www.finra.org.
2. A partial listing of key players implementing portfolio insurance strategies for large institutional investors during the period leading to the crash of 1987 includes: Leland O'Brien Rubinstein Associates,

Aetna Life & Casualty, Putnam Adversary Co., Chase Investors Mgmt., JP Morgan Investment Mgmt., Wells Fargo Investment Advisors and Bankers Trust Co. This list does not include the wannabes at Goldman Sachs, Salomon Bros., Nomura and other firms seeking to gain status in this area. Goldman Sachs was the firm which employed Fischer Black at this time.

3. US regulations for margin involve a number of different regulators, including the Federal Reserve Board, FINRA and, indirectly, the FDIC and the SEC. Regulation T administered by the Federal Reserve governs the extension of credit by securities brokers and dealers in the United States and applies to margin requirements for stocks bought with funds received from the broker-dealer. Since 1974, the initial margin for stock purchases is 50 per cent and the maintenance margin is 25 per cent. FINRA also establishes minimum margin requirements. In general, 'margin' describes necessary collateral to: purchase new securities; sell securities short; write options and other derivatives contracts; or withdraw cash without selling securities.
4. One particularly significant instance involved the CFTC's 1998 attempt to extend regulatory authority to OTC derivative trading that failed in the face of dissent from the Federal Reserve, the SEC and the Treasury. Such trading in credit default swaps and related derivatives was at the core of the subprime mortgage crisis that precipitated the financial collapse of 2008–09.
5. Position limits in the E-mini contract traded on the CME are set in conjunction with the S&P 500 contract which is 20000 net short or long. Given that the E-mini is one-fifth of the S&P contract, a position done completely in the E-mini would have a $100000 contract limit. For the S&P 500 index at 1200, the value of the position limit is $6 billion. By comparison, the important eurodollar futures contract has no position limit. Agricultural futures contracts, such as wheat and corn, work with limits on price moves instead of speculative position limits.
6. The approach suggested in SEC (2010a) is to define the short trade by the mutual fund complex as 'legitimate hedging activity' and, as a consequence, is an activity that requires support and encouragement. Poitras (2002, esp. pp. 132–5) details the difficulties that can arise with distinguishing hedging activity from speculation. Conventionally, a trader actively engaged in the cash market is considered a hedger in the futures market. However, such a definition ignores situations where the 'hedger' engages in futures trading activities that are purely speculative. Falloon (1998, Ch. 8) details a classical illustration of the distinction: the Cargill corn case of 1936–37. SEC (2010a) provides no information about the trading motives of the 'large mutual fund complex'. However, a trading strategy of placing a $4.1 billion short trade in one day that is unwound, say, a month later in one day would appear to be a speculation on market price movement; that is, a trade placed solely to benefit from price changes is 'speculation' by definition.
7. From SEC (2010c, p. 129): 'bona fide arbitrage transactions promote market efficiency because they equalize prices at an instant in time in different markets or between relatively equivalent securities'.
8. Long and short refer to the cash position in the arbitrage. The long arbitrage involves borrowing the funds to purchase the spot commodity that is simultaneously sold for future delivery. This arbitrage bounds the futures price above. The short arbitrage involves borrowing the spot commodity, investing the proceeds from the short sale and purchasing the commodity for future delivery. This arbitrage bounds the futures price from below. Financial futures as a group have tight bounds around the futures price because both the short and long arbitrages are readily executed. In eurodollars futures, for example, the short (long) arbitrage involves borrowing (lending) for T days in the eurodollar deposit market and using the funds to purchase (from borrowing with) a three-month + T day eurodollar, simultaneously undertaking a eurodollar futures contract to issue (purchase) a three-month eurodollar purchase in T days.
9. Such notional arbitrages are discussed in conventional textbooks on derivative securities, for example, Poitras (2002, Ch. 4). The arbitrage descriptions are only illustrative. For example, most stock index futures contracts are cash settled. In this case, the gain or loss on the futures position would offset the costs of buying the ETF in the cash market to return to the short. In addition, short positions have to return any pecuniary return earned during the time the short is in place. For example, the short T-bond position would owe the coupon that accrues.
10. This quote was obtained from the SEC at: http://www.sec.gov/answers/nakedshortsale.htm.

REFERENCES

Edwards, F. (1988), 'Futures trading and cash market volatility: stock index and interest rate futures', *Journal of Futures Markets*, **8**, 421–40.

Falloon, W. (1998), *Market Maker: A Sesquicentennial Look at the Chicago Board of Trade*, Chicago, IL: CBT.

Jonker, J. (2009), 'Isaac Le Maire's Memorandum to the Lord Advocate', *Shareholder Rights at 400*, Amsterdam: APG.

Haupt, O. (1870). *The London Arbitrageur; or, the English Money Market in connexion with foreign Bourses. A Collection of Notes and Formulae for the Arbitration of Bills, Stocks, Shares, Bullion and Coins, with all the Important Foreign Countries*, London: Trubner and Co.

Kirilenko, A, M. Samadi, A. Kyle and T. Tuzun (2010), 'The flash crash: the impact of high frequency trading on an electronic market', SSRN, http://ssrn.com/abstract=1686004.

Kramer, H. and J. Corcoran (2010), 'Assessing the shotgun volley of SEC market structure initiatives', *Journal of Securities Law, Regulation and Compliance*, **3** (Oct.), 294–306.

Macey, J., M. Mitchell and J. Netter (1989), 'Restrictions on short sales: an analysis of the uptick rule and its role in view of the October 1987 stock market crash', *Cornell Law Review*, **74**, 799–835.

Michie, R. (1986), 'The London and New York stock exchanges, 1850–1914', *Journal of Economic History*, **46**, 171-87.

Poitras, G. (2002), *Risk Management, Speculation and Derivative Securities*, New York: Academic Press.

Presidential Task Force on Market Mechanisms (1988), 'Report of the Presidential Task Force on Market Mechanisms, Nicholas F. Brady (Chairman)', Washington, DC: US Government Printing Office.

Securities and Exchange Commission (2010a), "Findings regarding the market events of May 6, 2010: report of the Staffs of the CFTC and SEC to the Joint Advisory Committee on Emerging Regulatory Issues', 30 September, Washington, DC.

Securities and Exchange Commission (2010b), 'Preliminary findings regarding the market events of May 6, 2010: report of the Staffs of the CFTC and SEC to the Joint Advisory Committee on Emerging Regulatory Issues', 18 May, Washington, DC.

Securities and Exchange Commission (2010c), 'Amendments to Regulation SHO", CFR Part 242 Release No. 34-61595, 27 February.

Tosini, P. (1988), 'Stock index futures and stock market activity in October 1987', *Financial Analysts Journal*, January–February, 28–37.

12 The impact of electronic communication networks on exchange trading floors and derivatives regulation[1]

Jerry W. Markham and Daniel J. Harty

The colorful 'open outcry' trading in the 'pits' of the Chicago futures exchanges and the bell-ringing opening of trading on the floor of the New York Stock Exchange (NYSE) has long dominated the public perception of how those markets operate. However, exchange trading floors are fast fading into history because the trading of stocks and derivative instruments are moving to electronic communications networks (ECNs) that simply match trades by computers through algorithms at incredibly high speeds and volumes.[2] Competition from ECNs has already forced the NYSE and the Chicago futures and options exchanges to demutualize, consolidate and reduce the role of their trading floors, while expanding their own electronic execution facilities.[3]

This chapter will describe the development of electronic trading through ECNs and how the futures, equity and equity options exchanges responded to that competition. As will be shown, the traditional exchanges paralleled each other in resisting electronic trading in order to preserve their traditional open outcry trading floors. Gradually, after much pressure from market users, those exchanges began to adopt computer-assisted executions as a way of speeding up the trading process, while still preserving their trading floors. That still left the exchanges exposed to competition from the newly arrived and fully electronic ECNs, which quickly grabbed market share from the traditional markets. Finally, the exchanges accepted the inevitable and became fully committed to electronic trading.

This chapter will also address the regulatory concerns raised by electronic traders. The ECNs have provided new trading opportunities for algorithmic traders, but their trading was soon causing regulatory concerns. High-frequency electronic traders are now dominating market volume in both the securities and derivatives markets, raising concerns on how their trading is affecting long-term investors. Some electronic trading practices such as 'naked access' and 'quote stuffing'[4] and trading in 'dark pools' are also under regulatory scrutiny.[5] High-frequency electronic traders were suspected as contributors to the 'flash crash' that resulted in a 1000-point drop in the Dow Jones Industrial Average in just a few minutes on 6 May 2010.[6]

AUTOMATION IN THE FUTURES INDUSTRY

The futures industry's approach to computerization has been schizophrenic. It early on embraced computers into its clearing and settlement processes, allowing it to match and clear all trades overnight. In contrast, as described below, the securities markets were slow to adopt computerization until a paperwork crisis in the 1960s caused the industry to embrace technology. The futures industry's pioneering efforts in automating clearing and settlement were not matched with equal zeal in automating trade executions. This was because it was obvious to the traders on the floors of the exchange that electronic executions posed a threat to their existence. Since the floor traders dominated the exchanges they were able to block any efforts to replace themselves with computers.[7]

In fact, there was little or no thought given to computerizing the trading floors on futures exchanges until the creation of the Commodity Futures Trading Commission (CFTC) by the Commodity Futures Trading Commission Act of 1974.[8] That legislation required the CFTC to study how computers could aid trading in the industry.[9] The CFTC held a conference on that topic in 1977. Papers presented at the conference were critical of the perceived inefficiencies of the open outcry trading system.[10] The response by the industry to that conference was harsh. Leo Melamed, a senior official at the Chicago Mercantile Exchange (CME) and a leading figure in the industry,[11] published a detailed and passionate defense of open outcry trading in a widely read article published in the *Hofstra Law Review*.[12] Melamed conceded that the open outcry trading system was not automated but argued that the exchanges were automating the order execution process outside the trading pits.[13] However, pit executions still required the manual transmission of orders into often overcrowded trading pits by written orders or hand signals and then the orders were bid or offered to the pit orally. After execution, the orders were transmitted back out of the pit manually. Melamed argued that the psychology of the trading pit generated information for price efficiency and brought liquidity to the market from the trading by locals.[14] This was the oft-cited defense of floor trading: that is, the physiological lift from the noise and energy of the trading crowd that inspires traders to take risks.[15]

The futures exchanges' defense of their trading floors came under increasing criticism as volume expanded. Pits trading popular products became overcrowded and execution times were delayed in high-volume periods. Orders were often traded through in 'fast market' conditions. The CME's computer system crashed during trading hours in 1984, causing much confusion,[16] but capacity constraints were an even more pressing issue.[17] John Conheeney, chairman of Merrill Lynch Futures, then noted that: 'There isn't a person in the industry who wouldn't agree that the system is breaking down, but we don't see any concrete moves toward a solution, which is the most frightening aspect of the problem.'[18] Conheeney concluded that merely adding more space on the trading floors, as the exchanges were then planning, was not the solution,[19] but he also asserted that 'black box' computer trading 'lacks the vital human element that makes a market work'. He asserted that: '"pit psychology," eye contact and the chemistry between traders, was often as important in determining prices as the market's technical factors and fundamentals of supply and demand'.

More presciently, Gerald Tellefsen, senior vice-president of the consulting firm of Booz Allen & Hamilton, Inc., stated in response to Conheeney's recommendations that:

> There is little chance of any progress toward any solution until their trading system falls apart; until their physical and financial pains become unbearable, which may be sooner than many of them think. While the futures industry has been and will remain the most innovative sector of the marketplace, it is also the most tradition-bound. Thus, the exchange members will not automate, for cultural reasons as well as the fear that they will lose control over their markets. . . . Eventually, futures trading will have to be automated, because their business is fast becoming global in scope. Whether or not the new innovators will, as the domestic automakers learned

the hard way, come from overseas, the losers will fight it at every turn and be unprepared for its inevitable introduction.[20]

The futures exchanges continued their ostrich-like approach to automated executions, but demand was growing for extended trading hours. Trading floors were open only for a limited number of hours permitted by the stamina of the floor traders, but that left market participants stranded until the next trading day. Worldwide events with market effect often occurred after the close of trading, but traders were helpless until the opening of trading on the next day and, therefore, sought access to trade outside the regular trading hours.[21] Futures exchanges and securities intermediaries sought to capture the additional revenues this interest represented by extending trading hours with three basic options: offering open outcry sessions at night,[22] establishing exchanges in non-US jurisdictions with local partners, and later developing electronic trading systems.

The demand for extended trading hours led to a linkage between the CME and the Singapore International Monetary Exchange (SIMEX) in 1984.[23] That link allowed trades to be opened on the SIMEX in the evening and reciprocally closed on the CME on the next day or at some other time.[24] The SIMEX link was a substitute for computerized executions, but it was limited in scope of the futures covered and still was tied to the floor trading operations of CME members.[25]

The International Futures Exchange Ltd. (INTEX) was created in 1984 by a former Merrill Lynch executive to operate as the first computerized commodity exchange. It was based in Bermuda in order to avoid the delay of seeking contract market status from the CFTC. INTEX traded futures on gold and other commodities and cleared its trades through the London International Commodity Clearinghouse.[26] Intex was not particularly successful, but it signaled the future.

The demand for after-hours trading continued to grow. In 1987, the Chicago Board of Trade (CBOT) began open outcry sessions at night, but those sessions were sparsely attended. The CME's response came in 1989 with its development of a computerized trading system called Globex (global exchange) with Reuters Holdings PLC. This system matched buy and sell orders on the basis of time and price after the trading pits closed.[27] The CBOT responded to Globex with an announcement that it was developing its own computerized trading system, named Aurora, that would compete with Globex and pose no threat to floor traders during normal trading hours.[28] Aurora never really got off the ground, and the CBOT joined Globex.[29]

Globex's limitations caused it to struggle to obtain a profit,[30] and the CBOT withdrew from the venture in 1994.[31] In the meantime, the CBOT and CME's share of futures and options trading also continued to plummet, dropping from about 75 percent of all futures trading in 1987 to under 50 percent in 1992. In particular, competition from new exchanges abroad was fierce. One such upstart was the London International Financial Futures Exchange (LIFFE) that began trading in 1982.[32] It initially modeled its trading operations after those in Chicago, utilizing open outcry pit trading for order executions,[33] but later became an all-electronic exchange.[34] More competition from Europe would follow. A 1992 *New York Times* article noted that: 'The [American] exchanges have been losing ground to the approximately 50 exchanges outside the United States, about half of which have been founded since 1985. Off-exchange deals between banks and other institutional investors are also a rapidly growing part of the derivatives business.'[35]

The CBOT opened a new trading floor in 1997 that was supposed to employ the newest technology, but it remained devoted to open outcry trading in the pits. New innovations were added elsewhere in the industry. Floor brokers adopted 'Electronic Clerk' and 'Cubs'[36] devices that allowed them to receive orders electronically in the pits, seeking to obviate the need for phone clerks and 'runners' who had traditionally relayed customer orders into the pits either in writing or by 'flashing' to the floor broker through hand signals.[37] Those efforts did not succeed in meeting the competition from foreign exchanges that were becoming increasingly all electronic.[38] The Deutsche terminborse, now called Eurex, a joint venture of the Deutsche Borse and the Swiss Stock Exchange, opened as an all-electronic exchange in 1989.[39] It took Eurex just two years to eclipse the largest futures exchange in America, the CBOT, in trading volume. Eurex also later bought the International Securities Exchange, an electronic exchange that became the largest equity options market in the United States, taking market share from the open outcry equity options exchanges.[40] Ironically, futures trading was not legalized in Germany until the 1980s when US brokers successfully advocated a change in German law that had, formerly, treated futures contracts as prohibited illegal gambling.[41]

Eurex was also competing with LIFFE, which operated a large trading floor and was the largest futures exchange in Europe until Eurex arrived. LIFFE was forced to switch from open outcry trading to electronic trading in 2000.[42] Similarity, MATIF, the Paris-based derivatives exchange, tried to offer both electronic and open outcry trading in April 1998. A month later, most trading migrated to computers and the trading floor was shut down.

The Chicago exchanges only slowly awakened to this threat, but by the end of the last century even Leo Melamed, the most ardent defender of open outcry trading, was in full retreat. He sounded the tocsin for this pull-back in a May 1999 address at an industry conference in New York. Melamed faulted the regulatory structure for the erosion of US market share in futures trading, but he also stated that 'If the futures exchanges fail to quickly embrace current technological and competitive demands, . . . then our exchanges may well be doomed.'[43]

The Chicago exchanges were still sluggish in their response to the electronic threat. They began a desperate effort to link with foreign electronic markets in order to cling to their remaining businesses. The CME announced a link with MATIF in Paris, which was then combined with its SIMEX program. The CBOT initially linked with Eurex, but then abandoned that arrangement for an electronic platform operated by LIFFE, which was then a unit of the pan-European exchange Euronext, the subsequent merger partner of the NYSE.[44] In response, Eurex announced that it was opening its own exchange in the United States to compete directly with the Chicago exchanges.[45] The Chicago exchanges then sought unsuccessfully to block Eurex from being designated as a contract market by the CFTC, which happened in 2004, but Eurex was not successful in that effort to compete.[46]

Domestic electronic futures exchanges were also appearing. FutureCom Ltd submitted the first application to the CFTC to be designated as a contract market for Internet trading only. BrokerTec Futures Exchange, an electronic futures market, had tried to compete with the CBOT but failed in that effort.[47] The New York Cotton Exchange merged with the Coffee, Sugar & Cocoa Exchange to become the Board of Trade of New

York.[48] It entered into a joint venture with Cantor Fitzgerald, a New York government securities trader, for the creation of an electronic futures exchange, the Cantor Financial Futures Exchange (CFFE), which would compete with the CBOT floor traders. The CBOT quickly announced that it was opening its own electronic market in those contracts.[49] Neither electronic trading system did very well, but CFFE responded with a completely interactive electronic trading platform.

Several other electronic futures markets followed, including the Chicago Board Options Exchange (CBOE) Futures Exchange, HedgeStreet, NASDAQ LIFFE Markets (NQLX), OneChicago, and US Futures Exchange. The Intercontinental Exchange (ICE), an electronic exchange based in Atlanta, Georgia, became a major global marketplace for trading futures and over-the-counter (OTC) energy derivative contracts.[50] The Chicago exchanges were paralyzed by this competition and exchange politics became divided between those favoring electronic trading and those seeking to preserve open outcry trading. In a hotly contested election in 1998, one candidate was labeled by his opponent as the 'President of the Flat Earth Society' for his defense of the pitch of trading desks on the floor, but the real criticism of his campaign was his desire to preserve pit trading and the value of exchange memberships that were then plunging in price.[51] Opponents of electronic trading narrowly won that election, unseating the incumbent who was seeking to modernize the exchange with more electronic trading. Compromise followed in the form of side-by-side trading of contracts electronically and in the pits.[52] However, that was only a compromise, not a winning strategy in the new world of all-electronic trading.

More pressure for electronic trading arrived in 1989 after a massive FBI sting operation on the CME and the CBOT exposed widespread fraud and questionable trading activities.[53] Those practices were made possible by archaic trading practices on the floor that involved 'dual' trading floor brokers and floor traders ('locals') and the lack of an adequate audit trail that shielded those activities.[54] Former senator (and briefly vice-presidential candidate) Thomas Eagleton made headlines by resigning from the CME board after charging that the exchange was driven with conflicts of interest.[55] He recommended that the trading floor be replaced with an electronic trading system that would provide a better audit trail.

Competition appeared from another source in the form of the OTC market in derivatives that exploded in the last part of the twentieth century. The swap became a classic in finance within ten years of its introduction in 1981.[56] A new phenomenon also appeared – the OTC derivative.[57] Unfortunately, trading in over-the-counter foreign currency derivatives began with some boiler room operations fraudulently selling derivative products disguised in a manner to avoid Commodity Futures Trading Commission (CFTC) regulation. The CFTC continued to wrestle with that problem, particularly in currency trading, for a number of years.[58] Commercial firms were also exploring OTC derivatives during the CFTC's formative years. The CFTC resisted that effort and sought to regulate these then-designated 'hybrid' instruments if their options or futures elements outweighed their securities elements.[59] The CFTC was reluctant to create a commercial trader exception that would allow OTC derivatives to be traded by institutions or sophisticated traders,[60] such as that employed by the SEC under the federal securities laws for 'accredited investors'.[61] However, the swaps market expanded so quickly that Congress and the CFTC adopted such an exemption for swaps.[62] An exemption was also granted for the Brent oil market that had been handicapped by a district court ruling that it was a futures exchange, a decision that would have required it to register as a contract market and destroy its viability in the United States.[63] The OTC derivative market continued to expand even after a series of large losses by numerous institutions, including the destruction of the venerable Barings Bank by a rogue trader.[64]

The open outcry trading systems on the futures exchanges' floors were clearly being overwhelmed as the new century began. Responding to those competitive threats, the CME and the CBOT merged their clearing operations in 2003, and both the CME (in 2002) and the CBOT (in 2005) demutualized and became public companies.[65] Still, the percentage of open outcry trades declined between 2000 and 2007 from 90 percent to 22 percent. Recognizing that the end was near, the CBOT and the CME merged all of their operations in 2007.[66] That merger was nearly spoiled by a competing bid from ICE for the CBOT in the amount of $11.9 billion, but in the end ICE lost out to the CME.[67] After their merger, the CME and CBOT announced that they were consolidating their trading floors and would be shifting several contracts to their electronic trading platform (Globex), including agricultural products such as the once very popular frozen pork belly futures contract.[68]

Resistance on the floor to electronic trading remained. That resistance was aided by no less a personage than former Federal Reserve Board chairman Alan Greenspan. In March 2007, Greenspan asserted at a futures industry conference that the open outcry system of trading is still 'the optimum model' because, while computers are useful, human beings always prefer personal interactions and that, therefore, open outcry markets will always be around.[69] However, the growth of electronic trading is calling that claim into question in both the securities and commodity futures industries.[70]

AUTOMATION IN THE SECURITIES INDUSTRY

The securities industry appeared in some ways more receptive than the futures industry to technological changes. That may have been due to the so-called paperwork crisis that occurred on the NYSE at the end of the 1960s. Increased trading volumes resulted in a massive number of unmatched trades ('fails' to deliver or receive, and 'DK' – don't know – trades) that were the result of the fact that bookkeeping was still largely being done by hand. Over 100 NYSE firms failed and many more were threatened and had to be rescued by the NYSE. The industry then began a broad-based effort to computerize the clearing and settlement process. Among the results of that effort was the creation of the Depository Trust and Clearing Corp.[71]

Although often accused of being hidebound, the NYSE was not oblivious to the need to adopt new technology into its operations. That exchange spent over $1 billion on technology between 1982 and 1995, allowing it to cut order execution time dramatically. Those improvements allowed the NYSE to handle daily order flows in excess of 1.4 billion shares as the market surged at the end of the last century.[72] That was in stark contrast to the 10 million share trading days that almost destroyed the NYSE during the 1960s 'paperwork crisis',[73] and the 600 million share days that shut down the trading floor in October 1987.[74] Still, the securities industry was unable to match the overnight clearing and settlement cycle (that is now becoming even intraday settlement) in the futures industry. Securities transactions were cleared on a five-day cycle until 1994, when a three-day cycle (T+3) was implemented.

Thomas Russo, a former senior executive at Lehman Brothers with experience in both the futures and securities industries, has noted that: 'While no futures exchange had yet taken major steps in the field of automation, the New York Stock Exchange was making some progress. In 1976, it launched the DOT (Designed Order Turnaround) system, followed by the Super-DOT system in 1984.'[75] Super-DOT allowed the transmission and execution of orders to buy and sell to the specialist electronically: 'The orders appear on a special electronic workstation often referred to as the "display book." Each Specialist Firm has a computerized "display book" at its trading post that permits the Firm to execute orders for the market.'[76] The Super-DOT system was handling 'some 80 percent of the NYSE's transactional volume' by 1992,[77] reaching 90 percent of volume in 2000, but large trades were still manually walked to the specialist post by a floor broker for execution.[78]

Other electronic improvements in the securities industry included automated systems for broker-dealer back-office processing of securities transactions, and improved screen-based information services provided to broker-dealers by private vendors such as Reuters, Quotron Systems, Telerate, Automatic Data Processing, Knight-Ridder and Bloomberg. However, these improvements did not create an electronic exchange; rather, it was called 'computer-assisted trading' (CAT), to signify that the technology was merely aiding, not replacing, the specialist. Signifying that distinction, a special edition of *Life Magazine* published in 1992 to celebrate the bicentennial of the founding of the NYSE contained an article decrying the growth of electronic trading and defending the trading floor. Mimicking Melamed's defense of open outcry trading in the futures industry, the article stated that:

> This, it seems to me, is the biggest problem with electronic trading and what it portends. . . . Do we advance business by making it more faceless and impersonal? Such a world not only threatens to overwhelm us with market choices, time zones and currencies, it likewise cuts us out of the deal as social creatures. It only further distances us from the rich and varied human affairs that are as much the soul of business as they are the essence of the social and inner life.[79]

However, a warning had already been sounded by a congressional staff study in 1990, which noted that financial information vendors may offer execution services using automated execution systems.

One such effort, GEMCO, had failed but the Instinet Corporation was more successful. Created in 1969 as the Institutional Network Corporation,[80] Instinet was later acquired by Reuters and began offering an electronic securities trading system that was executing an average of 13 million shares a day in NYSE and NASDAQ stocks as the 1990s began.[81] Instinet allowed broker-dealers and institutional traders to indicate their interest in purchasing or selling NYSE or NASDAQ securities. Participants could then respond to those indications of interest by making bids or offers. Instinet would then process and report executions.[82] Orders were not publicly disclosed, protecting the identity of the institution in the trade.[83] Instinet was processing 170 million shares per day at the end of the century. Twenty million of those trades were executed before and after traditional trading hours.[84]

Automation was seemingly more prevalent in the OTC market. NASDAQ was itself an electronic 'quotation' system that was developed in the 1960s after a special study of the securities markets by the Securities and Exchange Commission (SEC) staff suggested the desirability of such an automated system to replace the manual printing of quotes circulated to broker-dealers through the 'Pink Sheets'.[85] NASDAQ employed competing market makers, rather than a specialist auction system.[86] NASDAQ was broken down into tiers: the National Market System (NMS) for larger companies, a SmallCap Market for small and medium-sized companies, and a Bulletin Board for illiquid securities.[87]

NASDAQ did not initially provide for the automated execution of orders. Rather, a broker observing a quote on a computer screen for a stock posted on NASDAQ would contact the posting broker and negotiate the trade. NASDAQ developed a Small Order Execution System (SOES) for the automatic execution of small customer orders, but large trades still were negotiated orally with the market makers. Another improvement was SelectNet, a screen-based trading system that allowed National Association of Securities Dealers (NASD) members to enter and negotiate the terms of their trades utilizing that computer system. The NASDAQ market became successful. By 1992, NASDAQ volume was accounting for some 42 percent of total share volume on all US markets.[88] NASDAQ volume was sometimes in excess of 2.5 billion shares a day in 2000, which was sometimes a billion more shares than were traded on the NYSE.

Like the futures exchanges, both NASDAQ and the NYSE encountered scandals in their market-making operations. After NASDAQ market makers fled to avoid their market-making responsibilities during the stock market crash of 1987, the NASD required all market makers to participate in SOES and increased penalties for unexcused withdrawals. This gave rise to the so-called 'SOES Bandits' who entered orders in response to market movements before the NASDAQ market makers were able to update their SOES quotes.[89] This was made possible by the development of Internet trading by retail customers.[90]

The NASD tried to help the NASDAQ market makers by barring 'professional' traders from using SOES, but a court of appeals held that the rule was too vague.[91] Other efforts by the NASD also failed to deter the SOES Bandits, so the market makers began taking their own actions to stop the bandits' attacks. The effect of the market makers' response was revealed in an economic study published in 1994. It found that the spreads quoted by NASDAQ market makers were extraordinarily wide and suggested that they were the result of collusion among market makers.[92] The Justice Department then brought an antitrust action against the market makers.[93] The SEC also investigated and found a number of improper practices on the part of those market makers.[94] Among other things, the SEC found that bids and offers displayed by market makers on Instinet and another ECNs were almost always better than those they posted publicly on NASDAQ. This meant that the market makers had created a two-tiered market, in that retail customers using SOES were receiving less competitive prices than the institutional traders that could access ECNs.

As a result of this scandal, the NASD was censured by the SEC and agreed to spend $100 million to improve its self-regulatory program.[95] The NASD was also reorganized to obviate any conflicts between its role as the promoter of NASDAQ and its self-regulatory responsibilities. A separate subsidiary was given primary responsibility for regulatory matters. Another subsidiary was given responsibility over NASDAQ.[96] Numerous

NASDAQ market makers were also sanctioned for their role in this scandal.[97] Scandal also arrived on the floor of the NYSE. Floor brokers on the NYSE were engaged in 'flipping' and 'trading for eighths', a practice that the NYSE was aware of at the time but did not stop.[98] These practices involved the execution of opposite customer orders against a third-party account, allowing them to obtain a profit on the spread between the bid and the ask as well as commissions for executing the trades.[99] Several floor brokers and their clerks pleaded guilty to criminal charges for that conduct.[100]An even larger scandal arose over conduct by NYSE specialists. An SEC investigation discovered that NYSE specialists were trading ahead of customer orders and engaging in other misconduct such as front running and 'interpositioning' themselves between matchable customer orders in order to create and profit from a spread.[101] Several NYSE specialist firms agreed to pay over $250 million to settle SEC charges over that misconduct,[102] but criminal charges over this conduct were dropped.[103] The SEC also brought an action against the NYSE that was settled by the exchange.[104] The NYSE agreed to require all of its directors to be independent directors, create a new Chief Regulatory Officer position, and to hire an independent monitor to oversee its supervision of the floor at a cost of $20 million. The NYSE also agreed to film and tape-record the specialists' operations on the floor during the trading day. Several employees of the specialist firms were indicted for their role in this scandal.[105] The SEC also brought actions against three regional exchanges for allowing their specialists to engage in similar conduct.

THE ECNS ARRIVE

The ECNs arrived in force in the financial markets beginning in the early 1990s in the form of automated trading systems for institutional traders in the third market.[106] In some ways they were actually a creation of the exchanges' efforts to automate. 'Electronic trading'[107] encompasses a wide range of systems that facilitate the entry and execution of orders electronically by algorithms.[108] The exchanges had employed algorithms for their own trading activities, using different algorithms for different contracts,[109] often based on a contract's liquidity. They include a first-in, first-out allocation system for trade matching, a pro rata system,[110] or a system that combines some elements of each of the above.[111] Without the creation of trade-matching algorithms by exchanges, the development of electronic trading systems in the remainder of the financial services industry would likely have stalled. Some commentators view the development of trade-matching algorithms as the democratization of the financial markets. They suggest that the adoption of algorithms replaces the 'privileged market access'[112] conferred by open outcry trading and permits exchanges to differentiate between each order, let alone between members and non-members.[113] The exchanges were initially unwilling to use algorithms to replace their trading floor functions. However, where established exchanges did not willingly venture, many 'new kids on the block' began filling the void.[114] Participants in these new ventures soon learned the benefits of electronic trading systems and order-matching algorithms.[115] These benefits include the reduction in costs and trading errors, enhancement of operational efficiencies, and benefits associated with risk management.[116] All of the major algorithms share some common characteristics. In particular, they provide for the anonymity of market users, something more difficult to disguise when traders stand face to face.

Algorithms that survive the exchange development and consolidation phase will strike the right balance of fundamental qualities important to users: anonymity, speed, capacity and stability. Like any software program, however, these algorithms require regular maintenance and a certain level of revision over time.[117]

Non-exchange intermediaries, however, design their algorithms to manage risk[118] and profit from market-making type functions in the exchanges' electronic environment.[119] These algorithms are most profitable when they buy or sell an exchange's standardized product as quickly, efficiently and anonymously as possible. Other algorithms developed by non-exchange intermediaries profit from long-term market movements, often requiring the intermediaries to hold large positions over long periods of time. Often, the non-exchange intermediaries experienced 'excessive' costs when executing large orders.[120] One reason intermediaries encouraged exchanges to adopt electronic trade-matching systems was to reduce these external costs through their ability to execute smaller-sized orders and eliminate slippage and piggybacking.[121]

In contrast, an exchange's trade-matching algorithm is limited to execution functions. The trade-matching system's purpose is to provide a central trading environment and predictable methodology for matching buyers and sellers. Critical attributes of these algorithms are their liquidity and stability because the non-exchange intermediaries require reliable and consistent responses to their algorithms' buy and sell signals. However, the costs associated with maintaining a sufficient liquidity pool are expensive.[122] Exchanges soon realized that they could tweak their algorithms to maximize profits by providing platforms that execute large-sized orders or many orders. Unlike exchanges, intermediaries realize profits from the exchanges' trade-matching systems and their own order routing systems and trading strategy algorithms. Thus, while the exchanges developed electronic trade-matching systems, intermediaries developed or purchased order routing systems.[123] These systems are either developed by intermediaries or third parties focused on supplying information technology services.[124] In addition to these services, the third parties also introduced the patent process, and concomitant litigation, to the commodity futures industry.[125]

The ECNs were screen-based and were initially regulated as broker-dealers in the securities industry. The SEC did not require them to register as a national securities exchange like the NYSE because they were not making a continuous market in securities.[126] Registration as an exchange would have imposed self-regulatory and other requirements that those broker-dealers were unwilling to satisfy.[127] By 1994, those proprietary systems were executing about 13 percent of NASDAQ volume but only about 1.4 percent of NYSE volume. Broker-dealers were also operating automated systems that matched customer orders internally, but NYSE Rule 390, until it was repealed, required orders for stocks subject to that rule to be executed on the NYSE. In preserving market share, the NYSE was also reporting record profits in 1993. However, the battle with the ECNs was already joined by NASDAQ where market share would be greatly eroded by their trading. Instinet was processing some 170 million shares a day at the end of the last century. It partnered with several online brokers that were permitting their customers to enter orders through the Internet. In August 1999, Instinet also joined with several large brokerage firms, including Merrill Lynch, Goldman Sachs and Morgan Stanley, to form Primex Trading N.A., an electronic platform for institutional traders in NYSE stocks, a project NASDAQ also joined. Other ECNs included Wit Capital, OptiMark, Easdaq,

POSIT, Tradepoint, the TONTO System which became Archipelago, Bloomberg Tradebook, the Attain System, MarketXT, the BRUT System, GFINet System, Bridge Trader, the Strike System and the Trading System.

Charles Schwab, Fidelity Investments, DLJdirect and Spear, Leeds & Kellogg, a NYSE specialist firm, developed MarketXT, Inc. to trade the more active stocks on the NYSE and NASDAQ. Spear, Leeds & Kellogg also created the REDI System that matched mixed-lot orders. Bloomberg's TradeBook system traded NASDAQ stocks.[128] The BRASS Utility System was an ECN that provided automatic execution, clearance and settlement of trades in NASDAQ National Market System and Small-Cap stocks. The BRUT System matched orders in NASDAQ National Market and Small-Cap securities on an anonymous basis.[129] Some ECNs grew so big that they sought registration as an exchange in order to compete directly with the traditional markets through their electronic facilities.[130] Archipelago Holdings LLC became a stock exchange through an arrangement with the Pacific Exchange. Island ECN was a leading ECN at one point. It applied to the SEC to become a stock exchange, and the CFTC approved the designation of Island Futures Exchange, LLP as a contract market in February of 2002. The National Stock Exchange, an electronic stock exchange that was trading NASDAQ stocks, entered into a linkage agreement with Island ECN, the largest electronic communications network. Reuters PLC, the then owner of the Instinet Group, Inc., bought Island ECN. Those two firms accounted for about 22 percent of NASDAQ listed stocks.

More competition was added when the SEC allowed a London ECN to operate in the United States without requiring it to register as a national securities exchange under the Securities Exchange Act of 1934.[131] This led the NYSE and NASDAQ to seek linkages to markets in London, Paris, Tokyo, Mexico, São Paulo, Amsterdam and elsewhere.[132] Globalization was ripe for exploitation by foreign ECNs because they had the ability to overcome the 'home bias' that had caused American investors to favor domestic exchanges. This was because the ECNs were simply mathematical models that were pretty much unaffected by government intervention or uncertain rule interpretations:

> In electronic systems, the algorithm that matches orders or trades constitutes the trading and execution rules that govern the priority and manner of trading. This leaves no room for disputes as to the applicability of the trading rules contained in the system. . . . This eliminates disputes about the validity of, or uncertainty as to the legality of, that interest.[133]

SECURITIES MARKET RESPONSES

Some regional exchanges in the United States adopted electronic trading even before the ECN competitive threat arose. The transformation to electronic trading at the Cincinnati Stock Exchange began in 1976 and was led by Bernard Madoff, who was later sentenced to 150 years in prison for running a giant Ponzi scheme through his hedge funds.[134] That exchange changed its name in 1995 to the National Stock Exchange, Inc. and moved to Chicago. The Midwest Stock Exchange began electronic trading in 1982. It changed its name to the Chicago Stock Exchange in 1993 and became an all-electronic exchange trading NASDAQ, NYSE and American Stock Exchange (AMEX) stocks through the Internet.[135] However, those efforts to compete with the larger market centers paled in comparison to trading through ECNs.

The effects from electronic competition were more dramatic on the options exchanges. Initially, there was no competition in options trading on the stocks of the companies listed on those exchanges. The SEC ordered the exchanges to stop that practice and to permit multiple listings, but the option exchanges simply ignored that order until the Justice Department attacked that arrangement in 2000. The International Stock Exchange ('ISE'), a new all-electronic exchange, was then able to compete head to head with the floor trading operations of the stock options exchanges. ISE soon became the world's largest equity options exchange, supplanting the CBOE in that role.[136] The SEC found that this competition was beneficial; in addition to narrowing spreads, the expansion of multiple trading led to: 'market structure innovations that were designed to attract more order flow by enhancing the efficiency, transparency and liquidity of their markets'.[137] The Boston Options Exchange became all-electronic, and the AMEX began electronic trading in its options in 2004. The CBOE was forced to develop a new electronic exchange called 'C2'.[138]

In 2000, SEC Chairman Arthur Levitt noted that ECNs 'have provided investors with greater choices, and have driven execution costs down to a fraction of a penny. As a result, these networks presented serious competitive challenges to the established market centers.'[139] NASDAQ was reeling from ECN competition.[140] In 2002, ECNs accounted for some 70 percent of NASDAQ volume.[141] NASDAQ demutualized in order to gain access to a larger capital base. NASDAQ sold a portion of itself in private placements before registering for its initial public offering.[142] NASDAQ began competing with the ECNs through its own SuperMontage electronic trading program developed over the objections of competitors and at a cost of over $100 million.[143] NASDAQ subsequently went a step further and bought Instinet's ECN operations for about $1.9 billion in April 2005, after the NYSE announced its merger with another ECN, Archipelago Holdings Inc. NASDAQ also tried to stem its loss of market share by mergers, first with the AMEX in 1998. A merger with the Philadelphia Stock Exchange (PHLX), the nation's first stock exchange, initially fell through, but NASDAQ did later acquire it,[144] as well as the Boston Stock Exchange.[145]

More competition emerged from abroad. The London and Frankfurt stock exchanges merged,[146] and they entered into a linkage with NASDAQ.[147] The Canadian exchanges in Montreal, Vancouver, Toronto and Alberta reorganized into a Pan-Canadian exchange. NASDAQ responded by acquiring control of OMX, a Nordic market operator, in a joint venture with Borse Dubai for almost $5 billion.[148] However, NASDAQ failed in its efforts to gain control of the London Stock Exchange.[149] NASDAQ sold its 28 percent ownership interest in that exchange to Dubai World, a sovereign investment fund in that country, as well as a 20 percent stake in NASDAQ itself.[150]

The NYSE had successfully resisted competition from the ECNs until a scandal arose concerning the $187 million retirement package given to its chief executive officer (CEO), Richard Grasso, in 2003.[151] Under Grasso, NYSE volume had exploded, the exchange was still executing 85 percent of transactions in its listed stocks, the price of NYSE seats had doubled, and the exchange had total profits of over $2 billion between 1995 and 2000.[152] Grasso kept the NYSE competitive by constantly updating its technology even as the specialists continued to enjoy their floor monopoly.[153] The NYSE spent over $2 billion during the 1990s on technology and was spending $350 million per year on technology as the new century began. However, Grasso was forced from office after the scandal involving his salary, and his successors gave up the franchise. Although the NYSE had resisted electronic trading competition for many years, it threw in the towel in 2005, merging with Archipelago Holdings, a Chicago-based ECN[154] that was then trading about 500 million shares a day, mostly in NASDAQ stocks.[155] As a part of this merger, the NYSE gave up its not-for-profit status, demutualized, and became a public company, changing its name to NYSE Group, Inc.[156]

In 2006, the NYSE merged with Euronext,[157] an amalgamation of European exchanges that principally trade electronically.[158] The NYSE agreed to give up American control of the merged entity, NYSE Euronext, sharing control of the board of the merged company with its European counterpart.[159] Euronext was also given the right to withdraw from the combined operation in the event that the SEC tried to regulate its European operations.[160] The NYSE continued its global expansion by entering into an alliance with three foreign exchanges, one of which was the Tokyo Stock Exchange.[161]

NYSE market share plunged after these mergers. In September 2007, the NYSE 'executed only 56.1 percent of trades involving NYSE-listed stocks, down from 69.3 percent a year earlier, and 78.6 percent in September 2005'.[162] The NYSE–Euronext merger was followed by the dismantling of a considerable portion of the NYSE floor,[163] and resulted in lay-offs of hundreds of NYSE employees. The number of people employed by specialists on the NYSE floor was cut in half and the number of specialist firms was reduced to seven, down from 40 in the 1990s.[164] The specialist lost its icon status. The NYSE made a name change for the specialists, calling them 'liquidity providers' and allowing others to act as 'supplemental liquidity providers'.[165] Those were all blows to the NYSE's historical role, but its merger program showed signs of success. The NYSE's own stock was up 355 percent[166] as revenues and earnings soared in the first months after the merger.[167]

The NYSE–Euronext merger also had some other wide-ranging effects. In 2007, NASD Regulation merged with the NYSE Regulation to become the Financial Industry Regulatory Authority, Inc. (FINRA), thereby creating a single self-regulator and eliminating much overlap and redundancy.[168] The NYSE and the NASD additionally merged their arbitration programs.[169]

REGULATING THE ECNS: SECURITIES INDUSTRY

The growth of ECNs gave rise to the question of how they were to be regulated. If ECNs were viewed as securities exchanges, they would have to register with the SEC as a national securities exchange under the Securities Exchange Act of 1934.[170] It would have been difficult for most ECNs to operate as registered exchanges, which have self-regulatory responsibilities and, traditionally, no profit motive.[171] Imposing such requirements would have nipped the growth of ECNs in the bud. Instead, the SEC chose to regulate most ECNs as broker-dealers under the Securities Exchange Act.[172] Initially, the SEC staff applied this interpretation through the issuance of no-action letters.[173] The SEC later adopted Rule 11Ac1-1 under the Securities Exchange Act to regulate ECNs that were matching customer orders with those of an exchange specialist or an over-the-counter market maker.[174] This rule excluded from its reach ECNs that crossed multiple orders at a single price set by the ECN by an algorithm or any derivative pricing mechanism, and did not allow orders to be crossed or executed against orders or participants outside of such terms.[175]

In 1997, the SEC issued a massive 'concept release' in which the agency announced that it was 'reevaluating its approach to the regulation of exchanges and other markets in light of technological advances and the corresponding growth of alternative trading systems and cross-border trading opportunities'.[176] The SEC subsequently decided to throw a wider net over ECNs with Regulation ATS (the SEC liked the moniker 'alternate trading systems – (ATS) – rather than ECNs) that allowed ECNs to choose to register as national securities exchanges or as broker-dealers.[177] However, an ECN was required to register as an exchange when it exceeded certain volume levels.[178] The SEC adopted Rule 11Ac1-1 under the Securities Exchange Act[179] to define an ATS as any electronic system that widely disseminates to third parties orders entered by an exchange market maker or an over-the-counter market maker and permits such orders to be executed against each other in whole or in part. This rule excluded any system that crossed orders only at prices set by an algorithm or any derivative pricing mechanism.

Regulation ATS requires an ECN that has 20 percent or more of the average daily volume of a stock during four of the preceding six months to establish written standards for granting access to trading on its system and must not unreasonably limit access to its trading facilities. The SEC was concerned that the private nature of ECN trades provided institutional traders with an advantage, that is, more favorable trading opportunities were often available to institutional traders through ECNs. The SEC, therefore, required market makers and specialists to make publicly available superior prices that it privately offered through ECNs. This rule required market makers and specialists who were using ECNs to change their quotes on public quotation systems to reflect orders placed in the ECNs or to be sure that any ECN to which they sent an order was itself able to reflect that order on the public quotation system.[180]

A proposal surfaced from large broker-dealers that envisioned a centralized electronic trading system with a central limit order book (CLOB).[181] This raised concerns that those broker-dealers were seeking to internalize their order flow, keeping it from the exchanges.[182] The NYSE claimed that such internalization would fragment markets, impair liquidity and have other adverse effects. The SEC did not adopt this proposal, but did expand its trade-through rule with the controversial Regulation NMS.[183] The former trade-through rule had applied only to exchanges and had helped to shield the exchanges from ECN competition. There was no such rule for NASDAQ stocks so ECNs were better able to compete for NASDAQ volume.[184] Regulation NMS expanded the trade-through rule to NASDAQ, but that change came too late to stop the loss of market share from NASDAQ.

REGULATING ECNS: DERIVATIVES INDUSTRY

The CFTC ceded much of its jurisdiction to the ECNs in 2000. Ironically, that action came after a jurisdictional battle over the SEC's creation of a broker-dealer 'Lite' registration program for broker-dealers that were also acting as derivatives dealers.[185] The CFTC viewed that action as an encroachment on its turf, and it responded with a proposal to explore the expansion of its jurisdiction over the burgeoning OTC derivatives market, a proposal that was met first by industry and then by congressional opposition.[186] After a change in leadership at the CFTC, that agency executed a volte-face and adopted rules that implemented an almost complete deregulation of the OTC derivatives market for institutional participants.[187] That action was subsequently enacted into law in the form of the Commodity Futures Modernization Act of 2000 (CFMA),[188] which created a principles-based regulatory scheme. Among other instructions, Congress charged the CFTC with reviewing and adopting rules to implement a new regime based on regulatory principles.[189] Although the majority of the principles did not directly touch on electronic trading,[190] their implementation would speed up the CFTC's response to rule changes and the explosive growth associated with electronic trading systems.[191]

The CFMA created a multitiered derivatives market in which: 'Each tier is subject to a varying level of oversight, based primarily on the commodity traded, the type of trading, and the nature of the participants in the market.'[192] The most regulated tier is the 'designated contract markets' where retail traders are prevalent, but the nature of the regulation was changed to a principles-based regimen that allows the exchanges to have more control over their operations.[193] Nevertheless, that legislation left the traditional contract markets saddled with cumbersome regulatory requirements while upstart electronic execution facilities were left virtually unregulated. The CFMA separately regulated what it called derivatives transaction execution facilities (DTEFs), which may be either 'retail' or 'commercial' DTEFs. These operations were regulated more lightly than a contract market, but no trading platforms have yet been created that would fall within this category.[194]

The CFMA additionally created an exemption and exclusions from most regulation for electronic trading facilities used by institutional traders that were called exempt commercial markets (ECMs) under the CFMA.[195] The ECM exclusion is often referred to as the 'Enron loophole' because it was inserted into the CFMA at the last minute through the lobbying efforts of the Enron Corp.[196] At that time, Enron was operating a popular electronic trading platform called EnronOnline. After Enron imploded in scandal, this exemption became controversial. Nevertheless, this exemption was exploited by other trading operations to create a viable OTC institutional trading market.[197]

ECMs were required to restrict trading through their electronic facilities to principal-to-principal transactions between 'eligible commercial entities'.[198] These were large institutional traders, including hedge funds, that trade 'exempt' commodities, which included energy products, metals, chemicals and emission allowances.[199] The CFTC imposed registration and reporting requirements on ECMs, including a requirement that transactions be reported to the CFTC.[200] ECMs that were serving as a price discovery mechanism for the market must also publicly disseminate execution reports and volume.[201]

Another source of competition for domestic exchanges was located abroad. The CFTC approved a broad range of foreign futures contracts for trading in the United States, many of which are traded on electronic exchanges abroad.[202] The CFTC exempted foreign brokers from registration, provided that they limited their client base to persons located outside the United States and trade through a US Futures Commission Merchant on an omnibus basis.[203] Foreign futures exchanges, many of which were electronic, were also allowed to place terminals in the United States, adding another layer of competition to the traditional pit traders.[204] Since 2000, the number of foreign customers trading on US exchanges has more than tripled, while the number of US customers trading on foreign exchanges more than quintupled.[205] The Chicago exchanges also began a desperate quest for linkages with foreign exchanges, such as MATIF and even Eurex, in order to retain their market and 'supplement' the open outcry market by allowing access to after-hours trading systems abroad.[206]

REGULATORY CHALLENGES: DERIVATIVE MARKETS

The ECNs have revolutionized trading markets, but they also created some regulatory challenges. The CFTC encountered a number of problems from its deregulation under the CFMA that has caused the agency and Congress to review whether more regulation should be imposed on those entities. The bankruptcy of Enron resulted in a broad-ranging scandal that grew to include EnronOnline, Enron's proprietary ECN. Before its bankruptcy, EnronOnline was the world's largest online energy trading platform.[207] In *CFTC* v. *Enron Corp.*,[208] the CFTC complaint charged that Enron had sought to manipulate natural gas prices by rapidly purchasing a massive amount of natural gas through its electronic trading platform. The CFTC also charged that Enron's ECN was either an illegal futures exchange that should have been registered with the CFTC, or that the CFTC should have been notified that the platform was exempt from registration. The district court entered a consent order of permanent injunction in that case and imposed a $35 million civil penalty.

That incident was only the tip of a very large iceberg. Enron had also massively 'gamed' the California electricity market in 2000–2001, a period where the state was experiencing an electricity shortage caused by an incredibly inept attempt by the state to deregulate the wholesale electricity market.[209] During the California electricity crisis, the Federal Energy Regulatory Commission (FERC) concluded that natural gas prices rose to 'extraordinary' levels and facilitated the increased electricity prices.[210] The FERC staff found that false reporting of natural gas prices had become epidemic.[211]

This intrusion into the energy market aroused the ire of regulators and Congress.[212] The CFTC brought dozens of cases charging that round-trip trades and false reports of trading to industry publications constituted attempted manipulation and violated the prohibition in the Commodity Exchange Act on false price reports. The CFTC collected several hundred million dollars in civil penalties in settling those cases.[213] Criminal prosecutors made similar charges.[214] FERC brought a number of actions under its power to regulate natural gas and electricity.[215] The SEC jumped in with actions charging that round-trip trades had distorted the balance sheets of the public companies engaging in such activities.[216] Congress also responded with the Energy Policy Act of 2005,[217] which authorized FERC to investigate and prosecute energy price manipulations.[218] In implementing the provisions of the Energy Policy Act of 2005, FERC rules prohibit natural gas sales or resales that are without a legitimate business purpose and that are intended to or could foreseeably manipulate market prices, market conditions or market rules for natural gas.[219]

This meant that two agencies would be supervising price manipulation in the energy markets. In simultaneous actions filed by both the CFTC and FERC, Energy Transfer Partners, L.P. was charged with manipulating physical natural gas prices.[220] Another such dual prosecution was brought against a hedge fund, Amaranth Advisors, after it lost over $6 billion in a single week during 2006 from its trades in energy products.[221] The New York Mercantile Exchange (NYMEX) had forced Amaranth to reduce its positions on that exchange, and Amaranth, using a regulatory arbitrage, shifted its position to the unregulated market on ICE,[222] which operated an OTC electronic trading platform for institutional traders in the United States as an ECM. A district court refused to enjoin the joint proceedings even though both actions were directed at the same conduct.[223]

The grant of additional power to FERC still did not alleviate congressional concerns that more regulation was needed. Congress subsequently granted the Federal Trade Commission authority to prosecute false reporting and market manipulation in the wholesale petroleum market.[224] This means that there are now three agencies directly charged with regulating trading in the energy markets, that is, the Commodity Futures Trading Commission (CFTC), FERC, and the Federal Trade Commission (FTC).[225]

A new form of trader – index traders who passively trade an index of commodities (or securities) – accompanied the increase in energy and other commodity prices.[226] Those traders established long positions in those indexes, raising fears that they were artificially increasing prices.[227] Traders using the Goldman Sachs Commodity Index (GSCI) and the Dow Jones-AIG Commodity Index (DJ-AIG) were estimated to have collectively held positions valued at $100 billion. The Deutsche Bank index held additional funds. As a class, the index traders' interest represents a significant minority in the markets in which they participate.[228] Of particular interest is a comparison of the index traders' participation in wheat contracts offered by the Kansas City Board of Trade (KCBOT) and the CBOT.[229] Comparing the index traders' activity in these two markets can lead to the conclusion that exchanges that promote their electronic trading system will attract more market users.

In particular, the index traders' participation in the KCBOT and CBOT's wheat contracts presaged other participants' preference in choosing a market. The trend in commercial traders' participation is quite clear in this respect. Commercial traders migrated to the CBOT's wheat contract in large numbers despite the fact that a competing exchange offers a more accurate hedging product.[230] The migration suggests that hard red winter wheat commercial hedgers prefer to use a futures contract designed for another product type – the CBOT's wheat contract is designed for the soft red winter wheat – over the KCBOT's futures contract, a contract specifically designed for hard red winter wheat hedging. To create a mature, liquid market, exchanges must attract participants willing to trade volume.[231] In an effort to allow retail customers to trade so-called 'managed futures funds' were created, which acted like a regular mutual fund except that they traded in commodities. Those funds tried to mimic the strategies that resulted in large profits when commodity prices were rising in 2008, but those markets were languishing in 2010 and the managed futures fund profits were unimpressive.[232] Futures trading volumes soared as electronic trading increased and concern was raised that index traders were responsible for some of that growth and were placing pressures on prices. However, a CFTC investigation in 2008 could find no evidence that index traders were adversely affecting the market.[233]

Intermediaries involved in electronic trading developed order routing and strategy algorithms that required information on a sub-second basis.[234] This led to an ever-increasing demand for information from the ECNs' servers about the current market,[235] and could be the cause of some interruptions in trading operations early in their development.[236] To combat this unrelenting need for messages transmitted by market participants, exchange-operated ECNs developed rules and policies to regulate the contact that intermediaries may have with their servers.[237] The ECNs limit the entities that may 'write' to the servers and deliver messages to those who own trading rights, memberships, or satisfy their application program interface requirements. Exchange-operated ECNs then fine those permitted entities that send too many messages. Because the exchanges want to encourage trading, these fines are relatively light, do not appear on regulatory records and have a high minimum threshold.[238] Ultimately, intermediaries that are fined even a trivial amount will have violated the rule on a sustained and egregious level. There is also a national security element at play with the growth of ECNs. A significant concern that has developed is the question of when an exchange may close its doors due to external factors. As a result of the tragic events on 11 September 2001, all exchanges and intermediaries store critical documents, systems, and procedures at a back-up location.[239] In the event of a disaster, the back-up location shall become the fully functioning headquarters. The advent of electronic trading, however, brings new meaning to what is sufficient for an exchange to close. Before electronic trading became widespread, if members were unable to reach the exchange physically, the exchange staff and pit committee members would determine whether opening was unattainable. Now, with the majority of exchange trading happening through electronic matching systems, local failures will certainly not prevent a majority of participants from accessing the system. Absent a local failure in Chicago or New York, this will virtually guarantee that exchanges will remain open under most circumstances.

THE SUBPRIME CRISIS

One of the fastest-growing areas of derivatives trading in the new century was the unregulated credit default swaps ('CDS') market.[240] Although CDSs were widely used as a form of insurance for 'credit events',[241] what really amounts to a default of a borrower,[242] they were also used for speculation on whether a default will occur.[243] It was estimated that 80 percent or more of the giant CDS market was speculative.[244] The CDS, in all events, proved to be a popular instrument. Outstanding notional value of the CDS was over $42 trillion in debt at year-end 2007.[245]

CDSs were used to enhance the creditworthiness of subprime securitizations called collateralized debt obligations (CDOs).[246] As an April 2008 UBS shareholder report noted: 'Key to the growth of the CDO structuring business was the development of the credit default swap ("CDS")'.[247] With the credit enhancement of a CDS, the credit rating agencies often gave the 'Super Senior' tranches of CDOs their highest triple-A rating. This was the same credit rating enjoyed by the federal government, which signaled to the world that a default on those Super Senior tranches was highly unlikely. Unfortunately, the rating agencies' risk models for awarding the triple-A rating on CDOs did not take into account the possibility of a major downturn in the real estate market. That flaw was not spotted until the subprime crisis arose.

The high credit ratings given to the Super Senior tranches posed another problem. These securities were hard to market due to their lower interest rates, which was a function of their triple-A rating. That problem was solved after bank regulators in the United States allowed favorable capital treatment of Super Seniors on bank balance sheets, provided that the Super Senior had a triple-A credit rating.[248] This regulatory blessing removed any residual concerns on the part of the banks of undue risk from Super Seniors and created a demand for the Super Seniors by banks in the USA and abroad. As a result, a large portion of the Super Senior tranches were held on the books of many major investment banks such as Citigroup, Merrill Lynch, UBS AG and Lehman Brothers. The 25 largest banks were holding $13 trillion in CDS notionals on their books in March 2008.[249] Those companies faced massive losses when the market in CDOs collapsed in 2008. A credit downgrade at the American International Group, Inc. (AIG) in September 2008 raised additional concerns that large losses would be experienced in the financial community if AIG defaulted on its $500 billion CDS portfolio. This spurred the federal government to mount a $183 billion rescue of that firm.[250]

The CDS market was unregulated before the subprime crisis, but the International Swaps and Derivatives Association ('ISDA'), the industry trade group, provided a self-regulating structure for the business.[251] The failure of Lehman Brothers raised concerns that CDSs written on its debt obligations would be massive, but in the end the net exposure was a manageable $5.2 billion.[252] Indeed, a report from the senior financial supervisors of the G-7 nations concluded that the credit default swap market functioned well in the second half of 2008, despite 'an unprecedented 12 credit events' – or actions that obliged the sellers of credit protection to make payments to those who had bought protection.[253] Nevertheless, the AIG failure, which resulted in a US government bailout of over $180 billion, placed political pressure worldwide for regulation of the CDS market. Initially, that effort was directed at requiring CDS to be listed on a central clearing-house that would provide transparency and credit protection.

The SEC also sought regulatory authority over CDSs, claiming that they lacked transparency.[254] However, the Depository Trust & Clearing Corporation (DTCC) had established a Trade Information Warehouse (Warehouse), before the subprime crisis that was 'the only global repository and centralized post-trade processing infrastructure for over-the-counter (OTC) credit derivatives. The Warehouse maintains the vast majority of CDS contracts in the market place'.[255] The DTCC was able quickly to calculate Lehman's Brothers net exposure on its CDSs at the time of its failure, removing concerns by confirming that losses would be less than $6 billion, rather than the $400 billion bandied about in the press.[256]

The Obama administration nevertheless sought legislation that would repeal the 'Enron loophole' in the CFMA for OTC derivatives and give the SEC jurisdiction over securities-based swaps, including CDSs. That legislation was contained in the Dodd–Frank Wall Street Reform and Consumer Protection Act that was passed on 15 July 2010.[257] That legislation gave the SEC jurisdiction over security-based swaps and the CFTC jurisdiction over other swaps, except that joint regulatory authority is given to both agencies for 'mixed' swaps that have elements of both securities and commodities.[258] Most swaps will now be exchange traded and cleared through a regulated central counterparty and many swap market participants will now be regulated, including swap dealers and 'major swap participants'.[259] Firms acting as swap dealers and major swap participants must register with the CFTC or the SEC before they can engage in swap transactions. Firms engaged in securities-based swaps must register with the

SEC.[260] The CFTC may also require the registration of foreign boards of trade that allow US traders to access their electronic trading systems.[261]

Dodd–Frank requires parties to swap contracts to be eligible contract participants (institutions or wealthy individuals) if the swap is not traded on a regulated contract market.[262] Dodd–Frank also requires swaps to be cleared by a registered derivatives clearing organization (DCO) unless the CFTC rules otherwise.[263] Swaps cleared by a DCO must be maintained at a registered futures commission merchant that is subject to CFTC segregation requirements for customer funds. Segregation may also be demanded for non-cleared swaps.[264] The CFTC was allowed to regulate margin requirements when necessary to protect the integrity of derivative clearing organizations.[265] Dodd–Frank requires the CFTC to make public disclosures concerning the volume and nature of cleared swaps, but disclosure of trader identity is restricted.[266] The Act requires the reporting of non-cleared swaps to registered 'swap data repositories' or (if the former doesn't accept them) to the CFTC.[267] Dodd–Frank directs the CFTC to establish position limit requirements on swaps.[268] Federal assistance to any swap-related transaction or entity is prohibited, an apparent effort to assure no more bailouts like AIG.[269] The Dodd–Frank push toward exchange trading is a continuation of the regulatory scheme introduced in the commodity markets in the 1920s. Today, there is an almost complete domination of US futures contracts by a single exchange – the CME. The CME will, at least initially, have some competition from ICE in exchange traded swaps, but each will fight for dominance and likely only one will prevail.[270] This change will in all events result in more, not less, electronic trading.

Dodd–Frank also sought to enhance the CFTC's ability to deal with manipulations and disruptive trading practices in an electronic age. The CFTC was instituting enforcement actions against electronic trading abuses even before Dodd–Frank. In *In re Lui*,[271] the CFTC, by consent, imposed sanctions against a respondent for knowingly and illegally prearranging trades on the Globex electronic trading platform at the CME. The respondent was trading several of his accounts against each other, resulting in profits for the customers on one side of the trades and losses to customers on the other. In another case, *CFTC* v. *Optiver*,[272] which was still pending as of July 2011, the CFTC charged that defendants had sought to manipulate closing prices on the CME Globex trading system for energy futures contracts in order to benefit another position.[273]

The CFTC, however, has had a dismal record in prosecuting manipulation and improper trading claims.[274] Dodd–Frank sought to rectify that shortcoming by adding additional powers to the CFTC's arsenal. Section 4c of the Commodity Exchange Act of 1936 prohibits certain improper trading practices such as 'wash' sales, 'accommodation' trades and 'fictitious' trades.[275] Section 747 of Dodd–Frank has expanded those prohibited trading activities to include other 'disruptive' trading such as 'spoofing' (bidding or offering with the intent to cancel the bid or offer before execution), violating bids and offers and actions that 'demonstrates intentional or reckless disregard for the orderly execution of transactions during the closing period'.[276] Section 747 also authorizes the CFTC to promulgate rules that would prohibit 'any other trading practice that is disruptive of fair and equitable trading'.

Section 753 of Dodd–Frank also expands the thrust of the present manipulation provisions in the CEA.[277] Section 753 prohibits any 'manipulative or deceptive device or contrivance' in violation of CFTC rules adopted within one year of the enactment of

Dodd–Frank. The 'manipulative or deceptive device or contrivance' language in Section 753 is taken from Section 10(b) of the Securities Exchange Act ('34 Act').[278] Section 753 of Dodd–Frank also contains a provision specifically prohibiting 'false reporting', that adopts a 'reckless disregard' scienter standard as the basis for liability for such false reports, but not for other manipulative activity.

ELECTRONIC TRADING CHALLENGES: THE SECURITIES MARKETS

The securities markets were also encountering some regulatory challenges from electronic trading in the new century. In one instance, the SEC found that a large number of wash and matched trades had been executed on MarketXT, an ECN.[279] Those trades had been arranged in order to increase income from payments from vendors of trade data.[280] In another case, respondents were found to have used an ECN to engage in wash trades for tax purposes.[281] Still another case involved an ECN's failure to provide equal access to market information by subscribers.[282]

Electronic trading grew rapidly in the securities industry.[283] By 2009: 'More than two-thirds of stock-market volume comes from high-frequency traders, who can buy or sell in less than 400 microseconds, or nearly a thousand times faster than you can blink your eye.'[284] The growth of high-frequency trading caused concern at the SEC, which then published a rule proposal in January 2010 that would prohibit 'naked access' by high-frequency traders to exchange platforms. This is a reference to a practice by some broker-dealers that allowed high-frequency traders to access directly ('sponsored access') an exchange without broker-dealer intermediation or supervision. The SEC believed that allowing traders to avoid such supervision should not be permitted.[285] To mitigate this gap in oversight, in April 2010, the SEC proposed another rule that sought to track high-frequency traders by assigning them codes and requiring them to report their trading to the agency when requested.[286]

Proponents of algorithmic trading argue that increased volume creates liquidity from which all investors benefit.[287] However, this increased liquidity comes at a cost. Another high-frequency trading issue involves 'flash' orders. These are orders that are cancelled immediately upon communication or which are withdrawn if not executed immediately after communication.[288] The use of flash orders, or 'quote stuffing' as the practice is sometimes called, raised concerns after the SEC discovered that some firms were entering 90 orders for every one executed.[289] An SEC Rule had allowed exchanges to exclude such orders from consolidated quotation data because of their ephemeral nature.[290] However, electronic traders began using flash orders for a variety of purposes and in large amounts. Among other things, the SEC noted that: 'For those seeking liquidity, the flash mechanism may attract additional liquidity from market participants who are not willing to display their trading interest publicly.'[291]

Notwithstanding such benefits, the SEC sought public comment in September 2009 on whether its exception from quotation for flash orders should be continued for flash orders. Among other things, the SEC was concerned with the fact that flash orders provide professional short-term traders with an advantage over long-term investors.[292] However, the SEC deferred action on that proposal, and issued a concept release in January 2010 that launched a broad-based review of the current equity market structure. The SEC was seeking to determine whether its rules have kept pace with the growth of electronic trading, including the role of flash orders.[293] After a series of algorithmic errors in 2010, however, the SEC has sought additional public comment on eliminating the exemption for flash quotes, but only with respect to options exchanges.[294]

An algorithmic error occurred on 3 February 2010 on NYMEX, causing a sharp increase in price and volume on the close of the sweet crude futures contract.[295] As access to information becomes available to more investors through electronic communications and access is eased through ECNs, the herd impact will increase its influence in both the securities and commodities industries.[296] The effect on capital formation should make it easier to raise capital under most market circumstances, but blur the lines between grades of risk.[297] In the commodities markets, it may impair the ability of those markets to accomplish their original functions: price discovery and risk allocation.[298] High-frequency electronic traders caused grave concern on 6 May 2010 when the Dow Jones Industrial Average dropped by almost 1000 points in just a few minutes – the 'flash crash'. The sell-off was variously attributed to trading errors, uncertainty in Europe over economic conditions, a Procter & Gamble sell order, a large trade on the Chicago Mercantile Exchange by Waddell & Reed, a mutual fund, and a large options trade by a hedge fund advised by Nassim Taleb of 'Black Swan' fame which may have triggered high-frequency algorithmic sell orders.[299] The staffs of the SEC and CFTC mounted an intensive investigation of the flash crash and issued a preliminary report on 18 May 2010[300] and a final joint report on 30 September 2010.[301] The final report found that liquidity in the E-Mini S&P 500 futures contract ('E-Mini') and the S&P 500 SPDR exchange traded fund ('SPDR') had dropped and that volatility was up in the market on 6 May 2010. On that day, at 2.32 p.m., a large mutual fund complex (Waddell & Reed Financial Inc.) entered an automated algorithm order to sell 75 000 E-Mini futures contracts valued at over $4 billion in order to hedge an existing position. The algorithm dictated an execution rate of 9 percent of trading volume without regard to time or price. High-frequency traders (HFTs) then quickly responded to the order, thereby increasing volume and the rate of execution of this massive order. The joint report then describes the results:

> The combined selling pressure from the Sell Algorithm, HFTs and other traders drove the price of the E-Mini down approximately 3% in just four minutes from the beginning of 2.41 p.m. through the end of 2.44 p.m. During this same time cross-market arbitrageurs who did buy the E-Mini, simultaneously sold equivalent amounts in the equities markets, driving the price of SPY also down approximately 3%.
>
> Still lacking sufficient demand from fundamental buyers or cross-market arbitrageurs, HFTs began to quickly buy and then resell contracts to each other – generating a 'hot-potato' volume efect as the same positions were rapidly passed back and forth. Between 2.45.13 and 2.45.27, HFTs traded over 27 000 contracts, which accounted for about 49 percent of the total trading volume, while buying only about 200 additional contracts net.
>
> At this time, buy-side market depth in the E-Mini fell to about $58 million, less than 1% of its depth from that morning's level. As liquidity vanished, the price of the E-Mini dropped by an additional 1.7% in just these 15 seconds, to reach its intraday low of 1056. This sudden decline in both price and liquidity may be symptomatic of the notion that prices were moving so fast, fundamental buyers and cross-market arbitrageurs were either unable or unwilling to supply enough buy-side liquidity . . .

> Between 2.32 p.m. and 2.45 p.m., as prices of the E-Mini rapidly declined, the Sell Algorithm sold about 35000 E-Mini contracts (valued at approximately $1.9 billion) of the 75000 intended. During the same time, all fundamental sellers combined sold more than 80000 contracts net, while all fundamental buyers bought only about 50000 contracts net, for a net fundamental imbalance of 30000 contracts. This level of net selling by fundamental sellers is about 15 times larger compared to the same 13-minute interval during the previous three days, while this level of net buying by the fundamental buyers is about 10 times larger compared to the same time period during the previous three days.[302]

This sell-off then spread to the equities markets for individual stocks.[303]

The staff report noted that:

> One key lesson is that under stressed market conditions, the automated execution of a large sell order can trigger extreme price movements, especially if the automated execution algorithm does not take prices into account. Moreover, the interaction between automated execution programs and algorithmic trading strategies can quickly erode liquidity and result in disorderly markets. As the events of May 6 demonstrate, especially in times of significant volatility, high trading volume is not necessarily a reliable indicator of market liquidity.[304]

The final report also pointed to the important effect of the interconnectedness of the derivatives and securities markets,[305] a factor that was focused on by the Brady Commission after the stock market crash of 1987.[306]

The exchanges involved in the flash crash announced that trades executed at a price of more than 60 percent below the share prices at the time of the flash crash would be cancelled. This displeased traders with large profits from the fall. At the request of the SEC, the exchanges agreed to adopt circuit breakers to interrupt trading when such a sharp downturn begins. Schapiro blamed a lack of uniformity in exchange rules as furthering the problem and was urging the exchanges to build a trading data center so that future events could be more easily tracked.[307] Schapiro also raised a policy issue highlighted by the flash crash: the fact that the percentage of volume executed on dark venues plummeted from 30 percent to 10 percent during the height of the market disruption.[308] Put another way, Schapiro wonders whether the public markets can be expected 'to handle nearly all the order flow in tough times, yet be bypassed routinely by a large volume in normal times'.[309]

Another trading practice highlighted by the 'flash crash' was the presence, and lack of oversight of, stub quotes, which are quotations that market makers provide as the minimum to satisfy an exchange's 'market maker' qualification requirements, but are so far away from the current market price that they cannot reasonably be expected to be executed.[310] Currently, market makers' obligations vary by exchange, some of which do not require 'stub quotes' to be near the current market price.[311] Rule changes proposed by the NYSE,[312] NASDAQ[313] and BATS,[314] all impose requirements on market makers of the respective exchange to maintain quotes within a range of the current market.[315]

Senator Chuck Schumer from New York sought to impose market-maker obligations, like those imposed on exchange specialists, on high-frequency traders.[316] Supporters of high-frequency traders claimed that their trading resulted in tighter spreads, a factor indicative of an efficient and liquid market.[317] In fact, some exchanges anticipated a potential backlash from the elimination of the specialist and provide members with incentives to promote liquidity.[318] However, another Senator, Edward Kaufman from

Delaware, challenged that claim, suggesting that tight spreads might not be worth the price of giving high-frequency traders market advantage.[319] Another concern associated with electronic trading was over the so-called 'dark pools', which were trading platforms that did not publicly disclose their trading activity as is required for traditional exchanges.[320] In October 2009, the SEC proposed rules that would make dark pools more transparent. The SEC noted that the number of dark pools had grown from 10 in 2002 to 29 in 2009, and they were then executing 7.2 percent of share volume in the stocks they traded.[321] The SEC's concerns with this trading were described as follows:

> When investors place an order to buy or sell on an exchange, the exchange typically makes that order available for the public to view. With some dark pools, however, investors are able to signal that they have an interest in either buying or selling a security. But that so-called indication of interest (IOI) is communicated only to a subset of market participants.
>
> That means that investors operating with the dark pool have access to information about a potential trade that other investors using public quotations do not. As a result, dark pool participants are able to have their orders filled, while those on publicly displayed markets go unfilled, even though dark pools use the information from publicly displayed markets to price the dark pool transactions. When dark pools share information about their trading interest with other dark pools, they can function like private networks that exclude the public investor.[322]

ROLE OF REGULATORS

Regulators are charged with the difficult task of balancing the many policy issues presented by electronic exchanges,[323] and encouraging the development of electronic systems throughout the industry while maintaining the present supremacy of the US marketplace. One of the primary functions of regulators, however, is to guard against customer abuse. Traditionally, one of the most relied-upon oversight tools in this area was the regulation and supervision of the specialist. Although analysis of traditional fraud concepts remain valid because the use of computers did little to alter fundamental aspects of most fraud schemes,[324] regulatory investigations must change as the trading host evolves.[325] Regulators recognize that their surveillance of order execution on the exchanges must incorporate a review of electronic trade-matching algorithms. The adoption of electronic trading provides them with a mountain of detailed trade data.[326] As the importance of algorithms has grown, regulators understandably have taken the position that any changes to an exchange's algorithm carry the force of a rule change and the accompanying regulatory oversight.[327]

Since the flash crash, many industry observers have analyzed these data mountains; NASDAQ produces roughly 50 gigabytes of trade data every day.[328] Some suggest that these trading algorithms act as 'financial radar' while others confess to having no clue as to their purpose.[329] These algorithms use their speed to capture mispricing between instruments, the latest of which appears to be exchange-traded funds.[330] Whatever the reason, they produce a significant amount of data to review.

Some pundits believe that these circumstances have outpaced regulators' ability to detect unsuitable trading activities.[331] Dodd–Frank recognized that shortcoming and required the SEC to hire an independent consultant to, among other things, report on the effect of high-frequency trading and other technological advances on the market.[332]

Dodd–Frank also requires the SEC and the CFTC to conduct a joint study on the feasibility of requiring the derivatives industry to adopt computer-readable algorithmic descriptions for complex and standardized financial derivatives in order better to calculate net exposures to such instruments and to define regulated contracts.[333] Clearly these initiatives are intended as first steps and more surveillance activities are necessary.

Inevitably, the focus of regulators' market surveillance activities has changed as part of the 'cat and mouse' games among the regulators and some of the regulated. The adoption of electronic trade-matching systems, also inevitably, has rendered some of these games obsolete. Many regulators report that customer abuses, in particular, have declined. Electronic trading has virtually eliminated the 'trade-throughs' familiar in fast markets on commodity exchange floors, they allow real-time updates on changes in value of the trader's positions and a reliable audit trail. However, new forms of trading lead to new types of abuses that require the attention of regulators.[334] One of the more significant changes has been the regulators' allocation of resources away from floor activities towards order entry points, like the terminal operator's activities, short-term manipulations and other activities in illiquid markets, side-by-side trading products, and intermarket transactions.

Additional regulatory changes are necessary in light of the extent and ease with which intermediaries' and exchanges' interests cross jurisdictional borders. Cooperation among the regulatory bodies, inside and outside the United States, is vital in monitoring the industry.[335] In the international arena, cooperation among regulators has evolved from bilateral agreements to multilateral agreements to participation in international organizations. Information sharing in this arena often relates to the most fundamental market information, identifying market participants and the positions they hold.[336] Requests often occur when a participant engages in market activities in different countries, which is much easier with the advent of electronic trading.

Another critical challenge is the government's maintenance of surveillance over foreign exchanges in some form. The CFTC acknowledged this in its grant of a no-action letter to ICE Futures.[337] The grant of access to US customers without registering under the Commodity Exchange Act (CEA) of 1936 is dependent upon the CFTC's ability to obtain information about a contract's salient details and positions held by participants.[338] Both the CFTC and the SEC seek trade data from the ECNs. Those demands can be readily met in an electronic format, but one of the issues that ECNs had to address after developing their trade-matching systems was the desire for all participants to receive 'real-time' trade information. Dodd–Frank requires the SEC and CFTC to consult and coordinate with foreign regulatory authorities on the creation of consistent international standards for the regulation of swaps and futures and to create information-sharing agreements.[339] A joint study by the SEC and the CFTC of international swap regulation was also required by Dodd–Frank.[340]

ELECTRONIC TRADING: THE ROLE OF THE EXCHANGES

The role of the regulated exchange has been brought into question by the growth of electronic trading. The exchange's transparency traditionally provided a price discovery mechanism and liquidity so that investors, speculators and hedgers can quickly create and liquidate positions at current market prices. The exchanges also provide some quality control features. For example, the commodity exchanges standardize contract terms for such things as quantity, quality and delivery conditions. The exchange clearing-houses provide clearing and settlement functions that assure the smooth processing and confirmation of trades, overnight in the case of the commodity exchanges and within three days on the securities exchanges. The commodity exchange clearing-houses also provide a performance guarantee for counterparties, eliminating most concerns of counterparty default.[341]

The stock exchanges and NASDAQ impose minimum listing requirements as quality control mechanisms. When developing new products to trade, exchanges often seek the input from participants in the cash market or dealers.[342] For instance, in order for a company to obtain a listing on a national securities exchange, an indication of interest from brokers, dealers and underwriters is a virtual requirement.[343] The commodity exchanges also decide what products they will trade with a view toward preventing manipulation and are constantly testing new products.[344]

Market transparency allows regulators to follow market trends and adjust their regulation accordingly. To illustrate, the CFTC revised its Commitment of Traders Report in 2006 and formally recognized the new category of index trader.[345] The primary purpose of the report is to identify publicly the composition of participants in various commodity markets.[346] The report provides the public with a glimpse of what some exchanges already know, trends in market participants' positions; and something the exchanges do not know, a detailed comparison of their customers' activity relative to other exchanges.[347]

In addition to providing a marketplace, the exchanges are a natural entity to enforce federal commodity and securities laws. They are uniquely qualified to act as gatekeeper for membership,[348] resolve disputes, establish codes for acceptable trading practices, and implement other policies that are applicable to the industry and its trading requirements and standards.[349] These functions flow naturally to the exchange and lend themselves to revisions and a knowledge base that, over time, led to the exchanges' assumption of other complementary functions. For instance, exchanges have always performed some level of selection in qualifying new members. The exchanges benefited from the qualification process because they were able to identify and establish minimum financial and ethical criteria, fostering customer trust and encouraging trading. The very existence of a selection process also conferred benefits on existing members that were critical to their success as brokers. Obviously, regulators could easily tap this long-standing exchange service and establish additional requirements as they saw fit.[350]

Another natural service ripe for exchange assumption is the resolution of trading errors. Errors occur on a trading floor every day and usually result in someone losing money, if not jobs and clients.[351] Exchange rules attempt to speed up the identification and resolution of errors.[352] Oftentimes, members identify the trade as good, but some portion of it – price, quantity or contract month – is identified as an error, which results in an 'out trade' or the clearing-house's rejection of the trade.[353] Exchanges can easily prevent some types of errors, like trades beyond the daily price limits.[354] Although unpreventable, other types of errors can be easily identified and left to participants to resolve, like quantity errors.[355] Fortunately, electronic trading has resolved many of these problems, but other issues arise, as in the case of the 'fat finger' syndrome when an electronic trader mistakenly enters an order in an excessive size in error.

Clearly, not all errors can be eliminated. The exchanges themselves will continue to grapple with the system as they get acclimated to algorithmic trading. When they do occur, computer-generated errors can wreak havoc on the exchanges. The London Stock Exchange's computers malfunctioned on 8 September 2008, and traders were frozen out of that market, which was rallying, for more than seven hours. The Toronto Stock Exchange was closed on 17 December 2008 because of computer problems, and the Globex market was down for over three hours on 24 December 2008. More recently, on 14 September 2010, the CME entered some 30000 test trades by mistake into the live energy and metals markets, causing a drop in prices. The CME agreed to reimburse customers for any losses.[356] These errors are a slight embarrassment, but represent growing pains rather than the decline of exchanges' quality standards. They are, however, one example of why exchanges, and central counterparties, will eventually be designated as 'systemically significant'.[357]

Exchanges have always performed some dispute resolution function. The highly specialized nature of disputes and the industry norms for resolving such disputes are largely responsible for the exchange's willingness to undertake these functions. The exchanges and their national counterparts, the National Futures Association (NFA) and the NASD (now the Financial Industry Regulatory Authority, Inc., FINRA), also provide arbitration forums to resolve disputes with customers and among members. The Supreme Court's recognition of the enforceability of such contracts has led many, if not most, broker-dealer–customer disputes to be settled by arbitration rather than in the courts.[358] Electronic trading is unlikely to have a significant impact on dispute resolution. The most significant changes in this area would relate to the nature of the dispute, the legal arguments presented and the forms of acceptable evidence. Dodd–Frank, however, may have thrown a wrench into this highly efficient dispute-resolution mechanism. Section 921 of that Act authorized the SEC to limit pre-dispute arbitration clauses in broker-dealer or investment adviser agreements with customers.[359] There has been some consumer criticism of industry-administered arbitration,[360] and the SEC is currently on an aggressive anti-industry regulatory approach, so such restrictions on arbitration are not unlikely.

Most significantly, the exchanges and their counterparts (FINRA and the NFA) have provided a self-regulatory role that supplements governmental regulations.[361] Former SEC chairman and Supreme Court Justice William O. Douglas described the concept of self-regulation as requiring the exchanges to be the frontline regulator with the government playing only a residual role: 'Government will keep the shotgun, so to speak, behind the door, loaded, well oiled, cleaned, ready for use but with the hope it would never have to be used.'[362] However, the SEC and CFTC have never fully believed in the concept and have broadly exercised their powers to regulate the markets. Today, the self-regulatory bodies have become vast bureaucracies that impose regulations that in many instances are even more intrusive than those agencies. However, the exchanges and other self-regulators do impose education and other requirements designed to assure competency in industry professionals.[363] ECNs do not fulfill many of these traditional exchange functions.

Smaller commodity exchanges were also struggling in the face of the growth of electronic trading. For example, the KCBOT began offering electronic trading of agricultural products alongside floor-based trading in August 2006.[364] The KCBOT's volume increased, but relative to other major exchanges and similar products, it failed to keep pace. Crop size alone suggests that the KCBOT is underachieving. Although the index trader is trading KCBOT wheat,[365] it is doing so far less than it is at other exchanges. The US Department of Agriculture calculated that the United States produced 930 million bushels of hard red winter wheat (HRW) for the 2005–06 crop-year and 309 million bushels of soft red winter wheat (SRW) for the same period.[366] Converting these numbers, the US production of HRW translates into an open interest of 185 000 contracts. Despite the fact that the United States produced roughly 300 percent more HRW than SRW for the 2005–06 crop year, open interest in the CBOT's wheat contract exceeded the KCBOT's contract by 325 percent.[367] Moreover, the CBOT's open interest in wheat has increased by more than 45 percent since January 2006 while the KCBOT's open interest in wheat has declined by 22 percent during that same period.[368]

Exchange consolidation and adoption of electronic trading is expected to reduce costs,[369] but their demutualization raises some interesting issues. The roles and motivations of members and shareholders are different. Historically, exchanges limited membership to establish minimum financial and other industry standards and to bolster the exchanges' financial integrity and prominence. Although often in synchronicity, members could hold divergent views on the best course of action for the exchange.[370] Shareholders, conversely, provide capital for the operation of a venture with profit-seeking motivating their actions.

Many exchanges acknowledged these differences by extracting the trading rights from the ownership rights.[371] These differences are likely to become more pronounced over time.[372] Thus, exchanges are likely to face increasing pressures from shareholders to become more profitable, possibly at the expense of their regulatory requirements.[373] This conflict of interest, however, is already present at every other level throughout the financial service industry: the brokerage firm, the broker and the analyst. Exchanges are the only intermediaries in this group that are quasi-governmental.[374] They are responsible for providing a forum to resolve conflicts among their members and their clients. Historically, even conflicts that affected oversight were more difficult to detect because the exchanges were private organizations. Thus the fundamental changes, which are already taking place, are changing relationships between intermediaries and their customers and the intermediaries and their regulators.

Many believe that the reorganization of exchanges into for-profit, public companies was fundamental to their continued growth. As the exchanges began to focus on profitability, to most, an obvious conflict surfaced when attempting to regulate their customers from whom they derive their income. The exchanges rely on several alternatives to minimize the conflict: outsourcing their regulatory functions[375] or establishing prominent roles for independent directors in the regulatory and oversight areas of exchange governance are most common. The CFTC appears to be aware of this conflict. In its most recent rule enforcement review of the CME, the CFTC recommended that the CME: 'review [and report to the CFTC] the compliance staff size necessary to ensure that the compliance services provided to all CME Group exchanges'.[376] This recommendation was made while noting that the exchange reduced trade surveillance compliance staff by 22 percent, in comparison to the level of staff before its merger, while volume increased slightly.[377]

Dodd–Frank requires the CFTC to adopt conflict of interest rules, including numerical limits on voting rights for any swaps clearing organization, swap execution facilities and commodity exchanges that allow large financial institutions to trade swaps.[378] Independence requirements for public companies have already undergone recent revisions. Corporate activists claim that the more independent directors, the less likely a company will engage in fraud, but that is an uncertain proposition.[379] Exchanges that adopt this approach for the oversight of their regulatory functions have taken the 'more is better' philosophy and point to it as a perceived extra layer of caution. There is no indication, however, as to whether these minimal requirements lead to the same conclusions of effective independent directors in exchanges. Ultimately, however, this philosophical roadblock must face the reality that most public companies select their independent directors after approval by the chief executive officer. As existing exchanges transform into for-profit entities, they will look to achieve efficiencies in all aspects of their operations, regulatory consolidations being one of them.[380] New exchanges may also consider outsourcing regulatory functions, because as a business decision it reduces, or at least quantifies, a significant expense that the exchange will face. National industry associations, which already perform regulatory functions that overlap with exchanges, would likely satisfy federal regulators and speed up the approval process, FINRA being a good test case.[381] Other acceptable third parties could include affiliated or wholly owned existing exchanges that already provide support.[382]

FEE ISSUES

One service, and revenue source, for exchanges is fulfilling the demand for market data. As intermediaries found it profitable to develop trading strategies, they demanded and paid for trade data from the exchanges.[383] The exchanges' profitability from the dissemination of trade data is large; according to some researchers, market data fees accounted for 50 percent of the NYSE Group's total revenues in 2006 while those same fees represented about 80 percent of NASDAQ'S total revenue.[384] Exchanges have always charged for historical data, but demand for data was stoked by index traders, hedge funds and other quantitative traders. Quantitative traders, in particular, require a significant amount of data to test their programs during development. The costs associated with purchasing data reflects the dynamics of information flows in the financial world.[385]

ECNs sought to tap the data market. First, however, they began by highlighting the benefits of straight-through processing for market users.[386] That advantage is compelling to large money managers and hedge funds. Market users who established large positions, primarily hedge funds and money managers, were the most likely to suffer from information delays.[387] These customers are not new to the commodities markets, but the latest increase in the size of their positions is noticeably more significant than in recent times.[388] Moreover, the hedge funds' affection for electronic trading platforms is a likely factor in the exchanges' development of their trade-matching systems.[389]

The intermediaries' new role, in particular the ECN's new role, is reflected in the services they provide and the fees they charge.[390] 'Market participants have incorporated technology into their businesses to provide investors with an increasing array of services, and to furnish these services more efficiently, and often at lower prices.'[391] ECNs provide anonymous access to pools of liquidity. Their performance is measured in milliseconds and whether participants can peer through the opacity to determine the principal opposite to them in the transaction.[392] As competition among the intermediaries increases, their business margins continue to thin and they are left with the choice to consolidate or close.[393] To some, it is no surprise that shrinking margins are responsible for the decline in intermediaries.[394]

Many pundits suggest that electronic trading will also reduce trading fees. Indeed, some fees will likely be reduced or eliminated.[395] The more significant consequence, however, is who will receive the lion's share of fees. Electronically executed trades push the fees up the food chain.[396] Exchanges that charged fees under a floor-based system were part of a series of fees associated with the execution of the order, which included floor brokers, introducing brokers, clearing members, the clearing-house, and the exchange itself. With direct access to trade-matching systems through proprietary or third-party order routing or front-end systems, more intermediaries, including exchanges, are taking on customers directly.[397] An electronically processed trade could reduce that list to the clearing member and the exchange itself, providing these two entities with the opportunity to collect a larger piece of the fee pie. The fee battles are as much about services as they are about fees, with intermediaries continuously adding more offerings and sophistication to their list.[398] One common service the security and commodity industries both provide is the dissemination of news. Imperfect information across markets and investors is a common arbitrage from which intermediaries profit.[399] One reason asymmetrical information exists is the high level of complexity of the products financial intermediaries offer.[400] Financial intermediaries are particularly aware of the risks associated with asymmetric information. Large intermediaries absorb risk by disseminating information internally through devices like squawk boxes and research reports. Some analysts suggest that the federal securities laws were drafted to account for the likelihood that investors would not understand these complex instruments by imposing obligations on intermediaries to distribute and explain the instruments.[401] In the security and commodity markets: 'Complexity heightens ambiguity, which in turn . . . allows people to see what they are already inclined to believe.'[402] Some intermediaries attempt to fill the void and replicate the squawk box to the public.[403] News dissemination alone, however, may not be sufficient to balance the asymmetry of information distribution. Electronic trading may increase the flow and access to information, but it will not, ceteris paribus, decrease its complexity or the costs associated with its simplification.

In *NetCoalition* v. *SEC*,[404] the D.C. Circuit reversed an SEC order approving a proposed fee by NYSE Arca for access to its 'depth-of-book' (ArcaBook) data on outstanding limit orders, which had been the heart of the specialists' books for many years. That data is valuable to traders, providing them valuable information on market depth and trends. The SEC was required to pass on the fairness and reasonableness of the fees and to determine if they were discriminatory.[405] The Court of Appeals did not disagree with the SEC's methodology on making that assessment, but held that the SEC's decision on the fees was not supported by substantial evidence. This decision meant that exchange fees were now subject to public utility style rate regulation. Interestingly, the petitioner in this case, NetCoalition, was a public policy corporation representing some 20 Internet companies (including Google and Yahoo!) and the Securities Industry and Financial Markets Association (SIFMA), a trade association representing more than 600 securities firms and banks. Another fight was brewing over an SEC proposal that would limit fees charged by options exchanges for access to displayed bids and offers. This proposal was said to be unneeded price controls by the CBOE, which charges such fees.[406]

The battle over fees and services is also a battle over customers. Some intermediaries have grown so large that the possibility of owning their own exchange and ultimately capturing fees paid to exchanges for themselves is a reality.[407] As this new business model ripples through the industry, eventually, more exchanges will have 'members' that look like retail customers, thus competing directly with intermediaries for the same customers, 'direct access customers.'[408] Fees will fluctuate during this transition period, and after the consolidation phase ends they will probably increase.

GLOBAL COOPERATION

Algorithmic trading is moving forward and not waiting on regulators. For instance, high-frequency traders (HFTs) recently have focused on the physical barriers of algorithmic trading's limits,[409] including the speed of light.[410] They desire to reduce the delay between the moment an order is initiated via computer algorithm and the moment the algorithm receives a response from the trading venue where the order is to be executed, which is referred to as 'latency'.[411] HFTs focus on reducing the latency of their entire system, which can be accomplished by monitoring the connections and optimizing transmissions.[412] As the ability to reduce latency decreases, HFTs will seek other venues to exploit the benefits of super-fast trading algorithms, not all of which will be beneficial.[413]

Algorithmic trading is going global, and the most recent crisis is facilitating that trend.[414] Currently, regulatory cooperation consists of little more than memoranda of understanding and information-sharing agreements.[415] When the need for information becomes apparent, it is often the most basic of information that is shared: identification of market participants, the positions they hold and when the positions were established.[416] Thus, algorithmic issues must be viewed in context of an industry that is increasingly global in scope.[417] The interbank payment and settlement systems are growing more interconnected,[418] and by extension so is the trading industry that relies on the payment systems.[419] There is some evidence that the degree of interconnectedness played a role in the severity of the crisis of 2007–10.[420] Moreover, the interconnectedness is facilitated by the ease with which large volumes of data is transmitted.[421] Large data transmission is facilitated by the innovative forms of clearing and settlement arrangements that increase global interconnectedness.[422]

The increasing interconnectedness belies the need for effective coordination among international and domestic authorities.[423] This will be difficult in light of the fact that sovereign debt crises often follow banking crises,[424] and the possibility of 'currency wars' that follow.[425] To minimize the disparity between regulatory structures, the International Organization of Securities Commissions (IOSCO) published a set of principles for regulating electronic access to financial markets.[426] The stated purpose of the report is to standardize terminology associated with the direct electronic access to financial markets and provide guidance for the several challenges facing markets, intermediaries and regulators because of this access.[427]

Dodd–Frank recognizes the global implications of these interconnections and takes preliminary steps towards addressing them. Section 738 authorizes the CFTC to: 'adopt rules and regulations requiring registration with the [CFTC] for a foreign board of trade [FBOT] that provides the members of the FBOT or other participants located within the United States with direct access to electronic trading and order matching system'.[428] Cross-jurisdictional requirements could take a significant step forward if the CFTC exercises its authority to its maximum extent, particularly in this area.[429] However, the teeth of this authority have been filed down, if not removed, to the extent that Dodd–Frank provides little recourse for a party to a commodity futures or options contract executed through an FBOT because they cannot rescind or recover any payment made with respect to such contract even if the FBOT fails to comply with the CEA.[430]

While Dodd–Frank contains many similar delegations of authority, it is not the only legislation poised to change the landscape of market trading practices. The European Commission is in the process of adopting revisions to the Market in Financial Instruments Directive (MiFID).[431] The current review explores the role of liquidity, and to some extent the role of high-frequency trading, and their impact on transparency, efficiency and the soundness of markets.[432] Despite the review, these steps remain preliminary. Neither the MiFID review nor Dodd–Frank is specifically tailored to regulate high-frequency trading; neither specifically promotes jurisdictional cooperation. Moreover, with different standards being established by each country, there is the potential to engage in a 'race to the bottom'.[433] Regulators have a lot of catching up to do because algorithmic traders have the ability to exploit regulatory loopholes almost as fast as their order execution.[434]

CONCLUSION

ECNs and exchange electronic trading have led to a revolution in both the securities and derivatives markets. It has brought fairness in algorithmic executions, but also brought disparity between long-term and high-frequency traders, the latter now being accused of using their size and speed to take advantage of the former less nimble traders. Regulators will address these and other policy concerns in future months. Inevitably, as policy becomes regulation across different jurisdictions, market participants will exploit their disparities and adapt to the new rules. While high-frequency trading offers a quick and efficient vehicle for delivering access, it is still novel and its evolution will undoubtedly raise still more as yet unforeseen issues.

NOTES

1. Much of this chapter is drawn from previous work, Markham and Harty (2008). The opinions expressed herein are solely those of the authors and do not reflect those of the Federal Deposit Insurance Corporation.
2. One author was calling the exchange trading floor an 'anachronism' as early as 1993 (Nowak 1993). See generally Solomon and Corso (1991) (describing the effect of technology on trading).
3. As one author has noted: 'With increased competition caused by deregulation, technological advances, and globalization, the organization of stock exchanges is at a crossroads. Traditionally, stock exchanges were organized as not-for-profit organizations, founded and owned by brokers and dealers who managed "their" stock exchange like an exclusive club, with high barriers for new entrants and a regional or even national monopoly, comparable to a medieval gild [*sic*]. Today, domestic and international competition

increasingly compel stock exchanges to give up their exclusivity, undergo restructuring, and become publicly traded for-profit companies, a process referred to as demutualization' (Fleckner, 2006). See generally Karmel (2002) (discussing the implications of exchange demutualizations).
4. See *infra* notes 289, 293 and 314 and accompanying text.
5. See *infra* notes 321–323 and accompanying text.
6. See *infra* notes 303–314 and accompanying text.
7. For a description of that controlling role see Markham (1991).
8. Commodity Futures Trading Commission Act of 1974, Pub. L. No. 93-463, 88 Stat. 1389 (1974).
9. 7 U.S.C. § 22 (2000).
10. Conference on Automation in the Futures Industry (1977).
11. See Melamed and Tamarkin (1996); Tamarkin (1993) (describing Melamed's role in the industry).
12. Melamed (1977).
13. Melamed stated: '[I]t does not take many visits to realize that futures markets utilize every available form of modern technology, and that they have done so at great expense and much more quickly than their counterparts in the securities field. From the time a futures order is placed with an account executive or registered representative anywhere in the world to the time its execution is reported back, the transaction passes through many sophisticated electronic systems. Highly advanced technology is utilized to process the order, quotation, transaction, and confirmation and to complete the back-office requirements of the brokerage firm' (ibid. at 149–50).
14. Ibid. at 159–60.
15. See Koppel (2007) (stating that floor traders on the exchanges continue to make such arguments). Electronic trading creates a new dynamic. As an anthropologist noted in studying these new arrangements: 'The designers of the computer interfaces and dealing rooms were promoting a relationship to the market based on observation and more explicit analysis. Traders were now expected to watch the market and act on it, rather than being the market and acting in it. The technological possibilities of digital systems raised the interconnected problems of how the material form of the market and human form of market reason should be related' (Zaloom 2006).
16. See Maidenberg (1984b) (describing that event).
17. See Maidenberg (1984c) (noting the 'increasing congestion on the exchange floors').
18. Ibid. Inefficiencies in order execution can occur on exchange floors with large crowds, which can fragment when a crowd becomes so large that actors are unable to communicate effectively and efficiently. See Baker (1984). Upon exceeding a critical mass, like those in financial products such as the CME's eurodollar contract or the CBOT's Treasury bond contract, the effectiveness of traders' communication with each other on the exchange floor declines. See ibid.
19. Maidenberg (1984a, p. D6).
20. Ibid. There was some tension between the floors and firms like Merrill Lynch that handled customer orders for futures contract. They would like to internalize and match that order flow 'upstairs', thereby bypassing the floor ('Another unspecial study' 1995, pp. 485, 513, n. 120).
21. See 'Click boom' (2007, p. 26) (stating that 'CME Globex and other electronic platforms were initially intended to extend trading hours and provide overnight access to customers in different time zones'); see also Oesterle (1998, pp. 17, 18) (stating that the 'NYSE, since 1991, has had an after-hours crossing system . . . with automatic execution of single-stock orders and baskets of stock').
22. Roeder (1998) (describing the last night floor trading session); see also NASD (2000).
23. Lohr (1984).
24. Greenhouse (1984).
25. Gilpin (1987).
26. Ibid.
27. Shapiro (1989).
28. Flynn Siler (1989).
29. As one newspaper report noted: 'The Board of Trade pursued a wide range of actions aimed at sustaining pit trading, including investing in electronic systems that would handle some of its products during hours when the pits were closed. The most ambitious of those investments, a joint venture with the Chicago Mercantile Exchange and Reuters to start a worldwide computer-based trading system called Globex, floundered both before and after the Board of Trade dropped out in 1994' (Feder 1997, p. 41).
30. Ibid. Associated Press (1993, p. D12). The exchange has overcome these limitations of late as monthly volume data for trades executed on CME's Globex trading platform between 2004 through 2006 shows that 'average daily order volume grew by approximately 300 percent, while the time it takes to get a trade executed decreased by more than 50 percent' CME Group (2007).
31. Feder (1994).
32. Rattner (1982).
33. Ibid.

34. Ibid. The most visible example of an exchange's effort to sustain its existence by developing an electronic trading system is that of the London International Financial Futures and Optional Exchange (LIFFE), which transformed itself from an open outcry-based exchange to an electronic exchange exclusively. See Sun Microsystem (2005) (describing Sun's role in the transformation of LIFFE's exchange environment from open outcry to electronic trading via LIFE CONNECT® in less than one year).
35. Feder (1992).
36. See Commodity Futures Trading Commission (1999) (identifying electronic order routing systems then in use for COMEX to consider adopting).
37. Barboza (2000) (describing this process).
38. For a description of the growth of foreign electronic exchanges, see 'Regulation of Exchanges' Securities Exchange Act Release No. 38, 672, 64 SEC Docket 1631 (May 23, 1977).
39. Crawford Jr. (1991) (describing development of Eurex).
40. Associated Press (2007a, p. C10).
41. Rogers and Markham (1987).
42. See Cowell (2000b, p. C2) (stating '[o]pen outcry trading of financial options ended in May [2000]').
43. Melamed (1999).
44. (Kanter 2006); 'Germany moves to start central stock exchange', *New York Times*, 8 October 1992, at D2.
45. 'Eurex to open exchange in US', *New York Times*, 10 January 2003, at 18.
46. See Markham (2006) (this author was an expert witness in antitrust litigation involving that competition).
47. 'Board of Trade rival going out of business', *New York Times*, 13 November 2003, at C10 (describing BrokerTec Future's decision to stop doing business).
48. Pedersen-Pietersen (1998).
49. Chicago Board seeks to add contracts', *New York Times*, 10 August 1998, at D9.
50. See Timmons (2007) (describing competition between ICE and NYMEX, the leading traditional exchange for energy products).
51. Zaloom (2006) (describing the tension between candidates).
52. Barr (1998).
53. See generally Greising and Morse (1991) (describing the government's sting operation and resulting indictments).
54. See Markham (1989) (describing that sting operation). More recently, a NYMEX floor trader, who was also a former exchange official, pleaded guilty to criminal charges for engaging in such activities on the floor of that exchange. '7 are charged in illegal trading inquiry at NYMEX', *New York Times*, 9 April 2008, at C2.
55. Gutierres (1989).
56. See MacRae (1999) (quoting Leo Melamed's estimate that 'two-thirds' of the total financial derivative market in 1999 consisted of $80 trillion in outstanding contracts that were mostly swaps executed outside of the exchanges). See generally Eales and Choudry (2003) (describing some of these products).
57. Gilberg (1986) (describing the growth of those instruments).
58. The CFTC had sought to regulate the OTC currency market by deeming it to be a 'board of trade' within its jurisdiction. See 'Trading in foreign currencies for future delivery', 50 Fed. Reg. 12983 (Oct. 23, 1985) (regulating currency market); Tormey (1997) (describing the CFTC's effort); Webb (1994) (same). However, the Supreme Court ruled that the CFTC had gone too far in that effort. *Dunn* v. *Commodity Futures Trading Commission*, 519 U.S. 465 (1997) (exempting '"off-exchange" trading in options to buy or sell foreign currency' from CFTC regulation). The CFTC then sought and obtained corrective legislation that requires OTC currency trading to be conducted through regulated financial institutions or between institutional participants. See *Commodity Futures Trading Comm'n* v. *Gibralter Monetary Corp*., No. 04-80132-CIV, 2006 WL 1789018, at *19 (S.D. Fla. May 30, 2006) (describing that legislation). However, the CFTC suffered another setback after the Seventh Circuit ruled that speculative transactions in foreign currency were 'spot' transactions that were outside the CFTC's derivative instrument jurisdiction. *Commodity Futures Trading Comm'n* v. *Zelener*, 373 F.3d 861, 869 (7th Cir. 2004). This led to another round of legislation. See Markham (2010a).
59. See Markham (1990) (describing the CFTC's attempts to regulate certain hybrid instruments).
60. The CFTC had, early on, created an exception from its suspension of OTC options trading after retail market abuses became rampant. However, it rejected a petition from Merrill Lynch seeking an accredited investor exception for OTC currency trading. See 'Letter to the Office of the CFTC Secretariat from Merrill Lynch & Co. Inc.' (23 December 1985) (on file with the authors); *Salomon Forex, Inc.* v. *Tauber*, 8 F.3d 966 (4th Cir. 1993), cert. denied, 511 U.S. 1031 (1994) (rejecting the CFTC position).
61. 17 C.F.R. § 230.501(a) (2007) (defining 'accredited investor').

62. Department of the Treasury (2008).
63. *Transnor (Bermuda) Ltd.* v. *BP N. Am. Petroleum*, 738 F. Supp. 1472, 1489 (S.D.N.Y. 1990) (stating that the 15-day Brent oil market is a futures exchange); see also Bettelheim and Markham (1990); More on Transnor, 8 Oil Gas L. & Tax. Rev. 223-27 (1991) (describing that decision and CFTC action).
64. See Rawnsley (1996) (describing that debacle).
65. Cameron (2006).
66. Associated Press (2007b, p. C2).
67. Donville (2007).
68. Pit trading to end for pork bellies and selected products in Chicago', *New York Times*, 29 August 2007, at C7. The CME website now notes that: 'The CME open outcry platform and trading floor systems are linked to the CME® Globex® electronic trading platform, which allows market participants to buy and sell whether they're sitting at trading booths on our Chicago trading floors, working at offices or homes thousands of miles away, or making trades during and after regular trading hours. At CME, some traders prefer face-to-face interaction on the CME trading floors while an increasing number prefer to trade electronically' CME, 'Open outcry to eTrading', http://www.cme.com/about/ins/caag/index.html (visited 21 October 2007).
69. Greenspan (2007b).
70. Former Chairman Greenspan was less sanguine on the future of open outcry in his autobiography. There he stated: '[T]he never-ending jockeying for advantage among traders is continuously rebalancing supply and demand at a pace too fast for human comprehension. The trades, of necessity, are thus becoming increasingly computerized, and traditional 'outcry' trading on the floors of stock and commodity exchanges is rapidly being replaced by computer algorithms' (Greenspan, 2007a, p. 350).
71. Markham (2002b).
72. Hershey (2000).
73. See Eichenwald (1992) (discussing Haack's efforts to help the exchange move past the crisis it experienced in the late 1960s that was caused by the large amount of paperwork created by trading over 10 million shares daily).
74. Leigh Cowan (1987).
75. Russo (2006).
76. *In re NYSE Specialists Sec. Litig.*, 503 F.3d 89, 92 (2d Cir. 2007).
77. Schizer (1992, pp. 1551, 1556).
78. See Borrelli (2001) (describing the role of floor brokers on the NYSE under the Super-DOT system).
79. Duffy (1992, pp. 17, 18). For a countervailing view see Nowak (1993) (advocating for the elimination of physical exchanges in favor of 'a completely automated communication and exchange process').
80. Mittra (1971, p. 224).
81. Ibid. Instinet's ECN operations were later purchased by NASDAQ. Its remaining business was sold to a private equity group, Silver Lake Partners, which flipped it shortly after its acquisition by selling it to Nomura Holdings, Inc., a large Japanese brokerage company (Edmonston, 2006).
82. De Bel (1993).
83. Welles (1975).
84. Buckman (1999).
85. See Simon and Colby (1986) (describing the development of the NASDAQ market).
86. Gallagher (1998).
87. See Ketchum and Weimer (1994) (describing the NASDAQ market).
88. Ibid.
89. The SOES Bandits operated as follows: 'The [SOES] traders would . . . monitor news developments constantly and use the instantaneous execution feature of the SOES to purchase shares before the market makers – who frequently handle many stocks – could adjust their quotations to reflect the new information. By executing within a few seconds as many as five orders for up to 1000 shares each and liquidating the position shortly afterward at the new market price, a trader could profit handsomely at the expense of the market maker', *Timpinaro* v. *SEC*, 2 F.3d 453, 455 (D.C. Cir. 1993).
90. Although large broker-dealers were developing ECNs to compete with the exchanges, many of those same broker-dealers had fiercely resisted Internet trading for their own customers. As a result, discount brokers were able to grab much of that business.
91. *Timpinaro* v. *SEC* , 2 F.3d at 460 (D.C. Cir. 1993) (describing the rise in online trading).
92. Christie and Schultz (1994).
93. Report Pursuant to Section 21(a) of the Securities Act of 1934 Regarding the NASD and the NASDAQ Market, Exchange Act Release No. 37,542, 52 S.E.C. 882, 884 n.7 (Aug. 8, 1996).
94. See § 9.1 (describing those practices).
95. (Norris, 1996). A 'monitor' was appointed to assure compliance with this settlement. 'NASDAQ gets

a monitor', *New York Times*, 29 October 1996, at D2. Private suits that were brought against the NASDAQ market makers resulted in a settlement of about $1 billion (Lohse, 1998); 'What's news', *Wall Street Journal*, 19 December 1997, at A1.

96. (Norris, 1995). This reorganization was the result of an NASD internal study headed by former Senator Warren B. Rudman (idem).
97. Schroeder (1999).
98. *MFS Sec. Corp.* v. *SEC*, 380 F.3d 611, 613-14 (2d Cir. 2004).
99. Ibid.
100. '2 ex-brokers get one-week jail terms', *New York Times*, 20 January 2000, at C14. Despite their guilty pleas, two of those brokers sued the NYSE claiming that it was aware of and permitted those trading practices on its floor. 'Convicted brokers sue stock exchange', *New York Times*, 28 June 2000, at B8.
101. See Finnerty, Securities Act Release No. 8805, Exchange Act Release No. 55,805, 2007 SEC LEXIS 1083 (May 23, 2007) (describing these practices); *Calif. Pub. Employees' Ret. Sys.* v. *NYSE*, 503 F.3d 89 (2d Cir. 2007) (same).
102. For examples of those settlements, see Spear, Leeds & Kellogg Specialists, LLC, Exchange Act Release No. 49,501, 82 SEC Docket 1912 (Mar. 30, 2004); Van Der Moolen Specialists USA, LLC, Exchange Act Release No. 49, 502, 82 SEC Docket 1920 (Mar. 30, 2004).
103. Markham (2010b).
104. NYSE, Exchange Act Release No. 51,524, 85 SEC Docket 217 (2005).
105. See for example *United States* v. *Hunt*, No. 05 Cr. 395(DAB), 2006 WL 2613754, at *1 (S.D.N.Y. Sept. 6, 2006); *United States* v. *Bongiorno*, No. 05 Cr. 390(SHS), 2006 WL 1140864, at *1 (S.D.N.Y. May 1, 2006). However, the conviction of one of these employees was set aside because it was not shown that the customers were misled. *United States* v. *Finnerty*, 474 F. Supp. 2d 530 (S.D.N.Y. 2007).
106. See generally Cohen (1999) (describing various forms of ECNs).
107. See BIS (2001, p. 3) (defining electronic trading). The broad scope of this definition includes a system that: 'provides some or all of the following services: electronic order routing (the delivery of orders from users to the execution system), automated trade execution (the transformation of orders into trades) and electronic dissemination of pre-trade (bid/offer quotes and depth) and post-trade information (transaction price and volume data)' (ibid.).
108. For a description of algorithmic trading in the futures industry see Acworth (2007a). An algorithm has been defined as follows: 'A fixed step-by-step procedure for accomplishing a given result; usually a simplified procedure for solving a complex problem, also a full statement of a finite number of steps. 2. A defined process or set of rules that leads . . . and assures development of a desired output from a given input. A sequence of formulas and/or algebraic/logical steps to calculate or determine a given task; processing rules', Brief of Petitioner at 6 n.12, *Diamond* v. *Bradley*, No. 79-855 (U.S. June 10, 1980) (quoting Sippl and Sippl 1972); *Diamond* v. *Diehr*, 450 U.S. 175, 186 n. 9 (1981) (quoting above definition but applying a more narrow definition to patent claims). See also Finders (2007) (defining algorithmic trading as computer systems that 'buy shares automatically when predefined market conditions are met').
109. Exchanges typically employ a series of algorithms to address all of the different order issues the exchange may receive. For instance, the algorithms for recognizing user names or uncrossing orders can be applied to all markets exchange wide.
110. In pro rata systems, larger sized orders receive priority over smaller sized orders, regardless of when the exchange accepted the order relative to other orders. See for example Chicago Board of Trade (2006) (describing the nine steps in matching trades for its pro rata algorithm).
111. See Press Release (2003) (announcing the approval of the CBOE Futures Exchange and commenting that its 'trading system will match orders based anonymously either on a price-time priority or a pro-rata trade-matching algorithm, each similar to those employed by other automated trading systems at various existing futures exchanges').
112. See Commodity Futures Trading Commission (2002b) (defining privilege market access as 'any rule, policy or processing convention of organized markets that discriminates among classes of market participants when providing any of their services, access to their services or access to market critical information').
113. See for example Chicago Mercantile Exchange (2007a) (explaining circumstances where an order in the CME eurodollar algorithm designates an order with 'TOP order status when it betters the current bid (or ask) price and its quantity is at least 50 contracts'). For intermediaries who receive special treatment, see Chicago Mercantile Exchange (2007b) (explaining that the 'LMM designation is given to those individuals chosen by CME to make a two-sided market in an assigned contract. LMMs enjoy the benefit of LMM matching privileges (a guaranteed allocation percentage of incoming orders, as specified below) and associated pricing concessions in return for meeting CME-determined LMM market obligations'); see also Euronext (2007) (explaining that only user names 'that are registered to submit [market making

orders] in a contract will be allowed to do so. These [user names] will not be allowed to submit any other order type into that contract').

114. The appearance of new financial intermediaries is particularly visible in the securities industry where broker-dealers are just as likely as exchanges to develop trade-matching systems. Independent companies created networks for brokers and dealers to execute trades electronically soon after established national exchanges merged. See Schmerken (2005) (discussing the companies that emerged).
115. For instance, one reason why ECNs found fertile ground in the equities industry was their ability to engage in the practice of preferencing whereby the broker-dealer directs orders that, in effect, permit the broker-dealer to take the opposite side of a customer's order, a practice prohibited by the Commodity Exchange Act absent extenuating circumstances. Compare 17 CFR 240.11b-1(a)(2)(ii) (2007) (requiring as a condition of a specialist's registration, that a specialist engage in a course of dealings for his own account to assist in the maintenance, so far as practicable, of a fair and orderly market, and that a finding by the exchange of any substantial or continued failure by a specialist to engage in such a course of dealings will result in the suspension or cancellation of such specialist's registration in one or more of the securities in which such specialist is registered) with CFTC Reg. § 155.2(e) (2007) (prohibiting floor brokers 'from taking, directly or indirectly, the other side of any order of another person revealed to him by reason of his relationship to such other person, except with such other person's prior consent and in conformity with contract market rules'). The SEC has noted that: 'in its broadest sense, the term preferencing refers to the direction of order flow by a broker-dealer to a specific market maker or specialist, independent of whether or not some form of affiliation or inducement for the direction of order flow exists between the broker-dealer and the market maker or specialist. [Internalization, a subset of preferencing broadly defined, is the direction of order flow by a broker-dealer to an affiliated specialist or order flow executed by that broker- dealer as market maker.]' (Securities & Exchange Commission, Report on the Practice of Preferencing, available at http://sec.gov/news/studies/prefrep.htm). Often, an intermediary only realizes measurable profits after identifying trading strategies and establishing large positions. Intermediaries regularly saw a reduction in profits, often due to 'slippage' in execution and piggybacking of the trading desks through which they execute their orders. Because their strategies require large positions, the amount of time and slippage when executing the orders to establish or liquidate these large positions is magnified.
116. See CME Group (2007) (stating that monthly volume data for trades executed on CME's Globex trading platform between 2004 and 2006 show that 'average daily order volume grew by approximately 300%, while the time it takes to get a trade executed decreased by more than 50%').
117. See for example US Futures Exchange (2003, p. 2) (stating that 'Eurex continuously upgrades its trading software, releasing and installing significantly upgraded versions about every fifteen months').
118. See Scholtens and van Wensveen (2003, p. 35) (concluding that 'risk transformation, not dealing with information and agency problems, is at the heart of financial intermediation'). In this sense, 'risk' applies to its most expansive definition, 'maturity risk, counterparty risk, market risk (interest rate and stock prices), life expectancy, income expectancy risk, etc.' (ibid. at 34).
119. Market-makers never take 'long-term views on where stock prices [are] heading. Instead, [they] aim to profit off tiny differences between what investors [are] willing to pay for heavily traded stocks and what others [are] willing to sell them for' (Lucchetti 2006, p. A1).
120. Another strategy employed by intermediaries requires them to establish large positions. Often, an intermediary's profits are less than anticipated due to slippage in execution: 'The effective spread statistics for large, electronically-received market orders in NYSE stocks show significant "slippage" – the amount by which orders are executed at prices inferior to the national best bid or offer . . . at the time of order receipt. Slippage often results in effective spreads for large orders that are many times wider than the effective spreads for small orders in the same NYSE stocks', Regulation NMS, 70 Fed. Reg. 37,496, 37,513 (June 29, 2005) (to be codified at 17 C.F.R. pts. 200, 201, 230, 240, 242, 249 and 270).
121. '[T]here are two components in the cost of trading a stock: brokerage commissions and "friction" (i.e., slippage, market impact, liquidity cost, and dealer spread) . . . [F]riction results from the current market structure and averages about ten cents per share for a basket of stocks contained in the S&P 500.' See Division of Market Regulation, United States Securities and Exchange Commission (1994) at A VI-7 (comments of Jeffrey P. Ricker).
122. See Domowitz et al. (2008).
123. The term 'order routing system' originated from the system's process of directing an order to the applicable pit for execution. Order routing is also commonly referred to as order flow. See Opiela (2004).
124. See ibid. at 46–7 (quoting Dennis Dick, CFA, Bright Trading, LLC, as saying that: 'through the course of reducing the number of stocks that they [Charles Schwab] make markets in, they shifted a lot of the handling of order flow to automated systems. This allowed them to ramp back up again with about a

70 percent reduction in personnel.' Dick also sees 'the NYSE slowly turning into a [NASDAQ]-oriented market where you have everything trading on an automated system') (ibid. at 47).

125. See generally Acworth (2007b) (discussing these issues); *Trading Tech. Int'l, Inc.* v. *eSpeed, Inc.*, 595 F.3d 1340 (7th Cir. 2010) (litigating over an ECN-related patent). See *Bilski* v. *Kappos*, 561 U.S. (2010) (process explaining how energy market participants could hedge their risks was not patentable).
126. See generally Maynard (1992) (examining regulation of ECNs as exchanges under the Securities Act of 1934).
127. The SEC proposed a rule in 1989 that would have imposed exchange-like regulation on proprietary trading systems, but backed off from that proposal. For a description of the role of self-regulation, see generally Cleveland (2005) (securities industry); Keaveny (2005) (futures industry).
128. Symposium, What's New in the Financial Services Industry: New Initiatives, 3 Fordham Fin. Sec. & Tax L.F. 67, 68 (1998) (statement of Kim Bang).
129. Ibid.
130. See for example Basar (2007) (quoting Joe Ratterman, CEO of Bats, as saying: 'Our motivation to become an exchange stems from our desire to participate directly in the national market system. We also desire to be on the same regulatory playing field as our primary competitors, Nasdaq and the New York Stock Exchange').
131. McCarroll (2000).
132. Cox and Michael (1987); Markham (2002b); Ewing (1999).
133. Corcoran (2000, pp. 581, 588).
134. Madoff also introduced the concept of 'payment for order flow' that paid brokerage firms to direct customer order flow to a particular firm or exchange. See Markham (2010a).
135. http://www.economywatch.com/stockexchanges/chicago.html (visited 10 September 2010).
136. Markham (2010a).
137. 69 Fed. Reg. 6124, 6126 (Feb. 9, 1004).
138. Bunge (2010a).
139. Levitt (2000, p. 5).
140. See generally Ingebretsen (2002) (describing growth of NASDAQ and ECN competition).
141. Tarquinio (2002).
142. MacRae (2003).
143. Labaton (2002).
144. Reuters (2007).
145. Ibid.
146. Schumer (2000).
147. Cowell (2000a).
148. Raphaeli and Gersten (2008).
149. Gross (2007).
150. Timmons and Werdigier (2007). In 2006, NASDAQ decided to convert to the registration status of a national securities exchange and integrated its three execution systems – the NASDAQ Market Center, the Brut ECN and the INET ECN – into a single platform called the 'NASDAQ Single Book'. Securities Exchange Act Release No. 56708, 2007 WL 4236257 (Oct. 26, 2007).
151. This scandal was exploited by then New York Attorney General Eliot Spitzer in order to grab headlines and aid his gubernatorial campaign. After Spitzer left to become governor, the case against Grasso was dismissed by the New York courts. See Markham (2010a).
152. But see Morgenson (1999) (arguing that Grasso had opened the door to ECN competition by giving in to pressure from the SEC to eliminate NYSE Rule 390).
153. The NYSE also created a less-than-successful after-hours trading program where crosses could be executed after the close of trading on the floor. NASDAQ also introduced after-hours trading.
154. Grasso's biographer discovered that his dismissal by the NYSE board of directors was spearheaded by Henry Paulson, an NYSE board member and CEO of Goldman Sachs. Paulson had led an earlier effort to undermine the NYSE trading floor through a central limit order book (CLOB). At the time, Goldman Sachs was an investor in Archipelago Holdings. Grasso believed that Paulson was then trying to destroy the NYSE trading floor and strongly resisted Paulson's efforts. Paulson is now Secretary of the US Treasury Department (Gasparino 2007). See also Markham (2007) (describing this scandal).
155. Anderson (2005). See *Hyman* v. *NYSE*, 848 N.Y.S.2d 51, 52 (N.Y. Sup. Ct. 2007) (describing this merger and background).
156. Anderson and Thomas Jr. (2007).
157. Anderson and Fackler (2007).
158. de la Merced (2006). As a condition for that merger, the NYSE agreed to split management and board control of the new entity evenly with the European exchanges, thus giving up domestic control of one of America's oldest financial institutions (Kanter 2007).

159. Ceron (2007).
160. See Bickerton and Cohen (2006, p. 24), noting that: 'To guard against regulatory "creep," NYSE and Euronext have agreed to create a Foundation under Dutch law . . . that will have the power to take over . . . under certain circumstances'. This provided a mechanism for US firms to list their stocks on Euronext and avoid expensive SEC regulation. See Editorial, 'Europe wins another', *Wall Street Journal* 24 November 2007, at A10 (discussing the Tommy Hilfiger Corp. plan to go public on the Amsterdam exchange).
161. Henriques (2007).
162. Authers (2007, p. 1). The percentage of NYSE executions dropped a further 2 percent in October 2007 (Dowell, 2007).
163. McGeehan (2007); Bloomberg News (2007); Lucchetti (2007a). The NYSE acquired the American Stock Exchange in January 2008. It announced a few months later that about 75 percent of the AMEX employees would be laid off (Lucchetti, 2008).
164. Lucchetti (2007b).
165. 'Since these traders emerged in the 1870s, specialists – named because they each specialize in the trading of just a few stocks – have amassed profits and critics alike for their privileged role in putting together buyers and sellers of NYSE stocks' (Lucchetti 2007a, p. C14). The NYSE also automated its bond trading operations. Securities Exchange Act Release No. 55,496, 2007 WL 1260859 (S.E.C. Mar. 20, 2007). A further electronic improvement was the creation of Matchpoint, a system that will match orders at predetermined times during regular hours at a single trading price derived from externally derived algorithmic calculations. It was thought that this system would reduce market volatility risks. Securities Exchange Act Release No. 56,798, 2007 WL 4302678 (S.E.C. Nov. 15, 2007).
166. Posting of David Gaffen to Money Blogs, http://www.blogs.wsj.com, reprinted in 'Best of WSJ.com's Money Blogs: from Deal Journal, Market Beat and Wealth Report', *Wall Street Journal*, 17 November 2007, at B4.
167. 'Business brief: NYSE Euronext', *Wall Street Journal*, 3 November 2007.
168. Masters (2007).
169. Browning (2007).
170. 15 U.S.C. § 78s (2000).
171. See *Board of Trade of the City of Chicago* v. *SEC*, 923 F.2d 1270, 1272-73 (7th Cir. 1991) (describing these difficulties).
172. 15 U.S.C. § 78o (2000). See generally Borrelli (2001) (describing the SEC's regulatory approach towards ECNs).
173. See for example EJV Partners, L.P., SEC No-Action Letter, 1992 WL 372147 (Dec. 7, 1992); Instinet Real-Time Trading Service, SEC No-Action Letter, 1997 WL 18336 (Jan. 21, 1997).
174. 17 C.F.R. § 240.11Acl (2007). This rule was subsequently included in Regulation NMS. 70 Fed. Reg. 37,496, 37,618 (June 29, 2005). See generally Nyquist (1995) (describing the background of this regulation).
175. See generally Collins (2002) (describing regulatory issues associated with alternative trading systems which included ECNs).
176. 'Regulation of exchanges', Securities Exchange Act Release No. 38,672, 64 SEC Docket 1631 (May 23, 1997). This concept release was not entirely gratuitous. The National Securities Markets Improvement Act of 1996, Pub. L. 104-290, 110 Stat. 3416, § 510 (1996) required the SEC to report to Congress on the effect of technology in the securities markets.
177. 17 C.F.R. § 242.300 (2007). The SEC noted that ECNs have characteristics of both exchanges and broker-dealers. See generally Matus (2001) (describing Regulation ATS); Klock (1999) (same). In INET ATS, Inc., Securities Exchange Act Release No. 53,631, 2006 WL 938783, at *2 (S.E.C. Apr. 12, 2006), the SEC stated that: 'An ATS is any organization, association, person, group of persons, or system: (a) that constitutes, maintains, or provides a market place or facilities for bringing together purchasers and sellers of securities or for otherwise performing with respect to securities the functions commonly performed by a stock exchange within the meaning of Exchange Act Rule 3b-16; and (b) that does not: (i) set rules governing the conduct of subscribers other than the conduct of such subscribers' trading on such organization, association, person, group of persons, or system; or (ii) discipline subscribers other than by exclusion from trading.'
178. The SEC subsequently required ECNs to publish reports on the quality of their trade executions and to disclose information concerning their trading relationships. 17 C.F.R. §§ 240.11Acl-5, 11Acl-6. These rules were subsequently included in Regulation NMS. 70 Fed. Reg. 37496, 37618 (June 29, 2005).
179. 17 C.F.R. § 240.11Acl (2007). This rule was subsequently incorporated into Regulation NMS, 70 Fed. Reg. 37,496, 37,618 (June 29, 2005).
180. 17 C.F.R. § 240.11Acl-1(c) (2007). This rule was subsequently incorporated into Regulation NMS, 70 Fed. Reg. 37,496, 37,618 (June 29, 2005).

181. See Schroeder and Smith (2000) (noting the lobbying efforts by large broker-dealers to adopt a central display).
182. See Andersen (2000, p. A48) (noting the concern that a CLOB would 'deny an ECN's ability to compete with traditional players'). See generally Schizer (1992) (describing market problems raised by a CLOB). An SEC chairman responded with a proposal that would have created a CLOB across all markets, but it too proved too controversial to adopt.
183. Regulation NMS, Exchange Act Release No. 51,808, 85 SEC Docket 1642 (June 9, 2005); see Paredes (2006) (describing the trade-through rule).
184. Oesterle (2005).
185. See Gibson (1999) (describing the Broker-Dealer Lite Rule).
186. The CFTC was 'blasted' by Robert Rubin, the Secretary of the Treasury, Alan Greenspan, Chairman of the Federal Reserve Board, and Arthur Levitt, Chairman of the SEC, for the CFTCs effort to seek additional regulation of OTC derivatives. Congress then acted to prevent the CFTC from imposing unilateral regulation (Barboza and Gerth 1998).
187. Markham (2007) (noting that a 'change in leadership at the CFTC led to the proposal of an entirely new regulatory structure').
188. Commodity Futures Modernization Act of 2000, Pub. L. No. 106-554, 114 Stat. 2763A-365 (2000).
189. See Commodity Futures Modernization Act of 2000 § 125 (instructing the CFTC to complete a study of the Commodity Exchange Act and explain the rules it intends to adopt).
190. But see Commodity Futures Modernization Act of 2000 §§ 103, 104 (sections entitled 'Legal certainty for excluded derivative transactions' and 'Excluded electronic trading facilities').
191. See 'Written Testimony Before the S. Subcomm. On Fin. Servs. And Gen. Gov't Comm. On Appropriations', 110th Cong. 8 (2007) (hereinafter Jeffery Testimony) (statement of Reuben Jeffery III, Chairman, Commodity Futures Trading Commission) (noting that: 'technology is the single most effective tool in assisting those professionals who oversee the market'), available at http://www.cftc.gov/stellent/groups/public/@newsroom/documents/speechandtestimony/opajeffery-15.pdf.
192. Arbit (2007) (hereinafter Arbit, Hearing).
193. Ibid.
194. The CFTC General Counsel has noted that: 'Both DTEF categories have fewer regulatory requirements than a contract market, but are subject to differing limitations on eligible traders and the commodities that may be traded. Although subject to a "lighter" regulatory regime, this alternative exchange must have compliance and surveillance programs, and must undertake significant self-regulatory responsibilities. These include a requirement to establish and enforce rules to deter trading abuses and to monitor trading to ensure orderly trading' (ibid. at 2).
195. The CFTC General Counsel has also noted that: 'Exempt Commercial Markets are electronic trading facilities that restrict trading to principal-to-principal transactions between "eligible commercial entities." The term "eligible commercial entities," like the name "Exempt Commercial Markets," connotes a purely commercial marketplace among entities that can make or take delivery of the underlying commodity. But that also is not quite right. Under the statutory definitions of the CFMA, pooled investment vehicles such as hedge funds qualify as "eligible commercial entities," and their participation on certain Exempt Commercial Markets has become both active and significant', ibid. at 2–3.
196. Staff Of S. Permanent Subcomm. on Investigations of the Comm. on Homeland Security and Governmental Affairs, 110th Cong., Report on Excessive Speculation in the Natural Gas Market 41-42 (2007).
197. See Markham (2010a).
198. 7 U.S.C. § 2 (2000).
199. An exempt commodity is a non-agricultural commodity or one that is not an 'excluded commodity'. 7 U.S.C. § 1a(14) (2000). Excluded commodities include interest rates, currencies and credit exposures inter alia. 7 U.S.C. §1a(13) (2000).
200. 17 C.F.R. § 36.3 (2007).
201. 17 C.F.R. § 36.3(c) (2007).
202. CFTC Foreign Instrument Approval and Exemptions, 2005 CFTC Ltr. LEXIS 27, *1 (Nov. 28, 2005).
203. CFTC Adopts Rules Exempting Most Foreign Brokers From Registration, 39 Sec. Reg. & L. Rep. (BNA) 1798 (2007).
204. See for example Commodity Futures Trading Commission (2006a) (allowing the Parisbourse (SBF) SA to place terminals in the United States which access that exchange's electronic trading and order matching system without registration as a contract market).
205. Commodity Futures Trading Commission (2006c). Competition from Europe just got tougher. The European Union's (EU) Market in Financial Instruments Directive (MiFID) is now effective and is removing virtually all cross-border barriers to the offering of financial services within the EU (MacDonald 2007).

206. Berg (1989).
207. *In re Enron Corp.*, 274 B.R. 327, 334 (Bankr. S.D.N.Y. 2002).
208. *CFTC* v. *Enron Corp.*, Comm. Fut. L. Rep. (CCH) ¶ 29,811 (S.D. Tex. 2004).
209. See Markham and Hunt Jr. (2004) (describing these problems).
210. See for example Mirant Americas Energy Marketing, LP, Comm. Fut. L. Rep. (CCH) ¶ 29,925 (C.F.T.C. 2004).
211. Fed. Energy Regulatory Comm'n, FERC Docket No. PA02-2-000, Final Report on Price Manipulation of Electric and Natural Gas Prices, at ES-6 (2003).
212. See generally Brunet and Shafe (2007) (describing that response).
213. A spike in energy prices over the last few years has placed increased political pressure on the CFTC to attack traders profiting from those increases. The CFTC responded with gusto. For a description of CFTC cases involving energy market enforcement actions and the amounts of civil monetary penalties collected see Commodity Futures Trading Commission Energy Markets Enforcements Results, Comm. Fut. L. Rep. (CCH) ¶ 30,598 (C.F.T.C. 2007).
214. See *United States* v. *Valencia*, 394 F.3d 352, 354-55 (5th Cir. 2004) (describing elements of false reporting charges under Commodity Exchange Act); *United States* v. *Reliant Energy Servs., Inc.*, 420 F. Supp. 2d 1043, 1046-47 (N.D. Cal. 2006) (same).
215. See Horwich (2006) (describing those actions).
216. Dynegy, Inc., Securities Act Release No. 8134, Securities Exchange Act Release No. 46,537 (S.E.C. Sept. 24, 2002); Reliant Resources, Securities Act Release No. 8232, Securities Exchange Act Release No. 47,828 (S.E.C. May 12, 2003). The basis for the SEC's concern has been described as follows: 'In addition to producing energy, Dynegy also conducted energy trades through its online trading platform, DynegyDirect. On November 15, 2001, Dynegy contracted with another energy trading firm to conduct two large energy trades. Each company would send the other the same amount of energy, at the same time, and at the same price. Therefore, neither company would have to report any income from the trade, yet they would be able to report a large increase in overall trading volume. These trades are known as "round-trip" or "wash" trades. The resulting trading volume and operating cash flow was reported by Dynegy on its financial statements filed with the SEC. The increased trading volume was reflected in press releases from corporate headquarters as well as to employees who were being offered Dynegy shares. All of these statements combined to artificially create an increase in the value of Dynegy stock' (Miltich 2003, pp. 983, 985–6).
217. Energy Policy Act of 2005, Pub. L. No. 109-58, 119 Stat. 594 (2005).
218. A House bill had also proposed a specific prohibition on round trip trades. Energy Policy Act of 2005, S. Rep. No. 109-215, pt. 1, at 135 (2005).
219. 18 C.F.R. § 284.403(a) (2005) (since amended by 18 C.F.R. pt. 1c (2006) and no longer contains legitimate business purpose language). Under the FERC rule all participants in the energy market are subject to this prohibition.
220. *CFTC* v. *Energy Transfer Partners, L.P.*, CIV. NO. 07 CV1301-K (N.D. Tex. 2007); Matter of Energy Transfer Partners, L.P., Doc. No. IN06-3-002 (F.E.R.C. 2007).
221. de la Merced (2007).
222. Ibid. at 88. For a description of the debacle at Amaranth see Mallaby (2010).
223. *Commodity Futures Trading Comm'n* v. *Amaranth Advisors, LLC*, 523 F. Supp. 2d 328, 331-32 (S.D.N.Y. 2007).
224. Energy Policy Act of 2007, Pub. L. No. 110-140, § 811, 121 Stat. 1492 (2007). The terms of this prohibition (idem) are modeled after those of section 10(b) of the Securities Exchange Act of 1934, 15 U.S.C. § 78j(b) (2000).
225. However, section 720 of the Dodd–Frank Wall Street Reform and Consumer Protection Act requires the CFTC and FERC to 'negotiate a memorandum of understanding to establish procedures for applying their respective authorities in a manner so as to ensure effective and efficient regulation.' Dodd–Frank §720. Other than its participation in an interagency working group to study the carbon markets, the FTC is provided with no direction in resolving any jurisdictional disputes with other agencies in this area.
226. See Commodity Futures Trading Commission (2006d, p. 6) ('Comprehensive Review') (quoting MGEX comments that the current reporting system 'blends noncommercial open interest such as index funds with traditional noncommercial open interest . . . [and] enables index funds to potentially conceal their positions amongst other market participants'.). During the process of revising the report, the CFTC created another category, 'swap dealer', and published it in the disaggregated public report. See Commodity Futures Trading Commission (2006d–Present) ('Index Trader Supplement'). The index trader category, reported as 'Managed Money', included the relatively new instrument, exchange traded funds (ETFs) and proved prescient. ETF's average daily trading volume increased 60 percent in the first half of 2010 alone. See BlackRock (2010). The high volume and arbitrage opportunities are qualities

of ETFs that make them well suited for trading algorithms. This is evidenced by the high interest of institutional investors in ETFs. Dale (2010) (describing the holders of ETFs in Europe as 90 percent institutional and in the US as 50 percent institutional); but see Anand (2010) (explaining an adviser's reluctance to recommend ETFs to investors because of a lack of liquidity highlighted by the flash crash). For instance, the SPDR S&P 500 ETF's average daily trading volume is over $28 billion. See BlackRock (2010, p. 14). An algorithm is ideally suited to execute trades in the fund and its underlying components. This is evidenced by some estimates that institutional investors represent roughly half of the assets invested in ETFs in the US (BlackRock 2010, p. 4).

227. See Comprehensive Review (2006, p. 9) (noting that 'noncommercial traders generally use futures markets to speculate on the future direction of price movements and are generally sensitive to fundamental and/or technical factors that might influence prices').
228. During the period covered by the Supplement, index traders held as much as 51 percent of the open interest in CBOT wheat and as little as 12 percent in KCBOT wheat. See Index Trader Supplement.
229. The CBOT contract has seen a growing number of reportable index traders in the CBOT's wheat contract. The total positions held by index traders has also increased in the CBOT's wheat contract over the last year by 26 200 contracts while their positions in the KCBOT's wheat contract have only increased by 7000 contracts. See Index Trader Supplement.
230. During the initial period covered by the Supplement, commercial participants increased their interest in the CBOT's contract by 56 percent while at the same time they reduced their interest in the KCBOT's contract by 31 percent. On 3 January 2006, the two exchanges had nearly identical commercial participation, 103 commercial participants in the CBOT contract versus 102 in the KCBOT contract. See Commodity Futures Trading Commission (2006b) (showing a commercial long participation of 42 and commercial short participation of 61 for CBOT wheat, and showing a commercial long participation of 41 and commercial short participation of 61 for KCBOT wheat). Since then, the number of commercial participants has increased by approximately 40 percent at the CBOT and only 20 percent at the KCBOT. See Commodity Futures Trading Commission (2008) (showing a commercial long participation of 73 and commercial short participation of 112 for CBOT wheat, and showing a commercial long participation of 48 and commercial short participation of 80 for KCBOT wheat).
231. Thus, mature contracts are the result of an exchange's effort to produce a product both hedgers and speculators will trade.
232. Laise (2010).
233. See Markham (2010a).
234. See Lucchetti (2006, p. A1) (explaining the difference for a Kansas City-based broker that moved its servers closer to the New York exchanges and the resulting time delay that 'now takes . . . about 1/1000 of a second to trade a stock, compared with 20/1000 before the move').
235. The order routing and trading strategy systems that traders and intermediaries create send 'messages' with information about their orders to an exchange's server housing a trade-matching algorithm for each product in which they intend to trade. The servers receive information and respond with information about the market and whether the order has been received, accepted, executed in full or in part, and also with price and time information.
236. See for example CME (2007) (hereinafter CME, Messaging Policy) (recognizing that '[i]nefficient messaging slows system performance, negatively impacts other market participants and increases capacity requirements and costs').
237. See for example NYSE Rule 104(b)(i) (2008).
238. See ibid.
239. See Commodity Futures Trading Commission (2002b).
240. Parts of this discussion on CDS are drawn from Markham (2009). A CDS is an agreement by one party to make a series of payments to a counterparty, in exchange for a pay-off, if a specified credit instrument goes into default. As one court defined these instruments: 'a common type of credit derivative in which the protection buyer makes a fixed payment to the protection seller in return for a payment that is contingent upon a "credit event" – such as a bankruptcy – occurring to the company that issued the security (the "reference entity") or the security itself (the "reference obligation"). The contingent payment is often made against delivery of a "deliverable obligation" – usually the reference obligation or other security issued by the reference entity – by the protection buyer to the protection seller. This delivery is known as the "physical settlement."' (*Deutsche Bank AG* v. *Ambac Credit Products LLC*, 2006 U.S. Dist. LEXIS 45322 (S.D.N.Y. 2006)). Peter Wallison, an American Enterprise Institute Fellow, gave the following description of a credit default swap where: Bank A is trying to hedge its exposure from a $10 million loan to company B 'by going to C, a dealer in these swaps, who agrees to pay the $10 million to A if B defaults, in exchange for paying an annual premium to C for the protection. A will want collateral from C to be sure it's good for the debt' (Crovitz 2008, p. A17).
241. A 'credit event' is defined in standardized forms provided by ISDA, but counterparties can negotiate

variations to the term. A 'credit event', in part, means: 'with respect to a Credit Derivative Transaction, one or more of Bankruptcy, Failure to Pay, Obligation Acceleration, Obligation Default, Repudiation/ Moratorium or Restructuring, as specified in the related Confirmation. If an occurrence would otherwise constitute a Credit Event, such occurrence will constitute a Credit Event whether or not such occurrence arises directly or indirectly from, or is subject to a defense' (International Swaps and Derivatives Association, 2003 ISDA Credit Derivatives Definitions §4.1, 2003).

242. Ultimately, however, pursuant to the adoption of the 'Big Bang Protocol' parties to an ISDA Master Agreement authorize a committee appointed by ISDA to determine whether a credit event has occurred with respect to a reference entity. See ISDA (2009).
243. An ABX Index was created to track the value of mortgaged-backed securities based on credit default swaps: 'The ABX Index is a series of credit-default swaps based on 20 bonds that consist of subprime mortgages. ABX contracts are commonly used by investors to speculate on or to hedge against the risk that the underling mortgage securities are not repaid as expected. The ABX swaps offer protection if the securities are not repaid as expected, in return for regular insurance-like premiums. A decline in the ABX Index signifies investor sentiment that subprime mortgage holders will suffer increased financial losses from those investments. Likewise, an increase in the ABX Index signifies investor sentiment looking for subprime mortgage holdings to perform better as investments', Housing Derivatives: ABX Index, http://www.housingderivatives.typepad.com/housing_ Derivatives/abx_index/. The CBOE also began trading credit default options in 2007 that were automatically exercised upon the occurrence of specified credit events. Press Release (2007). The Chicago Board of Trade (CBOT) also developed CDS Index Futures contracts. 'CBOT Credit Default Swap Index Futures Reference Guide' (2008), http://www.cmegroup.com/trading/interest-rates/files/Swap_Futures_Reference_Guide_2008_Oct_doc.pdf.
244. See Postal (2009).
245. See International Swap and Derivatives Association, Inc. (2009).
246. Another credit enhancement device for CDOs was the use of credit insurance written by the 'monoline' insurance companies, such as MBIA Inc. and Ambac Financial Corp. Unfortunately, these insurers did not have sufficient capital to cover the losses they insured on CDOs. See *Landmen Partners Inc.* v. *Blackstone Group, L.P.*, 2009 U.S. Dist. LEXIS 87001 (S.D.N.Y. 20090) (describing monoline CDO insurance).
247. See UBS AG (2008, § 4.22).
248. See Markham (2010a).
249. See Morrissey (2008).
250. See Silva Laughlin (2009).
251. See International Swaps and Derivatives Association, Inc., http://www.isda.org/.
252. See Williams Walsh (2008) (describing that resolution).
253. See http://money.cnn.com/2009/03/16/markets/cds.bear.fortune/index.htm.
254. Cox (2009).
255. See Press Release (2009). 'DTCC provides data, for example, on the outstanding amounts of credit default swaps on 1000 different corporate and sovereign borrowers' (Council on Foreign Relations, 2009). Counsel for the DTCC has also advised the author that: 'DTCC Deriv/SERV LLC is a subsidiary of DTCC, which provides automated matching and confirmation services for OTC derivatives trades, including credit, equity and interest rate derivatives. It also provides related matching of payment flows and bilateral netting services. Deriv/SERV was established in 2003. In 2006, Deriv/SERV's global Trade Information Warehouse was launched. The Warehouse is the market's first and only comprehensive trade database and centralized electronic infrastructure for post-trade processing of OTC derivatives contracts over their lifecycles, from confirmation through to final settlement.

'One of the many central servicing functions of the Warehouse is to calculate payments due on registered contracts, including cash payments due upon the occurrence of the insolvency of any company on which the contracts are written. Calculated amounts are netted on a bilateral basis, and then, for firms electing to use the service, transmitted to CLS Bank (the world's central settlement bank for foreign exchange) where they are combined with foreign exchange settlement obligations and settled on a multilateral net basis. Currently, all major global credit default swap dealers use CLS Bank to settle obligations under credit default swaps.

'On September 1, 2009, DTCC and Markit announced the launch of MarkitSERV (http://www.markitserv.com), a new company that combined the two organizations' electronic trade confirmation and workflow platforms to provide a single gateway for OTC derivative trade processing . . . The partnership was first announced in July 2008, subject to regulatory filings and approval by regulators. MarkitSERV received regulatory approval from the UK Financial Services Authority and the US Department of Justice' (email from Scott Halvorsen, Counsel for DTCC, to the author, 22 September 2009) (on file with author).

256. See 'Central repository key to reducing systemic risk in OTC markets' (2009).

257. Pub. L. 111-203. The regulation of CDS was spurred by a sensational case brought by the SEC against Goldman Sachs. See Markham (2010b). That case was settled on the same day as the passage of the Dodd–Frank legislation. In addition to regulating CDS, Dodd–Frank added a provision to cover the SEC's case against Goldman Sachs by prohibiting conflicts of interest for one year on the part of underwriters or placement agents of asset-backed securities, including synthetic CDOs. However, underwriters could engage in hedging and market making activities. See also Dodd–Frank changes §764 (amending Sec. §27B of the Securities Act of 1933) (inserting section 15F(j)(5) in to the Securities Exchange Act imposing a duty on each registered security-based swap dealer or major security-swap participant to implement conflict-of-interest systems and procedures).
258. Dodd–Frank §722.
259. Ibid. at § 723.
260. Ibid. at § 764.
261. Ibid. at § 738a.
262. Ibid. at § 723.
263. Ibid. at § 725. However, a significant number of swap transactions may be exempt from many of these requirements if the CFTC interprets 'in connection with originating a loan with [a] customer' broadly (ibid. at §721, amending section 1a(49) of the Commodity Exchange Act).
264. Ibid. at § 724.
265. Ibid. at § 736, but see §731 (authorizing the prudential regulators to impose initial and variation margin requirements on swaps that are not cleared by a DCO).
266. Ibid. at § 727.
267. Ibid. at § 736.
268. Ibid. at § 733.
269. Ibid. at § 716.
270. Indeed, ICE will provide significant competition for the CME in this product class. CME and LCH. Clearnet have cleared a fraction of the swaps that ICE has cleared. Some attribute this to the fact that the top five largest dealers in swaps are members of the ICE clearing-house for CDS and combined receive as much as 50 percent of ICE's profits related to clearing these products. See Leising (2010).
271. Comm. Fut. L. Rep. (CCH) ¶ 30,491, 2007 CFTC LEXIS 36 (C.F.T.C. 2007).
272. 08 Civ. 6560 (S.D.N.Y. filed July 24, 2008).
273. The CFTC was also successful in prosecuting and settling disruptive trading practices by floor traders. See *In the Matter of ConAgra Trade Group Inc.* (firm agrees to pay $12 million to settle charges that one of its floor traders disrupted the crude oil futures market by engaging in a stunt to push that market over $100 per barrel for the first time in history); *In the Matter of Moore Capital Management, LP*, CFTC Doc. No. 10-09 (C.F.T.C. 2010) (charges that respondent was 'banging the close' were settled). In *In the Matter of DiPlacido*, Comm. Fut. L. Rep. (CCH) ¶30, 970 (C.F.T.C. 2008), *aff'd sub nom., DiPlacido* v. *CFTC*, 2009 U.S. App. LEXIS 22692 (2d Cir. 2009), *cert denied*, 2010 U.S. LEXIS 2461 (2010), the Second Circuit found manipulative activity where the floor trader was seeking an 'ugly' close, and traded through the orders of other market participants by violating bids and offers.
274. See Markham (1991) (describing that record).
275. 7 U.S.C. §6c.
276. Dodd–Frank §747.
277. Ibid. at §753.
278. (15 U.S.C. §78j(b)). The Supreme Court has held, in the context of Section 10(b) of the Securities Exchange Act of 1934 that 'manipulation' is 'virtually a term of art'. The term manipulation 'refers generally to practices, such as wash sales, matched orders, or rigged prices, that are intended to mislead investors by artificially affecting market activity'. *Santa Fe* v. *Green*, 430 U.S. 462, 476 (1977).
279. Report Regarding Investigation of NASDAQ and NASD, Exchange Act Release No. 51,163, 84 SEC Docket 2840 (Feb. 9, 2005) (hereinafter SEC, NASDAQ).
280. Ibid. The AMEX had experienced a problem with 'trade shredding' that involved splitting orders in order to increase revenues from the market data vendors. Self-Regulating Organizations, American Stock Exchange, LLC; Notice of Filing of Proposed Rule Change Relating to the Prohibition of Trade Shredding by Members, 71 Fed. Reg. 18,789 (proposed Apr. 12, 2006). SEC Regulation NMS subsequently changed the system for fees charged by SRO participants for market data in order to prevent such abuses. 70 Fed. Reg. 37,496, 37,562-63 (June 29, 2005).
281. Securities Exchange Act Release No. 48,261, SEC Docket 2220 (July 31, 2003) (judgment by consent).
282. INET ATS, Exchange Act Release No. 53,631, 2006 WL 938783 (Apr. 12, 2006).
283. Berman (2010).
284. Zweig (2009, p. B1). With speeds exceeding the sound barrier, some industry experts have begun to pose the obvious question: how fast is too fast? See Safarik (2005). The ability to place and cancel over 11 000 trades in less than a second begins to look a little extreme, especially if the 'liquidity' is likely to vanish

in times of stress. See Hendelman (2010, p. 38) (noting that while high-frequency trading accounts for 75 percent of US equity volumes, 'high-frequency traders – outside of [designated market makers and special liquidity providers] owe no fiduciary duty to anyone to create markets in stocks and thus should not be depended on for liquidity').
285. Peterson and Kardos Yesalavich (2010).
286. Johnson (2010).
287. See Spicer and Lash (2009) (quoting Manjo Narang, Chief Executive of Tradeworx as saying: 'People should expect and be willing to pay a price for the liquidity that they get. No one should expect that a provider of liquidity is just going to stand there while you bulldoze them into submission.').
288. Securities Exchange Act Release No. 34-60684, 74 Fed. Reg. 48632 (Sept. 23, 2009). These orders are also called 'quote stuffing' (Lauricella and Strasburg 2010, p. A1).
289. 'SEC to study rapid-fire orders', *New York Times*, 8 September 2010, at B9.
290. Although Regulation NMS requires 'fair and non-discriminatory access to quotations' and prohibits exchange 'members from engaging in a pattern or practice of displaying quotations that lock or cross automated quotations', this result is not always achieved. 70 Fed. Reg. 37,496, at 37,496 (June 29, 2005).
291. 74 Fed. Reg. at 48637. The SEC noted that: 'some market participants that choose to receive and respond to flash orders may represent large institutional investors that are reluctant to display quotations publicly to avoid revealing their full trading interest to the market, but are willing to step up on an order-by-order basis and provide liquidity to flash orders. Such investors may have the sophisticated systems themselves to respond to flash orders or may rely on the systems of their brokers. Executions against flash orders could help lower the transaction costs of these institutional investors.'
292. 74 Fed. Reg. at 48638.
293. Securities Exchange Release No. 32-61358 (Jan. 21, 2010).
294. Securities Exchange Release No. 34-62445 (Jul. 2, 2010).
295. Strasburg and Lynch (2010).
296. For example, an analysis of non-commercial market participants in crude oil suggests that: (1) they systematically shift their contract holdings between energy futures markets and Treasury bond markets; and (2) they follow price trends, rather than cause them. See Dale and Zyren (1996).
297. 'The speed of information dissemination via improved technology, and greater reliance by [large US banks] on capital markets for risk management and funding . . . are contributing factors to strong and sometime late-emerging forces of market discipline by creditors and counterparties' (BIS 2001).
298. Domanski and Heath (2007, pp. 53, 56–67). The increase in interest from non-traditional participants in the market may cause an evolution of the price behavior: '[the] emergence of trading among financial investors in commodity markets on a substantial scale suggests that the determinants of market liquidity may become more similar to those in traditional financial markets. These determinants include the amount of risk capital that financial investors allocate to commodities trading and the heterogeneity of opinions of market participants. One key risk in both regards is a high concentration of trading activity. The demise of Amaranth, which led to a sharp deterioration in liquidity conditions in those tenors of the natural gas futures market where the firm held extensive positions, provides a clear indication of these challenges' (ibid.).
299. Markham (2010a). See also Lauricella and Patterson (2010).
300. Report of the Staffs of the CFTC and SEC to the Joint Advisory Committee on Emerging Regulatory Issues, Preliminary Findings Regarding the Market Events on May 6, 2010, Comm. Fut. L. Rep. (CCH) ¶31,569 (May 18, 2010).
301. Report of the Staffs of the CFTC and SEC to the Joint Advisory Committee on Emerging Regulatory Issues, Findings Regarding the Market Events on May 6, 2010 (Sept. 30, 2010).
302. Ibid. at 3–4.
303. Ibid. at 4–5.
304. Ibid. at 6.
305. Ibid.
306. Markham and McCloy Stephanz (1988).
307. Markham (2010a). See also Lauricella and Patterson (2010).
308. Schapiro (2010).
309. Ibid.
310. Patterson (2010c).
311. See Bunge (2010c).
312. Securities Exchange Release No. 34-62946 (Sep. 20, 2010).
313. Securities Exchange Release No. 34-62950 (Sep. 20, 2010).
314. Securities Exchange Release No. 34-62945 (Sep. 20, 2010).
315. See, for example, Securities Exchange Release No. 34-62950 (Sep. 20, 2010) (deleting NASDAQ Rule 4613, titled 'Character of Quotations' that required 'minimum quotation increment for all quota-

tions of $1.00 or above in all System Securities shall be $0.01' and adding new Rule 4613 'Market Maker Obligations' requiring market makers to enter and maintain bids and offers not more than the Designated Percentage away from the then current' best bid or offer).

316. Bunge (2010b).
317. Patterson (2010a).
318. See Securities Exchange Release No. 34-61840 (Apr. 5, 2010) (NYSE filing of an immediately effective rule extending the operation of its supplemental liquidity provider pilot program under NYSE Rule 107B).
319. Berman (2010).
320. Paterson (2010b).
321. 'Strengthening the regulation of dark pools', http://www.sec.gov/news/press/2009/2009-223-fs.htm (visited September 12 2010).
322. Ibid.
323. Regulation NMS, 70 Fed. Reg. 37,496, 37,504 (June 29, 2005) (recognizing major changes in equities markets, which requires the SEC to handle many unresolved issues).
324. See Parker (1998); new fraud schemes directed at trading algorithms are already appearing. Two traders in Norway were recently convicted of sending false market signals in order to trigger the algorithmic orders of a brokerage firm based in the United States. This allowed the defendants to trade against and profit from those orders (Ward 2010).
325. See Government Accountability Office, GAO/T-GGD-99-34, Securities Fraud: The Internet Poses Challenges to Regulators and Investors 2 (Mar. 22, 1999) (testimony of Richard J. Hillman before the Permanent Subcomm. On Investigations, Comm. On Governmental Affairs) (noting that 'SEC and state regulatory agency programs to combat Internet securities fraud are new and face significant challenges that could limit their effectiveness in the long-term [absent changes]'); see also CFTC, Transcript of Meeting of the Technology Advisory Committee at 30 (Oct. 13, 2004) (comments of Kenneth Raisler) (hereinafter CFTC, Advisory Committee) (opining that 'issues about recording [telephone lines] certainly would be relevant to that market [the existing trading environment] as well' in response to the possibility that the CFTC would impose telephone recording requirements on terminal operators to fill in the last gap because the electronic order routing audit trail lacks this information), available at http:// www.cftc.gov/stellent/groups/public/ @aboutcptc/documents/file/tac_101304_transcript.pdf.
326. CFTC Regulation 1.35(g) requires exchanges to report trades in increments of no more than one minute. It also requires the 'actual time' a trade is executed. See 17 C.F.R. § 1.35(g) (2007) (stating 'actual times of execution shall be stated in increments of no more than one minute in length').
327. See generally CFTC Notice of Revision of Commission Policy Regarding the Listing of New Futures and Option Contracts by Foreign Boards of Trade That Have Received Staff No-Action Relief to Provide Direct Access to Their Automated Trading Systems From Locations in the United States, 71 Fed. Reg. 19,877, 19,878 (Apr. 18, 2006) (identifying the terms and conditions for approval of a foreign board of trade's access to US customers via electronic trading devices as 'requir[ing] that the foreign board of trade promptly provide the Division with written notice of any material change in the structure, operation or regulation of the foreign board of trade or its trading system').
328. See Spicer and Lash (2009).
329. Madrigal (2010).
330. See Walker and Cheang (2010, p. 14) (stating that 'the issue will only hedge a part and then seek to trade around his obligation through systemic statistical arbitrage – effectively high frequency trading efforts – to take advantage of miniature and monetary market mispricing relative to the benchmark composition'). Moreover, these trading vehicles now represent nearly one-third of total stock market turnover. See ibid.
331. See Tabb (2010, p. 41) (asserting that 'there are too many places to trade' and that 'the SEC needs to better monitor market activity').
332. Dodd–Frank §967.
333. Ibid. at §719.
334. See Smith (2007) (suggesting that the abuse of the odd-lot rules has 'gained more prominence with the advent of faster, electronic trading').
335. See Lukken (2006) (discussing the importance of coordinating 'regulatory efforts').
336. The International Securities Enforcement Cooperation Act of 1990 authorized the SEC to share information with international regulators and maintain the confidentiality of information shared with and by international regulators. See Roberts (1991) (detailing provisions of the Act).
337. See LIFFE No-Action Letter, 1999 CFTC Ltr. LEXIS 38, at *14 (July 23, 1999) (specifically conditioning the CFTC's no-action grant upon 'satisfactory information-sharing arrangements between the Commission and the FSA will remain in effect'), available at http:// www.cftc.gov/tmlletters199letters/ tmliffe_no-action.htm.

338. Boards of Trade Located Outside of the United States and No-Action Relief From the Requirement to Become a Designated Contract Market or Derivatives Transaction Execution Facility, 71 Fed. Reg. 64,443, 64,446-47 (Nov. 2, 2006) (reaffirming the CFTC's current approach, the no-action process, to 'facilitat[ing] direct access to the electronic trading system of a foreign board of trade by its US members or authorized participants' because the staff 'also reviews the adequacy of information sharing with the Commission by the market and its regulator').
339. Ibid. §752.
340. Ibid. at §719.
341. See *Merrill Lynch, Pierce, Fenner & Smith, Inc.* v. *Curran*, 456 U.S. 353, 357-59 (1982) (describing role of commodity exchanges and their clearinghouses).
342. Some studies suggest that the arbitrageurs and speculators and not the exchanges are the true designers of standardized contracts. See Nystedt (2004) (citing research by R. Rahi and J. Zigrand and paraphrasing that: '[r]ather than assuming, as is common in the literature, that exchanges design the innovations/contracts, Rahi and Zigrand argue that profit seeking agents that trade on the exchanges play an important role in the ultimate design of a financial contract').
343. See SEC 1934 Act Release No. 34-50896 (File No. SR-NYSE-2004-12) at 4 (2004) (describing NYSE proposed changes to listing requirements for initial public offerings on the exchange).
344. Although often considered the lifeblood of a commodity exchange, new contracts may prove detrimental.
345. 'Recognize' is a little misplaced here because the CFTC did not produce a definition of 'index trader', perhaps in keeping with the principles-based approach to regulation. The CFTC describes the category consisting of 'mostly . . . those that are seeking a more general exposure to commodity prices, typically in a long-only, unleveraged, and passively-managed manner using a standardized commodity index' (Commodity Futures Trading Commission, 2006d). Further clarifying the definition, the CFTC explained that: '[S]taff, having weighed all the available information, has used its best judgment to designate certain traders as Index Traders. Some traders assigned to this category are engaged in other futures activity that could not be disaggregated. As a result, the Index Traders category, which is typically made up of traders with long-only futures positions, will include some short futures positions where traders have multi-dimensional trading activities, the preponderance of which is index trading' (ibid., footnotes omitted).
346. See Commodity Futures Trading Comm'n, 'About the Commitments of Traders Report' (hereinafter CFTC, Commitments of Traders'), http://www.cftc.gov/marketreports/commitmentsoftraders/cot_about.html (last visited 1 April 2008).
347. Ibid.
348. All exchanges have a method of qualifying new members. See, for example, CBOT Rulebook Ch. 1 (2007). With respect to its gatekeeper functions, an exchange's membership department reviews applicants' financial and personal conduct, organizes information, processes applications, and typically presents them to a membership committee for review and action. See 17 C.F.R. § 1.52 (2007).
349. See 17 C.F.R. § 1.53 (2007).
350. See 17 C.F.R. § 1.53 (2007).
351. Foley (2007).
352. CFTC Reg. 1.35(j)(1) requires members of contract markets to collect cards for clearance not less than once every 15 minutes. 17 C.F.R. § 1.35(j)(1) (2007).
353. See Kansas City Board of Trade Clearing Corporation, Kansas City Board of Trade Rule Book Rule 1187.00 at 1123 (2007) (requiring all clearing members to settle their futures trades each day), available at http://www.kcbt.com/histdata/rule_book/CH11.pdf; see also Kansas City Board of Trade Clearing Corporation, Charter Provisions and By-Laws, arts. 6.04(b), 6.05, 6.11, at 6.2–6.3 (1999) (requiring all clearing members to deliver a report by 8.30 a.m. for the previous business day that 'shall reconcile all reported errors or discrepancies for the business day of the report' and imposing a fine for any clearing member who fails to deliver such a report and for reports that contain errors), available at http://www.kcbt.com/histdata/rule_book/rulebook_ kcbotcc.pdf.
354. Each day, for many commodity futures contracts, the exchanges establish the maximum daily high and low prices members are permitted to trade during that day's trading session. See for example CME Rulebook, R. 588.C; see also *Puckett* v. *Rufenacht, Bromagen & Hertz, & Co.*, 903 F.2d 1014, 1016 (5th Cir. 1990) (referencing these price limits). Trades made outside of this range established before the beginning of trading every day are simply deleted, or 'busted', as if they never occurred. See for example Chicago Board of Trade (2006) (stating all trades 'executed outside of the daily price limits will be busted by [the exchange] irrespective of any other circumstances).
355. 'Trading through the market' refers to trades made higher than the lowest current offer or lower than the highest current bid at the time of execution. See for example, Chicago Board of Trade (2006), Chicago Board of Trade Rulebook 514.A.1 (identifying any 'trade through the existing bid or offer' as a trading infraction), available at http://www.cbot.com/cbot/pub/cont_ detail/0,3206,931t53510,00.html.
356. Bunge et al. (2010).

357. Dodd–Frank §806 (authorizing the Federal Reserve Board of Governors to 'establish and maintain an account for a designated financial market utility' and provide 'discount and borrowing privileges').
358. See *Shearson/American Express, Inc.* v. *McMahon*, 482 U.S. 220 (1987) (upholding the enforceability of arbitration provisions in investment contracts); *Rodriguez De Quijas* v. *Shearson/American Express, Inc.*, 490 U.S. 477 (1989) (same). See generally, § 12:33 (2d ed. 2005).
359. Dodd–Frank §921.
360. For an analysis on how well customers fared in NASD (now FINRA) arbitration see Markham and Hazen (2010).
361. See *Silver* v. *N. Y. Stock Exch.*, 373 U.S. 341 (1963) (describing the role of self-regulation); Concept Release Concerning Self-Regulation, Exchange Act Release No. 50,700, 84 SEC Docket 619 (Nov. 18, 2004) (same), available at http://www.sec.gov/rules/concept/34-50700.htm; Sec. & Exch. Comm'n, Report of the Special Study of the Securities Markets ch. XII Over-the-Counter Markets (1963) (same), available at www.http://sechistorical.org/collection/papers/1960/1963_ss_sec_markets/chapter_07_1.pdf.
362. Douglas (1940 [1969], p. 82).
363. FINRA has continuing education programs for registrants and licensing series to assure competence. FINRA-Education & Programs, http:// www.finra.org/EducationPrograms/index.htm (visited 1 April 2008).
364. The KCBOT, CBOT and Minneapolis Grain Exchange all share the same electronic platform trading service provider. Before 2007, their provider was LIFFE Connect; since the CBOT's merger with the CME, the exchanges use the Globex platform. See Press Release (2008). Each exchange began offering electronic trading in agricultural products on a side-by-side basis the same month, August 2006. The exchanges, however, charge their customers different rates for trades executed electronically and on the floor of the respective exchange. See for example KCBT 'Exchange contract fees', http:// www.kcbt.com/fees.html (visited 27 April 2008) (identifying non-member exchange open outcry fee for wheat futures of $0.55 per contract and non-member electronic fee for wheat futures of $1.70 per contract).
365. See Commodity Futures Trading Comm'n, 'About the commitments of traders report', www.cftc.gov/opa/backgrounder/opacot596.htm (visited 11 April 2008).
366. USDA Nat. Agric. Statistics Serv., Crop Production 2006 Summary 16 (2007).
367. See Commodity Futures Trading Comm'n, 'Historical commitments of traders', www.cftc.gov/cftc/cftchistoricalcot.htm (visited 7 March 2007).
368. Since 3 January 2006, open interest in CBOT wheat increased 36 percent while it decreased 22 percent in KCBOT wheat. Compare Commodity Futures Trading Comm'n (2006b), Commitments of Traders Reports – 3 January 2006, http:// cftc.gov/marketreports/commitmentsoftraders/cot010306.html (visited 28 May 2008) (indicating total open interest in CBOT wheat of 339 284 contracts and KCBOT wheat with 143 580 contracts) with Commodity Futures Trading Comm'n (2008), Commitments of Traders Reports – 22 April 2008, http://cftc.gov/marketreports/commitmentsoftraders/cot042208.html (visited 28 May 2008) (indicating total open interest in CBOT wheat of 531 768 contracts and KCBOT wheat with 117 852 contracts).
369. (CME Group Inc., 2007, p. 15) (interview with Bryan Durkin and Phupinder Gill stating that 'consolidation of the CBOT and CME operations will result in annual cost savings to customers of $125 million'); NYSE Group, Inc (2000) (estimating annual cost savings after the first three years of combined operations at $155 million).
370. See Pirrong (1995, pp. 141, 158) (noting that 'exchanges are coalitions of individual members with divergent interests'). Some of the most significant decisions an exchange can make relate to the enforcement actions they take, or elect not to take. In this respect, the exchange members' interests are most starkly divided because inevitably, an enforcement action imparts a cost on some members, possibly to the benefit of other members. See idem at 159–60 (citations omitted). It has been noted that: 'exchange rule enforcers may not use their discretionary authority to stop manipulations because their decisions are intended to balance the interests of parties contending for [economic] rents, rather than to maximize efficiency. In the context of this analysis, an exchange's decision makers do not make decisions that maximize the wealth of its members. Instead, they trade off support from longs and shorts and settle on some intermediate outcome. Thus, one would not expect exchange directors to impose an efficient, competitive allocation' (ibid.).
371. See for example Memorandum from the Div. of Trading & Mkts. To the Commodity Futures Trading Comm'n (Feb. 6, 2006) (hereinafter CFTC, Memorandum), available at http://www.cftc.gov/tm/tmcme_demutualization_memo.htm.
372. See ibid. (forecasting that 'under a demutualization plan, over time the percentage of shareholders that are also market users may, and probably will, decrease').
373. See ibid. (qualifying its acknowledgement that '[i]t is possible that a for-profit exchange, interested in reducing expenses to enhance stockholder value, might consider reducing self-regulatory programs or

dedicate insufficient resources to its existing programs' by suggesting that 'this risk is also inherent for a mutual exchange whose members may also be interested in cutting costs to themselves').

374. Carson (2003) (hereinafter 'Carson, Conflicts') (acknowledging exchanges perform public service functions).
375. See for example, NASD Bylaw Amendments, Exchange Act Release No. 56145, 2007 SEC LEXIS 1640 (July 26, 2007) (approving rule changes 'to implement governance and related changes to accommodate the consolidation of the member firm regulatory functions of NASD and NYSE Regulation, Inc'). Although outsourcing these functions to national associations or private companies may be a viable option, apparently direct federal oversight is out of the question..
376. See CFTC (2010, pp. 3–4).
377. Ibid. at 11.
378. Dodd–Frank §726. This section of Dodd–Frank states that the CFTC must adopt rules that: 'are necessary or appropriate to improve the governance of, or to mitigate systemic risk, promote competition, or mitigate conflicts of interest in connection with a swap dealer or major swap participant's conduct of business with, a derivatives clearing organization, contract market, or swap execution facility that clears or posts swaps or makes swaps available for trading and in which such swap dealer or major swap participant has a material debt or equity investment.

    'In adopting rules pursuant to this section, the Commodity Futures Trading Commission shall consider any conflicts of interest arising from the amount of equity owned by a single investor, the ability to vote, cause the vote of, or withhold votes entitled to be cast on any matters by the holders of the ownership interest, and the governance arrangements of any derivatives clearing organization that clears swaps, or swap execution facility or board of trade designated as a contract market that posts swaps or makes swaps available for trading.'
379. Results of recent studies 'indicate that board composition and the structure of its oversight committees are significantly related to the incidence of corporate fraud' (Uzun et al. 2004, pp. 33, 41). However, other studies show that increasing the number of outside directors does not improve economic performance (Hamilton 1995). After the Enron scandal, the stock exchanges required public companies to appoint a majority of outside directors on their boards. However, no justification was show for this requirement. Indeed, some of the worst financial scandals in history occurred at public companies having a majority of outside directors on their boards, including Enron and Worldcom. Enron had a super-majority of outside directors on its board, as did WorldCom (Markham 2010a). Another reform measure is to separate the offices of CEO and board chairman, but both WorldCom and Enron had separated those posts (ibid. at 262). Dodd–Frank, nevertheless, requires public companies to disclose why they have or have not divided those roles (§972).
380. See Melamed (2006, pp. 44, 45) (predicting that 'technology will take us to another level of sophistication, the consolidation of markets').
381. For example, the NFA's contract to perform regulatory oversight services for the US Futures Exchange played a significant role in the CFTC's designation of the exchange as a contract market. See 'Letter from the Commodity Futures Trading Comm'n to Daniel Waldman' (Feb. 4, 2004) (approving the USFE's application for contract market designation based on the representations by USFE and NFA 'concerning how the NFA will, among other things, assist the USFE in meeting the Exchange's self-regulatory obligations'). The CFTC processed USFE's application and approved it in approximately five months, two months longer than LIFFE's application and three months longer than TFX's application. See CFTC US Futures Exchange, LLC (USFE) Contract Market Designation Application, Application Submissions, Public Comments Received and Approval Documents, http://www.cftc.gov/dea/deausfesubmissions_and_ comments_table.htm (visited 25 April 2008).
382. One such exchange is the CBOE futures exchange.
383. Today, exchanges customize trade data; one even offers a 'Hedge Fund' package. See CBOT, 'CBOT Data Exchange', http://cbotdataexchange.if5.com (visited 5 April 2008). The data purchased usually include volume, open interest, and each trade price, bid or offer quoted throughout the trading day. See ibid.; see also Wijnen (2002) (describing the prime broker's service of data production to hedge funds as a cost of doing business).
384. Ortega (2007).
385. See Haigh et al. (2005) (US Commodity Futures Trading Commission, unpublished manuscript) (explaining that hedge fund traders and money management traders 'appear to be, in econometric terms, an information sink – they do not cause any other participant to change their position in contemporaneous time (on the same day) but rather, information flows towards them rather than away').
386. See Sun Microsystem, Inc. (2002) (identifying that one of the key demands that the system Sun developed for LIFFE had to meet was its ability to 'provide a high level of integration for the front-, middle-, and back-office of [exchange] members reducing their cost and risk exposure'); see also Committee on

the Global Financial System (2001) (identifying straight-through processing as a primary benefit to adoption of electronic trading).

387. Order execution speeds remain of concern: 'The average NYSE floor execution time, even going back as little as three years ago, was approximately 14 seconds. Today most trading venues (including the NYSE floor) measure execution time in milliseconds and some in micro seconds and it is not rare for an order to be matched in 3 to 7 milliseconds.

'As execution times become measured in milliseconds, physics (more specifically – the speed of light) becomes an issue. If an exchange/ECN operates in single digit milliseconds and it takes 32 milliseconds for light (in a vacuum) to travel from San Francisco to New York and back, then by definition a trader in San Francisco will never be able to effectively trade fast-moving US Equities. This is no longer a theoretical problem. Speed has become so critical that distance and exchange-hosting has even become an issue for Eastern US-based firms that do not have local data centers', Tabb Group, US Equity Market Structure: Driving Change in Global Financial Markets (Executive Summary), http://www.tabbgroup.com/Page.aspx?MenuID=13&ParentMenuID=2&PageID=8.

388. The significance of hedge funds in commodity trading has grown significantly since 1994. See Bank for International Settlements (2007, p. 58). '[A]ssets under management by commodity trading advisers . . . rose from about $20 billion in 2002 to about $75 billion by end-2005' (ibid., citation omitted).

389. See ibid. at 59.

390. See Plasencia (1995, p. 14) (identifying financial advantages banks and brokerage firms receive if they employ clearinghouses with automated functions and services).

391. Regulation of Exchanges and Alternative Trading Systems, Exchange Act Release No. 40,760, 63 Fed. Reg. 70,844, 70,845 (Dec. 22, 1998).

392. See for example Brandes and Domowitz (2010) (comparing the cost, speed, and 'percentage of the order that is done in the dark' across primary exchanges, multilateral trading facilities, and dark pools in the wake of the Markets in Financial Instruments Directive).

393. See Schmerken (2005, p. 31) (describing the cause of consolidation as 'the ECN population plummeting from a dozen or so in the late 1990s to a handful today and the equity markets approaching a duopoly').

394. Arbor (1997) ('In 10 years the number of registered professionals have shrunk by about 8 percent. Even more telling, the number of FCMs has contracted by 39 percent. Today only 233 FCMs are sending orders to the seven unaffiliated exchanges, now actively trading future contracts down from nine in 1987.').

395. See 'Letter from Thomas W. Sexton, Vice President and Gen. Counsel, Nat'l Futures Ass'n to David Stawick, Office of the Secretariat, Commodity Futures Trading Commission' (20 November 2007) (attributing a fee reduction to the 'sustained strong growth in public trading volume'), http://www.nfa.futures.org/news/newsRuleSubletter.asp?ArticleID=1998; see also Ortega (2007, p. 1) (describing a BATS promotional event where the ATS charged 20 cents per 100 lot orders for the month of February 2007 and anticipating a doubling of its average daily volume).

396. SEC Regulation NMS has created a complex regulatory system for fees charged by SRO participants for market data. 70 Fed. Reg. 37,496, 37,562-3 (June 29, 2005).

397. See for example Hedgestreet, Inc., Rules, R. 3.1 (2008) (identifying the requirements for individuals to become a member as: US residency; 'old enough to enter into a legally enforceable contract'; maintain a bank account; complete an application; and fund the trading account with an initial deposit of $100 to HedgeStreet's 'customer segregated funds account'), available at http://www.hedgestreet.com/pdf/hedgestreet_rules.pdf.

398. 'Financial intermediaries perform gradually more sophisticated functions in the modern – more and more complex – economy' (Scholtens and van Wensveen, 2000, pp. 1243, 1247).

399. Interestingly, the existence of asymmetric information may lead to disintermediation, which is one of the reasons intermediaries reduce fees, but it is also at the heart of many other issues they face, like consolidation of the intermediaries and regulators: 'Financial intermediaries . . . make do with the market imperfections that mainly stem from informational asymmetries. They may reduce the information and transaction costs within the economy [motivating them to pass along these savings by reducing fees], but they still have to make do with agency problems and with moral hazard and adverse selection. In all, the financial intermediary is a more or less passive agent who intermediates between ultimate savers and investors. The process of disintermediation threatens the agent, as public financial markets promote a more efficient and transparent handling of the allocation of scarce resources in the economy, thanks to deregulation and information technology' (ibid. at 1249–50).

400. Intermediaries survive and profit from fragmented markets, where most investors have little or no knowledge of what the asset is, let alone its value. See Simon (1998, pp. 37–8) (finding that mutual fund investors did not correctly respond to 'basic questions about investment risks and strategies'). Thus, any device that increases transparency will increase competition among intermediaries. A counterintuitive conclusion drawn in some studies suggests that purchasers of securities originated by financial interme-

diaries may be more informed as to their value than the intermediaries themselves. See Mitchell (2004, p. 3) (identifying a type of asymmetric information problem unique to financial intermediaries). According to this theory: '[I]ntermediaries originating loans may be less informed about the ultimate market value of their assets than are investment banks which may serve as arrangers; i.e., who purchase the assets, repackage them by pooling them with assets originated by other intermediaries, and sell the repackaged assets or securities backed by them. Arrangers will have better information about market values of assets when their pricing models are better than those used by the originators. Also, whereas each originator may have good knowledge of the cash flows from its own assets or asset pools, it does not generally possess data on the cash flows from other originators' pools, in contrast to arrangers, who may have access to such information' (ibid.). However, this hypothesis may be challenged by the subprime crisis that arose in 2007 as the result of defaults on subprime mortgages that were often originated with little or no documentation. See Bajaj and Anderson (2008, p. A1) (describing these problems).

401. See Schwarcz (2004) (stating that same point).
402. Ibid. at 15.
403. See Trade The News, 'About us', http://www.tradethenews.com/about-company-history.asp (describing its service as 'a pioneer in the completely on-demand and independent research model built around a voice "hoot" network geared towards professional traders that require instant answers').
404. F.3d (D.C. Cir. Aug. 6, 2010).
405. 15 U.S.C. §78f.
406. DeCovny (2010).
407. Exchange ownership by intermediaries is nothing new in either the security or commodity industries. Prior to demutualization, clearing members were required to own a certain number of seats in each category of membership. See for example CME (2004) (highlighting the reduction of Class A shares the exchange required clearing members to own and reserve from 72093 to 30000). Most clearing members purchased the minimum required and did nothing more. Others, however, purchased additional seats for various reasons, but these additional purchases increased the number of votes come election time without much more. Many commodity firms do not have the same incentives, nor did they have the financing necessary to purchase such large stakes. A notable exception is Man Group, PLC's purchase of 70 percent of the US Futures Exchange's outstanding shares. See Press Release (2006).
408. See Futures Industry Association (2007) (summarizing risk management practices for clients with direct access to an exchange's trading system among specified exchanges and futures commission merchants generally).
409. See Hasbrouck and Saar (2010) (describing the advantages that accrue to HFTs).
410. See Kay (2009, pp. 5–6) (describing the speed of light as a fundamental barrier and the potential costs to HFTs).
411. See Budimir and Schweickert (2009, p. 47).
412. Ibid. at p. 50 (noting the importance of identifying where the measuring is being conducted and what is being measured).
413. See Madrigal (2010) (describing efforts to determine the trading strategy of 'trading bots' by reproducing pictures of their orders and trading prices). A trading bot is a software program that automatically generates orders.
414. See Rodier (2005, p. 3) (analyzing the development of algorithmic trading in emerging markets and stating that: 'exchanges in such places as Brazil and India have been actively increasing their capacity in terms of lower latency and throughput [while] regulators in these markets are relaxing their rules to boost electronic trading and their competitiveness in the global marketplace').
415. Regulators often base information sharing arrangements on delegations of authority provided the regulator establishes certain 'findings' with respect to the need to receive and provide information. For example, the International Securities Enforcement Cooperation Act of 1990 amended section 24 of the Securities Exchange Act of 1934 and authorized the SEC to 'in its discretion and upon a showing that such information is needed, provide all "records" . . . and other information in its possession to such persons, both domestic and foreign, as the Commission by rule deems appropriate.' Pub. L. 101–550, title II, § 202(c), Nov. 15, 1990, 104 Stat. 2715 (codified at 15 U.S.C. 78x(c)).
416. One of the most significant changes imposed by Dodd–Frank is the requirement for every swap or securities-based swap transaction to be reported to a trade repository regardless of whether the transaction is ultimately cleared through a central counterparty or not. See Dodd–Frank §712(d)(2)(B) (requiring the CFTC, SEC and Federal Reserve to establish rules that specify the data elements that shall be collected by swap repositories). Indeed, this is an indication of the difficulty facing all regulators of OTC derivatives. However, the requirement of parties to report into the repository is not the only issue, whether a repository, and the extent to which a repository can share information to regulators other than its primary regulator is an issue yet to be resolved by regulators. This is not so much an issue for repositories based in the US, where privacy laws are more permissive, but more so for those based

in jurisdictions with significant privacy protections. To the extent that these jurisdictions restrict the amount of data that supervisors outside of the jurisdiction receive data, regulators are less likely to agree that the sole repository for an asset class be domiciled there, and more likely market participants are likely to want it domiciled there.

417. See for example Danninger et al. (2009) (analyzing the effect of the current crisis on the transmission of banking crises between developed and emerging economies).
418. Bank for International Settlements (2008) ('BIS Interdependencies').
419. Bank for International Settlements (2005, p. 30) (noting that 'financial institutions have become more active in foreign markets, increasing the demand for cross-border payments in multiple currencies and contributing to the international integration of financial markets').
420. See Danninger et al. (2009, p. 144) (suggesting that the extent to which common global factors will have an impact on financial crises is 'likely related to the increasing financial integration of the majority of emerging economies in the past decades – in other words, financial globalization').
421. BIS Interdependencies (2008, p. 16).
422. Ibid.
423. Ibid. at 47; see also Rodier (2005, p. 34) (noting that Brazil recently passed new rules addressing sponsored access for equities markets that allow high-frequency traders to access low latency markets without pre-execution controls).
424. See Reinhart and Rogoff (2010, p. 73) (summarizing data that concludes 'a high incidence of global banking crises has historically been associated with a high incidence of sovereign defaults').
425. During the aftermath of global recessions, most countries have the same motivation to stimulate domestic production. By lowering the relative value of their currency, a central bank expects to stimulate external demand for products priced in its currency, presumably stimulating domestic production, thereby increasing domestic production and growth. See Kaminsky (1999, p. 6) (noting that 'with sticky prices, a devaluation may restore competitiveness and help in the elimination of unemployment, thus prompting [governments] to abandon the peg during recessions [and permit the currency to devalue]'). Thus, central banks, and the governments they serve, all share a bias towards 'competitive devaluations' or intervening in the currency markets to devalue their currency relative to others because monetary policies to combat inflation are easier to manage than those to manage deflation. See for example Eichengreen and Sachs (1986).
426. IOSCO (2010, p. 5) (noting that 'securities and derivatives exchanges are today overwhelmingly electronic, which has facilitated their operations globally through various forms of communication').
427. Ibid. at 5–6.
428. Dodd–Frank §738.
429. Congress provided regulators with a significant amount of latitude in defining many of the key elements that will implement Dodd–Frank. For instance, revised CEA section 4(b)(1)(A) states that registration requirements would be applied to FBOTs that provide 'an explicit grant of authority by a foreign board of trade to an identified member or other participant located in the [US] to enter trades directly into the trade matching system of the foreign board of trade.' If the CFTC defines 'explicit grant' narrowly, many FBOTs will escape cross-jurisdictional regulation. FBOTs could then focus on regulations issued by their primary regulator, keeping the cross-border regulatory scheme fractional.
430. Ibid. (adding section 22(e)(6) to the CEA).
431. Some members have suggested behind the scenes that a review of the impact of algorithmic trading on equities markets is necessary and might be forthcoming in June 2011.
432. See Program Guide for September 2010.
433. See note 409 and accompanying text.
434. See Sears (2010) (quoting a speech made by Thomas Peterffy, 'Technology, market structure and new products have evolved more quickly than our capacity to understand or control them.') Moreover, 'Peterffy has directed his trading firm, Timber Hill, to stop making markets in 50 exchange-traded funds' with a plan to eventually 'gradually widen quoted prices, and cut the size of trading commitments' (ibid.).

BIBLIOGRAPHY

Acworth, W. (2007a), 'Algorithmic trading, seeking an edge', *Futures Industry Magazine*, July–August, p. 2.

Acworth, W. (2007b), 'Intellectual property roundtable: what do current trends in patent law mean for the futures industry?' *Futures Industry Magazine*, November–December, p. 56.

Anand, S. (2010), 'Adviser says no to ETFs', *Wall Street Journal*, 4 October, p. R4.

Andersen, M. (2000), 'Manager's Journal: don't CLOBber ECNs', *Wall Street Journal*, 27 March, p. A48.
Anderson, J. (2005), 'Big board deal may tip world of floor trades', *New York Times*, 21 April, p. A1.
Anderson, J. and M. Fackler (2007), 'NYSE makes alliance with Tokyo exchange', *New York Times*, 1 February, p. C3.
Anderson, J. and L. Thomas Jr. (2007), 'Merrill Lynch to hire chief of big board', *New York Times*, 15 November, p. A1.
'Another unspecial study, the SEC's Market 2000 Report and competitive developments in the United States capital markets' (1995), *Business Lawyer*, **50**, 485–513.
Arbit, T.S. (2007), 'Commodity Futures Trading Commission General Counsel, testimony at the Hearing before the CFTC to examine trading on regulated exchanges and exempt commercial markets', 18 September, http://www.cftc.gov/stellent/groups/public/@newsroom/documents/speechandtestimony/opaarbit_091807.pdf.
Arbor, P. (1997), 'Statement of Patrick Arbor, Chairman, Chicago Board Of Trade', Testimony before the Risk Management and Specialty Crops Subcommittee of the US House Agriculture Committee, 29 October.
Associated Press (1993), 'Globex operating proposal', *New York Times*, 5 November, p. D12.
Associated Press (2007a), 'Deutsche Borse agrees to buy options market in New York', *New York Times*, 1 May, p. C10.
Associated Press (2007b), 'Shareholders approve Merc's buyout of CBOT', *New York Times*, 10 July, p. C2.
Authers, J. (2007), 'Nationalism Bites the Dust', *Financial Times*, 19 November, p. 1.
Bajaj, V. and J. Anderson (2008), 'Inquiry focuses on withholding of data on loans', *New York Times*, 12 January, p. A1.
Baker, W.E. (1984), 'Floor trading and crowd dynamics', in Patricia A. Adler and Peter Adler (eds), *The Social Dynamics Of Financial Markets*, Greenwich, CN: JAI Press.
Bank for International Settlements (BIS) (eds) (2001), 'Group of Ten report on consolidation in the financial sector', http://www.imf.org/external/np/g10/2001/01/Eng/pdf/file3.pdf.
Bank for International Settlements (BIS) (2007), 'Implications of electronic trading on the financial markets', *BIS Quarterly Review*, March, p. 58.
Barboza, D. (2000), 'In Chicago trading pits, this may be the final generation', *New York Times*, 6 August, § 3 p. 1.
Barboza, D. and J. Gerth (1998), 'Who's in charge? Agency infighting and regulatory uncertainty', *New York Times*, 15 December, p. C14.
Barr, P.G. (1998), 'US favors open outcry: international electronic derivatives exchange opens', *Pensions and Investments*, 14 December, p. 23.
Basar, S. (2007), 'Bats trading files for exchange status', *Financial News Online*, 6 November, http://www.financialnewsus.com/index.cfm?page=ushome&contentid=2349117265&printview=true, accessed 6 May 2008.
Berg, E.N. (1989), '2 big futures exchanges in a race', *New York Times*, 11 April, p. D2.
Berman, D.K. (2010), 'The game: saving the stock market only to destroy it', *Wall Street Journal*, 24 August, p. C1.
Bettelheim, E.C. and J.W Markham (1990), 'The Transnor decision and its aftermath', *Oil and Gas Law and Taxation Review*, **8**, 76.
Bickerton, I. and N. Cohen (2006), 'Dutch seek control of NYSE body', *Financial Times*, 19 December, p. 24.
BlackRock (2010), 'ETF landscape: a review of the exchange traded funds (ETFs) and exchange traded products (ETPs)', *Industry*, 15 July, p. 2.
Bloomberg News (2007), 'Trading-floor changes hurt LaBranche', *New York Times*, 10 July, p. C12.
Borrelli, M. (2001), 'Market making in the electronic age', *Loyola University Chicago Law Journal*, **32**, 815–23.
Brandes, Y. and I. Domowitz (2010), 'Alternative trading systems in Europe, trading performance by European venues post-MiFID', *Journal of Trading*, **5**, 17–30.
Browning, L. (2007), 'Decoding the markets 101, for the soon-to-retire', *New York Times*, 12 November, p. C8.
Brunet, A. and M. Shafe (2007), 'Beyond Enron: regulation in energy derivatives trading', *Northwestern Journal of International Law and Business*, **27**, 665.
Buckman, R. (1999), 'Plan by Chicago Exchange to offer extended trading is sign of the times', *Wall Street Journal*, 23August, p. C11.
Budimir, M. and U. Schweickert (2009), 'Latency in electronic securities trading: a proposal for systematic measurement', *Journal of Trading*, Summer, 47–55.
Bunge, J. (2010a), 'Plan would expand market makers', *Wall Street Journal*, 12 August, p. C3.
Bunge, J. (2010b), 'CBOE lures street banks, brokers', *Wall Street Journal*, 2 September, p. C3.
Bunge, J. (2010c), 'Exchanges propose new rules for market makers', *Wall Street Journal*, 20 September, p. C4.
Bunge, J., B. Baskin and S. Pulliam (2010), 'CME test orders went live', *Wall Street Journal*, 15 September, p. C3.
Cameron, D. (2006), 'Trading rivalry goes back 100 years', *Financial Times*, 18 October, p. 19.
Carson, J.W. (2003), 'Conflicts of interest in self-regulation: can demutualized exchanges successfully

manage them?' World Bank Policy Research Working Paper Series, Paper No. 3183, http://ssrn.com/abstract=636602.
'Central repository key to reducing systemic risk in OTC markets, DTCC says' (2009), *Securities Regulation and Law Report (BNA)* **41**, 1730, 21 September.
Ceron, G.F. (2007), 'Moving the market: NYSE to split board evenly with Euronext', *Wall Street Journal*, 24 January, C1.
CFTC (2010), 'Rule enforcement review of the Chicago Board of Trade and the Chicago Mercantile Exchange', 13 September.
Chicago Board of Trade (CBOT) (2006), *Electronic Trading Platform Reference Manual* (version 2.2), http://www.cbot.com/cbot/docs/74585.pdf.
Chicago Mercantile Exchange (2007a), 'Allocation algorithm for CME Eurodollar options', http://www.cme.com/trading/get/abt/functionality/edo.html (accessed 17 October 2007).
Chicago Mercantile Exchange (2007b), 'Lead Market Maker ("LMM") allocation algorithm', http://www.cme.com/trading/get/abt/functionality/lmm.html (accessed 17 October 2007).
Christie, W.G. and P.H. Schultz (1994), 'Why do NASDAQ market makers avoid odd-eighth quotes', *Journal of Finance*, **49**, 1813–14.
Cleveland, S.J. (2005), 'The NYSE as state actor? Rational actors, behavioral insights and joint investigations', *American University Law Review*, **55,** 1.
'Click boom: how electronic trading served as a catalyst in the creation of CME group' (2007), *CME Group Magazine*, Summer, p. 26.
CME (2004), 'CME reduces class a share requirement to attract new market participants', 9 September.
CME (2007), 'CME messaging policy for the Globex® Platform', 17 February.
CME Group (2007), 'CME Globex: the world's leading electronic trading platform', http://www.cmegroup.com/globex/files/CMEMessagingPolicy.pdf, accessed 28 May 2008.
Cohen, P.D. (1999), 'Securities trading via the Internet', *Stanford Journal of Law, Business and Finance*, **4**, 1.
Collins, A.L. (2002), 'Regulation of alternative trading systems: evolving regulatory models and prospects for increased regulatory coordination and convergence', *Law and Policy in International Business*, **33**, 481.
Committee on the Global Financial System (2001), 'Implications of Electronic Trading on the Financial Markets', Bank for International Settlements, January, p. 1.
Commodity Futures Trading Commission, 'About the commitments of traders report', www.cftc.gov/opa/backgrounder/opacot596.htm, accessed 11 April 2008.
Commodity Futures Trading Commission, 'Historical Commitments of Traders', www.cftc.gov/cftc/cftchistoricalcot.htm, accessed 7 March 2007.
Commodity Futures Trading Commission (1999), 'Report on gold options trading', 28 September, http://www.cftc.gov/tm/tmgold_options_report031000.htm.
Commodity Futures Trading Commission (2002a), 'Report on the futures industry response to September 11th', 11 March, http://www.cftc.gov/files/opa/opa9-11reportprintversion.pdf.
Commodity Futures Trading Commission (2002b), 'Technology advisory committee, best practices for organized electronic markets', 24 April, http://www.cftc.gov/stellent/groups/public/@aboutcftc/documents/file/acinterimmarketaccessreport.pdf.
Commodity Futures Trading Commission (2006a), 'Commission actions in response to the Comprehensive Review of the Commitments of Traders Reporting Program', http://www.cftc.gov/stellent/groups/public/@commitmentsoftraders/documents/file/noticeonsupplementalcotrept.pdf.
Commodity Futures Trading Commission (2006b), 'Commitments of traders reports', 3 January, http://cftc.gov/marketreports/commitmentsoftraders/cot010306.html, accessed 28 May 2008.
Commodity Futures Trading Commission (2006c), 'Commission action in response to the Comprehensive Review of the Commitments of Traders Reporting Program', 5 December, p. 6.
Commodity Futures Trading Commission (2006d – Present), 'Historical commitments of traders commodity index trader Supplement Reports', http://www.cftc.gov/marketreports/commitmentsoftraders/index.htm, accessed 27 April 2008.
Commodity Futures Trading Commission (2008), 'Commitments of traders reports', 22 April, http://cftc.gov/marketreports/commitmentsoftraders /cot042208.html, accessed 28 may 2008.
Conference on Automation in the Futures Industry (1977), Washington, DC, 15 June.
Corcoran, A.M. (2000), 'The uses of new capital markets: electronic commerce and the rules of the game in an international marketplace', *American University Law Review*, **49**, 581–8.
Council on Foreign Relations (2009), 'Credit default swaps, clearinghouses, and exchanges', Squam Lake Working Group on Financial Regulation, July, 1–8. Available at: http://www.cfr.org/financial-crises/credit-default-swaps-clearinghouses-exchanges/p19756.
Cowell, A. (2000a), '2 stock exchanges in Europe to merge, with Nasdaq', *Wall Street Journal*, 4 May, p. A1.
Cowell, A. (2000b), 'Liffe goes silent', *New York Times*, 25 November, p. C2.
Cox, C. (2009), 'Swapping secrecy for transparency', *New York Times*, 19 October, p. WK12.

Cox, C.C. and D.C. Michael (1987), 'The market for markets: development of international securities and commodities trading', *Catholic University Law Review*, **36,** 833–41.
Crawford Jr., W.B. (1991), 'German exchange plans broad computer trading', *Chicago Tribune*, 26 June, p. C3.
Crovitz, L.G. (2008), 'When even good news worsens a panic', *Wall Street Journal*, 24 November, p. A17.
Dale, C. and J. Zyren (1996), 'Noncommercial trading in the energy futures market', *Petroleum Marketing Monthly*, May, xiii–xxiv.
Dale, H. (2010), 'Opaque business holds back growth', *Financial Times*, 4 April, http://www.ft.com/cms/s/0/c829b812-3dbb-11df-bdbb-00144feabdc0.html.
Danninger, S., R. Balakrishnan, S. Elekdag and I. Tytell (2009), 'Chapter Four: How linkages fuel the fire: the transmission of financial stress from advanced to emerging economies', *World Economic Outlook*, April, 133–66.
De Bel, J. (1993), 'Automated trading systems and the concept of an "exchange" in an international context. Proprietary systems: a regulatory headache!', *University of Pennsylvania Journal of International Business Law*, **14**, 164–74.
DeCovny, S. (2010), To cap or not to cap', *Futures Industry Magazine*, September, p. 51.
de la Merced, M.J. (2006), 'Big board, moving toward electronic trading, to lay off 500', *New York Times*, 9 November, p. C3.
de la Merced, M.J. (2007), 'Citadel throws E*Trade a $2.55 billion lifeline', *New York Times*, 30 November, p.C3.
Department of the Treasury (2008), 'Blueprint for a modernized financial regulatory structure', March, http://www.treasury.gov.
Division of Market Regulation, United States Securities and Exchange Commission (1994), 'Market 2000: an examination of current equity market developments', January, Washington, DC: Division of Market Regulation, United States Securities and Exchange Commission. Available at: http://www.sec.gov/divisions/marketreg/market2000.pdf.
Domanski, D. and A. Heath (2007), 'Financial investors and commodity markets', *BIS Quarterly Review*, March, 53–67.
Domowitz, I., I. Finkelshteyn and H. Yegerman (2008), 'Cul de sacs and highways: an optical tour of dark pool trading performance', mimeo, August.
Donville, C. (2007), 'ICE to buy grain trader', *International Herald Tribune* (Paris), 25 June, p. 13.
Douglas, W.O. (1940), *Democracy and Finance: The Addresses and Public Statements of William O. Douglas as Member and Chairman of the Securities and Exchange Commission*, edited with an introduction and notes by James Allen (1969), Port Washington, NY: Kennikat Press.
Dowell, A. (2007), 'NYSE's floor suffers pair of defections', *Wall Street Journal*, 16 November, p. C2.
Duffy, B. (1992), 'The human element, one man's opinion: I trust a market when I can hear it breathing', *Life Magazine*, Spring, 17–18.
Eales, B. and M. Choudry (2003), *Derivative Instruments: A Guide to Theory and Practice,* Boston, MA: Butterworth-Heinemann.
Edmonston, P. (2006), 'Private firm sells broker and makes quick profit', *New York Times*, 3 November, p. C3.
Eichengreen, B. and J. Sachs (1986), 'Competitive devaluation and the great depression: a theoretical reassessment', *Economic Letters*, **22**, 67–71.
Eichenwald, K. (1992), 'Robert William Haack, 75, dies; led stock exchange during crisis', *New York Times*, 16 June, p. B8.
Euronext (2007), 'Functional overview of LIFFE CONNECT® market-making functionalities (ver. 0.3)', 22 May, http://www.euronext.com/fic/000/021/346/213462.pdf.
Ewing, T. (1999), 'NASD presents details of its plan for Nasdaq Europe', *Wall Street Journa*l, 5 November, p. C12.
Feder, B.J. (1992), 'Chicago's exchanges look toward an electronic salvation', *New York Times*, 29 November, §3, p. 5.
Feder, B.J. (1994), 'The Chicago Board of Trade will leave Globex network', *New York Times*, 16 April, §1, p. 35.
Feder, B.J. (1997), 'Face lift at Board of Trade: high tech, say hello to primal instinct', *New York Times*, 17 February, §1, p. 41.
Finders, K. (2007), 'Evolution of stock market technology', *Computerweekly.co*, 2 November, http://www.computerweekly.com/Articles/2007/11/02/227883/the-evolution-of-stock-market-technology.htm.
Fleckner, A.M. (2006), 'Stock exchanges at the crossroads', *Fordham Law Review*, **74**, 2541–42.
Flynn Siler, J. (1989), 'Board of Trade plans computerized trading', *New York Times*, 10 February, p. D6.
Foley, S. (2007), 'Single error costs mighty Morgan Stanley $8 bn', *Independent* (London), 20 December, http://findarticles.com/p/articles/mi_qn4158/is_20071220/ai_n21164197.

Futures Industry Association (2007), 'Profile of exchange and FCM risk management practices for direct access customers', http://www.futuresindustry.org/downloads/DMADecember32007.pdf.
Gallagher, D.M. (1998), 'Comment, move over tickertape, here comes the cyber-exchange: the rise of internet-based securities trading systems', *Catholic University Law Review*, **47**, 1009–25.
Gasparino, C. (2007), *King of the Club: Richard Grasso and the Survival of New York*, New York: Harper.
Gibson, W.E. (1999), 'Are swap agreements securities or futures?: the inadequacies of applying the traditional regulatory approach to OTC derivatives transactions', *Journal of Corporation Law*, **24**, 379–414.
Gilberg, D.J. (1986), 'Regulation of new financial instruments under the federal securities and commodities laws', *Vanderbilt Law Review*, **39**, 1599.
Gilpin, K.N. (1987), 'Early reviews favor Chicago night trading', *New York Times*, 18 May, p. D1.
Greenhouse, S. (1984), 'At the Merc: optimism hedged with caution', *New York Times*, 7 September, p. D1.
Greenspan, A. (2007a), *The Age of Turbulence, Adventures in a New World*, New York: Penguin Press.
Greenspan, A. (2007b), 'Remarks before the futures industry annual conference', *Commodity Futures Law Reporter* (CCH), 14 March, p. 782.
Greising, D. and L. Morse (1991), *Brokers, Bagmen and Moles, Fraud and Corruption in the Chicago Futures Markets*, New York: Wiley.
Gross, D. (2007), 'The capital of capital no more', *New York Times*, 14 October, §6, p. 62.
Gutierres, T. (1989), 'Scandals in Chicago; automate the futures exchanges', *New York Times*, 31 December, §3, p. 2.
Haigh, M.S., J. Hranaiova and J.A. Overdahl (2005), 'Price dynamics, price discovery and large futures trader interactions in the energy complex', 25 April, www.cftc.gov/files/opa/press05/opacftc-managed-money-trader-study.pdf.
Hamilton, R.W. (1995), 'Corporate governance in America 1950–2000: major changes but uncertain benefits', *Journal of Corporation Law*, **25**, 349–67.
Hasbrouck, J. and G. Saar (2010), 'Low Latency Trading', working paper, 2 October.
Hendelman, S. (2010), 'A flawed model: relying on HFT for liquidity', *Advanced Trading*, October, p. 38.
Henriques, D.B. (2007), 'Failed bid is setback for growth at Nasdaq', *New York Times*, 12 February, p. C1.
Hershey, R.D. (2000), 'The markets: stocks and bonds, Dow comes back from plunge but ends below 10000', *New York Times*, 19 October, p. C10.
Horwich, A. (2006), 'Warnings to the unwary: multi-jurisdictional federal enforcement of manipulation and deception in the energy markets after the energy Policy Act of 2005', *Energy Law Journal*, **27**, 363–8.
Ingebretsen, M. (2002), *Nasdaq: A History of the Market That Changed the World*, Roseville, CA: Forum Press.
International Swaps and Derivatives Association, Inc. (2009), 'Market survey', http://www.isda.org/statistics/pdf/ISDA-Market-Survey-historical-data.pdf, accessed 12 November 2009.
IOSCO (2010), 'Final report on principles for direct electronic access to markets', August, p. 5.
Johnson, F. (2010), 'SEC plans trader ID system – agency is trying to get its arms around "high frequency" transactions', *Wall Street Journal*, 15 April.
Kaminsky, G.L. (1999), 'Currency and banking crises: the early warnings of distress', IMF Institute Working Paper, December.
Kanter, J. (2006), 'Deustche Borse ends its quest for Euronext', *New York Times*, 16 November, p. C14.
Kanter, J. (2007), 'Trans-Atlantic exchange to be listed today', *New York Times*, 4 April, p. C2.
Karmel, R.S. (2002), 'Turning seats into shares: causes and implications of demutualization of stock and futures exchanges', *Hastings Law Journal*, **53**, 367.
Kay, R. (2009), 'Pragmatic network latency engineering fundamental facts and analysis', cPacket Networks.
Keaveny, J. (2005), 'In defense of market self-regulation: an analysis of the history of futures regulation and the trend toward demutalization', *Brooklyn Law Review*, **70**, 1419.
Ketchum R.G. and B.E. Weimer (1994), 'Market 2000 and the Nasdaq stock market', *Journal of Corporation Law*, **19**, 559–77.
Klock, M. (1999), 'The SEC's new regulation ATS: placing the myth of market fragmentation ahead of economic theory and evidence', *Florida Law Review*, **51**, 753–68.
Koppel, N. (2007), 'In Chicago, a rowdy trading scene grows quieter', *New York Times*, 29 October, p. A10.
Labaton, S. (2002), 'Nasdaq wins battle at SEC on new system for trading', *New York Times*, 29 August, p. C5.
Laise, E. (2010), 'Futures flounder', *Wall Street Journal*, 4–5 September, p. B9.
Lauricella, T. and S. Patterson (2010), 'Legacy of the flash crash: enduring worries of repeat', *Wall Street Journal*, 6 August, p. A1.
Lauricella, T. and J. Strasburg (2010), 'SEC probes cancelled trades', *Wall Street Journal*, 2 September, p. A1.
Leigh Cowan, A. (1987), 'Exchange employees begin strike', *New York Times*, 11 November, p. D1.
Leising, M. (2010), 'How Wall Street gamed derivatives reform', *Bloomberg*, 27 May.
Levitt, A. (2000), 'The future of our markets: dynamic markets, timeless principles', *Columbia Business Law Review*, **1**, 5.
Lohr, S. (1984), 'Singapore's link to Chicago', *New York Times*, 7 September, p. D3.

Lohse, D. (1998), 'Nasdaq investors as late as July 1996 may be eligible for stake in settlement', *Wall Street Journal*, 5 January, p. C17.
Lucchetti, A. (2006), 'Fast lane: firms seek edge through speed as computer trading expands – Tradebot moves its machines into exchange buildings; competitors follow suit – 100 million shares in a day', *Wall Street Journal*, 15 December, p. A1.
Lucchetti, A. (2007a), 'Niederauer's first challenge: NYSE floor traders' future', 21 January, *Wall Street Journal*, p. C1.
Lucchetti, A. (2007b), 'The NYSE: faster (and lonelier)', *Wall Street Journal*, 24 January, p.C1.
Lucchetti, A. (2007c), 'Hi, "Designated Market Makers"', *Wall Street Journal*, 30 November, p. C14.
Lucchetti, A. (2008), 'NYSE deal may force Amex to eliminate 75% of staff', *Wall Street Journal*, 5 May, p. C1.
Lukken, W. (2006), Comm'r, Commodity Futures Trading Commission, 'The derivatives world is flat, address at the ISDA Energy, Commodities and Developing Products Conference', 14 June, http://www.cftc.gov/newsroom/speechestestimony/opalukken-20.html.
MacDonald, A. (2007), 'New rules to cut hassle, expense of trades in EU', *Wall Street Journal*, 29 October, p. C1.
MacRae, D. (1999), 'The future of futures: two big steps to a level playing field', December, http://www.leomelamed.com/articles/mar1299.htm.
MacRae, D. (2003), 'A bad bet for public exchanges? Demutualization is not the only answer', *Traders Magazine*, January, p. 2, http://www.tradersmagazine.com/issues/20030131/1493-1.html?page=1.
Madrigal, A. (2010), 'Explaining bizarre robot stock trader behavior', *Atlantic*, 6 August.
Maidenberg, H.J. (1984a), 'Futures/options; big growth in orders paralyzing trading pits', *New York Times*, 19 March, p. D6.
Maidenberg, H.J. (1984b), 'Influencing cash markets', *New York Times*, 28 April, p. D12.
Maidenberg, H.J. (1984c), 'Futures/options; automation in trading', *New York Times*, 10 December, p. D4.
Mallaby, S. (2010), *More Money Than God*, New York: Penguin Press.
Markham, J.W. (1989), 'Prohibited floor trading activities under the Commodity Exchange Act', *Fordham Law Review*, **58**, 1–52.
Markham, J.W. (1990), 'Regulation of hybrid instruments under the Commodity Exchange Act: a call for alternatives', *Columbia Business Law Review*, **1**, 40–53.
Markham, J.W. (1991), 'The commodity exchange monopoly – reform is needed', *Washington and Lee Law Review*, **48**, 977–1009.
Markham, J.W. (2002a), *A Financial History of the United States, From J.P. Morgan to the Institutional Investors (1900–1970)*, Vol. 2, Armonk, NY: M.E. Sharpe.
Markham, J.W. (2002b), *A Financial History of the United States, From the Age of Derivatives to the Internet (1970–2001)*, Vol. 3, Armonk, NY: M.E. Sharpe.
Markham, J.W. (2006), *A Financial History of Modern US Corporate Scandals: From Enron to Reform*, Armonk, NY: M.E. Sharpe.
Markham, J.W. (2007), 'Regulating excess executive compensation – why bother?', *Journal of Business and Technology Law*, **2**, 277–317.
Markham, J.W. (2009), 'Regulating credit default swaps in the wake of the subprime crisis', Working Paper for the International Monetary Fund Seminar on Current Developments in Monetary and Financial Law, 2 December, Washington, DC.
Markham, J.W. (2010a), *A Financial History of the United States, From Enron Era Scandals to the Subprime Crisis (2004–2006)*, Armonk, NY: M.E. Sharpe.
Markham, J.W. (2010b), 'SEC v. Goldman Sachs & Co. – Serious fraud or just more banker bashing', *Futures and Derivatives Law Report*, **30**, 8.
Markham, J.W. and D. Harty (2008), 'For whom the bell tolls: the demise of exchange trading floors and the growth of ECNs', *Iowa Journal of Corporation Law*, **33**, 865–939.
Markham, J.W. and T.L. Hazen (2010), '23A broker dealer operations under securities and commodities law: financial responsibilities, credit regulation, and customer protection', §12:33; and '13A Commodities regulation: fraud, manipulation and other claims', §27:14.50.
Markham, J.W. and L. Hunt Jr. (2004), 'The California energy crisis – Enron's gaming of Governor Gray's imperfect market', *Futures and Derivatives Law Report*, April, p. 1.
Markham, J.W. and R. McCloy Stephanz (1988), 'The stock market crash of 1987: the United States looks at new recommendations', *Georgetown Law Journal*, **76**, 1993–2010.
Masters, B. (2007), 'US investors gain "top cop" to police brokers', *Financial Times*, 31 July, p. 4.
Matus, G. (2001), 'Note, the regulation of alternative trading systems: market fragmentation and new market structure', *New York Law School Law Review*, **44**, 583–93.
Maynard, T.H. (1992), 'What is an "exchange?" Proprietary electronic securities trading systems and the statutory definition of an exchange', *Washington and Lee Law Review*, **49**, 833–912.

McCarroll, E.M. (2000), 'Regulation of electronic communications networks: an examination of Tradepoint Financial Network's SEC approval to become the first non-American exchange to operate in the United States', *Cornell International Law Journal*, **33**, 211–62.
McGeehan, P. (2007), 'Next to downsize on Wall Street? The exchange floor', *New York Times*, 23 September, § 1, p. 37.
Melamed, L. (1977), 'The mechanics of a commodity futures exchange: a critique of automation of the transaction process', *Hofstra Law Review*, **6**, 149–72.
Melamed, L. (1999), 'Address before the derivatives and risk expo', *Futures Markets in the Digital Century*, 11–12 May, http://www.leomelamed.com/essays/99-fow.htm.
Melamed, L. (2006), 'The future of futures in the twenty-first century', *Futures Industry Magazine*, March–April, 44–5.
Melamed, L. and B. Tamarkin (1996), 'Escape to the futures', http://www.leomelamed.com/essays/99-fow.htm.
Miltich, K.M. (2003), 'A slap on the wrist: Dynegy, Inc. v. Securities and Exchange Commission', *North Carolina Journal of International Law and Commercial Regulation*, **28**, 983.
Mitchell, J. (2004), 'Financial intermediation theory and the sources of value in structured finance markets', National Bank of Belgium working paper, http://www-bis-org/publ/cgfs23mitchell.pdf.
Mittra, S. (1971), *Inside Wall Street*, Homewood, IL: Dow-Jones Irwin.
Morgenson, G. (1999). 'Big board ready to open the e-gates', *New York Times*, 28 November, § 3, p. 1.
Morrissey, J. (2008), 'Credit default swaps: the next crisis', *Time Magazine*, 17 March, http://www.time.com/time/business/article/0,8599,1723152,00.html.
NASD (2000), 'Notice to Members 00-07, Disclosure to customers engaging in extended hours trading', January, http://www.finra.org/RulesRegulation/NoticestoMembers/2000NoticestoMembers/P003862.
Norris, F. (1995), 'Investors to get bigger role in running Nasdaq market', *New York Times*, 20 September, p. D1.
Norris, F. (1996), 'Tough crackdown on Nasdaq market announced by US', *New York Times*, 8 August, http://www.nytimes.com/1996/08/09/business/tough-crackdown-on-nasdaq-market-announced-by-us.html.
Nowak, G.T. (1993), 'Note, a failure of communication: an argument for the closing of the NYSE floor', *University of Michigan Journal of Law Reform*, **26**, 485.
Nyquist, P. (1995), 'Failure to engage: the regulation of proprietary trading systems', *Yale Law and Policy Review*, **13**, 281–338.
Nystedt, J. (2004), 'Derivative market competition: OTC markets versus organized derivative exchanges', International Monetary Fund, Working Paper No. WP/04/61, http://ssrn.com/abstract=878884.
Oesterle, D.A. (1998), 'The SEC's assault on electronic trading, regulation', *Regulation: The Cato Review of Business and Government*, Summer, 17, 18.
Oesterle, D.A. (2005), 'Regulation NMS: has the SEC exceeded its congressional mandate to facilitate a "National Market System" in securities trading?' *New York University Journal of Law and Business*, **1**, 613.
Opiela, N. (2004), 'Why is it so quiet in the trading room? Change in order flow characteristics is likely culprit', *CFA Magazine*, January–February, p. 46.
Ortega, E. (2007), 'Bats market doubles its business after cutting trading fees', *Bloomberg News*, 4 January, http://www.batstrading.com/news_articlepdf/Bats%20Doubles%CC20its%CC20Business%CC20After%CC20uCtting%CC20Trading% 20Fees.pdf.
Paredes, T.A. (2006), 'On the decision to regulate hedge funds: the SEC's regulatory philosophy, style, and mission', *University of Illinois Law Review*, **2006**, 975–1027.
Parker, Donn B. (1998), *Fighting Computer Crime*, New York: John Wiley & Sons.
Patterson, S. (2010a), 'Superfast traders' new edge – investment firms grab stock data first, and use it seconds before others', *Wall Street Journal*, 4 June, p. C1.
Patterson, S. (2010b), 'Fast traders face off with big investors over "Gaming"', *Wall Street Journal*, 30 June, p. C1.
Patterson, S. (2010c), 'Market makers push change', *Wall Street Journal*, 13 July, p. C3.
Pedersen-Pietersen, L. (1998), 'Minding your business: how do you keep them in the casino once they've seen the cocoa pit?' *New York Times*, 13 September, § 3, p. 10.
Peterson, K. and Kardos Yesalavich, D. (2010), 'Lime brokerage introduces "Naked" trading platform', *Wall Street Journal*, 25 March, p. C9.
Pirrong, S.C. (1995), 'The self-regulation of commodity exchanges: the case of market manipulation', *Journal of Law and Economics*, **38**, 141–206.
Plasencia, W. (1995), 'Clearing firms gain new clout by supplying investment services that can provide edge', *American Banker*, 20 July, p. 14.
Postal, A.D. (2009), 'Credit default swaps belong under supervision of states', *P&C National Underwriter*, 23 February, http://www.property-casualty.com/Issues/2009/7/Pages/Credit-Default-Swaps-Belong-Under-Supervision-Of-States.aspx, accessed 12 November 2009.

Press Release (2003), 'Commodity Futures Trading Commission, recognizes new exchange', 7 August, http://www.cftc.gov/opa/press03/opa4831-03.htm.

Press Release (2006), 'US Futures Exchange, LLC, Man Group closes transaction on US Futures Exchange', 3 October, http://www.usfe.com/pr/USFECloseRelease-Final_Web.pdf.

Press Release (2007), 'Chicago Board Options Exchange, CBEO to launch exchange-traded credit default options in second quarter', 14 May, http://www.cboe.com/AboutCBOE/ShowDocument.aspx?DIR=ACNews&FILE=cboe_20070314a.doc.

Press Release (2008), 'CME group to host KCBT, MGEX electronic trading on CME Globex', CME Group, Inc., 11 January, http://cmegroup.mediaroom.com/index.php?s=43&item=672.

Press Release (2009), 'The Depository Trust & Clearing Corporation', DTCC Media Statement on General Motors Credit Default Swaps, 4 June, http://www.dtcc.com/news/press/releases/2009/gm_credit_default_swaps.php.

Raphaeli, N. and B. Gersten (2008), 'Sovereign wealth funds: investment vehicles for the Persian Gulf countries', *Middle East Quarterly*, Spring, 15.

Rattner, S. (1982), 'Financial futures set brisk pace in London', *New York Times*, 5 October, p. D9.

Rawnsley, J.H. (1996), *Total Risk: Nick Leeson and the Fall of Barings Bank*, New York: Harper-Collins.

Reinhart, C.M. and K.S. Rogoff (2010), *This Time is Different: Eight Centuries of Financial Folly*, Princeton, NJ: Princeton University Press.

Reuters (2007), 'Nasdaq to add an exchange', *New York Times*, 8 November, p. C7.

Roberts, R.Y. (1991), Comm'r, Securities & Exchange Commission, 'SEC progress towards internationalization, remarks before the Securities and Exchange Commission', 22 March.

Rodier, M. (2005), 'Global domination?' *Wall Street and Technology*, October, p. 3.

Roeder, D. (1998), 'CBOT pulls plug on night session; computer trades to replace evening floor action', *Chicago Sun-Times*, 30 January, p. 53.

Rogers, W.P. and J.W. Markham (1987), 'The application of West German statutes to United States commodity futures contracts: an unnecessary clash of policies', *Law and Policy in International Business*, **19**, 273–93.

Russo, T.A. (2006, April 20), 'A tribute to Leo Melamed in honor of the presentation of the 2005 CME Fred Arditti Innovation Award', http://www.leomelamed.com/currentevents/06-ArdittiRussoRemarks.htm (accessed 29 October 2007).

Safarik, D. (2005), 'How fast is fast enough?' *Wall Street and Technology*, 1 October, p. 33.

Schapiro, M.L. (2010), 'Written remarks "Strengthening our equity market structure"', http://www.sec.gov.

Schizer, D.M. (1992), 'Benign restraint: the SEC's regulation of execution systems', *Yale Law Journal*, **101**, 1551–75.

Schmerken, I. (2005), 'New ATSs arise to fill a void', *Wall Street and Technology*, 1 October, p. 31.

Scholtens, B. and D. van Wensveen (2000), 'A critique on the theory of financial intermediation', *Journal of Banking and Finance*, **24**, 1243–5.

Scholtens, B. and D. van Wensveen (2003), 'The theory of financial intermediation: an essay on what it does (not) explain', European Money and Finance Forum, Paper No. 2003/1, http://www.suerf.org/download/studies/study20031.pdf.

Schroeder, M. (1999), 'Nasdaq probe leads to fines, suspensions', *Wall Street Journal*, 12 January, p. B6.

Schroeder, M. and R. Smith (2000), 'Sweeping change in market structure sought: major firms propose central order system and single regulator', *Wall Street Journal*, 29 February, p. C1.

Schumer, C. (2000), 'A shot across the trading floor', *New York Times*, 5 May, p. A27.

Schwarcz, S.L. (2004), 'Rethinking the disclosure paradigm in a world of complexity', *University of Illinois Law Review*, **2004**, 1–37.

Sears, S.M. (2010), 'Confessions of a market maker', *Barron's*, 16 October, http://www.interactivebrokers.com/en/general/about/commentLetters.php?ib_entity=llc.

Securities & Exchange Commission (1963), *Report of the Special Study of the Securities Markets, Ch. VII: Over-the-Counter Markets*, http://sechistorical.org/collection/papers/1960/1963_SSMkt_Chapter_07_1.pdf.

Shapiro, E. (1989), 'Globex trading system delayed and disputed', *New York Times*, 26 December, p. D2.

Silva Laughlin, L. (2009), 'Is the A.I.G. rally a little early?', *New York Times*, 8 September, p. B2.

Simon, M.J. and R.L.D. Colby (1986), 'The national market system for over-the-counter stocks', *George Washington Law Review*, **55**, 17–29.

Simon, R. (1998), 'We put investors to the test-and boy, did they ever flunk', *Money*, March, 37–8.

Smith, R. (2007), 'NYSE moves to prevent abuses in odd-lot trades: specialist firms complained some traders took advantage of program for small investors', *Wall Street Journal*, 14 November, p. C5.

Solomon, L.D. and L. Corso (1991), 'The impact of technology on the trading of securities: the emerging global market and the implications for regulation', *John Marshall Law Review*, **24**, 299.

Sippl, C. and R. Sippl (1972), *Computer Dictionary and Handbook*, 2nd edn, Indianapolis, IN: H.W. Sams.

Spicer, J. and H. Lash (2009), 'Who's afraid of high-frequency trading?' *Reuters*, 2 December.

Strasburg, J. and S.N. Lynch (2010), 'Infinium is focus of CME', *Wall Street Journal*, 26 August, p. C3.
Sun Microsystem, Inc. (2002), 'Best practices: exchanging electronically at record pace', December, http://www.sun.com/br/financial-sucs/Article_best-practices.html.
Sun Microsystem, Inc. (2005), 'Best practices: exchanging electronically at record pace', November, http://www.sun.com/solutions/documents/articles/fn_liffe2_aa.xml.
Tabb, L. (2010), 'Rethinking our markets', *Advanced Trading*, October, p. 41.
Tamarkin, B. (1993), *The Merc: The Emergence of a Global Powerhouse*, New York: HarperBusiness.
Tarquinio, J.A. (2002), 'Investing; electronic trading networks look toward the big board', *New York Times*, 29 December, § 3, p. 7.
Timmons, H. (2007), 'Nymex abandoning plans for British futures market', *New York Times*, 24 January, p. C4.
Timmons, H. and J. Werdigier (2007), 'For Abu Dhabi and Citi, credit crisis drove deal', *New York Times*,28 November, p. C1.
Tormey, T.A. (1997), 'A derivatives dilemma: the treasury amendment controversy and the regulatory status of foreign currency options', *Fordham Law Review*, **65**, 2313–79.
UBS AG (2008), 'Shareholder report on UBS's write-downs'.
US Futures Exchange (2003), LLC, CFTC Release No. dcm037f, September, Responses to CFTC Technical Questionnaire, p. 2, http://www.cftc.gov/files/submissions/dcodcm/dcm037f.pdf.
Uzun, H., S.H. Szewczyk and R. Varma (2004), 'Board composition and corporate fraud', *Financial Analysts Journal*, May–June, 33–41.
Walker, E. and D. Cheang (2010), 'The Asian angle: the rise of the machines', Royal Bank of Scotland, 15 September, p. 14.
Ward, A. (2010), 'Norwegians convicted for tricking broker's automated trade system', *Financial Times*, 14 October, p. 1.
Webb, C.R. (1994), 'Salomon Forex, Inc. v. Tauber – The 'sophisticated trader' and foreign currency derivatives under the Commodity Exchange Act', *North Carolina Journal of International Law and Commercial Regulation*, **19**, 579–94.
Welles, C. (1975), *The Last Days of the Club*, New York: Dutton.
Wijnen, R. (2002), 'Keeping pace with hedge funds', *Waters*, 1 February, http://db.riskwaters.com/public/showPage.html?page=153101.
Williams Walsh, M. (2008), 'Tracking firm says bets placed on Lehman have been quietly settled', *New York Times*, 23 October, p. A20.
Zaloom, C. (2006), *Out of the Pits: Traders and Technology, From Chicago to London*, Chicago, IL: University of Chicago Press.
Zweig, J. (2009), 'The intelligent investor: staying calm in a world of dark pools, dark doings', *Wall Street Journal*, 24 October, p. B1.

Index

Titles of publications are in *italics*.